Global Management

Strategic and Interpersonal

Helen Deresky

State University of New York—Plattsburgh

Prentice Hall

Upper Saddle River, New Jersey 07458

Library of Congress Cataloging-in-Publication Data

Deresky, Helen.
   Global management : strategic and interpersonal / Helen Deresky.
     p. cm.
   Includes bibliographical references and index.
   ISBN 0-13-061964-7
   1. Strategic planning—Cross-cultural studies. 2. Management—Cross-cultural
   studies.
   I. Title.

HD30.28 .D459 2002
658'.049—dc21   2001053131

AVP/Executive Editor: David Shafer
Editor-in-Chief: Jeff Shelstad
Senior Managing Editor (Editorial): Jennifer Glennon
Assistant Editor: Melanie Olsen
Editorial Assistant: Kim Marsden
Media Project Manager: Michele Faranda
Marketing Manager: Shannon Moore
Marketing Assistant: Christine Genneken
Managing Editor (Production): John Roberts
Production Editor: Maureen Wilson
Production Assistant: Dianne Falcone
Permissions Coordinator: Suzanne Grappi
Associate Director, Manufacturing: Vincent Scelta
Production Manager: Arnold Vila
Manufacturing Buyer: Michelle Klein
Cover Design: Bruce Kenselaar
Cover Illustration/Photo: Peter Scholey/Stone
Full-Service Project Management and Composition: UG / GGS Information
   Services, Inc.
Project Manager: Denise May
Printer/Binder: RR Donnelley-Harrisonburg

Credits and acknowledgements borrowed from other sources and reproduced, with permission, in this textbook appear on appropriate page within text.

Pearson Education LTD.
Pearson Education Australia PTY, Limited
Pearson Education Singapore, Pte. Ltd
Pearson Education North Asia Ltd
Pearson Education, Canada, Ltd
Pearson Educación de Mexico, S.A. de C.V.
Pearson Education–Japan
Pearson Education Malaysia, Pte. Ltd

10 9 8 7 6 5 4 3 2 1
ISBN 0-13-061964-7

BRIEF CONTENTS

CONTENTS

PART 2 - THE CULTURAL CONTEXT OF GLOBAL MANAGEMENT   61

PART 4 - GLOBAL HUMAN RESOURCE MANAGEMENT   253

Preface

The hypercompetitive global arena of the twenty-first century mandates that managers develop the skills necessary to design and implement global strategies, to conduct effective cross-national interactions, and to manage daily operations in foreign subsidiaries. Companies operating abroad often report that their global strategy is undermined by expatriate failure—the ineffective management of intercultural relations. This means that the fate of overseas operations depends at least in part on the international manager's cultural skills and sensitivity, as well as the ability to carry out the company's strategy within the host country's business practices.

Clearly, the skills needed for effective management of people and processes in a global context are crucial for the twenty-first century. There is thus a pronounced need for a comprehensive textbook that addresses the actual management functions and behaviors necessary to develop global vision and management skills at both an organizational or **strategic** (macro) level and an **interpersonal** (micro) level. *Global Management: Strategic and Interpersonal*, fills this need.

This text places the executive or student in the role of a manager of any nationality, encouraging the student to take a truly global perspective in dealing with dynamic management issues in both foreign and diverse host environments. Competitive strategy is evaluated in the context of global changes—the European Union, the North American Free Trade Agreement (NAFTA), the liberalization of Eastern Europe, and the evolving marketplace of the Commonwealth of Independent States—that require new management applications. Throughout, the text emphasizes how the variable of culture interacts with other national and international factors to affect managerial processes and behaviors. In addition, the growing competitive influence of technology is emphasized, with boxes featuring the use of e-business for global competitive strategic positioning.

This book is designed as a concise, practitioner-oriented alternative to the typical 600-plus page textbook. It is especially useful for executive training and graduate courses, and for undergraduate courses in global management, international management or business, and cross-cultural management where the professor wishes to use his or her own pedagogical supplements. The emphasis is on practical currency, research grounding, and the integration of technology, business ethics, and global managerial skills.

DISTINCTIVE TEXT FEATURES

- **Chapter opening profiles** give practical and current illustrations of the chapter topics, such as "Nokia's China Strategy" and "The DaimlerChrysler AG Global Alliance Backfires."

- **Comparative Management in Focus** narratives provide in-depth comparative application of chapter topics in specific countries. Some examples are "Strategic Planning for the EU market," "Motivation in Mexico," "Communicating with Arabs," "Negotiating with the Chinese."
- **E-Biz Boxes** offer examples of the application of IT, specifically B2B, around the world. These include "Siemens AG Launches Global E-Company," "Covisint, LLC," and "FedEx E-Commerce Solutions in Asia."
- **Comprehensive Cases** place the manager in a decision-making role to wrestle with situations regarding strategy, culture, HRM, social responsibility, politics, and technology in the global arena.

SUPPLEMENTS PACKAGE

Instructor's Manual with Test Item File: For each chapter, the Instructor's Manual provides a comprehensive lecture outline, chapter discussion questions, and "Student Stimulation" questions and exercises, as well as additional Teaching Resources and Lecture Notes annotated in the lecture outline. There are also additional Experiential Exercises for selected chapters. The Test Item File consists of multiple choice questions (with page references for instructors), discussion questions, and longer essay questions.

Instructor's Resource CD-ROM, including PowerPoint slides: The Instructor's Resource CD-ROM contains the computerized Test Item File, PowerPoint Electronic Transparencies, and Instructor's Manual. A revised, comprehensive package of text outlines and figures corresponding to the text, the PowerPoint Electronic Transparencies are designed to aid the educator and supplement in-class lectures. Containing all of the questions in the printed Test Item File, Test Manager is a comprehensive suite of tools for testing and assessment. Test Manager allows educators to easily create and distribute tests for their courses, either by printing and distributing through traditional methods or by on-line delivery via a Local Area Network (LAN) server.

PH International Custom Video: This video, drawn from Prentice Hall's custom On Location! video series, features experts discussing a wide range of issues in the global marketplace. By focusing on the ways in which well-known companies (including Yahoo!, MTV Europe, Sebago Shoes, and Nivea) become successful beyond their home markets, these videos bring to life chapter concepts and terms, tying them together in a real-world context.

Companion web site: The companion web site for this text, located at www.prenhall.com/deresky, contains valuable resources for both students and professors, including an interactive student study guide.

About the Author

Helen Deresky (Ph.D., Concordia University, Montreal) is Professor of Strategic Management and International Management and Director of the International Business Program at the State University of New York, Plattsburgh. She is a Canadian Studies Associate and a member of the U.S.–Canada Business Council. She is a consultant for the Institute for International Business Education, Research, and Training (IBERT). Professor Deresky was born in England and worked and con-

sulted in various industries in Europe for a number of years before settling in the United States and entering academia. Since then, her research interests have been in strategic implementation and also in management in Latin American countries and in Canada, for which she has developed teaching modules under U.S.D.E. research grants. Professor Deresky has published in various journals, including the *Strategic Management Journal*, *Organizational Dynamics*, and the *Journal of Business Education*, and has presented papers at numerous conferences in the United States and Canada. She consults for regional universities and colleges wishing to internationalize their curricula. She teaches courses in strategic management and international management. This is her fourth book on the subject of international management.

Chapter

1

Assessing the Environment—Political, Economic, Legal, Technological

1

Opening Profile: Nokia's China Strategy: Exchanging Technology for Market Access

The Finnish company's China chairman talks about the challenges of doing business under Beijing's watchful eye.

When Folke Ahlback, chairman of Nokia (China) Investment Co., arrived in Beijing six years ago, the local office consisted of about 250 staffers working in a former Beijing movie theater. Since then, he's built Nokia's China operation into a sales powerhouse with 5,000 employees. In 1999, it contributed 14% of Nokia Corp's global sales.

Small wonder Nokia has invested more than $1 billion in the Chinese market. Already, there are more than 70 million wireless subscribers in the Middle Kingdom, with 2 million new users signing up each month. Ahlback, also a Nokia senior vice-president, recently spoke about his company's operations in China with Irene M. Kunii, a Business Week correspondent covering telecommunications. Here are excerpts from their conversation:

Q: Has there been any downturn in your China business?
A: There have been no cancellation of orders. Growth has continued to climb steadily . . . We're satisfied, since China's gross domestic product is on the 8% level.

Q: Nokia seems to have good relations with its Chinese partners. Why is that? And how many partners are there?
A: Chinese and Finns have some common characteristics. They don't brag and are modest. They are aware that life isn't easy. It makes you a little more humble. We have seven joint ventures, and all but one are state-owned.

Q: You're transferring sophisticated technology to these partners. Aren't you concerned that they might take your market share in the future?
A: Because the telecom industry is so important [in China], there are rules and regulations. You transfer technology and you get market access. It's a mix between a central and a planned economy. We've learned that every country has its own characteristics. In 1998, China became the second most important market for Nokia [after the U.S.].

Q: How much market share do Chinese handset makers have?
A: The MII's [Ministry of Information Industry] task is to make sure that 30% will be Chinese. It's likely to be in the range of 5% to 10% now.

Q: Are you concerned that China is backing the development of yet another third-generation, or 3G, cellular standard, TD-SCDMA?

A: We are firm believers that . . . regardless of what choice will be made, the point is to make an evolutionary path to wide-band CDMA (or W-CDMA, the 3G standard backed by Japan and Europe). If we don't do this, we haven't achieved our path.

Q: But what of this new standard under development with Siemens?

A: As with any standard, there are two steps. First is to make it a standard. We welcome the fact that China is involved in standardization. Consumers are interested only in features, and not the technology. So the test for TD-SCDMA will be the market. Nokia is supporting this standard and is involved in R&D.

Q: Will the mobile Internet take off in China the way it has in Japan? As you know, there the emphasis is on entertainment sites.

A: China is a big country, and it's [in the process of] building one of the world's biggest and most modern mobile-phone systems. But it is a developing country, so it will be very careful about how it's going to use it. So, for 3G, we shouldn't talk about content but rather how to enhance the business. The target for the Chinese government is to make investment decisions that will help industry to be more efficient.

Q: Does that mean Chinese won't be downloading games to their handsets?

A: The Chinese government's first concern is to give the Chinese [mobile] infrastructure to business. They'll get the state-of-the-art technology first. Then the government will give consumers what they want. Big consumer segments will want the same as everyone else. The whole of Chinese society would like to be connected [to the mobile Internet.]

Q: Will Chinese companies contribute to the development of content and applications for the mobile Net?

A: We think there will be hundreds of companies [doing this] in China and thousands worldwide. I'm sure the Chinese government wants Chinese businesses to play a big role in wireless cellular operations.

Q: Would it be possible for Nokia to operate independently in China and thus protect its intellectual property?

A: In China, it's very advisable to work with partners. I would not advise anyone to go to China without a partner for such a complicated business like telecoms. After building a business together, your joint-venture partner becomes your trusted partner.

cont.

cont.

Q: That's fine, but look what happened to the foreign partners of mobile operator China Unicom [which had its foreign joint-venture agreements with Unicom terminated last year].
A: It was political. They developed an investment structure that went against the government's policies, so Chinese officials decided they should dissolve it.

Q: Is this a good place to set up a business in terms of being able to hire promising engineers?
A: In China, we have a big supply of educated people. It didn't take us long to ramp up operations—less than 12 months per factory. Between 1996 [and] 1999, we have built manufacturing capability in China, not only for China but also the world. We made China a manufacturing center, along with the U.S. and Europe.

Q: What does Nokia headquarters think of your China strategy, where you offer technology in exchange for market access?
A: My message to headquarters is that nothing comes easy.

Managers in the twenty-first century are being challenged to operate in an increasingly complex, interdependent, and dynamic global environment. Those involved in global business have to adjust their strategies and management styles to those regions of the world in which they want to operate, whether directly or through some form of alliance. This global arena is illustrated in the opening profile—an interview with the Finnish company Nokia's Folke Ahlback, chairman of the Nokia (China) Investment Company.[1] Typical challenges that he has faced are those involving politics, culture, and the use, transfer, and protection of technology. In addition, the opportunities and risks of the global marketplace increasingly bring with them the societal obligations of operating in a global community. An example is the dilemma faced by western drug manufacturers, which came to the forefront in spring 2001, of how to fulfill their responsibilities to stockholders, acquire capital for research, protect their patents, and also be good global citizens by responding to the cry for free or low-cost drugs for AIDS in poor countries.[2] Managers in those companies are struggling to find ways to balance their social responsibilities, their image, and their competitive strategies.

To compete aggressively, firms must make considerable investments overseas—not only capital investment but also investment in well-trained managers with the skills essential to working effectively in a multicultural environment. In any foreign environment, managers need to handle a set of dynamic and fast-changing variables, including the all-pervasive variable of culture, which affects every facet of daily management. Added to this "behavioral software" is the challenge of the burgeoning use of technological software and the borderless Internet that is rapidly changing the dynamics of competition and operations.

Global management, then, is the process of developing strategies, designing and operating systems, and working with people around the world to ensure sustained competitive advantage. Those management functions are shaped by the prevailing conditions and ongoing developments in the world, as outlined in the following sections.

THE GLOBAL BUSINESS ENVIRONMENT

Globalism

Business competitiveness has now evolved to a level of sophistication that many term **globalism**: global competition characterized by networks that bind countries, institutions, and people in an interdependent global economy. The invisible hand of global competition is being propelled by the phenomenon of an increasingly borderless world. As described by Kenichi Ohmae, "The nation-state itself—that artifact of the eighteenth and nineteenth centuries—has begun to crumble, battered by a pent-up storm of political resentment, ethnic prejudice, tribal hatred, and religious animosity."[3]

As a result of global economic integration, extrapolation of current trends will lead to world exports of goods and services of $11 trillion by the year 2005, or 28 percent of world gross domestic product (GDP).[4] As reported by the World Trade Organization, differences in regional output growth rates have narrowed as economic activity picked up in Western Europe and the transition economies.[5] It is clear that world trade is phenomenal and growing and, importantly, is increasingly including the developing nations.

Almost all firms around the world are affected to some extent by globalism. Firms from any country now compete with your firm both at home and abroad, and your domestic competitors are competing on price by outsourcing resources anywhere in the world. It is essential, therefore, for managers to go beyond operating only in their domestic market, because by doing so they are already behind the majority of managers who recognize that they must have a global vision for their firms and that such a vision starts with preparing themselves with the skills and tools of managing in a global environment. Companies that desire to remain globally competitive and to expand their operations to other countries will have to develop a top management cadre who have experience operating abroad and who understand what it takes to do business in other countries and to work with people in and from other cultures.

As another indicator of globalism, foreign direct investment has grown more than three times faster than the world output of goods. The European Union (EU) has now caught up with the United States to share the position of the world's largest investor. Investment by global companies benefits developing economies through the transfer of financial, technological, and managerial resources and through the development of local allies, which later become self-sufficient and have other operations. Global companies are becoming less tied to specific locations, and their operations and allies are spread around the world, as they source and coordinate resources and activities wherever is most suitable, and as technology allows faster and more flexible interactions and greater efficiencies.

Small companies are also affected by and, in turn, effect globalism. They play a vital role in contributing to their national economies—through employment, new job creation, development of new products and services, and international operations, typically exporting. The vast majority (about 98 percent) of businesses in developed economies are small and medium-sized enterprises (SMEs), typically referred to as those having fewer than 500 employees. Though many small businesses are affected by globalism only to the extent that they face competing products from abroad, an increasing number of entrepreneurs are being approached by potential offshore customers, thanks to the burgeoning number of trade shows, federal and state export initiatives, and the growing use of Websites, with the ease of making contact and placing orders on-line. In the United States, for example, more than half of the companies with annual revenue under $100 million export their products.[6]

Regional Trading Blocs—The TRIAD

Much of today's world trade takes place within three regional free-trade blocs (Western Europe, Asia, and North America), called the TRIAD market, grouped around the three dominant currencies (the euro, the yen, and the dollar).[7] One researcher summarizes the impact this new order has had on our perception of national boundaries in the following way:

> Today, if you look closely at the world TRIAD companies inhabit, national borders have effectively disappeared and, along with them, the economic logic that made them useful lines of demarcation in the first place.[8]

The European Union

> We are very conscious about the euro because our main market is Europe; we told clients that as soon as they are ready, we will be ready [by pricing his products in euros].

> WILLY LIN, MILOS MANUFACTURING, HONG KONG (FAMILY-OWNED KNITWEAR COMPANY)
> *FAR EASTERN ECONOMIC REVIEW*, SEPTEMBER 3, 1998

With 12 of the 15 member states of the European Community adopting a common currency and monetary policy, the EU—a single, borderless western European market—is now a reality. And, as negotiations continued in 2001, voting rights were being negotiated for up to 13 new members to join the EU.[9] With the euro now as legally tradable currency, Europe's business environment is being transformed. Legislative measures have been adopted to create an internal market with free movement of goods and people among the European Union (EU) countries, creating the largest and most integrated common market in the world, with 376 million consumers. However, the elimination of internal tariffs and customs, as well as financial and commercial barriers, has not eliminated national pride. While most people in Western Europe are being thought of simply as Europeans, they still think of themselves first as British, French, Danish, or Italian. They are wary of giving up too much power to centralized institutions and of giving up their national culture.

Global managers face two major tasks. One is strategic (dealt with more fully in Chapter 6)—how firms outside of Europe can deal with the implications of the EU, of what some have called a "fortress Europe," that is, a market giving preference to insiders. The other is cultural—how to deal effectively with multiple sets of national cultures, traditions, and customs within Europe, such as differing attitudes about how much time should be spent on work versus leisure activities.

Asia

Japan and the Four Tigers—Singapore, Hong Kong, Taiwan, and South Korea, each of which has abundant natural resources and labor—provide most of the capital and expertise for Asia's developing countries.[10] Economists observe a growing integration of the region, with Japan as a catalyst and a dominant, but welcome, partner.

In the 1980s and early 1990s, much of Asia's economic power and competitive edge was attributed to Japan's *keiretsu* and South Korea's *chaebol*. Both are large conglomerates of financially linked groups of companies that play a significant role in their countries' economies. Japanese keiretsus—Mitsubishi and Toyota, to name two of the most powerful—are regarded in Washington as forms of trade barriers.[11] Recently, however, Japan's economic slide has been partially attributed to the closed system of the keiretsu, including political protection and influence for the keiretsu and dubious financial backing. As a result, such conglomerates have been forced to break up and restructure. As an example, in March 2000 Toshiba Corporation announced a three-year reorganization plan.[12]

In all, the economic woes in Southeast Asia have severely slowed the growth in the region, and in fact have had a ripple effect on the sales and earnings of companies around the world. However, in 2001, Washington and Tokyo renewed efforts toward a more open marketplace.[13]

North America

The goal of the North American Free Trade Agreement (**NAFTA**) between the United States, Canada, and Mexico, was to bring faster growth, more jobs, better working conditions, and a cleaner environment for all as a result of increased exports and trade. This "one America" trading bloc has 360 million consumers and the potential for expansion in South America as trade liberalization among the Latin American countries progresses.[14]

Reflecting optimism about investment opportunities resulting from the NAFTA, foreign companies have invested billions in Mexico. To take advantage of increased trade, American companies have set up new manufacturing facilities in Mexico or extended their manufacturing and assembly operations in the **maquiladoras**—U.S. manufacturing facilities that have operated just south of the Mexican–American border since the 1960s under special tax concessions. Many

Mexican and American companies have set up joint ventures, such as the one between Wal-Mart and Cifra, the largest retailers in the United States and Mexico, respectively; in fact, as of 2001, WalMex is the country's biggest chain.[15] Already known as "Detroit South," the car industry south of the border is taking over more and more factory production for the Big Three carmakers in the United States, taking advantage of lower Mexican wages. However, recurring problems with the infrastructure and the declining value of the peso continue to depress trade.

Other Regions in the World

Sweeping political, economic, and social changes around the world present new challenges to global managers. The worldwide move away from communism, together with the trend toward privitization, has had an enormous influence on the world economy; economic freedom is a critical factor in the relative wealth of nations.

One of the most striking changes today is that almost all nations have suddenly begun to develop decentralized, free-market systems in order to manage a global economy of intense competition, the complexity of high-tech industrialization, and an awakening hunger for freedom.[16]

Central and Eastern Europe

An area greatly affected by these recent developments is the Central and Eastern European bloc, where communism proved unworkable and crumbled. World attention is now focused on a new market of 430 million people whose invitingly low wage rates offer investors an unexplored, low-cost manufacturing opportunity. Many impediments remain that will hamper business growth, however, because East European countries lack the capitalist structure and systems to reproduce Western management practices easily. As one researcher notes, "Market research is unfamiliar. The closest thing to a market survey that many East Europeans have experienced is a government interrogation."[17] However, growing stability and economic gains in Central Europe—Poland, Hungary, and the Czech Republic—are attracting a flood of foreign investment. These include an Opel car plant in southern Poland, expansion by IBM of its disk-drive plant in Hungary, and a new TV plant by Matsushita in the Czech Republic.[18]

China

China has enjoyed recent success as an export powerhouse, a status built on its strengths of low costs and a constant flow of capital. Its GDP growth rate, though slowing, was the fastest growth rate in the world for several consecutive years.

President Jiang Zemin has made state-enterprise reform his priority. Though it can hardly be called mass privatization, his plan is to save China's 1,000 largest state enterprises, and privatize or dissolve smaller, money-losing ones. His goal is to invigorate Chinese industry so it can compete in the global economy. As a result, millions of surplus industrial workers will lose their jobs, and the others will no longer receive free lifelong social benefits.[19] In early 2002, China will join the World Trade Organization (WTO), opening its state-dominated economy to imports, foreign investment, and increased exports.[20]

Unfortunately, privatization is not as easy as it sounds; whether in Pakistan, China, Russia, or Argentina, the problems involved with selling state-owned companies—monsters of inefficiency that have incurred colossal losses over the years—are not easily solved.

Less Developed Countries

Change in less developed countries (**LDCs**) has come about more slowly as they struggle with low GNP and low per capita income as well as the burdens of large, relatively unskilled populations and high international debt. Their economic situation and the often unacceptable level of government intervention discourage the foreign investment they need. Many countries in Central and South America, the Middle East, India, and Africa desperately hope to attract foreign investment to stimulate economic growth. For firms willing to take the economic and political risks, there is considerable potential for international business in the LDCs. Assessing the risk-return trade-offs and keeping up with political developments in these developing countries are two of the many demands on international managers.

Information Technology

> From his London office, Richard J. Callahan, the U.S. West International chief, . . . begins a turbocharged conference call with seven division presidents in five countries. They hash over cellular-phone sales in the Czech Republic, forecast long-distance hookups in Russia, and give a thumbs-up to opening an office in Japan.[21]

Of all the developments propelling global business today, the one that is transforming the international manager's agenda more than any other is the rapid advances in **information technology (IT)**. The speed and accuracy of information transmission are changing the nature of the global manager's job by making geographic barriers less relevant. Indeed, the necessity of being able to access IT is being recognized by managers and families around the world, who are giving priority to being "plugged in" over other lifestyle accoutrements.

Information can no longer be centrally or secretly controlled by governments; political, economic, market, and competitive information is available almost instantaneously to anyone around the world, permitting informed and accurate decision making. Even cultural barriers are being gradually lowered by the role of information in educating societies about one another. Indeed, as consumers around the world become more aware, through various media, about how people in other countries live, their tastes and preferences begin to converge:

> Global brands of colas, blue jeans, athletic shoes and designer ties and handbags are as much on the mind of the taxi driver in Shanghai as they are in the home of the schoolteacher in Stockholm.[22]

The explosive growth of information technology is both a cause and an effect of globalism. The information revolution is boosting productivity around the world. In addition, the use of the Internet is propelling electronic commerce around the world, as discussed later in this chapter. Companies around the world are linked electronically to their employees, customers, distributors, suppliers, and alliance partners in many countries. Technology, in all its forms, gets dispersed around the world by multinational corporations (MNCs) and their alliance partners in many countries. However, some of the information intended for electronic transmission is currently subject to export controls by an EU directive intended to protect private information about its citizens. So, perhaps IT is not yet "borderless" after all, but rather as subject to the same norms, preferences, and regulations as "human" cross-border interactions.

Workforce Diversity

In many countries around the world, the workforce is becoming increasingly diverse because of the erosion of rigid political boundaries, the rapidity of travel, and the quick spread of information. Propelled by globalism, the world labor force is undergoing considerable change as a result of (1) the increasing movement across borders of workers at all skill levels; (2) the rising average age of employees; and (3) the addition of great numbers of women to the workforce (particularly in developing countries), many with higher levels of education.[23] In the United States, for example, demographic information from the Bureau of Labor Statistics indicates that, by the year 2050, Hispanic Americans will represent 25 percent, and Asian/Pacific Americans 9 percent, of the U.S. population.[24] Thus, workforce diversity is becoming a crucial managerial issue. In essence, cross-cultural management worldwide is as much the task of managing multiculturalism at home as it is of managing a workforce in a foreign country. In fact, it often means both: managers operating in a foreign environment also manage a culturally diverse local workforce.

Effective management increasingly depends on the ability to design and implement programs, throughout an organization, that value diversity and pluralism. Such programs enable the organization to enjoy the benefits of multiculturalism, including the possibility of more creativity, innovation, and flexibility; they heighten sensitivity to foreign customers, and provide a greater and more varied pool of talent.[25]

The Global Manager's Role

Whatever your level of involvement, you need to understand the global business environment and its influence on the manager's role. This complex role demands a contingency approach to dynamic environments, each of which has its own unique requirements. Within the larger context of global trends and competition, the rules of the game for the global manager are set by each country (as depicted in Exhibit 1-1): its political and economic agenda, its technological status and level of development, its regulatory environment, its comparative and competitive advantages, and its cultural norms. The astute manager will analyze the new environment, anticipate how it may affect the future of the home company, and then develop appropriate strategies and operating styles.

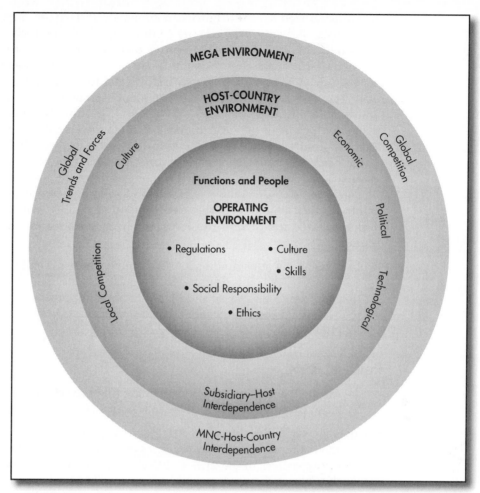

Exhibit 1-1
An Open Systems Model: The Contingency Role of the Global Manager

THE POLITICAL AND ECONOMIC ENVIRONMENT

Proactive globally oriented firms maintain an up-to-date profile of the political and economic environment of the countries in which they maintain operations (or have plans for future investment). In the early 1990s, the formerly rigid ideological systems of capitalism, communism, and socialism underwent profound changes, and the lines of demarcation between those systems increasingly blurred. It is now best to measure such systems along a continuum of economic systems—from those that operate primarily according to market forces (such as the United States) to those that use central planning for resource allocation (such as the People's Republic of China). Near the center of the continuum lie the industrialized Western European countries and Japan. Some countries in Africa, Asia, and Latin America are continuing to develop their market mechanisms and economic systems to improve their economic health.

An important aspect of the political environment is the phenomenon of ethnicity—a driving force behind political instability around the world. In fact, many uprisings and conflicts which are thought to be political in nature are actually expressions of differences among ethnic groupings. Often, it is religious disputes which lie at the heart of those differences. Uprisings based on religion operate both in conjunction with ethnic differences (as probably was the case in the former Yugoslavia), or separate from them (as in Northern Ireland). Many terrorist activities are also based on religious differences, as in the Middle East. Managers must understand the ethnic and religious composition of the host country to anticipate how problems of general instability will affect operations: your workforce, production and access to raw materials, and your market.[26] For example:

> In Pakistan one must understand the differences between Punjabi and Sindi. In Malaysia it is essential to recognize the special economic relationship between Chinese and Malay. In the Philippines it is important to understand the significant and lead financial role played by the Filipino-Chinese.[27]

Political Risk

> Increasingly, investors are understanding that projects can be derailed by little "p" political risk . . . the death from 1,000 cuts.[28]

The managers of a global firm need to investigate the political risks to which they expose their company in certain countries and the implications of those risks for the economic success of the firm. **Political risks** are any governmental action or politically motivated event that could adversely affect the long-run profitability or value of a firm.[29] The Middle East, as we have seen, has traditionally been an unstable area where political risk heavily influences business decisions.

In unstable areas, multinational corporations weigh the risks of nationalization or expropriation. **Nationalization** refers to the forced sale of the MNC's assets to local buyers, with some compensation to the firm, perhaps leaving a minority ownership with the MNC. **Expropriation**, very rare in the last decade, occurs when the local government seizes the foreign-owned assets of the MNC, providing inadequate compensation; in the case of no compensation, it is known as confiscation. In countries that have a proven history of stability and consistency, the political risk to a multinational corporation is relatively low. The risk of expropriation is highest in countries that experience continuous political upheaval, violence, and change. Events that affect all foreign firms doing business in a country or region are called macropolitical risk events. In the Middle East, Iraq's invasion of Kuwait in 1990 abruptly halted all international business with and within both those countries and caught businesses wholly unprepared. In China, the Tiananmen Square crackdown on student protestors in 1989 interrupted much foreign business in the Far East. After years of increasing international investment in China (the United States had reached the $3-billion mark in direct foreign investment at the time of the crackdown), many companies closed and withdrew their personnel. Concerned about the government's response to student unrest, these businesses were wary about the future.[30]

The political uncertainty and unrest in the newly independent countries of Eastern Europe are a prime example of the risk-return trade-off that companies must assess. The attraction in Russia, for example, though it struggles in its transition to a market economy, is the considerable potential profits available to investors in the consumer goods sector which can accrue from the pent-up demand for goods for 150 million people who are beginning to realize some economic growth.[31] The continuing uncertainty has also not deterred Japan from setting up bases in Eastern Europe to penetrate the European Community market.[32]

In many regions, terrorism poses a severe and random political risk to company personnel and assets and can, obviously, interrupt the conduct of business. According to Micklous, **terrorism** is "the use, or threat of use, of anxiety-inducing . . . violence for ideological or political purposes."[33] The increasing incidence of terrorism, especially in Latin America, concerns MNCs. In particular, the kidnapping of business executives has become quite common. Those events that affect one industry or company or only a few companies are called **micropolitical risk events**.[34] These types of events have become more common than macrorisk events. Such microaction is often called creeping expropriation, indicating a government's gradual and subtle action against foreign firms.[35] This is when the "death from a 1,000 cuts" comes in—"when you haven't been expropriated, but it takes ten times longer to do anything."[36] Such continuing problems with an investment present more difficulty for foreign firms, typically, than major events which are insurable by political-risk insurance agencies. The following list describes seven typical political risk events common today (and possible in the future).

1. Expropriation of corporate assets without prompt and adequate compensation
2. Forced sale of equity to host-country nationals, usually at or below depreciated book value
3. Discriminatory treatment against foreign firms in the application of regulations or laws
4. Barriers to repatriation of funds (profits or equity)
5. Loss of technology or other intellectual property (such as patents, trademarks, or trade names)
6. Interference in managerial decision making
7. Dishonesty by government officials, including cancelling or altering contractual agreements, extortion demands, and so forth[37]

Political Risk Assessment

International companies must conduct some form of **political risk assessment** to manage their exposure to risk and to minimize financial losses. Typically, local managers in each country assess the potentially destabilizing issues and evaluate their future impact on the company, making suggestions for dealing with possible problems. Corporate advisers then establish guidelines for each local manager to follow in handling these problems. Dow Chemical has a program in which it uses line managers trained in political and economic analysis as well as executives in foreign subsidiaries to provide risk analyses of each country.[38]

Risk assessment by multinational corporations usually takes two forms. One is through the use of experts or consultants familiar with the country or region under consideration. Such consultants, advisers, and committees usually monitor important trends that may portend political change, such as the development of opposition or destabilizing political parties. They then assess the likelihood of political change and develop several plausible scenarios to describe alternative political conditions in the future.

A second and increasingly common means of political risk assessment used by MNCs is through the development of their own internal staff and in-house capabilities. This type of assessment may be accomplished by having staff assigned to foreign subsidiaries or affiliates monitor local political activities or by hiring people with expertise in the political and economic conditions in regions critical to the firm's operations. Frequently, both means are used. The focus must be on monitoring political issues before they become headlines; the ability to minimize the negative effects on the firm—or to be the first to take advantage of opportunities—is greatly reduced once CNN has put out the news.

No matter how sophisticated the methods of political risk assessment become, however, nothing can replace timely information from people on the front line. In other words, sophisticated techniques and consultations are useful as an addition to, but not as a substitute for, the line managers in the foreign subsidiaries, many of whom are host-country nationals. These managers represent the most important resource for current information on the political environment and how it might affect their firm because they are uniquely situated at the meeting point of the firm and the host country. Prudent MNCs, however, weigh the subjectivity of these managers' assessments and also realize that similar events will have different effects from one country to another.

An additional technique, the assessment of political risk through the use of computer modeling, is now becoming fairly common. One firm, American Can, uses a program called PRISM (primary risk investment screening matrix). This program digests information from overseas managers and consultants on 200 variables and reduces them to an index of economic desirability and an index of political and economic stability. Those countries with the most favorable PRISM indices are then considered by American Can for investment.[39] Such a program, of course, is only as good as its input data, which is often of doubtful quality because of inadequate information systems in many countries and because the information is processed subjectively.

To analyze their data on potential risks, some companies attempt to quantify variables into a ranking system for countries. They use their staff or outside consultants to allocate a minimum and a maximum score for criteria they deem important to them (1) on the political and economic environment, (2) on domestic economic conditions, and (3) on external economic relations. The sum of the individual scores for each variable represents a total risk evaluation range for each country.[40]

An actual risk ranking of selected countries for 1997 is shown in Exhibit 1-2. The country risk assessment is a comparative ranking of those countries based on

Exhibit 1-2
Comparative Country Risk Rankings

COUNTRY	OVERALL RATING	POLITICAL RISK	GDP GROWTH	PER CAPITA INCOME	TRADE FLOW WITH U.S.
Italy	4.13	5	3	5	4
Denmark	4.25	5	3	5	2
Netherlands	4.63	5	3	5	4
Japan	4.19	5	3	5	5
Australia	4.5	5	4	5	4
Ireland	4.38	5	3	5	3
Germany	4.5	5	3	5	5
Sweden	4	5	3	5	3
France	4.38	5	3	5	5
Switzerland	4.5	5	3	5	4
Singapore	4.88	5	5	5	5
Belgium	4.38	5	3	5	4
United Kingdom	4.63	5	3	5	5
Canada	4.38	5	3	4	5
Israel	4	4	4	4	4
Malaysia	3.75	4	4	—	4
Chile	2.88	4	3	—	2
Thailand	3.5	4	4	—	4
South Korea	3.63	4	4	3	5
Spain	3.5	4	3	4	3
Hong Kong	4.5	4	4	5	4
Saudi Arabia	3.38	4	3	2	4
Taiwan	4.13	4	4	4	5
Turkey	2.13	3	—	—	2
South Africa	2.75	3	3	—	2
Argentina	3.25	3	4	3	3
Poland	2.75	3	4	—	2
Indonesia	2.63	3	4	—	3
Philippines	3	3	4	—	4
Costa Rica	2.38	3	3	—	2
Czech Republic	2.75	3	3	—	—
Colombia	3.25	3	4	3	3
India	2.75	3	3	—	3
China	2.88	3	4	—	5
Mexico	3.38	3	3	2	5
Brazil	3	3	4	—	4
Egypt	2.38	2	3	—	2
Venezuela	2.38	2	2	—	4
Peru	2.56	2	4.5	—	2
Russia	2	—	—	2	2

Source: Data from T. Morrison, W. Conaway, J. Douress, Dun & Bradstreet's *Guide to Doing Business Around the World* (Englewood Cliffs, N.J.: Prentice-Hall, 1997).

cont.

Exhibit 1-2

cont.

COUNTRY	MONETARY POLICY	TRADE POLICY	PROTECTION OF PROPERTY RIGHTS	FOREIGN INVESTMENT CLIMATE
Italy	4	4	4	4
Denmark	5	4	5	5
Netherlands	5	5	5	5
Japan	5	4	4	2.5
Australia	5	4	5	4
Ireland	5	4	5	5
Germany	5	4	5	4
Sweden	4	4	4	4
France	5	4	5	3
Switzerland	5	4	5	5
Singapore	5	5	4	5
Belgium	5	4	5	4
United Kingdom	5	4	5	5
Canada	5	4	5	4
Israel	3	4	4	5
Malaysia	5	4	4	4
Chile	3	3	3	4
Thailand	5	3	3	4
South Korea	5	3	3	2
Spain	3	4	3	4
Hong Kong	4	5	5	5
Saudi Arabia	5	3	3	3
Taiwan	5	4	4	3
Turkey	—	3	2	4
South Africa	4	3	3	3
Argentina	4	3	3	3
Poland	2	3	3	4
Indonesia	3	2	3	2
Philippines	4	2	4	4
Costa Rica	2	2	3	3
Czech Republic	3	4	3	4
Colombia	4	3	3	3
India	4	2	3	3
China	3	2	2	3
Mexico	4	3	3	4
Brazil	3	3	3	3
Egypt	4	2	2	3
Venezuela	2	2	3	3
Peru	2.5	2.5	3	3
Russia	—	3	3	3

Ranking Scale: 1–5, with 5 = best, or lowest risk.

factors such as GDP growth, trade policy, and foreign investment climate—that is, economic, not just political, factors. The comparison is on a scale of 1 to 5, with 5 being the highest ranking, or lowest relative risk. Thus, Russia and Turkey have the most risk in the overall rating of these countries, with Singapore and the Netherlands having relatively low risk.[41]

One drawback of these quantitative systems is that they rely on information based primarily on past events. They are therefore limited in their ability to predict political events in a volatile environment.

Still another method, more rapidly responsive to and predictive of political changes, is called the early-warning system. This system uses lead indicators to predict possible political dangers, such as signs of violence or riots, developing pressure on the MNC to hire more local workers, or pending import-export restrictions.[42] The early-warning analysis is typically separated into macrorisk and microrisk elements.

In addition to assessing the political risk facing a firm, alert managers also assess the specific types of impact that such risks may have on the company. For an autonomous international subsidiary, most of the impact from political risks (nationalization, terrorism) will be at the level of the ownership and control of the firm because its acquisition by the host country would provide the state with a fully operational business.[43] For global firms, the primary risks are likely to be from restrictions (on imports, exports, currency, and so forth), with the impact at the level of the firm's transfers (or exchanges) of money, products, or component parts.[44,45]

Managing Political Risk

After assessing the potential political risk of investing or maintaining current operations in a country, managers face perplexing decisions on how to manage that risk. On one level, they can decide to suspend their firm's dealings with a certain country at a given point—either by the **avoidance** of investment or by the withdrawal of current investment (by selling or abandoning plants and assets). On another level, if they decide that the risk is relatively low in a particular country or that a high-risk environment is worth the potential returns, they may choose to start (or maintain) operations there and to accommodate that risk through **adaptation** to the political regulatory environment. That adaptation can take many forms, each designed to respond to the concerns of a given local area. Some means of adaptation suggested by Taoka and Beeman are given here:

1. **Equity sharing** includes the initiation of joint ventures with nationals (individuals or those in firms, labor unions, or government) to reduce political risks.
2. **Participative management** requires that the firm actively involve nationals, including those in labor organizations or government, in the management of the subsidiary.
3. **Localization of the operation** includes the modification of the subsidiary's name, management style, and so forth, to suit local tastes. Localization seeks to transform the subsidiary from a foreign firm to a national firm.

4. **Development assistance** includes the firm's active involvement in infrastructure development (foreign-exchange generation, local sourcing of materials or parts, management training, technology transfer, securing external debt, and so forth).[46]

In addition to avoidance and adaptation, two other means of risk reduction available to managers are **dependency** and **hedging**. Some means that managers might use to maintain dependency—keeping the subsidiary and the host nation dependent on the parent corporation—are listed here:

1. **Input control** means that the firm maintains control over key inputs, such as raw materials, components, technology, and know-how.
2. **Market control** requires that the firm keep control of the means of distribution (for instance, by only manufacturing components for the parent firm or legally blocking sales outside the host country).
3. **Position control** involves keeping certain key subsidiary management positions in the hands of expatriate or home-office managers.
4. **Staged contribution strategies** mean that the firm plans to increase, in each successive year, the subsidiary's contributions to the host nation (in the form of tax revenues, jobs, infrastructure development, hard-currency generation, and so forth). For this strategy to be most effective, the firm must inform the host nation of these projected contributions as an incentive.[47]

Finally, even if the company cannot diminish or change political risks, it can minimize the losses associated with these events by hedging. Some means of hedging are as follows:

1. **Political risk insurance** is offered by most industrialized countries. In the United States, the Overseas Private Investment Corporation (OPIC) provides coverage for new investments in projects in friendly, less developed countries. Insurance minimizes losses arising from specific risks—such as the inability to repatriate profits, expropriation, nationalization, or confiscation—and from damage as a result of war, terrorism, and so forth.[48] The Foreign Credit Insurance Association (FCIA) also covers political risks caused by war, revolution, currency inconvertibility, and the cancellation of import or export licenses. However, political risk insurance only covers the loss of a firm's assets, not the loss of revenue resulting from expropriation.[49]
2. **Local debt financing** (money borrowed in the host country), where available, helps a firm hedge against being forced out of operation without adequate compensation. In such instances, the firm withholds debt repayment in lieu of sufficient compensation for its business losses.

Multinational corporations also manage political risk through their global strategic choices. Many large companies diversify their operations both by investing in many countries and by operating through joint ventures with a local firm or government or through local licensees. By involving local people, companies, and agencies, firms minimize the risk of negative outcomes due to political events. (We discuss these and other global strategies in Chapters 6 and 7.)

Managing Terrorism Risk

Terrorists attack New York City World Trade Center and The Pentagon.

NEWS SOURCES AROUND THE WORLD, SEPTEMBER 11, 2001

Eighty countries lost citizens in the World Trade Center

SEC. COLIN POWELL, SEPTEMBER 23, 2001

No longer is the risk of terrorism for global businesses focused only on certain areas such as South America or the Middle East. That risk now has to be considered in countries such as the United States, which had previously been regarded as safe. Many companies from Asia and Europe had office branches in the towers of the World Trade Center in New York; most of those offices, along with the employees from those countries, were destroyed in the attack. Thousands of lives and billions of dollars were lost, not only by those immediately affected by the attack, but to countless small and large businesses impacted by the ripple effect; global airlines and financial markets were devastated.

As incidents of terrorism accelerate around the world, such as the 2000 bombing of the USS *Cole* in Yemen, many companies are also increasingly aware of the need to manage the risk of terrorism. Both IBM and Exxon try to develop a benevolent image in high-risk countries through charitable contributions to the local community. They also try to maintain low profiles and minimize publicity in the host countries by using discreet corporate signs at the company sites, for instance.[50] Some companies have put together teams to monitor the patterns of terrorism around the world. Kidnappings are common in Latin America (as a means of raising money for political activities). Abductions in Colombia hit a record 3,029 in 2000.[51] In the Middle East, airplane hijackings, the kidnapping of foreigners, and blackmail (for the release of political prisoners) are common. In Western Europe, typically, terrorists aim bombs at U.S. banks and computer companies. Almost all MNCs have stepped up their security measures abroad, hiring consultants in counterterrorism (to train employees to cope with the threat of terrorism) and advising their employees to avoid U.S. airlines when flying overseas.[52]

Economic Risk

In one month, you see your net income wiped out before your eyes.

JOHN VONDRAS, U.S. WEST MANAGER IN INDONESIA.[53]

Closely connected to a country's political stability is its economic environment, and the relative risk that it may pose to foreign companies. A country's level of economic development generally determines its economic stability and therefore its relative risk to a foreign firm. Most industrialized nations pose little risk of economic instability; less developed nations pose more risk.

A country's ability or intention to meet its financial obligations determines its economic risk. The economic risk incurred by a foreign corporation usually falls into one of two main categories: its subsidiary (or other investment) in a specific country may become unprofitable (1) if the government abruptly changes its domestic monetary or fiscal policies or (2) if the government decides to modify its foreign-investment policies. The latter situation would threaten the ability of the company to repatriate its earnings and would create a financial or interest-rate risk.[54] Furthermore, exchange-rate volatility results in currency translation exposure to the firm when the balance sheet of the entire corporation is consolidated. This risk may cause a negative cash flow from the foreign subsidiary. Currency translation exposure occurs when the value of one country's currency changes relative to another. For a U.S. company operating in Mexico, for example, the peso devaluation meant that the company's assets in that country were worth less when translated into dollars on the financial statements; on the other hand, the firm's liabilities in Mexico were less also. When exchange-rate changes are radical, as with the devaluation of the Russian ruble in 1998, there are repercussions around the world. Not only is it unfortunate for the Russian people whose money suddenly can buy so much less, but it also means that Russian firms do not have enough buying power to buy products from overseas, which means that the sales of foreign companies will go down. On the other hand, foreign companies have more purchasing power in Russia to outsource raw materials, labor, and so on.

Because every MNC operating overseas exposes itself to some level of economic risk, often affecting its everyday operational profitability, managers constantly reassess the level of risk the company may face in any specific country or region of the world. Four methods of analyzing economic risk, or a country's creditworthiness, are recommended by John Mathis, a professor of international economics who has also served as senior financial policy analyst for the World Bank. These methods are (1) the quantitative approach, (2) the qualitative approach, (3) a combination of both of these approaches, and (4) the checklist approach.

The quantitative method, says Mathis, "attempts to measure statistically a country's ability to honor its debt obligation."[55] This measure is arrived at by assigning different weights to economic variables to produce a composite index used to monitor the country's creditworthiness over time and to make comparisons with other countries. A drawback of this approach is that it does not take into account different stages of development among the countries it compares.

The qualitative approach evaluates a country's economic risk by assessing the competence of its leaders and analyzing the types of policies they are likely to implement. This approach entails a subjective assessment by the researcher in the process of interviewing those leaders and projecting the future direction of the economy.

The checklist approach, explains Mathis, "relies on a few easily measurable and timely criteria believed to reflect or indicate changes in the creditworthiness of the country."[56] Researchers develop various vulnerability indicators that categorize countries in terms of their ability to withstand economic volatility. Most corporations recognize that neither this, nor any single approach, can provide a comprehensive economic risk profile of a country, and therefore they try to use a combination of approaches.

In 2002, companies around the world are still feeling the effects of their exposure to economic risk in Asian countries as the economic decline that began with Thailand in 1997 deepened. It also appeared that Japan was not taking sufficiently radical steps to turn around its economy. The reverberations on the earnings of MNCs and on the world's stockmarkets, felt around the world, reconfirmed for everyone the interdependence of world economies. It clarified the points of interface between world economic issues and business, and indeed that of the individual welfare. See Comparative Management in Focus for further details.

Comparative Management in Focus

Global Managers Respond to Economic Slide in Indonesia[57]

As one Asian economy after another appeared to be melting down in 1998, one of the first to fall, and the hardest hit, was Indonesia, the world's fourth largest country. The result was devastating for the people in Indonesia as the rupiah lost 75 percent of its value over a period of a few months. Inflation seemed to be out of hand, and there was considerable unrest and rioting. It wasn't long before President Suharto was forced to resign.

Foreign companies operating in Indonesia were also hit hard; their managers struggled with how to respond to the events and how much economic risk to take for the potential long-term rewards of a vast market opening up to foreigners. Japanese and British companies have an even greater investment to date in Indonesia than do American companies, which alone have invested some $9 billion there. Lured by abundant natural resources, companies such as Goodyear Tire & Rubber have long had a presence in Indonesia. Unocal has been there for 30 years and plans to stay. Barry Lane, of Unocal notes that "major infrastructure projects are so integrated into a country, it's not like we could pack up our bags and leave at any moment." Interdependence of country and foreign investment is further evidenced by Freeport McMoRan, Inc., which mines copper, gold, and silver in the Irian Jaya province; that region is the company's entire mining resource, and the company is the largest corporate taxpayer for Indonesia.

One of the managers caught in the downdraft was John Vondras, U.S. West's top manager in Indonesia, in charge of running a 500,000-line telephone system in Indonesia. His problems were many: as a result of the devaluation of the rupiah, the company was losing a great deal in dollar terms, even though the local revenues in rupiahs were up 26 percent. In addition, his joint venture has to repay a $615 million loan in dollars, though it earns revenues in rupiahs. "In one month," says Vondras, "you see your net income wiped out before your eyes."[58]

A number of companies, such as a KFC franchise, were in partnership with a member of the Suharto family, often the only entry mode in the past for foreign firms trying to gain a foothold in Indonesia. Other companies, such as General Motors, have been able to get out of this relationship. GM, which has been making cars in Indonesia since 1994, was able to buy out its Indonesian partner, a Suharto half-brother, in 1997. While the local partner has since gone bankrupt—not able to withstand the Asian economic crisis—GM has been able to keep afloat. However, GM cars lost two-thirds of their dollar value within a few days. GM now makes monthly price revisions in anticipation of currency exchange fluctuations. Other strategies to combat the problem have been to increase the GM cars' local content in order to take advantage of lower local costs. Bill Botwick, president of GM's Indonesian operation, says he is hanging in there for the long run because they expect to have a good market share.

As the IMF pressures the Indonesian government to privatize state-owned companies in the banking, telecommunications, mining, steel, shipbuilding, and aerospace sectors, investment opportunities will become available and help to reverse the economic decline. Meanwhile foreign managers there assess their exposure to continued economic risk compared to the potential long-term market opportunities.

THE LEGAL ENVIRONMENT

The prudent global manager consults with legal services, both locally and at her or his headquarters, to comply with host-country regulations and to maintain cooperative long-term relationships in the local area. If the manager waits until a problem arises, little legal recourse may be available outside of local interpretation and enforcement. Indeed, this has been the experience of many foreign managers in China, where financial and legal systems remain rudimentary in spite of attempts to show the world a capitalist face. Managers there often simply ignore their debts to foreign companies as they did under the old socialist system.[59] The painful lesson to many foreign companies in China is that they are losing millions because Beijing often does not stand behind the commitments of its state-owned enterprises. Although still no guarantee, ways to minimize the risk of massive losses include making sure you get approval from related government offices (national, provincial, and local), making sure you are not going to run amok of long-term government goals, and getting loan guarantees from the headquarters of one of Beijing's main banks.[60] In addition, don't assume there will be legal recourse in China. Mr. Cheng, an American businessman who grew up in Hunan, was thrown in jail in China because a Chinese businessman changed his mind about investing in Mr. Cheng's safety-helmet factory in Zhuhai. Only after two months and his son's visit to the U.S. Embassy in Beijing was Mr. Cheng freed. Mr. Cheng asks, "[without even a trial] how could the court render a decision just one hour after Mr. Liu and my general manager had signed a new contract?"[61] Some of the contributing factors, he has realized since then, were the personal connections—*guanxi*—involved and the fact that some courts offer their services to the business community for profit; in addition many judges get their jobs through nepotism rather than by virtue of a law degree.

While the regulatory environment for the international manager consists of the many local laws and the court systems in those countries in which he or she operates, certain other legal issues are covered by international law. International law is the law that governs relationships between sovereign countries, the basic units in the world political system.[62] One such agreement, which regulates international business by spelling out the rights and obligations of the seller and the buyer, is the United Nations Convention on Contracts for the International Sale of Goods (CISG). This convention became law on January 1, 1988, and applies to contracts for the sale of goods between countries that have adopted the convention.

Generally speaking, the manager of the foreign subsidiary or foreign operating division will comply with the host country's legal system. Such systems, derived from common law, civil law, or Muslim law, are a reflection of the country's culture, religion, and traditions. Under **common law**, used in the United States and 26 other countries of English origin or influence, past court decisions act as precedents to the interpretation of the law and to common custom. **Civil law** is based on a comprehensive set of laws organized into a code. Interpretation of these laws is based on reference to codes and statutes. About 70 countries, predominantly in Europe (e.g., France and Germany), are ruled by civil law, as is Japan. In Islamic countries, such as Saudi Arabia, the dominant legal system is Islamic law; based on religious beliefs, it dominates all aspects of life. **Islamic law** is followed in approximately 27 countries and combines, in varying degrees, civil, common, and indigenous law.[63]

Contract Law

> In China, the old joke goes, a contract is a pause in the negotiation.
>
> VANESSA CHANG, KPMG PEAT MARWICK.[64]

A **contract** is an agreement by the parties concerned to establish a set of rules to govern a business transaction. Contract law plays a major role in international business transactions because of complexities arising from the differences in participating countries' legal systems and because the host government in many developing and communist countries is often a third party in the contract. Both common-law and civil-law countries enforce contracts, although their means of resolving disputes differ. Under civil law, it is assumed that a contract reflects promises that will be enforced without specifying the details in the contract; under common law, the details of promises must be written into the contract to be enforced.[65] Astute international managers recognize that they will have to draft contracts in legal contexts different from their own, and so they prepare themselves accordingly by consulting with experts in international law before going overseas. In China, for example, "The risk is, you could have a contract torn up or changed. We're just going to have to adjust to that in the West," says Robert Broadfoot, who heads the Political & Economic Risk Consultancy in Hong Kong.[66] He says that western companies think that they can avoid political risk by spelling out every detail in a contract, but "in Asia, there is no shortcut for managing the relationship." In other words, the contract is in the relationship, not on the paper, and the way to ensure the reliability of the agreement is to nurture the relationship.

Even a deal that has been implemented for some time may start to get watered down at a time when you cannot do anything about it. A Japanese-led consortium experienced this problem after it built an expressway in Bangkok. The Thai government later lowered the toll that they had agreed could be charged for use of the road. This is a subtle form of expropriation, since a company cannot simply pack up a road and leave.[67] Neglect regarding contract law may leave a firm burdened with an agent who does not perform the expected functions or faced with laws that prevent management from laying off employees (often the case in Belgium, Holland, Germany, Sweden, and elsewhere).[68]

Other Regulatory Issues

Differences in laws and regulations from country to country are numerous and complex. These and other issues in the regulatory environment that concern multinational firms are discussed briefly here.

Countries often impose protectionist policies, such as tariffs, quotas, and other trade restrictions, to give preference to their own products and industries. The Japanese have come under much criticism for protectionism, which they use to limit imports of foreign goods while they continue exporting consumer goods (e.g., cars, electronics) on a large scale. The American auto industry continues to ask the U.S. government for protection from Japanese car imports. Calls to "buy American," however, are thwarted by the difficulty of identifying cars that were truly American-made; the intricate web of car-manufacturing alliances between Japanese and American companies often makes it difficult to distinguish the maker.

A country's tax system influences the attractiveness of investing in that country and affects the relative level of profitability for an MNC. Foreign tax credits, holidays, exemptions, depreciation allowances, and taxation of corporate profits are additional considerations the foreign investor must examine before acting. Many countries have signed tax treaties (or conventions) that define terms such as income, source, and residency and spell out what constitutes taxable activities.

The level of government involvement in the economic and regulatory environment varies a great deal among countries and has a varying impact on management practices. In Canada, the government has a significant involvement in the economy. It has a powerful role in many industries, including transportation, petrochemicals, fishing, steel, textiles, and building materials—forming partly owned or wholly owned enterprises. Wholly owned businesses are called Crown Corporations (Petro Canada, Ontario Hydro Corporation, Marystown Shipyard, Saskatchewan Telephones, and so forth), many of which are as large as the major private companies. The government's role in the Canadian economy, then, is one of both control and competition.[69] Government policies, subsidies, and regulations directly affect the manager's planning process, as do other major factors in the Canadian legal environment, such as the high proportion of unionized workers (30 percent). In Quebec, the law requiring official bilingualism imposes considerable operating constraints and expenses. For a foreign subsidiary, this regulation forces managers to speak both French and English and to incur the costs of language training for employees, translators, the administration of bilingual paperwork, and so on.[70]

THE TECHNOLOGICAL ENVIRONMENT

The effects of technology around the world are pervasive in business and in private lives. In fact in many parts of the world, whole generations of technological development are being skipped over; for example, many people will go straight to a digital phone without ever having their houses wired under the analog system. Even in a remote village such as Bario, Malaysia—still lacking traditional roads in 2001—an information highway is under way.[71] Advances in information technology are bringing about increased productivity, for employees, for companies, and for countries.

Now that we are in a global information society, it is clear that corporations must incorporate into their strategic planning and their everyday operations the accelerating macro-environmental phenomenon of **technoglobalism**, in which the rapid developments in information and communication technologies (**ICTs**) are propelling globalization and vice-versa.[72] Investment-led globalization is leading to global production networks, which result in global diffusion of technology to link parts of the value-added chain in different countries. That chain may comprise parts of the same firm, or it may comprise suppliers and customers, or it may comprise technology-partnering alliances among two or more firms. These technological developments are facilitating, indeed necessitating, the network firm structure which allows flexibility and rapid response to local needs. Clearly there is no ignoring the effects of technology on global trade and business transactions; in addition, the **Internet** is propelling electronic commerce around the world. In fact, the ease of use and pervasiveness of the Internet raises difficult questions about ownership of intellectual property, consumer protection, residence location, taxation, and other issues.[73]

New technology specific to a firm's products represents a key competitive advantage to firms and challenges international businesses to manage the transfer and diffusion of proprietary technology, with its attendant risks. Whether it is a product, a process, or a management technology, an MNC's major concern is the **appropriability of technology**: that is, the ability of the innovating firm to profit from its own technology by protecting it from competitors.

An MNC can enjoy many technological benefits from its global operations. Advances resulting from cooperative research and development (R&D) can be transferred among affiliates around the world, and specialized management knowledge can be integrated and shared. However, the risk of technology transfer and pirating is considerable and costly. Although firms face few restrictions on the creation and dissemination of technology in developed countries, less developed countries often impose restrictions on licensing agreements, royalties, and so forth, and have other legal constraints on patent protection.

In Germany, for example, royalties on patents are limited to 10 percent of sales, but the patent and trademark durations are 20 years and 10 years, respectively, with 45 percent the highest tax bracket allowed on royalties. Less developed countries tend to be comparatively more restrictive on the patent and trademark durations and on the range of unpatentable items. Egypt has no limits on royalties, but will only patent production processes, and then only for 15 years.

In most countries, governments use their laws to some extent to control the flow of technology. These controls may be in place for reasons of national security. Other countries, LDCs in particular, use their investment laws to acquire needed technology (usually labor-intensive technology to create jobs), to increase exports, to use local technology, and to train local people.

The most common methods of protecting proprietary technology are the use of patents, trademarks, trade names, copyrights, and trade secrets. Various international conventions do afford some protection in participating countries; over 80 countries adhere to the International Convention for the Protection of Industrial Property, often referred to as the Paris Union, for the protection of patents. However, restrictions and differences in the rules in some countries not signatory to the Paris Union, as well as industrial espionage, pose continuing problems for firms trying to protect their technology. In 2001, western pharmaceutical companies were embroiled in the difficult battle to protect their patents for drugs while some less developed economies felt they had a right to override patents in order to provide low-cost drugs to fight AIDs epidemics.

One of the risks to a firm's intellectual property is the inappropriate use of the technology by joint-venture partners, franchisees, licensees, and employees (especially those who move to other companies). Some countries rigorously enforce employee secrecy agreements.

As another major consideration, global managers will want to evaluate the appropriateness of technology for the local environment—especially in less developed countries. Managers must study the possible cultural consequences of the transfer of technology to assess whether the local people are ready and willing to change their values, expectations, and behaviors on the job to apply new technological methods to production, research, marketing, finance, or some other aspect of business. Often, the decision regarding the level of technology transfer is dominated by the host government's regulations or requirements. In some instances, the host country may require that foreign investors import only their most modern machinery and methods so that the local area may benefit from new technology. In other cases, the host country may insist that foreign companies only use labor-intensive processes to help reduce high unemployment in the area. When the choice is left to international managers, experts in economic development recommend that managers make an informed choice of appropriate technology; the choice of technology may be capital-intensive, labor-intensive, or intermediate, but the key is that it should suit the level of development in the area and the needs and expectations of the people who will use it.[74]

As an example of the successful use of appropriate technology, we can point out a small manufacturer of detergent in India called Patel. Patel has taken over three-quarters of the detergent market from Lever, a multinational company whose Surf brand detergent had formerly dominated the market in India. Managers at Patel realized that, although Surf was a high-quality, high-priced product, it was clearly not suitable for a poor country. They set up a chain of stores in which people mixed their own detergent ingredients by hand. This primitive method has enabled Patel to tailor its technology to the conditions and expectations in India and to outsell Lever on the basis of price; its annual sales are now over $250 million.[75]

Global E-Business

Internet-based electronic trading and data exchange is changing the way companies do business and breaking down global barriers of time, space, logistics and culture. It has introduced a new level of global competition by providing efficiencies through reducing the number of suppliers and slashing administration costs throughout the value chain. **E-business** is "the integration of systems, processes, organizations, value chains and entire markets using Internet-based and related technologies and concepts."[76] **E-commerce** refers directly to the marketing and sales process. E-business is used by firms to help build new relationships between businesses and customers.[77] The Internet and e-business provide with the following global businesses advantages:[78]

1. Convenience in conducting business worldwide; facilitating communication across borders contributes to the shift toward globalization and a global market.

2. An electronic meeting and trading place, which adds efficiency in conducting business sales.
3. A corporate intranet service, merging internal and external information for enterprises worldwide.
4. Limitless options and price differentials for consumers.
5. A link and efficiency in distribution.[79]

While most of the early attention was on e-commerce, experts now believe the real opportunities are in business-to-business (**B2B**) transactions. And, while the scope, complexity, and sheer speed of the B2B phenomenon, including e-market-places, have global executives scrambling to assess the impact and their own competitive roles, estimates for growth in the e-business marketplace may have been overzealous. The global economic slowdown and its resultant dampening of corporate IT spending has caused various research groups such as AMR Research and the Gartner Group to revise downwards their projections for B2B Internet transactions, as shown in Exhibit 1-3. Still the growth projections are considerable, with an estimated $6 trillion in B2B transactions expected in 2004.

While we hear mostly about large companies embracing B2B, it is noteworthy that a large proportion of the current and projected B2B use is by small- and

Exhibit 1-3
Revised Forecast

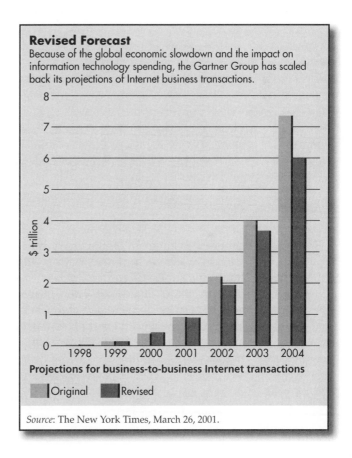

Revised Forecast
Because of the global economic slowdown and the impact on information technology spending, the Gartner Group has scaled back its projections of Internet business transactions.

$ trillion

Projections for business-to-business Internet transactions

Original   Revised

Source: The New York Times, March 26, 2001.

Exhibit 1-4
It's Barely Started

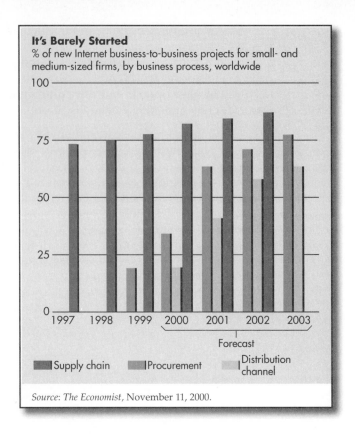

It's Barely Started
% of new Internet business-to-business projects for small- and medium-sized firms, by business process, worldwide

Supply chain ▪ Procurement ▪ Distribution channel

Source: *The Economist*, November 11, 2000.

medium-sized firms. This is shown in Exhibit 1-4, broken down by three common purposes: supply chain, procurement, and distribution channel.

Of course, a successful Internet strategy—especially on a global scale—is not easy. Potential problems abound, as experienced by the European and U.S. companies surveyed by Forrester Research, and shown in Exhibit 1-5. These include internal obstacles and politics, problems in regional coordination and in balancing global versus local e-commerce, and cultural differences. It is clear that such a large-scale change in organizing business calls for absolute commitment from the top, empowered employees with a willingness to experiment, and good internal communications.[80]

Barriers to the adoption and progression of e-business include lack of readiness of partners in the value chain, such as suppliers. Typically, companies must invest in increasing their trading partners' readiness and their customers' capabilities if they want to have an effective marketplace. Other barriers are cultural. In Europe, for example:

> Europe's e-commerce excursion has been hindered by a laundry list of cultural and regulatory obstacles, like widely varying tax systems, language hurdles and currency issues.

"E-COMMERCE REPORT", *THE NEW YORK TIMES*, MARCH 26, 2001

Exhibit 1-5

Why It Isn't Easy

Why It Isn't Easy

"What is the major pain in doing global e-commerce?"
% of 40 US and European companies interviewed

Source: *The Economist*, November 11, 2000.

Other problems relate to the difficulty within industries of agreeing on common formats for transmitting data—a problem experienced by Milan Turk, Jr., director of global customer business development for Procter and Gamble.[81]

In spite of various problems, the use of the Internet to facilitate and improve global competitiveness continues to be explored and discovered. In the public sector in Europe, for example, the European Commission has started advertising tender invitations on-line in order to transform the way public-sector contracts are awarded, using the Internet to build a truly single market:

> With public procurement accounting for 11.5 percent of the European Union's GDP, the initiative could result in increased cross-border trade, improved transparency and openness, and better value-for-money for taxpayers.
>
> *THE FINANCIAL TIMES.* www.ft.com/eprocurement, WINTER 2000

Global professional service organizations are successfully using all aspects of e-business, and helping their clients to do so. One example is Pricewaterhouse-Coopers. The company's employees, operating in over 150 countries, provide clients with expertise in solving complex business problems, including the sectors of Global Human Resources, Business Process Outsourcing, Financial Advisory, Audit and Advisory, Management Consulting, and Global Tax Services.[82,83]

Clearly, as the PricewaterhouseCoopers executives claim, e-business is not only a new Web site on the Internet, but, "a source of significant strategic

France-based Airbus Industrie is joining the Global Aerospace and Defense Exchange for aircraft parts under development by Boeing, Lockheed Martin, Raytheon, and BAE Systems. The open aerospace and defense exchange is based on the Commerce One MarketSite Portal Solution which provides an electronic marketplace where buyers and sellers around the world can conduct business. The founding industry partners have an agreement to share equal ownership stakes in the new entity, with adjustments over time to be based on each partner's flow of its e-commerce through the exchange. Commerce One has a 5 percent equity, and 20 percent equity has been set aside for other industry participants and employees of the new venture.

The partner companies, their manufacturers, and suppliers expect to realize enormous cost savings in the $400 billion industry by buying and selling parts over the Internet in the on-line exchange. The companies involved currently do business with over 37,000 suppliers, hundreds of airlines, and national governments globally, all of whom will be invited to join the Web-based marketplace. Most commercial airplanes contain up to six million parts and are supported by millions of pages of technical data. The partners expect to be able to deliver greater value and to realize significantly lower transaction costs. The exchange will also be an e-marketplace for the indirect products and services that the partner companies, the airlines, and their suppliers need for daily operations.

Plans for the Website now include the world's five largest aerospace companies, and the biggest manufacturers of commercial airliners, Boeing and Airbus. Airbus Industrie is a European consortium comprising France's Aerospatiale Matra, Germany's DaimlerChrysler Aerospace, Spain's Construcciones Aeronauticas, and UK's BAE Systems.

While the combined exchange is being developed, the partners involved continue their own e-commerce sites, such as Raytheon's www.Everythingaircraft.com., and Airbus Online Services. Meanwhile, other alliances among various parters continue, such as that between Aerospatiale, DaimlerChrysler Aerospace, and Construcciones, who formed the European Aeronautic Defence and Space Company. The company also plans to pull Italy's Finmeccanica into the fold. The Brits, retaining their usual independence, have decided to keep their aerospace company BAE Systems, 20 percent owner of airbus, independent.

But, no one said it would be easy. Commerce One, developer of the five-member Global aerospace site, faces considerable technical hurdles because of the tremendous red tape and regulatory clearances involved with aerospace transactions.

SOURCE: Adapted from: www.commerceone.com, www.Airbus.com, www.herring.com, www.FT.com, www.Boeing.com, www.baesystems.com, www.raytheon.com, www.lockheedmartin.com (all 2000).

advantage; one that will distinguish one company from another and transform business relationships as they are known today."[84] Hoping to capture this strategic advantage, the European Airbus venture, a public and private sector combination, has joined a global aerospace B2B exchange for aircraft parts, as detailed in the accompanying *E-Biz Box*. The exchange illustrates two major trends in global competition: (1) those of cooperative global alliances, even among competitors, to achieve synergies, and (2) the use of technology to enable those connections and synergies.

Conclusion

In conclusion, a skillful global manager cannot develop a suitable strategic plan or consider an investment abroad without first assessing the environment—political, legal, regulatory, and technological—in which the company will operate. This assessment should result not so much in a comparison of countries as in a comparison of (1) the relative risk and (2) the projected return on investments among these countries. Similarly, for ongoing operations, the subsidiary manager and headquarters management both must continually monitor the environment for potentially unsettling events or undesirable changes that may require the redirection of certain subsidiaries or the entire company. Some of the critical factors affecting the global manager's environment (and therefore requiring monitoring) are listed in Exhibit 1–6.

Environmental risk has become the new frontier in global business. The skills of companies and the measures taken to really manage their exposure to environmental risk on a world scale will soon largely replace their ability to develop, produce, and market global brands as the key element in global competitive advantage.[85]

As we shall see, the managerial functions and the daily operations of a firm are also affected by a subtle, but powerful, environmental factor in the host country—that of culture. The pervasive role of culture in international management will be discussed fully in Part 2.

In the next chapter we will assess some more subtle, but critical, factors in the global environment: social responsibility and ethical behavior. We will consider

Exhibit 1-6

The Environment of the International Manager

Political Environment	Economic Environment
Form of government	Economic system
Political stability	Stage of development
Foreign policy	Economic stability
State companies	GNP
Role of military	International financial standing
Level of terrorism	Monetary/fiscal policies
Restrictions on imports/exports	Foreign investment
Regulatory Environment	Technological Environment
Legal system	Level of technology
Prevailing international laws	Availability of local technical skills
Protectionist laws	Technical requirements of country
Tax laws	Appropriability
Role of contracts	Transfer of technology
Protection for proprietary property	Infrastructure
	Internet usage

Cultural Environment (see Part 2)

such questions as: What is the role of the firm in the future of other societies and their people? What stakeholders do managers need to consider in their strategic and operational decisions in other countries? How do the expectations of firm behavior vary around the world and should those expectations influence the international manager's decisions? What role does long-term global economic interdependence play in the firm's actions in other countries?

INTERNET RESOURCES

 Visit the Deresky companion Web site at http://prenhall.com/Deresky for this chapter's Internet resources.

1. Competing in the twenty-first century requires firms to invest in the increasingly refined managerial skills needed to perform effectively in a multicultural environment. Managers need a global orientation to meet the challenges of world markets and rapid, fundamental changes in a world of increasing economic interdependence.

2. Global management is the process of developing strategies, designing and operating systems, and working with people around the world to ensure sustained competitive advantage.

3. One major direction in world trade is the development of regional free-trade blocs. The TRIAD market refers to the three trade blocs of Western Europe, Asia, and North America.

4. New markets and trading opportunities are emerging in Eastern Europe (in countries like Hungary and those of the Commonwealth of Independent States), in China, and in less developed countries.

5. Drastic worldwide changes present dynamic challenges to global managers, including the political and economic trend toward the privatization of businesses, rapid advances in information technology, and a growing culturally diverse workforce.

6. Global managers must be aware of political risks around the world. Political risks are any governmental actions or politically motivated events that adversely affect the long-run profitability or value of a firm.

7. Political risk assessment by MNCs usually takes two forms: consultation with experts familiar with the area and the development of internal staff capabilities. Political risk can be managed through (1) the avoidance or withdrawal of investment; (2) adaptations to the political regulatory environment; (3) maintaining the host country's dependency on the parent corporation; and (4) hedging potential losses through political risk insurance and local debt financing.

8. Economic risk refers to the ability of a country to meet its financial obligations. The risk is that the government may change its economic policies, thereby making a foreign company unprofitable or unable to repatriate its foreign earnings.

9. The regulatory environment comprises the many different laws and courts of those nations in which a company operates. Most legal systems derive from the common law, civil law, or Muslim law.

10. Use of the Internet in e-commerce—particularly in business-to-business transactions—and for intracompany efficiencies is rapidly becoming an important factor in global competitiveness.

11. The appropriability of technology is the ability of the innovating firm to protect its technology from competitors and to obtain economic benefits from that technology. Risks to the appropriability of technology include technology transfer and pirating and legal restrictions on the protection of proprietary technology. Intellectual property can be protected through patents, trademarks, trade names, copyrights, and trade secrets.

Chapter 2

Managing Interdependence: Social Responsibility and Ethics

For the Nestlé Corporation of Switzerland, its 2001 moral dilemma regarding distribution of its baby formula in Africa was an ironic turnaround from its 1981 dilemma. Then, a seven-year boycott of Nestlé's baby products and a United Nations code on selling baby formula in LDCs pressured Nestlé to change its marketing strategy for Similac baby formula. Nestlé had promoted Similac in LDCs as a replacement for breast milk, giving out free samples of the baby formula without proper instructions for preparing it. Public outcry arose over the massive number of infant deaths that resulted primarily from the lack of information about sterilizing the bottles and the water to mix with the formula and from the lack of facilities to do so. In addition, poverty-stricken mothers resorted to overdiluting the formula or not buying any more when the samples ran out; meanwhile, they found that their own breast milk had stopped flowing from lack of use.[1] Nestlé agreed to a voluntary marketing code and agreed not to distribute free or low-cost formula.

In 2001, however, many thought that UNICEF should reconsider that code because of the modern scourge of AIDS in Africa. The problem is that mothers infected with the AIDS virus are transmitting it to their babies through breast-feeding, with estimates of infected babies well over a million.[2] And, while Nestlé has volunteered to donate free formula to HIV-infected women, UNICEF still refuses to endorse the $3 billion infant-formula industry. So, even though the situation has changed, unless UNICEF also changes the requirements, Nestlé does not want to go against the code and risk a repeat of the situation twenty years ago.[3]

Global interdependence is a compelling dimension of the global business environment, creating demands on international managers to take a positive stance on issues of social responsibility and ethical behavior, economic development in host countries, and ecological protection around the world.

Managers today are usually quite sensitive to issues of social responsibility and ethical behavior because of pressures from the public, from interest groups, from legal and governmental concerns, and from media coverage. It is less clear where to draw the line between socially responsible behavior and the corporation's other concerns, or between the conflicting expectations of ethical behavior among different countries. In the domestic arena, managers are faced with numerous ethical complexities. In the global arena, such concerns are compounded by the larger numbers of stakeholders involved, including customers, communities, and owners in various countries.

Our discussion will focus separately on issues of social responsibility and ethical behavior, but there is considerable overlap between them. The difference is a matter of scope and degree. Whereas ethics deals with decisions and interactions on an individual level, decisions about social responsibility are broader in scope, tend to be made at a higher level, affect more people, and reflect a general stance taken by a company or a number of decision makers.

The Social Responsibility of MNCs

As illustrated in the opening profile, multinational corporations have been and—to a lesser extent—continue to be at the center of debate regarding social responsibility, particularly the benefits versus harm wrought by their operations around the world, especially in less developed countries. The criticisms of MNCs have been lessened in recent years by the decreasing economic differences among countries, by the emergence of LDC multinationals, and by the greater emphasis on social responsibility by MNCs. However, concerns still remain about the exploitation of LDCs, fueled by such incidents as the Union Carbide gas leak in Bhopal, India, in December 1984, which killed 2,500 people and injured over 200,000 others. Such incidents raise questions about the use of hazardous technology in developing economies.

Issues of social responsibility continue to center on the poverty and lack of equal opportunity around the world, the environment, consumer concerns, and employees' safety and welfare. Many argue that, since MNCs operate in a global context, they should use their capital, skills, and power to play a proactive role in handling worldwide social and economic problems and that, at the least, they should be concerned with host-country welfare. Others argue that MNCs already have a positive impact on LDCs by providing managerial training, investment capital, and new technology as well as by creating jobs and improving the infrastructure. Certainly, multinational corporations (now often called transnational corporations [TNCs]) constitute a powerful presence in the world economy and often have a greater capacity than local governments to induce change. The sales, debts, and resources of the largest multinationals exceed the gross national product, the public and private debt, and the resources, respectively, of some nations.[4]

The concept of international social responsibility includes the expectation that MNCs concern themselves with the social and economic effects of their decisions. The issue is how far that concern should go and what level of planning and control that concern should take. Such dilemmas are common for MNC managers. Del Monte managers, for example, realize that growing pineapples in the rich coastal lands of Kenya brings mixed results there. While badly needed foreign exchange earnings are generated for Kenya, there are adverse effects for poor Kenyans living in the region because less land is available for subsistence agriculture to support them.[5]

Opinions on the level of social responsibility that a domestic firm should demonstrate range from one extreme—the only responsibility of a business is to make a profit, within the confines of the law, in order to produce goods and services and serve its shareholders' interests[6]—to another extreme—companies should anticipate and try to solve problems in society. In between these extremes are varying positions described as socially reactive, in which companies respond,

Exhibit 2-1

A Three-Dimensional Model of Corporate Social Responsibility

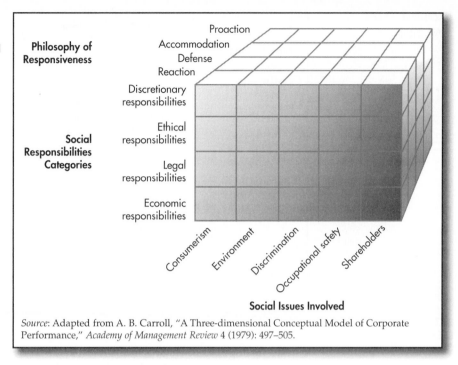

Source: Adapted from A. B. Carroll, "A Three-dimensional Conceptual Model of Corporate Performance," *Academy of Management Review* 4 (1979): 497–505.

to some degree of currently prevailing social expectations, to the environmental and social costs of their actions.[7] Carroll's classic model illustrates the relationships among the social issues involved, the categories of social responsibilities, and the four levels of the philosophy of reaction, or responsiveness: reaction, defense, accommodation, and proaction.[8] Carroll's model is shown in Exhibit 2-1. The levels of philosophy (proaction, accommodation, etc.), at the top, correspond to the levels of social responsibility on the side in the same order as shown (from top to bottom). Thus, usually a company with a proactive philosophy will put in the extra effort to fulfill discretionary responsibilities, whereas a company with a defensive philosophy will not be concerned beyond its legal responsibilities. In applying those dimensions to the typical social issues facing a corporation, the model suggests that a company with a defensive philosophy toward the social issue of discrimination typically meets its legal responsibilities only when compelled to by outside forces, as compared with a company with a proactive philosophy, which would meet its ethical and discretionary responsibilities by setting up positive programs to value diversity in the company. For example, the Denny's chain of restaurants in the United States was forced by lawsuits in 1997–98 to diversify its management structure; a more proactive stance would have called for that change to be made much earlier, perhaps as the growing diversity of its clientele was noted.

The stance toward social responsibility that a firm should take in its international operations, however, is much more complex—ranging perhaps from assuming some responsibility for economic development in a subsidiary's host country to taking an active role in identifying and solving world problems. The increased complexity regarding social responsibility and ethical behavior of firms

Exhibit 2-2
MNC Stakeholders

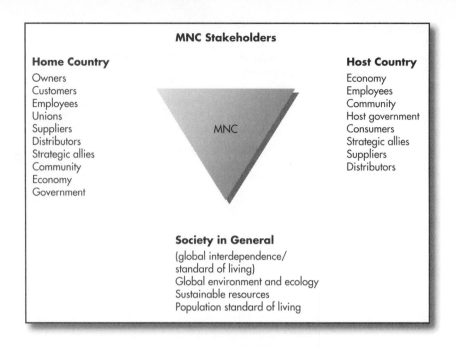

MNC Stakeholders

Home Country
Owners
Customers
Employees
Unions
Suppliers
Distributors
Strategic allies
Community
Economy
Government

MNC

Host Country
Economy
Employees
Community
Host government
Consumers
Strategic allies
Suppliers
Distributors

Society in General
(global interdependence/
standard of living)
Global environment and ecology
Sustainable resources
Population standard of living

across borders is brought about by the additional stakeholders in the firm's activities through operating overseas. As illustrated in Exhibit 2-2, managers are faced not only with considering stakeholders in the host country, but also with weighing their rights against the rights of their domestic stakeholders. Most managerial decisions will have a trade-off of the rights of these stakeholders—at least in the short term. For example, a decision to discontinue the use of children in Pakistan to sew soccer balls means the company will pay more for adult employees, and therefore reduce the profitability to its owners. That same decision—while taking a stand for human rights according to the social and ethical expectations in the home country, and bowing to consumers' demands—may mean that those children and their families go hungry or are forced into worse working situations. Another decision to keep jobs at home to satisfy local employees and unions will mean higher prices for consumers and less profit for stakeholders. Moreover, if competitors take their jobs to cheaper overseas factories, then your company may go out of business, which will mean no jobs at all for the domestic employees and a loss for the owners.

With the growing awareness of the world's socioeconomic interdependence, global organizations are beginning to recognize the need to reach a consensus on what should constitute moral and ethical behavior. Some think that such consensus is emerging because of the development of a global corporate culture—an integration of the business environments in which firms currently operate.[9] This integration results from the gradual dissolution of traditional boundaries and from the many intricate interconnections among MNCs, internationally linked securities markets, and communication networks.[10]

Although it is very difficult to implement a generalized code of morality and ethics in individual countries, such guidelines do provide a basis of judgment regarding specific situations. Bowie uses the term *moral universalism* to address the need for a moral standard that is accepted by all cultures.[11] He says that this approach to doing business across cultures is far preferable to other approaches, such as ethnocentrism or ethical relativism. With an *ethnocentric approach*, a company applies the morality used in its home country, regardless of the host country's system of ethics.

A company subscribing to *ethical relativism*, on the other hand, simply adopts the local moral code in whatever country it is operating. With this approach, companies run into value conflicts, such as continuing to do business in China despite home-country objections to China's continued violation of human rights. In addition, public pressure in the home country often forces the MNC to act in accordance with ethnocentric value systems anyway. In one instance, public outcry in the United States and most of the world resulted in major companies (IBM, General Motors, Coca-Cola, and Eastman Kodak) either selling or discontinuing their operations in South Africa during the 1980s to protest that country's apartheid policies. More recently, the FDA has been pressuring U.S. manufacturers of silicone-filled breast implants (prohibited in the United States for cosmetic surgery because of health hazards) to adopt a voluntary moratorium on exports. While Dow Corning has ceased its foreign sales—citing its responsibility to apply the same standards internationally as it does domestically—the other three major manufacturers continue to export the implants, often from their factories in other countries.

The difficulty, even in adopting a stance of moral universalism, is in deciding where to draw the line. Which kinds of conflicts of values, asks Wicks, are "conversation stoppers" or "cooperation enders"? Individual managers must at some point decide, based on their own morality, when they feel a situation is simply not right and withdraw their involvement.

> There are practical limitations on our ability to act in the modern world, . . . but a systematic infringement of basic personal rights is generally grounds for ending cooperation. Less blatant violations, or practices which are not abhorrent to our basic values, are treated as items which are negotiable.[12]

MNC Responsibility Toward Human Rights

Whereas many situations regarding the morality of the MNC's presence or activities in a country are quite clear, other situations are not, especially when dealing with human rights. The role of MNCs in pulling out of South Africa in the 1980s as part of the movement against apartheid has now played out and many cautiously return to the now multiracial democracy. In many other areas of the world, the question of what role MNCs should play regarding human rights is at the forefront. So loud has been the cry about products coming from "sweatshops" around the world that President Clinton established an Anti-Sweatshop Code of Conduct which includes a ban on forced labor, abuse and discrimination, and requires companies to provide a healthy and safe work environment and to pay at least the prevailing local minimum wage, among other requirements. A group has been named to monitor compliance; enforcement is difficult, of course, but publicity helps! The

Department of Labor publishes the names of companies who comply with the code, including Nike, Reebok, Liz Claiborne, Wal-Mart, and Phillips-Van Heusen.[13] Those companies can be identified on the department's home page Website (http://www.gov./nosweat.htm). Even so, in a study commissioned by Nike in 2000 to review personnel activities at its contractors in Indonesia, it was found that

> . . . 56 percent of the 4,004 workers told researchers that they had witnessed supervisors verbally, sexually, or physically abusing other employees.
>
> WALL STREET JOURNAL, FEBRUARY 22, 2001

The study, by nonprofit Global Alliance, concludes that workers at the Indonesian factories contracted by Nike had limited access to medical care, were exposed to sexual molestation by managers, and were often forced to work overtime.[14]

What constitutes "human rights" is clouded by the perceptions and priorities of people in different countries. While the United States often takes the lead in the charge against what they consider human rights violations around the world, other countries point to the homelessness and high crime statistics in the United States. Often the discussion of human rights centers around Asia, because many of the products in the West are imported from there by western companies using manufacturing facilities located there.[15] It is commonly held in the West that the best chance to gain some ground on human rights issues is for large MNCs and governments around the world to take a unified stance; many global players now question the morality of trading for goods that have been produced by forced labor or child labor. Though laws in the United States ban prison imports, shady deals between the manufacturers and companies acting as intermediaries make it difficult to determine the origin of many products—and make it easy for companies wanting access to cheap products or materials to ignore the law. However, under pressure from their labor unions (and, perhaps, their conscience), a number of large image-conscious companies have established corporate codes of conduct for their buyers, suppliers, and contractors and have instituted strict procedures for auditing their imports.[16] Reebok has audited all its suppliers in Asia. Levi Strauss has gone a step further. After sending teams of investigators around the world, Levi announced a new company policy: "We should not initiate or renew contractual relationships in countries where there are pervasive violations of basic human rights."[17] In fact, after that study, Levi withdrew its contracts in China and Burma, citing pervasive violation of human rights and continuing labor inequities. Of course, the company was also concerned that its brand image would suffer and that customers would not want to buy a shirt made by children in Bangladesh or by forced labor in China. Levi's top managers concluded that decisions focusing only on cost factors undermine the long-term interests of the company. They feel that more benefits accrue from an ethical approach, such as loyalty among its employees, partners, suppliers and customers. Levi has adopted strict guidelines for its foreign contractors, such as:

- Suppliers must provide safe and healthy conditions that meet Levi's standards.
- Suppliers must pay workers no less than prevailing local wages.
- Company inspectors will make surprise visits to contractors to ensure compliance.[18]

Exhibit 2-3
International Codes of Conduct for MNEs

ECONOMIC AND DEVELOPMENTAL POLICIES

- MNEs should consult with governmental authorities and national employers' and workers' organizations to assure that their investments conform to the economic and social development policies of the host country. (ICC; OECD; ILO; UN/CTC)

- MNEs should not adversely disturb the balance-of-payments or currency exchange rates of the countries in which they operate. They should try, in consultation with the government, to resolve balance-of-payments and exchange rate difficulties when possible. (ICC; OECD; UN/CTC)

- MNEs should cooperate with governmental policies regarding local equity participation. (ICC; UN/CTC)

- MNEs should not dominate the capital markets of the countries in which they operate. (ICC; UN/CTC)

- MNEs should provide to host government authorities the information necessary for correctly assessing taxes to be paid. (ICC; OECD)

- MNEs should not engage in transfer pricing policies that modify the tax base on which their entities are assessed. (OECD; UN/CTC)

- MNEs should give preference to local sources for components and raw materials if prices and quality are competitive. (ICC; ILO)

- MNEs should reinvest some profits in the countries in which they operate. (ICC)

LAWS AND REGULATIONS

- MNEs are subject to the laws, regulations, and jurisdiction of the countries in which they operate. (ICC; OECD; UN/CTC)

- MNEs should respect the right of every country to exercise control over its natural resources, and to regulate the activities of entities operating within its territory. (ICC; OECD; UN/CTC)

- MNEs should use appropriate international dispute settlement mechanisms, including arbitration, to resolve conflicts with the governments of the countries in which they operate. (ICC; OECD)

- MNEs should not request the intervention of their home governments in disputes with host governments. (UN/CTC)

- MNEs should resolve disputes arising from expropriation by host governments under the domestic law of the host country. (UN/CTC)

POLITICAL INVOLVEMENT

- MNEs should refrain from improper or illegal involvement in local political activities. (OECD, UN/CTC)

- MNEs should not pay bribes or render improper benefits to any public servant. (OECD, UN/CTC)

- MNEs should not interfere in intergovernmental relations. (UN/CTC)

TECHNOLOGY TRANSFER

- MNEs should cooperate with governmental authorities in assessing the impact of transfers of technology to developing countries, and should enhance the technological capacities of developing countries. (OECD; UN/CTC)

- MNEs should develop and adapt technologies to the needs and characteristics of the countries in which they operate. (ICC; OECD; ILO)

- MNEs should conduct research and development activities in developing countries, using local resources and personnel to the greatest extent possible. (ICC; UN/CTC)

- When granting licenses for the use of industrial property rights, MNEs should do so on reasonable terms and conditions (ICC; OECD)

- MNEs should not require payment for the use of technologies of no real value to the enterprise. (ICC)

ENVIRONMENTAL PROTECTION

- MNEs should respect the laws and regulations concerning environmental protection of the countries in which they operate. (OECD; UN/CTC)

- MNEs should cooperate with host governments and with international organizations in the development of national and international environmental protection standards. (ICC; UN/CTC)

- MNEs should supply to appropriate host governmental authorities, information concerning the environmental impact of the products and processes of their entities. (ICC; UN/CTC)

cont.

Exhibit 2-3
cont.

MNES AND PERSONS

CONSUMER PROTECTION

- MNEs should respect the laws and regulations of the countries in which they operate with regard to consumer protection. (OECD; UN/CTC)
- MNEs should preserve the safety and health of consumers by disclosure of appropriate information, proper labeling, and accurate advertising. (UN/CTC)

EMPLOYMENT PRACTICES

- MNEs should cooperate with host governments' efforts to create employment opportunities in particular localities. (ICC)
- MNEs should support representative employers' organizations. (ICC; ILO)
- MNEs should try to increase employment opportunities and standards in the countries in which they operate. (ILO)
- MNEs should provide stable employment for their employees. (ILO)
- MNEs should establish nondiscriminatory employment policies, and promote equal employment opportunities. (OECD; ILO)
- MNEs should give priority to the employment and promotion of nationals of the countries in which they operate. (ILO)
- MNEs should assure that adequate training is provided to all employees. (ILO)
- MNEs should contribute to the managerial and technical training of nationals of the countries in which they operate, and should employ qualified nationals in managerial and professional capacities. (ICC, OECD, UN/CTC)
- MNEs should respect the right of employees to organize for the purpose of collective bargaining. (OECD; ILO)

- MNEs should provide workers' representatives with information necessary to assist in the development of collective agreements. (OECD; ILO)
- MNEs should consult with workers' representatives in all matters directly affecting the interests of labors. (ICC)
- MNEs, in the context of negotiations with workers' representatives, should not threaten to transfer the operating unit to another country. (OECD; ILO)
- MNEs should give advance notice of plant closures, and mitigate the resultant adverse effects. (ICC; OECD; ILO)
- MNEs should cooperate with governments in providing income protection for workers whose employment has been terminated. (ILO)
- MNEs should provide standards of employment equal to or better than those of comparable employers in the countries in which they operate. (ICC; OECD; ILO)
- MNEs should pay, at minimun, basic living wages. (ILO)
- MNEs should maintain the highest standards of safety and health, and should provide adequate information about work-related health hazards. (ILO)

HUMAN RIGHTS

- MNEs should respect human rights and fundamental freedoms in the countries in which they operate. (UN/CTC)
- MNEs should not discriminate on the basis of race, color, sex, religion, language, social, national and ethnic origin, or political or other opinion. (UN/CTC)
- MNEs should respect the social and cultural objectives, values, and traditions of the countries in which they operate. (UN/CTC)

International agency sources:
OECD: The Organization for Economic Cooperation and Development Guidelines for Multinational Enterprises.
ILO: The International Labor Office Tripartite Declarations of Principles Concerning Multinational Enterprises and Social Policy.
ICC: The International Chamber of Commerce Guidelines for International Investment.
UN/CTC: The United Nations Universal Declaration of Human Rights.
The UN Code of Conduct on Transnational Corps.

Codes of Conduct

A considerable number of organizations have developed their own codes of conduct; some have gone further to group together with others around the world to establish standards to improve the quality of life for workers around the world. Companies such as Avon, Sainsbury Plc., Toys 'R' Us and Otto Versand have joined with the Council on Economic Priorities (CEP) to establish SA8000 (Social Accountability 8000, on the lines of the manufacturing quality standard ISO9000). Their proposed global labor standards would be monitored by outside organizations to certify if plants are meeting those standards, among which are the following:

- Do not use child or forced labor.
- Provide a safe working environment.
- Respect workers' rights to unionize.
- Do not regularly require more than 48-hour work weeks.
- Pay wages sufficient to meet workers' basic needs.[19]

Also, there are four international codes of conduct that provide some consistent guidelines for multinational enterprises (MNEs). These codes were developed by the International Chamber of Commerce, the Organization for Economic Cooperation and Development, the International Labor Organization, and the United Nations Commission on Transnational Corporations. Getz has integrated these four codes and organized their common underlying principles, thereby establishing MNE behavior toward governments, publics, and people, as shown in Exhibit 2-3 (the originating institutions are in parentheses). She concludes, "As international organizations and institutions (including MNEs themselves) continue to refine the codes, the underlying moral issues will be better identified, and appropriate MNE behavior will be more readily apparent."[20]

ETHICS IN GLOBAL MANAGEMENT

> The computer is on the dock, it's raining, and you have to pay $100 [bribe] to get it picked up.
>
> WM. C. NORRIS, CONTROL DATA CORP.

Globalization has multiplied the ethical problems facing organizations. Yet business ethics have not yet globalized. While domestic American companies may use general guidelines for appropriate behavior based on federal law and the value structure rooted in the nation's Judeo-Christian heritage, such guidelines are not consistently applicable overseas. Attitudes toward ethics are rooted in culture and business practices. American businesses have a high degree of institutionalized ethics, such as codes of ethics and tax breaks for socially responsible behavior. Swee Hoon Ang found, for example, that, while East Asians tended to be less ethical than their expatriate counterparts from the United States and Britain, it was because they considered deception as amoral and acceptable if it had a positive effect on larger issues such as the company, the extended family, or the state.[21] For an MNC, it is very difficult to reconcile consistent and acceptable behavior around the world with home-country standards. One question, in fact, is whether they even should be reconciled; it seems that the United States is the driving force to legislate moral business conduct overseas.[22]

The term **international business ethics** refers to the business conduct or morals of MNCs in their relationships with individuals and entities.[23] Such behavior is based largely on the cultural value system and the generally accepted ways of doing business in each country or society, as we have discussed throughout this book. Those norms, in turn, are based on broadly accepted guidelines from religion, philosophy, the professions, and the legal system. Should managers of MNC subsidiaries, then, base their ethical standards on those of the host country or those of the home country—or can the two be reconciled? What is the moral responsibility of expatriates regarding ethical behavior, and how do these issues affect business objectives? How do expatriates simultaneously balance their responsibility to various stakeholders: owners, creditors, consumers, employees, suppliers, governments, and societies? The often conflicting objectives of host and home governments and societies also must be balanced.[24]

The approach to these dilemmas varies among MNCs from different countries. While the American approach is to treat everyone the same by making moral judgments based on general rules, managers in Japan and Europe tend to make such decisions based on shared values, social ties, and their perception of their obligations.[25] According to many U.S. executives, there is little difference in ethical practices among the United States, Canada, and Northern Europe. In fact according to Bruce Smart, former U.S. Undersecretary of Commerce for International Trade, the highest ethical standards seem to be practiced by the Canadians, British, Australians, and Germans. He says, "a kind of noblesse oblige still exists among the business classes in those countries" compared with the prevailing attitude among many American managers which condones making it whatever way you can.[26] Another who experienced few problems with ethical practices in Europe is Donald Petersen, former CEO of Ford Motor Company, but he warns us about underdeveloped countries, in particular those under a dictatorship, where bribery is generally accepted practice. And in Japan, says Petersen, the idea behind "give me the business and I'll give you a gift" is simply an accepted part of Japanese culture.[27]

The biggest single problem for MNCs in their attempt to define a corporatewide ethical posture is the great variation of ethical standards around the world. Many practices that are considered unethical or even illegal in some countries are accepted ways of doing business in others. More recently, this dilemma has taken on new forms because of the varied understandings of the ethical use of technology around the world, as illustrated in the accompanying *E-Biz Box*.

U.S. companies are often caught between being placed at a disadvantage by refusing to go along with a country's accepted practices, such as bribery, or being subject to criticism at home for using "unethical" tactics to get the job done. Large companies that have refused to participate have led the way in taking a moral stand because of their visibility, their potential impact on the local economy, and, after all, their ability to afford such a stance.[28]

Most people in the United States have wished for more privacy of personal data; they receive mailings, solicitations, and other information about themselves that make them wonder where that source acquired the personal information. Not so in Europe. In fact, the Europeans are determined that they won't get on any unwanted mailing list from the United States or elsewhere. As of October 25, 1998, when the European Union Directive on Data Protection went into effect, commissioners in Brussels have resolved to prosecute companies and block Websites that fail to live up to Europe's standards on data privacy. The directive guarantees European citizens absolute control over data concerning them. A U.S. company wanting personal information must get permission from that person and explain what the information will be used for; the company must also guarantee that the information won't be used for anything else without the person's consent. EU citizens have the right, under this directive, to file suits against a company if they feel it is abusing their private data.

Such protections seem admirable, but free marketers across the ocean are worried about the prospect of Europe being able to regulate the computer databases and the Internet, which are vital to the information economy. They feel that regulations should be agreed upon for a global system. It is a stalemate situation of protection of privacy versus freedom of information, which is protected by the First Amendment in the United States. At the heart of the standoff is a basic cultural difference: Europeans trust their governments over companies, whereas in the United

States, it is the opposite. Already, European inspectors travel to Sioux City, South Dakota, to Citigroup's giant data processing center, where computers store financial information about millions of German credit card holders, to make sure that Citigroup is complying with the privacy data protection law. Citigroup accepted the supervision as a condition to market a credit card in Germany.

U.S. companies are concerned that the EU directive will force them to establish separate data networks for Europe, making it impossible to conduct business as usual with EU member countries. The privacy rules are already having an effect—prohibiting U.S. airlines and hotels, for example, from storing information about their clients that they would normally use to provide better service for them. Third parties to business transactions, such as FedEx delivering a package across the ocean, could also be held responsible. There is considerable concern that the EU directive will imperil the future of electronic commerce.

The question of protection of export of private data is but one of the complexities brought about by the use of technology in international business. For now, on your next trip to Europe, bringing back the contact information that you entered on your laptop computer is illegal!

In 2001, some agreement between the EU and the U.S. had been reached on "safe harbor" principles allowing transfer of data. However one still must convince authorities in each country that the data was obtained lawfully and that you have sufficient security provisions for that data.

SOURCES: H. J. Smith, "Information Privacy and Marketing: What the U.S. Should (and Shouldn't) Learn from Europe," *California Management Review*, Winter 2001. v 43, i2, p. 8; R. Howells, "Update on Safe Harbor for International Data Transfer," (European Data Protection Directive), *Direct Marketing*, August 2000, v 63, i4. p. 40. "Europe's Privacy Cops," *Business Week*, November 2, 1998; "Eurocrats Try to Stop Data at the Border," *Wall Street Journal*, October 30, 1998.

Whereas the upper limits of ethical standards for international activities are set by the individual standards of certain leading companies—or, more realistically, by the moral values of their top managers—it is more difficult to set the lower limits of those standards. Laczniak and Naor explain:

> The laws of economically developed countries generally define the lowest common denominator of acceptable behavior for operations in those domestic markets. In an underdeveloped country or a developing country, it would be the actual **degree of enforcement** of the law that would, in practice, determine the lower limit of permissible behavior [boldface added].[29]

The bribery of officials is prohibited by law in many countries, but it still goes on as an accepted practice; often, it is the only way to get anything done. In such cases, the MNC managers have to decide what standard of behavior they will follow. What about the $100 bribe to get the computer off the rainy dock? According to William Norris he told them to pay the $100 because to refuse would be taking things too far. Generally, Control Data did not yield to such pressure, though they say they lost sales as a result.[30]

Questionable Payments

A specific ethical issue for managers in the international arena is that of **questionable payments**. These are business payments that raise significant questions of appropriate moral behavior either in the host nation or in other nations. Such questions arise out of differences in laws, customs, and ethics in various countries, whether the payments in question are political payments, extortion, bribes, sales commissions, or "grease money" (payments to expedite routine transactions).[31] Other common types are payments to speed the clearance of goods at ports of entry and to obtain required certifications. They are called different names: tokens of appreciation, la mordida (the bite, in Mexico), bastarella ("little envelope" in Italy), pot-de-vin (jug of wine in France). For the sake of simplicity, we will categorize all these different types of questionable payments as some form of bribery.

In South Korea, for example, the bribery scandal that put former President Roh Tae Woo behind bars in 1996 spread to the top 30 chaebol (which account for 14 percent of gross domestic product). Any ensuing changes to the close relationship between politics and business in South Korea are likely to reshape, and perhaps slow down, the Korean economy. But executives in those chaebols say they still expect to pay the Huk Kab, or "rice-cake expenses," which run thousands of dollars, as "holiday gifts" to cabinet ministers as a hedge against disadvantageous treatment.

The dilemma for Americans operating abroad is how much to adhere to their own ethical standards in the face of foreign customs, or how much to follow local ways to be competitive. Certainly, in some societies, gift giving is common to bind social and familial ties, and such gifts incur obligation. However, Americans must be able to distinguish between harmless practices and actual bribery, between genuine relationships and those used as a cover-up. To help them distinguish, the **Foreign Corrupt Practices Act (FCPA)** of 1977 was established, which prohibits

U.S. companies from making illegal payments or other gifts or political contributions to foreign government officials for the purposes of influencing them in business transactions. The goal was to stop MNCs from contributing to corruption in foreign government and to upgrade the image of the United States and its companies operating overseas. The penalties include severe fines and sometimes imprisonment. Many managers feel the law has given them a more even playing field, and they have been more willing to do business in certain countries where before it seemed impossible to do business without bribery and kickbacks. Unfortunately, bribery still continues, mostly on a small scale, where it often goes undetected. But, the U.S. Government does vigorously pursue and prosecute bribery cases. Even the mighty IBM's Argentine subsidiary has been accused of paying a bribe of $249 million to get the contract to install computers at all the branches of Argentina's largest commercial bank, Banco de la Nacion.[32] Companies from the U.S. claim that they are placed at a competitive disadvantage in Latin America and elsewhere because their competitors overseas do not face the same home-country restrictions on bribery.

If we agree with Carson that "accepting a bribe involves the violation of an implicit or explicit promise or understanding associated with one's office or role, and that, therefore, accepting (or giving) a bribe is always prima facie wrong," then our decisions as a manager, salesperson, or whatever are always clear, no matter where we are.[33]

However, if we accept that in some cases—in "morally corrupt contexts," as Philips calls them—"there may be no prima facie duty to adhere to the agreements implicit in one's role or position," then the issue becomes situational and a matter of judgment, with few consistent guidelines.[34] If our perspective, continues Philips, is that "the action purchased from the relevant official does not count as a violation of his [or her] duty," then the American managers or other foreign managers involved are actually victims of extortion rather than guilty of bribery.[35] That is the position taken by Gene Laczniak of Marquette Company, who says that it is just part of the cost of doing business in many countries to pay small bribes to get people just to do their jobs; but he is against paying bribes to persuade people to make a decision that they would not otherwise have made.[36]

Whatever their professed beliefs, many businesspeople are willing to engage in bribery as an everyday part of meeting their business objectives. Many corporate officials, in fact, avoid any moral issue by simply "turning a blind eye" to what goes on in subsidiaries. Some companies avoid these issues by hiring a local agent who takes care of the paperwork and pays all the so-called fees in return for a salary or consultant's fee.[37] However, while the FCPA does allow "grease" payments to facilitate business in a foreign country, if those payments are lawful there, other payments prohibited by the FCPA are still subject to prosecution even if the company says it did not know that its agents or subsidiaries were making such payments—the "reason to know" provision.[38,39]

Critics of the FCPA contend that the law represents an ethnocentric attempt to impose U.S. standards on the rest of the world and puts American firms at a competitive disadvantage.[40] In fact, the United States is the only country prohibiting firms from making payments to secure contracts overseas.[41] In any event, business activities that cannot stand scrutiny, many feel, are clearly unethical, corrupt, and, in the long run, corrupting.[42] Bribery fails three important tests of ethical corporate actions: (1) Is it legal? (2) Does it work (in the long run)? (3) Can it be talked about?[43]

Many MNCs have decided to confront concerns about ethical behavior and social responsibility by developing worldwide practices that represent the company's posture. Among those policies are the following:

- Develop worldwide codes of ethics.
- Consider ethical issues in strategy development.
- Given major, unsolvable, ethical problems, consider withdrawal from the problem market.
- Develop periodic "ethical impact" statements.[44]

Most of the leadership in developing ethical postures in international activities comes from the United States. Although this move toward ethics and social responsibility is spreading, both in the United States and around the world, problems still abound in many countries.

Heightened global competition encourages companies to seek advantages through questionable tactics. A 1995 Commerce Department study revealed many incidents of improper inducements by companies and governments around the world (such as Germany's Siemens and the European airframe consortium Airbus Industrie) which undercut U.S. companies. Indeed, American companies are not all clean. In October 1995, Lockheed Martin Corporation's former vice-president was sentenced to 18 months in prison and a $125,000 fine for bribing a member of the Egyptian Parliament to win an order for three C-130 cargo planes.[45] So much for Lockheed's consent decree to refrain from corrupt practices, which they signed 20 years ago following their bribery scandal in Japan.

Japan also continues to have its share of internal problems regarding the ethical behavior of its officials and businesspeople. In the scandal involving Nippon Telephone and Telegraph Company (NTT), the chairman of the board of NTT was involved in obtaining cut-rate stock in a real estate subsidiary of the Recruit Company in exchange for helping the company obtain two U.S. supercomputers. When the stock went public, the chairman and other NTT executives made a lot of money. They were later arrested and charged with accepting bribes.[46]As the scandal unfolded, it appeared that government members were involved, including the prime minister, Noboru Takeshita, who had received $1.4 million in questionable, albeit legal, donations from the Recruit Company. Takeshita subsequently resigned, as did other government officials, and the incident became known as Recruitgate, in reference to the Watergate scandal that forced President Nixon to resign.[47]

Making the Right Decision

How is a manager operating abroad to know what is the "right" decision when faced with questionable or unfamiliar circumstances of doing business? The first line of defense is to consult the laws of both the home and the host countries, such as the FCPA. If any of those laws would be violated, then you, the manager, must look to some other way to complete the business transaction or withdraw altogether. Secondly, you could consult the International Codes of conduct for MNEs, as shown in Exhibit 2-2. These are broad and cover various areas of social responsibility and ethical behavior; however, while they are comprehensive, many issues are subject to interpretation.

If legal consultation does not provide you with a clear answer about what to do, you should consult the company's code of ethics (if there is one). You, as the manager, should realize that you are not alone in making these kinds of decisions; it is also the responsibility of the company to provide guidelines for the actions and decisions made by its employees. In addition, you are not the first, and certainly not the last, to be faced with this kind of situation. This also allows for a collective experience in the company about what kinds of decisions your colleagues typically make in various circumstances. Those norms or expectations (assuming they are honorable) can supplement the code of ethics or substitute for the lack of a formal code. If your intended action runs contrary to the norms or the formal code, then discontinue that plan. If you are still unsure of what to do, you have the right and the obligation to consult your superiors. Unfortunately, often the situation is not that clear cut, or your boss will tell you to "use your own judgement." Sometimes your superiors back at the home office just want you to complete the transaction to the benefit of the company, and don't want to be involved in what you have to do to get the deal done. It is at this point that, if your dilemma continues, you must fall back to your own moral code of ethics. One way to consider the dilemma is to ask yourself what are the rights of the various stakeholders involved (see Exhibit 2-2) and how should you weigh those rights? First, does the proposed action (rigged contract bid, bribe, etc.) harm anyone? What are the likely consequences of your decision both in the short run and in the long run? Who would benefit from your contemplated action? What are the benefits to some versus potential harm to others? In the case of a rigged contract bid through bribery, for example, people are put at a disadvantage, especially over the long term with a pattern of this behavior. This is because if competition is unfair, not only are your competitors harmed by losing the bid, but also the consumers of the products or services are harmed because they will pay more to attain them than they would under an efficient market system.

In the end, you have to follow your own conscience and decide where to draw the line in the sand in order to operate with integrity—otherwise the line moves further and further away with each transgression. In addition, what can start with a small bribe or cover-up (a matter of personal ethics) can, over time and in the aggregate of many people covering up, result in a situation of a truly negligent, and perhaps criminal, stance toward social responsibility to society as that revealed by investigations of the tobacco industry in the United States. Indeed, executives are increasingly being held personally and criminally accountable for their decisions; this is true even for people operating on the board of directors of a company.

MANAGING INTERDEPENDENCE

Because multinational firms (or other organizations, such as the Red Cross) represent global interdependency, their managers at all levels must recognize that what they do, in the aggregate, has long-term implications for the socioeconomic interdependence of nations. Simply to describe ethical issues as part of the general environment does not address the fact that managers need to control their activities at all levels—from simple, daily business transactions involving local workers, intermediaries, or consumers to global concerns of ecological responsibility—for the future benefit of all concerned. Whatever the situation, the powerful long-term effects of MNC and MNE action (or inaction) should be planned for and controlled, not done haphazardly as part of the side effects of business. The profitability of individual companies depends on a cooperative and constructive attitude toward global interdependence.

Foreign Subsidiaries in the United States

Much of the preceding discussion has related to U.S. subsidiaries around the world. However, to highlight the growing interdependence and changing balance of business power globally, we should also consider foreign subsidiaries in the United States. Since much criticism about a lack of responsibility has been directed toward MNCs with headquarters in the United States, we need to think of these criticisms from an outsider's perspective. The number of foreign subsidiaries in the United States has grown and continues to grow dramatically; foreign direct investment (FDI) in the United States by other countries is in many cases far more than U.S. investment outward. Americans are thus becoming more sensitive to what they perceive as a lack of control over their own country's business.

Things look very different from the perspective of Americans employed at a subsidiary of some overseas MNC. Interdependence takes on a new meaning when people "over there" are calling the shots regarding strategy, expectations, products, and personnel. Often, resentment by Americans over different ways of doing business by "foreign" companies in the United States inhibits cooperation, which gave rise to the companies' presence in the first place.

Today, managers from all countries must learn new ways, and most MNCs are trying to adapt. Sadahei Kusumoto, president and CEO of the Minolta Corporation, says that Japanese managers in the United States need to recognize that they are "not in Honshu [Japan's largest island] anymore" and that one very different aspect of management in the United States is the idea of corporate social responsibility.[48]

In Japan, corporate social responsibility has traditionally meant that companies take care of their employees, whereas in the United States the public and private sectors are expected to share the responsibility for the community. Part of the explanation for this difference is that American corporations get tax deductions for corporate philanthropy, whereas Japanese firms do not. Furthermore, Japanese managers are not familiar with community needs. For these and other reasons, Japanese subsidiaries in the United States have not been active in U.S. philanthropy. However, Kusumoto pinpoints why they should become more involved in the future:

> In the long run, failure to play an active role in the community will brand these companies as irresponsible outsiders and dim their prospects for the future.[49]

Whether Kusomoto's motives for change are humanitarian or just good business sense does not really matter. The point is that he recognizes interdependence in globalization and acts accordingly.

Managing Subsidiary and Host-Country Interdependence

When managing interdependence, international managers must go beyond general issues of social responsibility and deal with the specific concerns of the MNC subsidiary and host-country relationship. Outdated MNC attitudes that focus only on profitability and autonomy are shortsighted and usually result in only short-term realization of those goals; MNCs must learn to accommodate the needs of other organizations and countries:

> Interdependence rather than independence, and cooperation rather than confrontation are at the heart of that accommodation . . . the journey from independence to interdependence managed badly leads to dependence, and that is an unacceptable destination.[50]

Most of the past criticism levied at MNCs has focused on their activities in LDCs. Their real or perceived lack of responsibility centers on the transfer-in of inappropriate technology, causing unemployment, and the transfer-out of scarce financial and other resources, reducing the capital available for internal development. In their defense, MNCs help LDCs by bringing in new technology and managerial skills, improving the infrastructure, creating jobs, and bringing in investment capital from other countries by exporting products. The infusion of outside capital provides foreign-exchange earnings that can be used for further development. The host government's attitude is often referred to as a love–hate relationship: it wants the economic growth that MNCs can provide but does not want the incursions on national sovereignty or the technological dependence that may result.[51] Most criticisms of MNC subsidiary activities, whether in less developed or more developed countries, are along these lines:

1. MNCs raise their needed capital locally, contributing to a rise in interest rates in host countries.
2. The majority (sometimes even 100 percent) of the stock of most subsidiaries is owned by the parent company. Consequently, host-country people do not have much control over the operations of corporations within their borders.
3. MNCs usually reserve the key managerial and technical positions for expatriates. As a result, they do not contribute to the development of host-country personnel.
4. MNCs do not adapt their technology to the conditions that exist in host countries.
5. MNCs concentrate their research and development activities at home, restricting the transfer of modern technology and know-how to host countries.
6. MNCs give rise to the demand for luxury goods in host countries at the expense of essential consumer goods.

7. MNCs start their foreign operations by purchasing existing firms rather than by developing new productive facilities in host countries.
8. MNCs dominate major industrial sectors, thus contributing to inflation by stimulating demand for scarce resources and earning excessively high profits and fees.
9. MNCs are not accountable to their host nations but only respond to home-country governments; they are not concerned with host-country plans for development.[52]

Specific MNCs have been charged with tax evasion, union busting, and interference in host-country politics. Of course, MNCs have both positive and negative effects on different economies; for every complaint about MNC activities (whether about capital markets, technology transfer, or employment practices), we can identify potential benefits, as shown in Exhibit 2-4.

Numerous conflicts arise between MNC companies or subsidiaries and host countries, including conflicting goals (both economic and noneconomic) and con-

Exhibit 2-4
MNC Benefits and Costs to Host Countries

BENEFITS	COSTS
CAPITAL MARKET EFFECTS	
• Broader access to outside capital • Foreign-exchange earnings • Import substitution effects allow governments to save foreign exchange for priority projects • Risk sharing	• Increased competition for local scarce capital • Increased interest rates as supply of local capital decreases • Capital service effects of balance of payments
TECHNOLOGY AND PROTECTION EFFECTS	
• Access to new technology and R&D developments • Infrastructure development and support • Export diversification	• Technology is not always appropriate • Plants are often for assembly only and can be dismantled • Government infrastructure investment is higher than expected benefits
EMPLOYMENT EFFECTS	
• Direct creation of new jobs • Opportunities for indigenous management development • Income multiplier effects on local community business	• Limited skill development and creation • Competition for scarce skills • Low percentage of managerial jobs for local people • Employment instability because of ability to move production operations freely to other countries

Source: R. H. Mason and R. S. Spich, *Management: An International Perspective* (Homewood, IL: Irwin, 1987), 202.

flicting concerns, such as the security of proprietary technology, patents, or information. Overall, the resulting trade-offs create an interdependent relationship between the subsidiary and the host government based on relative bargaining power. The power of MNCs is based on their large-scale, worldwide economies, their strategic flexibility, and their control over technology and production location. The bargaining chips of the host governments include their control of raw materials and market access and their ability to set the rules regarding the role of private enterprise, the operation of state-owned firms, and the specific regulations regarding taxes, permissions, and so forth.[53]

MNCs run the risk of their assets becoming hostage to host control, which may take the form of nationalism, protectionism, or governmentalism. Under nationalism, for example, public opinion is rallied in favor of national goals and against foreign influences. Under protectionism, the host institutes a partial or complete closing of borders to withstand competitive foreign products, using tariff and nontariff barriers, such as those used by Japan. Under governmentalism, the government uses its policy-setting role to favor national interests, rather than relying on market forces. An example is the decision of Britain to privatize its telephone system.[54]

Ford Motor Company came up against many of these controls when it decided to produce automobiles in Spain. The Spanish government set specific restrictions on sales and export volume: the sales volume was limited to 10 percent of the previous year's total automobile market, and the export volume had to be at least two-thirds of the entire production in Spain. Ford also had to agree that it would not broaden its model lines without the authorization of the government.[55] The intricacies of the relationship and the relative power of an MNC subsidiary and a host-country government are situation specific. Clearly, such a relationship should be managed for mutual benefit; a long-term, constructive relationship based on the MNC's socially responsive stance should result in progressive strategic success for the MNC and economic progress for the host country. The effective management of subsidiary and host-country interdependence must have a long-term perspective. Although temporary strategies to reduce interdependence via controls on the transnational flows by firms (for example, transfer-pricing tactics) or by governments (such as new residency requirements for skilled workers) are often successful in the short run, they result in inefficiencies that must be absorbed by one or both parties, with negative long-term results.[56] In setting up and maintaining subsidiaries, managers are wise to consider the long-term trade-offs between strategic plans and operational management. By finding out for themselves the pressing local concerns and understanding the sources of past conflicts, they can learn from mistakes and recognize the consequences of the failure to manage problems. Further, managers should implement policies that reflect corporate social responsibility regarding local economic issues, employee welfare, or natural resources.[57] At the least, the failure to manage interdependence effectively results in constraints on strategy. In the worst case, it results in disastrous consequences for the local area, for the subsidiary, and for the global reputation of the company.

The interdependent nature of developing economies and the MNCs operating there is of particular concern when discussing social responsibility because of the tentative and fragile nature of the economic progression in those countries. MNCs need to set a high moral standard and lay the groundwork for future economic development; at the minimum they should ensure that their actions will do no harm. Some recommendations by De George for MNCs operating in, and doing business with, developing countries are as follows:

1. Do no intentional harm. This includes respect for the integrity of the ecosystem and consumer safety.
2. Produce more good than harm for the host country.
3. Contribute by their activity to the host country's development.
4. Respect the human rights of their employees.
5. To the extent that local culture does not violate ethical norms, MNCs should respect the local culture and work with and not against it.
6. Pay their fair share of taxes.
7. Cooperate with the local government in developing and enforcing just background (infrastructure) institutions (i.e., laws, governmental regulations, unions, consumer groups, which serve as a means of social control).[58]

One issue that illustrates conflicting concerns about social responsibility and interdependence is the North American Free Trade Agreement (NAFTA), discussed in the Comparative Management in Focus.

Comparative Management in Focus

Interdependence:
The NAFTA—Perspectives from the South and the North

By 2001, about half of all new jobs created in Mexico since the NAFTA [will have] stemmed directly from that agreement, fostering a burgeoning middle class of consumers.

FORTUNE INVESTORS' GUIDE, DECEMBER 18, 2000

It may be too soon to judge the long-run success of NAFTA, but early results do reinforce the interdependent nature of the agreement between the three economies (Mexico, United States, and Canada) and the relative level of success attained for business firms, environmental issues, and people. Now, several years since NAFTA took effect, the Mexican border factories have boomed, with employment there rising to over one million. More importantly, many of those jobs are now high-tech, bringing training and a higher standard of living for many Mexicans. Indeed, Mexico's President Vincente Fox, a former Coca-Cola executive, set 2001 budget goals of 4% to 5% GDP growth.[59]

It seems that because of lower labor costs for "foreign" companies, the devalued peso, and NAFTA-reduced tariff levels, NAFTA had a mitigating effect on the Mexican economic crisis.[60] In a touch of irony, Asia's problems caused some global companies to relocate factories from Asia to Mexico. In fact, Mexico has overtaken mainland China as the volume leader of exports of textiles and garments to the United States. But, do the trade numbers tell it all? Perhaps we can compare perspectives from south and north of the border by looking at some examples and issues.

From the South Looking North

> It's not like ten years ago, when we wanted to talk to [U.S.] customers and no one would talk to us. Now, big [U.S.] customers are calling us.
>
> VICTOR ALMEIDA, CEO, INTERCERAMIC.[61]

The Almeida family of Interceramic (Internacional de Ceramica SA, Chihuahua, Mexico), always wanted to export to the United States, but it took the heightened interest in Mexico through the NAFTA agreement to really give them their breakthrough.

The manufacturer of glazed floor and wall tile is just one of the many savvy Mexican firms making inroads into the U.S. market. But in many ways it is harder for Mexican managers to go north than for U.S. managers to go south. While they both face the same sorts of cross-cultural managerial problems, Mexican companies are typically at a competitive disadvantage in the United States because they are not as advanced in technology or efficiency as American firms.

Interceramic, a traditional Mexican family business, had to learn the hard way that business is done differently in the United States. Victor Almeida, the CEO, found that contractors buy most of the tile in the United States, compared to the homeowner in Mexico, and that customers in the United States demanded a much better level of service.[62] He had to convince U.S. distributors that Interceramic had high-quality products and that the company was reliable, and it took some time to find the right U.S. managers to represent the company and interact with people on both sides of the border. He encouraged them to be more like Mexicans by showing their emotions more openly. In addition, he opened offices in Texas so that the export managers could be closer to the customer and thus get more input to custom design the tiles to suit American tastes. Although it has taken a few years, Mr. Almeida's efforts are now paying off, and he attributes much of that to NAFTA, as well as to his hard work.

But it's a different story for smaller, less efficient firms: many simply cannot compete with the resources of technology and access to capital that U.S. firms are bringing to Mexico. Corner stores and small businesses are getting driven out by the Wal-Marts, Grossmans, and Dunkin' Donuts—the same competitive situation that has hit towns in the United States. Mexican factories are finding it difficult to compete for employees with companies like GM which are offering subsidized housing. However, other businesses, in towns such as Nuevo Laredo, are booming as a result of servicing large companies such as Wal-Mart (known locally as Walmex), Mexico's biggest chain as of 2001.[63]

From the North Looking South

> If you don't have trustworthy Mexican partners, you can get into trouble here; only idiots try to figure it out themselves.
>
> R. HECKMANN, CEO, U.S. FILTER[64]

"For every factory opened in Mexico (whether by Asian, Canadian, European, or American firms), the U.S. wins service, transportation, or distribution jobs."[65] Also, American firms which supply components to those factories are profiting from the boom south of the border. This is because primary components in products such as VCRs must be made in North America to benefit from NAFTA. U.S. and Mexican companies also benefit from orders for supplies from European and Asian firms.

While many Canadian and American companies are expanding into Mexico, taking advantage of the increased confidence and opportunities resulting from passage of NAFTA, most firms face an uphill battle because they make incorrect assumptions about the similarity of the market and distribution system. Problems include corruption, American arrogance, red tape on both sides of the border, and misunderstandings about the Mexican culture and how to do business there.

Coupling these problems with those in the infrastructure, it is easy to see why many foreign firms have had difficulties expanding into Mexico, often giving up. While it is easier now to get a business phone line, transportation and mail systems are still behind American expectations, and bill collecting often must be done in person because of numerous problems with the mail and required documentation. Electricity is sometimes cut off without notice, and the legal system is so difficult to figure out that foreigners risk going to jail without being accused of a crime. Mexican partners and alliances seem to be the answer—as even the giant Wal-Mart Stores Inc. found out when it ran into so many distribution problems in Mexico that it decided it would cost no more in the long run to use local distributors.

So why do American companies bother? Typically, because they want to take advantage of market expansion opportunities. One example is U.S. Filter, a water-purification company whose target in Mexico is "90 million people who can't trust their tap water, and a slew of companies under government pressure to clean up waste water."[66]

Interdependence: South–North Strategic Alliances   Richard Heckmann, U.S. Filter's CEO, realized early on that alliances with trustworthy Mexican partners provided the answer to many problems and to achieving the interdependent goals of both countries and their firms. He knew, for example, that the political reality was that Mexican officials would favor their ties to Mexican firms and steer bids to those companies. So he contracted with a Mexican construction company, Plar SA, with strong political connections. Plar SA benefits from the deal by getting technical and financial help from U.S. Filter to upgrade its technology. Also, in order to reach his smaller potential customers, Mr. Heckmann has formed a joint venture with Enrique Anhalt, a local Mexico City water-purification supplier to 250 manufacturers and other customers with small systems, assuming that when they upgrade they will turn to a local supplier.

The environmental cleanup efforts in Mexico clearly exhibit the interdependence of NAFTA and will benefit everyone in the long run. Funding from the United States is helping with projects such as the sewage-treatment plants at 11 cities south of the border. In turn, that business is going to many U.S. environmental-services companies, such as San Diego Gas & Electric Co., which is building natural gas pipelines to Mexicali and Tijuana to supply clean fuel to industrial plants.

The auto industry is another agent of massive change in Mexico—building an industrial base south of the border that will help strengthen the Mexican economy. "The auto industry has the unusual ability to . . . jump start a middle class," according to David Cole, director of the University of Michigan's automotive-studies office.[67] While the average Ford worker in Hermosillo still earns considerably less than his counterpart in Wayne, Michigan, that wage does represent a considerable increase for Mexican workers. In addition, every new auto plant in Mexico trains thousands of Mexicans, most of them new to factory work. While those factors don't console auto workers in the United States who have lost their jobs, it does mean that American auto manufacturers can be more globally competitive.

There is likely to be increasing interdependence among the Americas in the future as agreements open up further trade with other South American countries such as Chile and Brazil. These countries are tearing down their internal trade barriers also, in a wave that may eventually form a free-trade zone from Alaska to Tierra del Fuego. South Americans are realizing that they may get left out in the cold as both the European Community and North America form their own huge markets. As noted by Mr. Grisetti, an Argentine businessman, "If the world is dividing into blocs, we have to form a bloc or disappear . . . it's a necessity."

Managing Environmental Interdependence

International managers—and all people—can no longer afford to ignore the impact of their activities on the environment. As Ward and Dubois put it:

> Now that mankind is in the process of completing the colonization of the planet, learning to manage it intelligently is an urgent imperative. [People] must accept responsibility for the stewardship of the earth. The word stewardship implies, of course, management for the sake of someone else. . . . As we enter the global phase of human evolution, it becomes obvious that each [person] has two countries, his [or her] own and the planet earth.[68]

Effectively managing environmental interdependence includes considering ecological interdependence as well as the economic and social implications of MNC activities. There is an ever-increasing awareness of, and a mounting concern, worldwide, about the effects of global industrialization on the natural environment. This concern was evidenced by the gathering of world leaders at the Earth Summit in Rio de Janeiro to discuss ecological preservation and decide on action. Government regulations and powerful interest groups are demanding ecological responsibility regarding the use of scarce natural resources and production processes that threaten permanent damage to the planet. MNCs have to deal with each country's different policies and techniques for environmental and health protection. Such variations in approach reflect different levels of industrialization, living standards, government–business relations, philosophies of collective intervention, patterns of industrial competition, and degrees of sophistication in public policy.[69] For an MNC to take advantage of less stringent regulations (or expectations) is not only irresponsible but also invites disaster, as illustrated by the Union Carbide accident in Bhopal.

In recent years, the export of hazardous wastes from developed countries to less developed ones has increased considerably. One instance was the dumping of over eight thousand drums of waste, including drums filled with polychlorinated biphenyl (PCB), a highly toxic compound, in Koko, Nigeria.[70] While not all dumping is illegal, the large international trade in hazardous wastes (as a result of the increasing barriers to domestic disposal) raises disturbing questions regarding social responsibility. Although the importer of waste must take some blame, it is the exporter who shoulders the ultimate responsibility for both generation and disposal. Often, companies choose to dispose of hazardous waste in less developed countries to take advantage of weaker regulations and lower costs. Until we have strict international regulation of trade in hazardous wastes, companies should take it upon themselves to monitor their activities, as Singh and Lakhan demand:

> To export these wastes to countries which do not benefit from waste-generating industrial processes or whose citizens do not have lifestyles that generate such wastes is unethical. It is especially unjust to send hazardous wastes to lesser developed countries which lack the technology to minimize the deleterious effects of these substances.[71]

The exporting of pesticides poses a similar problem, with the United States and Germany being the main culprits. The United States exports about 200 million pounds of pesticides each year that are prohibited, restricted, or not registered for use in the United States.[72] One MNC, Monsanto Chemical Corporation, for example, sells DDT to many foreign importers, even though its use in the United States has been essentially banned. Apart from the lack of social responsibility toward the people and the environment in the countries that import DDT, this action is also irresponsible to American citizens because many of their fruits and meat products are imported from those countries.[73]

These are only two of the environmental problems facing countries and large corporations today. According to Graedel and Allenby, the path to truly sustainable development is for corporations to broaden their concept of industrial ecology:

> The concept [of industrial ecology] requires that an industrial system be viewed not in isolation from its surrounding systems, but in concert with them. It is a systems view in which one seeks to optimize the total materials cycle from virgin material, to finished material, to component, to product, to obsolete product, and to ultimate disposal.[74]

Essentially, this perspective supports the idea that environmental citizenship is necessary for a firm's survival as well as responsible social performance.[75]

It is clear then, that MNCs must take the lead in dealing with ecological interdependence by integrating environmental factors into strategic planning. Along with an investment appraisal, a project feasibility study, and operational plans, such planning should include an environmental impact assessment.[76] At the least, MNC managers must deal with the increasing scarcity of natural resources in the next few decades by (1) looking for alternate raw materials, (2) developing new methods of recycling or disposing of used materials, and (3) expanding the use of by-products.[77]

Multinational corporations already have had a tremendous impact on foreign countries, and this impact will continue to grow and bring about long-lasting changes. Even now, U.S. multinational corporations alone account for about 10 percent of the world's GNP. Because of interdependence both at the local level and the global level, it is not only moral but also in the best interest of MNCs to establish a single clear posture toward social and ethical responsibilities worldwide and to ensure that it is implemented. In a real sense, foreign firms enter as guests in host countries and must respect the local laws, policies, traditions, and culture as well as those countries' economic and developmental needs.

Conclusion

In conclusion, when research findings and anecdotal evidence indicate differential attitudes toward ethical behavior and social responsibility across cultures, MNCs must take certain steps. For example, they must be careful when placing a foreign manager in a country whose values are incongruent with his or her own, because this could lead to conflicts with local managers, governmental bodies, customers, and suppliers. As discussed earlier, expatriates should be oriented to the legal and ethical ramifications of questionable foreign payments, the differences in environmental regulations, and the local expectations of personal integrity, and they should be supported as they attempt to integrate host-country behaviors with the expectations of the company's headquarters.[78]

Social responsibility, ethical behavior, and interdependence are important concerns to be built into management control—not as afterthoughts, but as part of the ongoing process of planning and controlling international operations for the long-term benefit of all.

In Part 2, we will focus on the pervasive and powerful influence of culture in the host-country environment in which the international manager operates. In Chapter 3, we will examine the nature of culture: What are its various dimensions and roots? How does culture affect the behavior and expectations of employees and what are the implications for how managers operating in other countries should behave?

INTERNET RESOURCES

Visit the Deresky companion Web site at http://prenhall.com/Deresky for this chapter's Internet resources.

SUMMARY OF KEY POINTS

1. The concept of international social responsibility includes the expectation that MNCs should be concerned about the social and the economic effects of their decisions regarding activities in other countries.
2. Moral universalism refers to the need for a moral standard that is accepted by all cultures.
3. Concerns about MNC social responsibility revolve around issues of human rights in other countries, such as South Africa and China. Many organizations develop codes of conduct for their approach to business around the world.
4. International business ethics refers to the conduct of MNCs in their relationships to all individuals and entities with whom they come into contact. Ethical behavior is judged and based largely on the cultural value system and the generally accepted ways of doing business in each country or society. MNC managers must decide whether to base their ethical standards on those of the host country or those of the home country and whether these different standards can be reconciled.
5. MNCs must balance their responsibility to various stakeholders, such as owners, creditors, consumers, employees, suppliers, governments, and societies.
6. Questionable payments are those payments that raise significant questions about appropriate moral behavior either in the host nation or other nations. The Foreign Corrupt Practices Act prohibits most questionable payments by U.S. companies doing business in other countries.
7. Managers must control their activities relative to interdependent relationships at all levels, from simple, daily business transactions involving local workers, intermediaries, or consumers to global concerns of ecological responsibility.
8. The MNC-host country relationship is generally a love–hate relationship from the host-country's viewpoint in that it wants the economic growth that the MNC can provide but does not want the dependency and other problems that result.
9. The failure to effectively manage interdependence will result in constraints on strategy, in the least, or in disastrous consequences for the local area, the subsidiary, and the global reputation of the company.
10. Managing environmental interdependence includes the need to consider ecological interdependence as well as the economic and social implications of MNC activities.

Chapter

3

Understanding the Role of Culture

Opening Profile: Telmex's Cultural Advantage Undermined by Global Competition

We speak to our customers in a language they can understand about benefits they can understand

—FRANCISCO CAMACHO, TELMEX MANAGER,
WALL STREET JOURNAL, 1998.

This is a watershed in the history of telecommunications competition in Mexico.

—ROLAND ZUBIRAN, PRESIDENT OF ALESTRA,
www.FT.com, JANUARY 2, 2001.

When U.S. phone giants AT&T and MCI Communications started up long-distance business in Mexico in 1997, they got a surprising lesson about competition from Telefonos de Mexico SA (Telmex), the former state-owned monopoly. At that time, AT&T and MCI (now MCI Worldcom, Inc. after the merger) had a combined market share of about 25 percent.

Telmex, apparently, has shown them how to do business in the developing world, by understanding its markets and its people. The company used its understanding of the way of life of Mexican people, took advantage of its familiarity of Mexico's feeble regulatory and legal systems, and engaged in smart marketing.

Much of Telmex's success, according to AT&T and MCI executives, comes from intricate cultural understanding in a country where influence often counts more than the law.

In 2001, however, the tables turned on Telmex, ending years of legal clashes designed to open up Mexico's $12 billion telecom market. Avantel and Alestra (partly owned by U.S. carriers Worldcom and AT&T), had claimed that Telmex was operating a near-monopoly. The United States had a complaint before the World Trade Organization. Mexico's antitrust agency declared that Telmex was in fact dominant in its services, but Telmex still evaded court efforts to restrict its reach. However, Telmex eventually agreed to provide fair access. This set the stage for President Vicente Fox's efforts to open up a new era of investment and economic development. Mexico has a population of 97 million, but only 11.5 million telephone lines—one of the lowest penetration rates compared with other large Latin American countries. As part of the agreement, Alestra and Avantel agreed to pay Telmex for past interconnection fees, amounting to $180 million.

As of February 2001, however, Telefonos de Mexico S.A. still controlled 98 percent of local lines and 81 percent market share for long-distance service. Perhaps its cultural savvy has given it a foothold difficult to penetrate by outsiders.

SOURCES: "Mexican Telcos Agree Pact," www.FT.com, January 2, 2001; "Pacts May give AT&T, Worldcom, Better Access in Mexico Market," *The Dallas Morning News*, January 8, 2001, in www.Chicagotribune.com, January 28, 2001; "U.S. Phone giants find Telmex can be a Bruising Competitor," *The Wall Street Journal*, October 23, 1998.

This chapter's Opening Profile describes how understanding of the local culture and business environment can give managers an advantage in competitive industries; foreign companies—no matter how big—can ignore those aspects to their peril. Such differences in culture and the way of life in other countries necessitate that managers develop international expertise to manage on a contingency basis according to the host-country environment. Powerful, interdependent factors in that environment—political, economic, legal, technological, and cultural—influence management strategy, functions, and processes.

A critical skill for managing people and processes in other countries is **cultural savvy**: that is, a working knowledge of the cultural variables affecting management decisions. Managers have often seriously underestimated the significance of cultural factors. According to numerous accounts, many blunders made in international operations can be attributed to a lack of cultural sensitivity.[1] Examples abound. Scott Russell, senior vice president for human resources at Cendant Mobility in Danbury, Connecticut, recounts that:

> An American company in Japan charged its Japanese HR manager with reducing the workforce. The Japanese manager studied the issue but couldn't find a solution within cultural Japanese parameters; so when he came back to the Americans, he reduced the workforce by resigning— which was not what they wanted.[2]

Cultural sensitivity, or **cultural empathy**, is an awareness and an honest caring about another individual's culture. Such sensitivity requires the ability to understand the perspective of those living in other (and very different) societies and the willingness to put oneself in another's shoes.

International managers can benefit greatly from understanding the nature, dimensions, and variables of a specific culture and how these affect work and organizational processes. This cultural awareness enables them to develop appropriate policies and determine how to plan, organize, lead, and control in a specific international setting. Such a process of adaptation to the environment is necessary to implement strategy successfully. It also leads to effective interaction in a workforce of increasing cultural diversity, both in the United States and in other countries.

Company reports and management studies make it clear that a lack of cultural sensitivity costs businesses money and opportunities. One study of U.S. multinational corporations found that poor intercultural communication skills still constitute a major management problem; American managers' knowledge of other cultures lags far behind their understanding of other organizational processes.[3] In a synthesis of the research on cross-cultural training, Black and Mendenhall found that up to 40 percent of expatriate managers leave their assignments early because of poor performance or poor adjustment to the local environment. About half of those who do remain are considered only marginally effective. Further, they found that cross-cultural differences are the cause of failed negotiations and interactions, resulting in losses to U.S. firms of over $2 billion a year for failed expatriate assignments alone.[4]

We also have evidence, however, that cross-cultural training is effective in developing skills and enhancing adjustment and performance. In spite of such evidence, little is done by U.S. firms to take advantage of such important research and to incorporate it into their ongoing training programs, whose purpose is ostensibly to prepare managers before sending them overseas. Too often, the importance of such training in developing cultural sensitivity is realized much too late, as seen in the following account of the unhappy marriage between America's AT&T and Italy's Olivetti, the office-equipment maker:

> One top AT&T executive believes that most of the problems in the venture stemmed from cultural differences. "I don't think we or Olivetti spent enough time understanding behavior patterns," says Robert Kayner, AT&T group executive. "We knew the culture was different, but we never really penetrated. We would get angry, and they would get upset." Mr. Kayner says AT&T's attempts to fix the problems, such as delays in deliveries, were transmitted in curt memos that offended Olivetti officials. "They would get an attitude, 'Who are you to tell us what to do,'" he says. Or the Olivetti side would explain its own problems, and AT&T managers would simply respond, "Don't tell me about your problems. Solve them." AT&T executives are the first to admit, now, that one of the greatest challenges of putting a venture together is that partners frequently see the world in very different—and potentially divisive—ways.[5]

In this chapter, we provide a conceptual framework with which companies and managers can assess relevant cultural variables and develop cultural profiles of various countries. We then use this framework to consider the probable effects of cultural differences on an organization and their implications for management. To do this, we need to examine the powerful environmental factor of cultural context. First, we explore the nature of culture, its variables and dimensions, and then we consider specific differences in cultural values and their implications for the on-the-job behavior of individuals and groups. We discuss cultural variables in general in this chapter. The impact of culture on specific management functions and processes will be discussed in later chapters.

CULTURE AND ITS EFFECTS ON ORGANIZATIONS

As generally understood, **the culture of a society** comprises the shared values, understandings, assumptions, and goals that are learned from earlier generations, imposed by present members of a society, and passed on to succeeding generations. This shared outlook results, in large part, in common attitudes, codes of conduct, and expectations that subconsciously guide and control certain norms of behavior.[6,7,8] One is born into, not with, a given culture, gradually internalizing its subtle effects through the socialization process. Culture results in a basis for living grounded in shared communication, standards, codes of conduct, and expectations.[9] A U.S. manager assigned to a foreign subsidiary, for example, must expect to find large and small differences in the behavior of individuals and groups within that organization. As depicted in Exhibit 3-1, these differences result from the societal, or sociocultural, variables of the culture, such as religion and language, in addition to prevailing national variables, such as economic, legal, and political factors. National and sociocultural variables thus provide the context for the development and perpetuation of cultural variables. These cultural variables, in turn, determine basic attitudes toward work, time, materialism, individualism, and change. Such attitudes affect an individual's motivation and expectations regarding work and group relations, and they ultimately affect the outcomes that can be expected from that individual.

The way these sets of variables can interact is illustrated by a policy change made by KLM Royal Dutch Airlines, where the organizational culture responded to national cultural values and accepted practices. The culture of social responsiveness in the Netherlands was incorporated into business policy when the airline revised its travel-benefits policy for families of employees. For some time, many KLM stewards had protested the rule that only immediate family were eligible for low fares on KLM flights. They found it discriminatory that even just-married heterosexual spouses received the benefit, while long-term homosexual partners were not eligible. Upon reconsideration, KLM responded that any couple who formally registered

Exhibit 3-1
Environmental Variables
Affecting Management
Functions

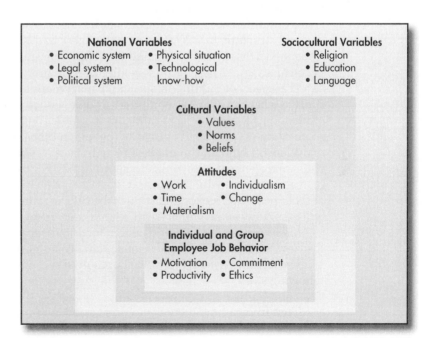

as living together, which is a normal legal practice in the Netherlands, would be eligible for the low fares. However, a year had to elapse between partners before a new partner could be registered. By changing its policy, KLM put the emphasis on committed relationships rather than on marital status or sexual preference.[10]

As of 2001, McDonald's had 58 restaurants in Russia. Their experience with setting up businesses there for the last eleven years since the first restaurant opened in Moscow demonstrates the combined effects of national and cultural variables on work. There, local employees require lengthy training to serve up "Bolshoi Maks" in the "McDonald's way." Unfortunately, Russians are still for the most part not familiar with working under the capitalist system; they have been victims of the inertia brought about by the old system of central planning for so long that productivity still remains low. As a result, Russians have few goods to buy, and the new free-market prices are so high that there is little motivation for them to work for rubles that won't buy anything.[11] (McDonald's in Moscow is further profiled in the opening profile at the beginning of Chapter 8.)

It is thus clear that cultural variables—shared beliefs, values, and attitudes—can greatly affect organizational processes. In fact, one example of how culture affects organizational processes is frequently evident as the use of technological applications in those processes spreads around the world. The result can be a clash between culture and technology, as illustrated in the accompanying *E-Biz Box*. Which organizational processes are most affected, and how, is the subject of ongoing cross-cultural management research and debate.[12] Some argue that the effects of culture are more evident at the individual level of personal behavior than at the organizational level, as a result of convergence.[13] Convergence describes the phenomenon of the shifting of individual management styles to become more similar to one another. The convergence argument is based on the belief that the demands of industrialization and worldwide coordination and competition tend to factor out differences in organizational-level processes, such as choice of technology and structure. In a 2000 study of Japanese and Korean firms, Lee, Roehl, and Choe found that globalization and firm size were sources of convergence of management styles.[14] These factors are discussed in more detail later in this chapter.

The effects of culture on specific management functions are particularly noticeable when we attempt to impose our own values and systems on another society. Exhibit 3-2 gives some examples of the values typical of U.S. culture, compares some common perspectives held by people in other countries, and shows which management functions might be affected, clearly implying the need for the differential management of organizational processes. For example, American managers plan activities, schedule them, and judge their timely completion based on the belief that people influence and control the future, rather than assuming that events will occur only at the will of Allah, as managers in an Islamic nation might believe.

Many people in the world understand and relate to others only in terms of their own culture. This unconscious reference point of one's own cultural values is called a *self-reference criterion*.[15] The result of such an attitude is illustrated in the following story:

> Once upon a time there was a great flood, and involved in this flood
> were two creatures, a monkey and a fish. The monkey, being agile and

Many managers in Asia cling to the standard corporate practice of doling out information on a need-to-know basis.

—www.businessweek.com, OCTOBER 23, 2000.

Asia is a world leader in wireless technology, broadband communications, and electronic government; it has tremendous potential as a center for B2B e-commerce. Yet advancements into e-business are hindered by a culture-internet clash. There are several problem areas:

While Asia is home to 60 percent of the world's people—creating the potential for huge pan-Asian e-marketplaces—those people speak hundreds of languages, creating a web of Babble. Also, the Internet is about giving workers access to information so they can move at Net speed. Yet many managers in Asia cling to the standard corporate practice of doling out information on a need-to-know basis.

Another hindrance to e-commerce is the way Asian companies deal with suppliers. Supply chains in Asia typically involve three or four middlemen—twice as many as in Europe. In Japan, for instance, retailers pay for what they receive and wholesalers eat the cost of missing items. To protect themselves, wholesalers get dozens of workers to unpack boxes, count the contents, and repack the boxes before they are shipped. Wholesalers, therefore, see the Internet as a threat to their jobs.

Costs of connecting to the Internet are high, also hindering e-business. While logging on in Hong Kong and Seoul is still a third more expensive than in the United States, Japan is even worse off. Leased lines are three times pricier in Tokyo than in New York and twice the cost of those in Germany. Meanwhile the phone system is so underpowered in India, most businesses can't even get Internet connections.

Other problems include commercial transactions, which in Asia still involve cash or letters of credit, with written receipts often required. In addition, a lack of comprehensive credit services also means each e-marketplace buyer and seller must be painstakingly screened, which can take weeks.

E-Zaiko, for example, a venture between Mitsui & Co. and Itochu Corp., two of Japan's largest trading houses, has created an electronic marketplace for excess inventory that matches buyers and sellers of clothing, furniture, and other goods. It is a first in Japan, and e-Zaiko has a ready-made list of clients from their *keiretsu* industrial groups. Yet the company must reach thousands of small businesses that don't even have computers, let alone connections to the Internet.

One company that isn't waiting for its customers to get wired is Asia-Steel.com. For the past few years, CEO Justin Chu has been giving away computers to get customers hooked into their online service. The Hong Kong company, which lets buyers and sellers trade steel electronically, has handed out more than 1,000 PCs to steel mills in China and trained purchasing managers to use them, resulting in attracting 200,000 tons of steel to its site per month.

To close the Internet divide, Asian companies need deep pockets, strong connections between their on-line and off-line businesses, and most importantly, tremendous skill at translating to the Web the networks of business relationships that make Asia a complicated place to operate.

SOURCE: Adapted from "The Net Is Transforming the West, But Companies in the East Lag Behind," www.businessweek.com, October 23, 2000.

Exhibit 3-2

U.S. Values and Possible Alternatives

ASPECTS OF U.S. CULTURE*	ALTERNATIVE ASPECT	EXAMPLES OF MANAGEMENT FUNCTION AFFECTED
The individual can influence the future (where there is a will there is a way).	Life follows a preordained course, and human action is determined by the will of God.	Planning and scheduling
The individual can change and improve the environment.	People are intended to adjust to the physical environment rather than to alter it.	Organizational environment, morale, and productivity
An individual should be realistic in his or her aspirations.	Ideals are to be pursued regardless of what is "reasonable."	Goal setting and career development
We must work hard to accomplish our objectives (Puritan ethic).	Hard work is not the only prerequisite for success; wisdom, luck, and time are also required.	Motivation and reward system
Commitments should be honored (people will do what they say they will do).	A commitment may be superseded by a conflicting request, or an agreement may only signify intention and have little or no relationship to the capacity for performance.	Negotiating and bargaining
One should effectively use one's time (time is money that can be saved or wasted).	Schedules are important, but only in relation to other priorities.	Long- and short-range planning
A primary obligation of an employee is to the organization.	The individual employee has a primary obligation to his or her family and friends.	Loyalty, commitment, and motivation
The employer or employee can terminate the relationship.	Employment is for a lifetime.	Motivation and commitment to the company
The best-qualified people should be given the positions available.	Family, friendship, and other considerations should determine employment practices.	Employment, promotions, recruiting, selection, and reward

*Aspect here refers to a belief, value, attitude, or assumption that is a part of a culture in that it is shared by a large number of people in that culture.

Source: Excerpted from *Managing Cultural Differences* by Philip R. Harris and Robert T. Moran, 5th ed. Copyright © 2000 by Gulf Publishing Company, Houston, TX. Used with permission. All rights reserved.

experienced, was lucky enough to scramble up a tree and escape the raging waters. As he looked down from his safe perch, he saw the poor fish struggling against the swift current. With the very best of intentions, he reached down and lifted the fish from the water. The result was inevitable.[16]

The monkey assumed that its frame of reference applied to the fish and acted accordingly. International managers from all countries thus must understand and adjust to unfamiliar social and commercial practices—especially the practices of that mysterious and unique nation, the United States. Japanese workers at a U.S.

manufacturing plant learned to put courtesy aside and interrupt conversations with Americans when there were problems. Europeans, however, are often confused by the Americans' apparent informality, which then backfires when the Europeans do not get work done as the Americans expect.[17]

As a first step toward cultural sensitivity, an international manager should understand her or his own culture. This awareness helps to guard against adopting either a parochial or ethnocentric attitude. **Parochialism** occurs when a Frenchman, for example, expects those from or in another country to automatically fall into patterns of behavior common in France. **Ethnocentrism** describes the attitude of those who operate from the assumption that their ways of doing things are best—no matter where or under what conditions they are applied. Companies both large and small have demonstrated this lack of cultural sensitivity in countless subtle (and not so subtle) ways, with varying disastrous effects.

Procter & Gamble was one such company. In an early Japanese television commercial for Camay soap, a Japanese woman is bathing when her husband walks into the bathroom. She starts telling him about her new beauty soap. Her husband, stroking her shoulder, hints that he has more on his mind than suds. The commercial, which had been popular in Europe, was a disaster in Japan. For the man to intrude on his wife "was considered bad manners," says Edwin L. Artzt, P&G's vice-chairman and international chief. "And the Japanese didn't think it was very funny." P&G has learned from its mistakes and now generates about half of its revenue from foreign sales.[18]

After studying his or her own culture, the manager's next step toward establishing effective cross-cultural relations is to develop cultural sensitivity. Managers not only must be aware of cultural variables and their effects on behavior in the workplace but also must appreciate cultural diversity and understand how to build constructive working relationships anywhere in the world. In the next sections, we explore cultural variables and dimensions. In later chapters, we suggest specific ways in which managers can address these variables and dimensions to help build constructive relationships.

CULTURAL VARIABLES AND DIMENSIONS

Given the great variety of cultures and subcultures around the world, how can a student of cross-cultural management, or a manager wishing to be culturally savvy, develop an understanding of the specific nature of a certain people? With such an understanding, how can a manager anticipate the probable effects of an unfamiliar culture within an organizational setting and thereby manage human resources productively and control outcomes?

One approach is to develop a cultural profile for each country or region with which the company does or is considering doing business. Developing a cultural profile requires some familiarity with the cultural variables universal to most cultures. From these universal variables, managers can identify the specific differences found in each country or people and hence anticipate their implications for the workplace.

Managers should never assume that they can successfully transplant American, or Japanese, or any other country's styles, practices, expectations, and processes. Instead, they should practice a basic tenet of good management—contingency management. Contingency management requires managers to adapt to the local environment and people and to manage accordingly.

Subcultures

Managers should recognize, of course, that generalizations in cultural profiles will produce only an approximation, or stereotype, of national character. Many countries, in fact, comprise diverse subcultures whose constituents conform only in varying degrees to the national character. In Canada, distinct subcultures include anglophones and francophones (English-speaking and French-speaking people) and indigenous Canadians. The United States, too, has varying subcultures. Americans abroad are almost always dealt with in the context of the stereotypical American, but Americans recognize differences among themselves due to ethnic, geographic, or other subcultural backgrounds. Americans should extend the same insight toward people in other countries and be extremely careful not to overgeneralize or oversimplify. For example, although Americans tend to think of Chinese as homogeneous in their culture, there are in fact considerable differences due to regional diversity—including distinct ethnic groups with their own local customs and a multitude of dialects. A study by Ralston, et al. concluded that, although adherence to traditional Confucian values was common to all regions, there were considerable differences among regions on variables such as individualism and openness to change (with Guangzhou and Shanghai ranking the highest on those dimensions, followed by Beijing and Dalian and then Chengdu and Lanzhou).[19] This implies that Chinese in Guangzhou and Shanghai may be somewhat more "westernized" and more open to doing business with westerners.

Above all, good managers treat people as individuals, and they consciously avoid any form of stereotyping. However, a cultural profile is a good starting point to help managers develop some tentative expectations—some cultural context—as a backdrop to managing in a specific international setting. It is useful, then, to look at what cultural variables have been studied and what implications can be drawn from the results.

Cultural Variables

To develop cultural profiles we first need to be familiar with the kinds of universal cultural variables found in most societies that make up unique clusters and provide a snapshot of the overall character of a specific group. While there are countless individual variables, one approach to categorizing interdependent variables is given by Harris and Moran, who identified eight categories that form the subsystems in any society.[20] This systems approach to understanding cultural and national variables—and their effects on work behavior—is consistent with the model shown in Exhibit 3-1. The following sections describe these eight categories and explain their implications.

Kinship

A kinship system is the system adopted by a given society to guide family relationships. Whereas in the United States this system primarily consists of the nuclear family (which is increasingly represented by single-parent families), in many other parts of the world the kinship system consists of an extended family with many members, spanning several generations. This extended, closely knit family, typical in many eastern nations, may influence corporate activities in cases where family loyalty is given primary consideration—such as when contracts are awarded or when employees are hired (and a family member is always selected over a more suitable candidate from outside the family). In these family-oriented societies, such practices are pervasive and are taken for granted. Foreign managers often find themselves locked out of important decisions when dealing with family businesses. If, however, they take the time to learn the local cultural expectations regarding families, they will notice predictable patterns of behavior and be better prepared to deal with them. Such traditional practices are exemplified in the experience of an Asian MBA, educated in the United States, when he presented a more up-to-date business plan to his uncle, the managing director of a medium-sized firm in India:

> The family astrologer attended the meeting and vetoed the plan. Later, the nephew persisted and asked the astrologer to reconsider the plan. The astrologer recommended various ceremonies after which the astral signs would probably bend toward the plan.[21]

Education

The formal or informal education of workers in a foreign firm, received from whatever source, greatly affects the expectations placed on those workers in the workplace. It also influences managers' choices about recruitment and staffing practices, training programs, and leadership styles. Training and development programs, for example, need to be consistent with the general level of educational preparation in that country.

Economy

Whatever the economic system, the means of production and distribution in a society (and the resulting effects on individuals and groups) has a powerful influence on such organizational processes as sourcing, distribution, incentives, and repatriation of capital. At this time of radically changing political systems, it appears that the drastic differences between capitalist and socialist systems will have less effect on MNCs than in the past.

Politics

The system of government in a society, whether democratic, communist, or dictatorial, imposes varying constraints on an organization and its freedom to do business. It is the manager's job to understand the political system and how it affects organizational processes, to negotiate positions within that system, and to manage effectively the mutual concerns of the host country and guest company. As demonstrated by the difficulties that McDonald's had in training

Russian workers for its Moscow restaurant (discussed earlier in the chapter), the political and economic subsystems of a country often dominate other cultural systems.

Religion

The spiritual beliefs of a society are often so powerful that they transcend other cultural aspects. Religion commonly underlies both moral and economic norms. In the United States, the effects of religion in the workplace are limited (other than a generalized belief in hard work, which stems from the Protestant work ethic), whereas in other countries religious beliefs and practices often influence everyday business transactions and on-the-job behaviors. For example, in a long-standing tradition based on the Qur'an and the sayings of Muhammad, Arabs consult with senior members of the ruling families or the community regarding business decisions. Hindus, Buddhists, and some Muslims believe in the concept of destiny, or fate. In Islamic countries, the idea of *inshallah*, that is, "God willing," prevails. In some Western countries, religious organizations, such as the Roman Catholic Church, play a major cultural role through moral and political influence.

One of the ways that the Islamic faith affects the operations of international firms involves the charging of interest:

> The kingdom of Saudi Arabia observes Sharia, which is Islamic law based on both the Qur'an and the Hadith—the traditions of the Prophet Muhammad. Under these codes, interest is banned, and both the giver and the taker of interest are equally damned. This means that the modern Western banking system is technically illegal. A debate has begun on the interpretation of the concept of interest. The kingdom's religious scholars, the ulema, view all interest, or rib'a, as banned. Some have challenged that interpretation as too restrictive, however, and have called for a more liberal interpretation. Their view is that Muhammad referred only to excessive interest when he condemned usury. Should something come of this debate, it would help establish a legal framework for dealing with Saudi Arabia's banking problems, such as steep drops in profits, and end the legal limbo of Western-style banking in the kingdom.[22]

Associations

Many and various types of associations arise out of the formal and informal groups that make up a society. Whether these associations are based on religious, social, professional, or trade affiliations, managers should be familiar with them and the role they may play in business interactions.

Health

The system of health care in a country affects employee productivity, expectations, and attitudes toward physical fitness and its role in the workplace. These expectations will influence managerial decisions regarding health care benefits, insurance, physical facilities, sick days, and so forth.

Recreation

Closely associated with other cultural factors, recreation includes the way in which people use their leisure time, as well as their attitudes toward leisure and their choice of whom to socialize with. Workers' attitudes toward recreation can affect their work behavior and their perception of the role of work in their lives.

Technology and Its Effects on Culture

> This is how many Koreans become versed in the Internet [at PC parlors]
>
> WON JUN YOUNG, MANAGER, YECA STATION (A PARLOR THAT SELLS THE USE OF PCS FOR GAMES, SHARE TRADING, TEMPORARY OFFICES). www.businessweek.com, SEPTEMBER 25, 2000.

We would be remiss if we did not acknowledge the contemporary phenomenon of the increasingly pervasive use of technology in society as it seems to be encroaching on most of the foregoing social variables—in particular associations, education, and the economy. In South Korea, for example, where information technology makes up about 10 percent of the $400 billion economy and is expected to reach 20 percent by 2010, there is an obsession for anything digital. This seems to be changing the lives of many Koreans. Teenagers, used to hanging out at the mall, now do so at the country's 20,000 PC parlors to watch movies, check e-mail and surf the Net for as little as $1. Korean housewives are on a waiting list for ADSL lines when the $35 billion high-speed government telecommunications project is completed in 2005. By then 95 percent of Korean households will have Internet access.[23]

Value Dimensions

Cultural variables result from unique sets of shared values among different groups of people. Most of the variations between cultures stem from underlying value systems, which cause people to behave differently under similar circumstances. **Values** are a society's ideas about what is good or bad, right or wrong—such as the widespread belief that stealing is immoral and unfair. Values determine how individuals will probably respond in any given circumstance. As a powerful component of a society's culture, values are communicated through the eight subsystems just described and are passed from generation to generation. Interaction and pressure among these subsystems (or more recently from foreign cultures) may provide the impetus for slow change. The dissolution of the Soviet Union and the formation of the Commonwealth of Independent States is an example of extreme political change resulting from internal economic pressures and external encouragement to change.

Hofstede's Value Dimensions

One useful framework for understanding how basic values underlie organizational behavior is proposed by Hofstede, as the result of his research on over 116,000 people in 50 countries. He proposes four value dimensions: (1) power distance, (2) uncertainty avoidance, (3) individualism, and (4) masculinity.[24] We should be cautious when interpreting these results, however, because his research findings are based on a sample drawn from one multinational firm, IBM, and because he does not account for within-country differences in multicultural countries. Although we introduce these value dimensions here to aid in the understanding of different cultures, their relevance and application to management functions will be discussed in later chapters.

The first of these value dimensions, **power distance**, is the level of acceptance by a society of the unequal distribution of power in institutions. In the workplace, inequalities in power are normal, as evidenced in hierarchical boss–subordinate relationships. However, the extent to which subordinates accept unequal power is societally determined. In countries in which people display high power distance (such as Malaysia, the Philippines, and Mexico), employees acknowledge the boss's authority simply by respecting that individual's formal position in the hierarchy, and they seldom bypass the chain of command. This respectful response results, predictably, in a centralized structure and autocratic leadership. In countries where people display low power distance (such as Austria, Denmark, and Israel), superiors and subordinates are apt to regard one another as equal in power, resulting in more harmony and cooperation. Clearly, an autocratic management style is not likely to be well received in low-power-distance countries.

*Not to scale—indicates relative magnitude.
ARA = Arab countries
AUT = Austria

Based on G. Hofstede, "National Cultures in Four Dimensions," *International Studies of Management and Organization*, Spring–Summer, 1983.

The second value dimension, **uncertainty avoidance**, refers to the extent to which people in a society feel threatened by ambiguous situations. Countries with a high level of uncertainty avoidance (such as Japan, Portugal, and Greece) tend to have strict laws and procedures to which their people adhere closely, and there is a strong sense of nationalism. In a business context, this value results in formal rules and procedures designed to provide more security and greater career stability. Managers have a propensity for low-risk decisions, employees exhibit little aggressiveness, and lifetime employment is common. In countries with lower levels of uncertainty avoidance (such as Denmark, Great Britain, and, to a lesser extent, the United States), nationalism is less pronounced, and protests and other such activities are tolerated. As a consequence, company activities are less structured and less formal, some managers take more risks, and there is high job mobility.

*Not to scale—indicates relative magnitude.
AUL = Australia

Based on G. Hofstede.

The third of Hofstede's value dimensions, **individualism**, refers to the tendency of people to look after themselves and their immediate family only and neglect the needs of society. In countries that prize individualism (such as the United States, Great Britain, and Australia), democracy, individual initiative, and achievement are highly valued; the relationship of the individual to organizations is one of independence on an emotional level, if not on an economic level.

In countries such as Pakistan and Panama, where low individualism prevails—that is, where collectivism predominates—one finds tight social frameworks, emotional dependence on belonging to "the organization," and a strong belief in group decisions. People from a collectivist country, like Japan, believe in the will of the group rather than that of the individual, and their pervasive collectivism exerts control over individual members through social pressure and the fear of humiliation. The society valorizes harmony and saving face, whereas individualistic cultures generally emphasize self-respect, autonomy, and independence. Hiring and promotion practices in collectivist societies are based on paternalism rather than achievement or personal capabilities, which are valued in individualistic societies. Other management practices (such as the use of quality circles in Japanese factories) reflect the emphasis on group decision-making processes in collectivist societies.

Hofstede's findings indicate that most countries scoring high on individualism have both a higher gross national product and a freer political system than those scoring low on individualism: that is, there is a strong relationship among individualism, wealth, and a political system with balanced power. Other studies have found that the output of individuals working in a group setting differs between individualistic and collectivist societies. In the United States, a highly individualistic culture, social loafing is common: that is, people tend to perform less when working as part of a group than when working alone.[25] In a comparative study between the United States and the People's Republic of China (a highly collectivist society), Earley found that the Chinese did not exhibit as much social loafing as the Americans.[26] This result can be attributed to Chinese cultural values, which subordinate personal interests to the greater goal of helping the group succeed.

*Not to scale—indicates relative magnitude.

Based on G. Hofstede.

The fourth value dimension, **masculinity**, refers to the degree of traditionally "masculine" values—assertiveness, materialism, and a lack of concern for others—that prevail in a society. In comparison, femininity emphasizes "feminine" values—a concern for others, for relationships, and for the quality of life. In highly masculine societies (Japan and Austria, for example), women are generally expected to stay home and raise a family. In organizations, one finds considerable job stress, and organizational interests generally encroach on employees' private lives. In countries with low masculinity (such as Switzerland and New Zealand), one finds less conflict and job stress, more women in high-level jobs, and a reduced need for assertiveness. The United States lies somewhat in the middle, according to Hofstede's research. American women typically are encouraged to work and usually are able to get some support for child care (through day-care centers and maternity leaves).

*Not to scale—indicates relative magnitude.

Based on G. Hofstede.

The four cultural value dimensions proposed by Hofstede do not operate in isolation; rather, they are interdependent and interactive—and thus complex—in their effects on work attitudes and behaviors. For example, in a 2000 study of small-to-medium-sized firms in Australia, Finland, Greece, Indonesia, Mexico, Norway, and Sweden, based on Hofstede's dimensions, Steensma, Marino, and Weaver found that "entrepreneurs from societies that are masculine and individualistic have a lower appreciation for cooperative strategies as compared to entrepreneurs from societies that are feminine and collectivist. Masculine cultures view cooperation in general as a sign of weakness and individualistic societies place a high value on independence and control."[27] In addition, they found that high levels of uncertainty avoidance prompted more cooperation, such as developing alliances to share risk.

Geographic Clusters

Nath and Sadhu summarized and categorized by geographic region the four value dimensions by Hofstede as well as other cultural dimensions, as shown in Exhibit 3-3.

Based on a synthesis of Hofstede's research and other cluster studies, Ronen and Shenkar developed eight country clusters grouped according to the similarities found in those studies of employee attitudes toward (1) the importance of work goals, (2) need fulfillment and job satisfaction, (3) managerial and organizational variables, and (4) work role and interpersonal orientation.[28] These country

Exhibit 3-3

The Cultural Milieu

| REGION/COUNTRY | HOFSTEDE'S DIMENSIONS | | | | |
	INDIVIDUALISM–COLLECTIVISM	POWER DISTANCE	UNCERTAINTY AVOIDANCE	MASCULINITY–FEMININITY	OTHER DIMENSIONS
North America (USA)	Individualism	Low	Medium	Masculine	
Japan	Collectivism	High and low	High	Masculine and feminine	*Amae* (mutual dependence); authority is respected but superior must be a warm leader
Europe:					
Anglo	Individualism	Low/medium	Low/medium	Masculine	
Germanic West Slavic West Urgic	Medium individualism	Low	Medium/high	Medium/high masculine	
Near Eastern Balkanic	Collectivism	High	High	Medium masculine	
Nordic	Medium/high individualism	Low	Low/medium	Feminine	
Latin Europe	Medium/high individualism	High	High	Medium masculine	
East Slavic	Collectivism	Low	Medium	Masculine	
China	Collectivism	Low	Low	Masculine and feminine	Emphasis on tradition, Marxism, Leninism, and Mao Zedong thought
Africa	Collectivism	High	High	Feminine	Colonial traditions; tribal customs
Latin America	Collectivism	High	High	Masculine	Extroverted; prefer orderly customs and procedures

Source: Raghu Nath and Kinal K. Sadhu, "Comparative Analysis, Conclusions, and Future Directions," in *Comparative Management—A Regional View*, ed. Raghu Nath (Cambridge, MA: Ballinger Publishing Company, 1988): 273. Based on G. Hofstede, "National Cultures in Four Dimensions," *International Studies of Management and Organization*, Spring–Summer 1983.

Exhibit 3-4
Clusters of
Countries
Based on
Attitudinal
Dimensions

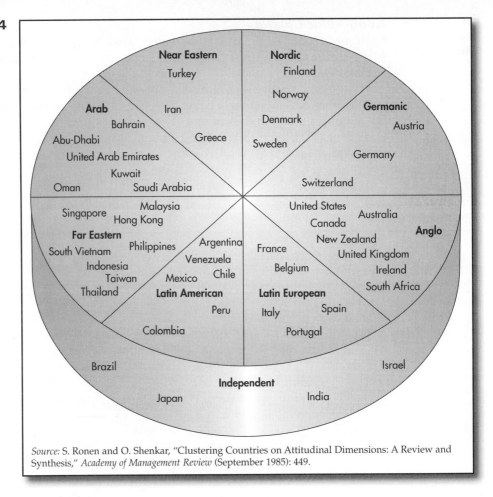

Source: S. Ronen and O. Shenkar, "Clustering Countries on Attitudinal Dimensions: A Review and Synthesis," *Academy of Management Review* (September 1985): 449.

clusters are shown in Exhibit 3-4. In addition, per capita gross national product (GNP) at that time (1985) was used to determine placement in the figure, with the most highly developed countries close to the center. This may indicate some relationship between a country's level of development and its generally accepted values and attitudes, although the variables are too complex to draw conclusions about any direction of causality among them.

Trompenaar's Findings

Fons Trompenaar also researched value dimensions; his work was spread over a ten-year period, with 15,000 managers from 28 countries, representing 47 national cultures.[29] Some of those dimensions which we are not discussing elsewhere and which affect daily business activities are shown in Exhibit 3-5, along with the descriptions and the placement of nine of the countries in approximate relative order. If we view the placement of these countries along a range from personal to

Exhibit 3-5
Trompenaar's Value Dimensions

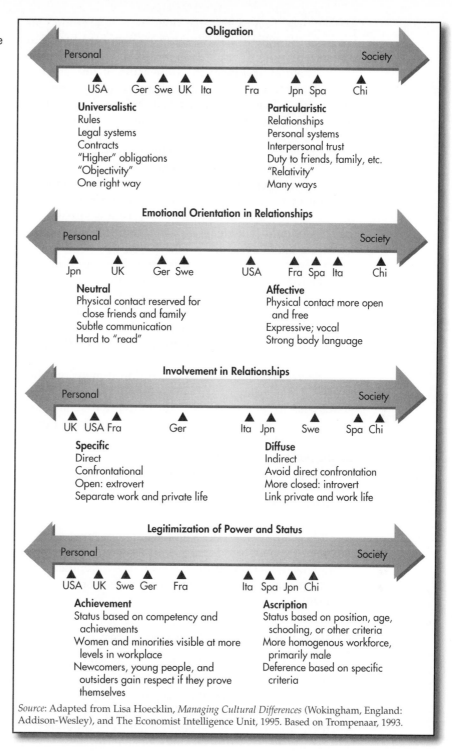

Obligation

Personal ⟷ Society

USA   Ger Swe UK Ita   Fra   Jpn Spa   Chi

Universalistic
Rules
Legal systems
Contracts
"Higher" obligations
"Objectivity"
One right way

Particularistic
Relationships
Personal systems
Interpersonal trust
Duty to friends, family, etc.
"Relativity"
Many ways

Emotional Orientation in Relationships

Personal ⟷ Society

Jpn   UK   Ger Swe   USA   Fra Spa Ita   Chi

Neutral
Physical contact reserved for
 close friends and family
Subtle communication
Hard to "read"

Affective
Physical contact more open
 and free
Expressive; vocal
Strong body language

Involvement in Relationships

Personal ⟷ Society

UK USA Fra   Ger   Ita Jpn   Swe   Spa Chi

Specific
Direct
Confrontational
Open: extrovert
Separate work and private life

Diffuse
Indirect
Avoid direct confrontation
More closed: introvert
Link private and work life

Legitimization of Power and Status

Personal ⟷ Society

USA UK Swe Ger   Fra   Ita Spa Jpn Chi

Achievement
Status based on competency and
 achievements
Women and minorities visible at more
 levels in workplace
Newcomers, young people, and
 outsiders gain respect if they prove
 themselves

Ascription
Status based on position, age,
 schooling, or other criteria
More homogenous workforce,
 primarily male
Deference based on specific
 criteria

Source: Adapted from Lisa Hoecklin, *Managing Cultural Differences* (Wokingham, England: Addison-Wesley), and The Economist Intelligence Unit, 1995. Based on Trompenaar, 1993.

societal, based on each dimension, some interesting patterns emerge.[30] One can see from the exhibit that the same countries tend to be at similar positions on all dimensions, with the exception of the emotional orientation.

Looking at Trompenaar's dimension of **universalism versus particularism**: the Universalistic approach applies rules and systems objectively, without consideration for individual circumstances; whereas the particularistic approach—more common in Asia and in Spain, for example—puts the obligation toward relationships first and is more subjective. Trompenaars found, for example, that people in particularistic societies are more likely to pass on insider information to a friend than those in universalistic societies.

In the **neutral versus affective** dimension, the focus is on the emotional orientation of relationships. The Italians, Mexicans, Chinese, for example, would openly express emotions even in a business situation, whereas the British and Japanese would consider such displays unprofessional; they, in turn would be regarded as hard to "read."

As far as involvement in relationships goes, people tend to be either **specific or diffuse** (or somewhere along that dimension). Managers in specific-oriented cultures—the United States, U.K., France—separate work and personal issues and relationships; they compartmentalize their work and private lives, and they are more open and direct. In diffuse-oriented cultures—Sweden, China—there is spill-over from the work into the personal relationships and vice-versa.

The **achievement versus ascription** dimension, the question is what is the source of power and status in society. In an achievement society the source of status and influence is based on individual achievement—how well one performs the job and what level of education and experience one has to offer. Therefore, women, minorities, and young people usually have equal opportunity to attain position based on their achievements. In an ascription-oriented society, people ascribe status on the basis of class, age, gender, and so on; one is more likely to be born into a position of influence. Hiring in Indonesia, for example, is more likely to be based on who you are than hiring for a position in Germany or Australia.

It is clear, then, that a lot of what goes on at work can be explained by differences in people's innate value systems, as described by Hofstede and Trompenaars, based on their research. Awareness of such differences and how they influence work behavior can be very useful to you as a future international manager.

Critical Operational Value Differences

After studying various research results about cultural variables, it helps to identify some specific culturally based variables that cause frequent problems for Americans in international management. Important variables are those involving conflicting orientations toward time, change, material factors, and individualism. We try to understand these operational value differences because they strongly influence a person's attitudes and probable response to work situations.

Time

Americans often experience much conflict and frustration because of differences in the concept of time around the world—that is, differences in temporal values. To Americans, time is a valuable and limited resource, to be saved, scheduled, and spent with precision, lest we waste it. The clock is always running; time is money. Therefore, deadlines and schedules have to be met. When others are not on time for meetings, Americans may feel insulted; when meetings digress from their purpose, Americans tend to become impatient. Similar attitudes toward time are found in Western Europe and elsewhere.

In many parts of the world, however, people view time from different and longer perspectives, often based on religious beliefs (such as reincarnation, in which time does not end at death), on a belief in destiny, or on pervasive social attitudes. In Latin America, for example, a common attitude toward time is *mañana*, a word that literally means "tomorrow"; a Latin American person using this word, however, usually means an indefinite time in the near future. Similarly, the word *bukra* in Arabic can mean "tomorrow" or "some time in the future." While Americans usually regard a deadline as a firm commitment, Arabs often regard a deadline imposed on them as an insult. They feel that important things take a long time and therefore cannot be rushed; to ask an Arab to rush something, then, would imply that you have not given him an important task, or that he would not treat that task with respect. International managers have to be careful not to offend people—or lose contracts or employee cooperation—because they misunderstand the local language of time.

Change

Based largely on long-standing religious beliefs, values regarding the acceptance of change and the pace of change can vary immensely among cultures. Western people generally believe that an individual can exert some control over the future and can manipulate events, particularly in a business context: that is, individuals feel they have some internal control. In many non-Western societies, however, control is considered external; people generally believe in destiny, or the will of Allah, and therefore adopt a passive attitude or even feel hostility toward those introducing the "evil" of change. In societies that place great importance on tradition (such as China), one small area of change may threaten an entire way of life. Webber describes just how difficult it is for an Asian male, concerned about tradition, to change his work habits:

> To the Chinese, the introduction of power machinery meant that he had to throw over not only habits of work but a whole ideology; it implied dissatisfaction with the ways of his father's way of life in all its aspects. If the old loom must be discarded, then 100 other things must be discarded with it, for there are somehow no adequate substitutes.[31]

International firms are agents of change throughout the world. Some changes are more popular than others: McDonald's hamburgers are apparently one change the Chinese are willing to accept.

Material Factors

Americans consume resources at a far greater rate than most of the rest of the world. Their attitude toward nature—that it is there to be used for their benefit—differs from the attitudes of Indians or Koreans, for example, whose worship of nature is part of their religious belief.[32] Whereas Americans often value physical goods and status symbols, many non-Westerners find these things unimportant; they value the aesthetic and the spiritual realm. Such differences in attitude have implications for management functions, such as motivation and reward systems, because the proverbial carrot must be appropriate to the employee's value system.

Individualism

In general, Americans tend to work and conduct their private lives independently, valuing individual achievement, accomplishments, promotions, and wealth above any group goals. In many other countries, individualism is not valued (as previously discussed in the context of Hofstede's work). In China, for example, much more of a "we" consciousness prevails, and the group is the basic building block of social life and work. For the Chinese, conformity and coopera-

Exhibit 3-6

Fundamental Differences Between Japanese and Mexican Culture That Affect Business Organizations

DIMENSION	JAPANESE CULTURE	MEXICAN CULTURE
Hierarchical nature	Rigid in rank and most communication; blurred in authority and responsibility	Rigid in all respects
Individualism vs. collectivism	Highly collective culture; loyalty to work group dominates; group harmony very important	Collective relative to family group; don't transfer loyalty to work group; individualistic outside family
Attitudes toward work	Work is sacred duty; acquiring skills, working hard, thriftiness, patience and perseverance are virtues	Work is means to support self and family; leisure more important than work
Time orientation	Balanced perspective; future oriented; monochronic in dealings with outside world	Present oriented; time is imprecise; time commitments become desirable objectives
Approach to problem solving	Holistic, reliance on intuition, pragmatic; consensus important	Reliance on intuition and emotion; individual approach
Fatalism	Fatalism leads to preparation	Fatalism makes planning, disciplined routine unnatural
View of human nature	Intrinsically good	Mixture of good and evil

Source: J. J. Lawrence and Ryh-song Yeh, "The Influence of Mexican Culture on the Use of Japanese Manufacturing Techniques in Mexico," *Management International Review* 34, no. 1 (1994): 49–66.

tion take precedence over individual achievement, and the emphasis is on the strength of the family or community—the predominant attitude being "we all rise or fall together."

International managers often face conflicts in the workplace as a result of differences in these four basic values of time, change, materialism, and individualism. If these operational value differences and their likely consequences are anticipated, managers can adjust expectations, communications, work organization, schedules, incentive systems, and so forth, to provide for more constructive outcomes for the company and its employees. Some of these operational differences between Japanese and Mexican cultures in shown in Exhibit 3-6. Note, in particular, the factors of time, individualism change (fatalism) and materialism (attitudes toward work), expressed in the exhibit.

DEVELOPING CULTURAL PROFILES

Managers can gather considerable information on cultural variables from current research, personal observation, and discussions with people. From these sources, managers can develop cultural profiles of various countries—composite pictures of working environments, people's attitudes, and norms of behavior. As we have previously discussed, these profiles are often highly generalized; many subcultures, of course, may exist within a country. But managers can use these profiles to anticipate drastic differences in the level of motivation, communication, ethics, loyalty, and individual and group productivity that may be encountered in a given country. More such homework may have helped the GM–Daewoo joint venture in Korea, which is coming to an end after years of acrimonious relations. Executives from both sides acknowledge that they "seriously underestimated the obstacles posed to their three-continent car-making experiment by divergent cultures and business aspirations, not to mention the different languages."[33]

It is relatively simple to pull together a descriptive profile for American culture, even though there are regional and individual differences, because we know ourselves and because researchers have thoroughly studied American culture. The results of one such study by Harris and Moran are shown in Exhibit 3-7, which provides a basis of comparison with other cultures and thus suggests the likely differences in workplace behaviors.

It is not so easy, however, to pull together descriptive cultural profiles of peoples in other countries unless one has lived there and been intricately involved with those people. But managers can make a start by using what research and literature is available on a comparative basis. The following section provides brief, generalized country profiles based on a synthesis of research, primarily from Hofstede[34] and England[35] as well as numerous other sources.[36] These profiles illustrate how to synthesize information and gain a sense of the character of a society from which implications may be drawn about how to manage more effectively in that society. More extensive implications and applications related to managerial functions are drawn in later chapters.

Exhibit 3-7
Americans at a Glance

1. *Goal and achievement oriented*—Americans think they can accomplish just about anything, given enough time, money, and technology.

2. *Highly organized and institutionally minded*—Americans refer a society that is strong institutionally, secure, and tidy or well kept.

3. *Freedom-loving and self-reliant*—Americans fought a revolution and subsequent wars to preserve their concept of democracy, so they resent too much control or interference, especially by government or external forces. They believe in an ideal that all persons are created equal; though they sometimes fail to live that ideal fully, they strive through law to promote equal opportunity and to confront their own racism or prejudice.

    They also idealize the self-made person who rises from poverty and adversity, and think they can influence and create their own futures. Control of one's destiny is popularly expressed as "doing your own thing." Americans think, for the most part, that with determination and initiative, one can achieve whatever one sets out to do and thus fulfill one's individual human potential.

4. *Work oriented and efficient*—Americans possess a strong work ethic, though they are learning in the present generation to enjoy leisure time constructively. They are conscious of time and efficient in doing things. They tinker with gadgets and technological systems, always searching for easier, better, more efficient ways to accomplish tasks.

5. *Friendly and informal*—Americans reject the traditional privileges of royalty and class, but defer to those with affluence and power. Although informal in greeting and dress, they are a noncontact culture (e.g., avoid embracing in public usually) and maintain a certain physical/psychological distance with others (e.g., about 2 feet).

6. *Competitive and aggressive*—Americans in play or business generally are so oriented because of their drives to achieve and succeed. This is partially traced to their heritage of having to overcome a wilderness and hostile elements in their environment.

7. *Values in transition*—Traditional American values of family loyalty, respect and care of the aged, marriage and the nuclear family, patriotism, material acquisition, forthrightness, and the like are undergoing profound reevaluation as people search for new meanings.

8. *Generosity*—Although Americans seemingly emphasize material values, they are a sharing people, as has been demonstrated in the Marshall Plan, foreign aid programs, refugee assistance, and their willingness at home and abroad to espouse a good cause and to help neighbors in need. They tend to be altruistic and some would say naive as a people.

Source: From *Managing Cultural Differences* by Philip R. Harris and Robert T. Moran, 5th ed. Copyright © 2000 by Gulf Publishing Company, Houston, TX. Used with permission. All rights reserved.

Comparative Management in Focus

Profiles in Culture

Japan

> Now I have to stand firmly on my own and think for myself. I wish I had realized this earlier in life. . . . Building my life around the company was a big mistake.
>
> AKIO KUZUOKA, 40-YEAR EMPLOYEE AT A JAPANESE COMPANY, *WALL STREET JOURNAL*, DECEMBER 29, 2000.

In 2002, we see evidence in cities of changes in Japan's business culture as a result of economic decline and global competition (discussed at the end of this section). However, the underlying cultural values still predominate—for now anyway.

Much of the Japanese culture, and the basis of working relationships, can be explained by the principle of *wa*, "peace and harmony." This principle, embedded in the value they attribute to *amae* ("indulgent love"), probably originated in the Shinto religion, which focuses on spiritual and physical harmony. Amae results in *shinyo*, which refers to the mutual confidence, faith, and honor necessary for successful business relationships. Japan ranks high on pragmatism, masculinity, and uncertainty avoidance, and fairly high on power distance. At the same time, much importance is attached to loyalty, empathy, and the guidance of subordinates. The result is a mix of authoritarianism and humanism in the workplace, similar to a family system. These cultural roots are evident in a very homogeneous managerial value system, with strong middle management, strong working relationships, strong seniority systems that stress rank, and an emphasis on looking after employees. The principle of wa carries forth into the work group—the building block of Japanese business. The Japanese strongly identify and thus seek to cooperate with their work groups. The emphasis is on participative management, consensus problem solving, and decision making with a patient, long-term perspective. Open expression or conflict is discouraged, and it is of paramount importance to avoid the shame of not fulfilling one's duty. These elements of work culture result in a devotion to work, collective responsibility, and a high degree of employee productivity.

If we extend this cultural profile to its implications for specific behaviors in the workplace, we can draw a comparison with common American behaviors. As shown in Exhibit 3-8, most of those behaviors seem to be opposite to those of their counterparts; it is no wonder that there are many misunderstandings and conflicts in the workplace between Americans and Japanese. For example, a majority of the attitudes and behaviors of many Japanese stems from a high level of collectivism, compared with a high level of individualism common to Americans. This contrast is highlighted in the center of Exhibit 3-8 by "maintain the group," compared with "protect the individual." In addition, the strict social order of the Japanese permeates the workplace in adherence to organizational hierarchy and seniority and in loyalty to the firm. This contrasts markedly with the typical American responses to organizational relationships and duties based on equality. In addition, the often blunt, outspoken American businessperson offends the indirectness and sensitivity of the Japanese for whom the virtue of patience is paramount, causing the silence and avoidance that so frustrates Americans.[37] As a result, Japanese businesspeople tend to think of American organizations as having no spiritual quality and little employee loyalty, and of Americans as assertive, frank, and egotistic. Their American counterparts, in turn, respond with the impression that Japanese businesspeople have little experience and are secretive, arrogant, and cautious.[38]

In 2002, however, anecdotal evidence indicates that some convergence with western business culture is taking place—resulting from Japan's economic contraction and subsequent bankruptcies. Focus on the group, lifetime employment and a pension, have given way to a more competitive business environment, with job security no longer guaranteed, and an emphasis on performance-based

Exhibit 3-8

The American-Japanese Cultural Divide

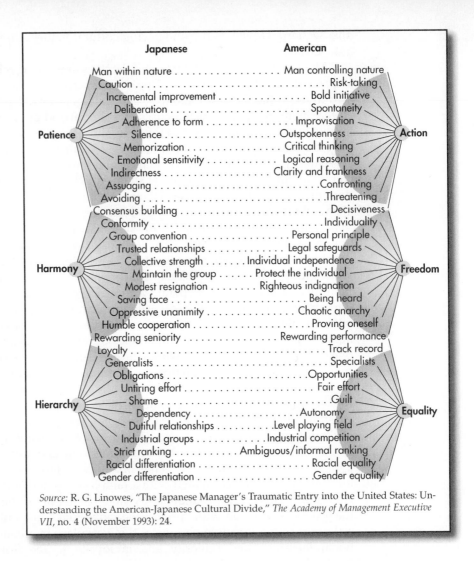

Japanese	American
Man within nature	Man controlling nature
Caution	Risk-taking
Incremental improvement	Bold initiative
Deliberation	Spontaneity
Adherence to form	Improvisation
Silence	Outspokenness
Memorization	Critical thinking
Emotional sensitivity	Logical reasoning
Indirectness	Clarity and frankness
Assuaging	Confronting
Avoiding	Threatening
Consensus building	Decisiveness
Conformity	Individuality
Group convention	Personal principle
Trusted relationships	Legal safeguards
Collective strength	Individual independence
Maintain the group	Protect the individual
Modest resignation	Righteous indignation
Saving face	Being heard
Oppressive unanimity	Chaotic anarchy
Humble cooperation	Proving oneself
Rewarding seniority	Rewarding performance
Loyalty	Track record
Generalists	Specialists
Obligations	Opportunities
Untiring effort	Fair effort
Shame	Guilt
Dependency	Autonomy
Dutiful relationships	Level playing field
Industrial groups	Industrial competition
Strict ranking	Ambiguous/informal ranking
Racial differentiation	Racial equality
Gender differentiation	Gender equality

(left poles: Patience, Harmony, Hierarchy; right poles: Action, Freedom, Equality)

Source: R. G. Linowes, "The Japanese Manager's Traumatic Entry into the United States: Understanding the American-Japanese Cultural Divide," *The Academy of Management Executive VII*, no. 4 (November 1993): 24.

pay. This has led Japan's "salarymen" to recognize the need for personal responsibility on the job and in their lives. While only a few years ago emphasis was on the group, Japan's long slump seems to be causing some cultural restructuring of the individual. Corporate Japan is changing from a culture of consensus and group think, to touting the need for an "era of personal responsibility" as a solution to revitalize their competitive position in the global marketplace.[39]

> To tell you the truth, it's hard to think for yourself, says Mr. Kuzuoka [but, if you don't] . . . in this age of cutthroat competition, you'll just end up drowning.[40]

Germany   The reunited Germany is naturally fairly culturally diverse, as the country borders several nations. Generally, Germans rank quite high on Hofstede's dimension of individualism, though their behaviors seem less individualistic than those of Americans. They score fairly high on uncertainty avoidance and masculinity, and have a relatively small need for power distance. These cultural norms show up in the Germans' preference for being around familiar people and situations; also in their propensity to do a detailed evaluation of business deals before committing themselves.

Christianity underlies much of German culture—over 96 percent of Germans are Catholics or Protestants. This may be why Germans tend to like rule and order in their lives, and why there is a clear public expectation of the acceptable and the unacceptable way to do things. Public signs everywhere in Germany dictate what is allowed or *verboten* (forbidden). Germans are very strict with their use of time, whether for business or pleasure, frowning on inefficiency or on tardiness. In business, Germans tend to be assertive, but they downplay aggression. Decisions are not as centralized as one would expect, with hierarchical processes often giving way to consensus decision making. However, there is strict departmentalization in organizations, with centralized and final authority at the departmental manager level. Hall and Hall describe the German preference for closed doors and private space as evidence of the affinity for compartmentalization in organizations and in their own lives. They also prefer more physical space around them in conversation than do most other Europeans, and privacy in aural distance. In fact, German law prohibits loud noises in public areas on weekend afternoons. Germans are conservative, valuing privacy, politeness, and formality; they usually use last names and titles for all except those close to them.

In negotiations, Germans want detailed information before and during discussions, which can become lengthy. Factors such as voice and speech control are given much weight. But, since Germany is a low-context society, communication is explicit and Americans find negotiations easy to understand.[41]

Korea Koreans rank high on collectivism and pragmatism, fairly low on masculinity, moderate on power distance, and quite high on uncertainty avoidance. Although greatly influenced by American culture, Koreans are still very much bound to the traditional Confucian teachings of spiritualism and collectivism. Korea and its people have undergone great changes, but the respect for family, authority, formality, class, and rank remain strong. Koreans are quite aggressive and hard-working, demonstrative, friendly, and very hospitable. For the most part, they do not subscribe to participative management. Family and personal relationships are important, and connections are vital for business introductions and transactions. Business is based on honor and trust; most contracts are oral. While achievement and competence are important to Koreans, a driving force in relationships is the priority of guarding both parties' social and professional reputations. Thus, praise predominates, and honest criticism is rare.

Further insight into the differences between American and Korean culture can be derived from the following excerpted letter from Professor Jin K. Kim in Plattsburgh, New York, to his high school friend, MK, in South Korea, who just returned from a visit to the United States. MK, whom Dr. Kim had not seen for 20 years, is planning to emigrate to the United States, and Dr. Kim wants to help ward off his friend's culture shock by telling him about American culture from a Korean perspective.

DEAR MK,

I sincerely hope the last leg of your trip home from the five-week fact-finding visit to the United States was pleasant and informative. Although I may not have expressed my sense of exhilaration about your visit through the meager lodging accommodations and "barbaric" foods we provided, it was sheer joy to spend four weeks with you and Kyung-Ok. (Please refrain from hitting the ceiling. My use of your charming wife's name, rather than the usual Korean expression, "your wife" or "your house person," is not an indication of my amorous intentions toward her as any red-blooded Korean man would suspect. Since you are planning to immigrate to this country soon, I thought you might as well begin to get used to the idea of your wife exerting her individuality. Better yet, I thought you should be warned that the moment the plane touches American soil, you will lose your status as the center of your familial universe.) At any rate, please be assured that during your stay here my heart was filled with memories of our three years together in high school when we were young in Pusan.

During your visit, you called me, on several occasions, an American. What prompted you to invoke such a reference is beyond my comprehension. Was it my rusty Korean expressions? Was it my calculating mind? Was it my pitifully subservient (at least when viewed through your cultural lens) role that I was playing in the family life? Or, was it my familiarity with some facets of the American cultural landscape? This may sound bewildering to you, but it is absolutely true that through all the years I have lived in this country, I never truly felt like an American. Sure, on the surface, our family followed closely many ritualistic routines of the American culture: shopping malls, dining out, PTA, Little League, picnics, camping trips, credit card shopping sprees, hot dogs, etc. But mentally I remained stubbornly in the periphery. Naturally, then, my subjective cultural attitudes stayed staunchly Korean. Never did the inner layers of my Korean psyche yield to the invading American cultural vagaries, I thought. So, when you labeled me an American for the first time, I felt a twinge of guilt.

Several years ago, an old Korean friend of mine, who settled in the United States about the same time I did, paid a visit to Korea for the first time in some 15 years. When he went to see his best high school friend, who was now married and had two sons, his friend's wife made a bed for him and her husband in the master bedroom, declaring that she would spend the night with the children. It was not necessarily the sexual connotation of the episode that made my friend blush; he was greatly embarrassed by the circumstance in which he imposed himself to the extent that the couple's privacy had to be violated. For his high school friend and his wife, it was clearly their age-old friendship to which the couple's privacy had to yield. MK, you might empathize rather easily with this Korean couple's state of mind. But it would be a gross mistake even to imagine there may be occasions in your adopted culture when a gesture of friendship breaks the barrier of privacy. Zealously guarding their privacy above all, Americans are marvelously adept at drawing the line where friendship—that elusive "we" feeling—stops and privacy begins. . . .

Indeed, one of the hardest tasks you will face as an "alien" is how to find that delicate balance between your individuality (for example, privacy) and your collective identity (for example, friendship or membership in social groups).

Privacy is not the only issue that stems from this individuality–collectivity continuum. Honesty in interpersonal relationships is another point that may keep you puzzled. Americans are almost brutally honest and frank about issues that belong to public domains; they are not afraid of discussing an embarrassing topic in most graphic details as long as the topic is a matter of public concern. Equally frank and honest gestures are adopted when they discuss their own personal lives once the presumed benefits from such gestures are determined to outweigh the risks involved. Accordingly, it is not uncommon to encounter friends who volunteer personally embarrassing and even shameful information lest you find it out from other sources. Are Americans equally straightforward and forthcoming in laying out heartfelt personal criticisms directed at their friends? Not likely. Their otherwise acute sense of honesty becomes significantly muted when they face the unpleasant task of being negative toward their personal friends. The fear of an emotion-draining confrontation and the virtue of being polite force them to put on a facade or mask.

The perfectly accepted social behavior of telling "white lies" is a good example. The social and personal virtues of accepting such lies are grounded in the belief that the potential damage that can be inflicted by directly telling a friend the hurtful truth far outweighs the potential benefit that the friend could gain from it. Instead of telling a hurtful truth directly, Americans use various indirect communication channels to which their friend is likely to be tuned. In other words, they publicize the information in the form of gossip or behind-the-back recriminations until it is transformed into a sort of collective criticism against the target individual. Thus objectified and collectivized, the "truth" ultimately reaches the target individual with a minimal cost of social discomfort on the part of the teller.

There is nothing vile or insidious about this communication tactic, since it is deeply rooted in the concern for sustaining social pleasantry for both parties.

This innocuous practice, however, is bound to be perceived as an act of outrageous dishonesty by a person deeply immersed in the Korean culture. In the Korean cultural context, a trusted personal relationship precludes such publicizing prior to direct, "honest" criticism to the individual concerned, no matter what the cost in social and personal unpleasantry. Indeed, as you are well aware, MK, such direct reproach and even recrimination in Korea is in most cases appreciated as a sign of one's utmost love and concern for the target individual. Stressful and emotionally draining as it is, such a frank expression of criticism is done out of "we" feeling. Straight-talking friends did not want me to repeat undesirable acts in front of others, as it would either damage "our reputation" or go against the common interest of "our collective identity." In Korea, the focus is on the self-discipline that forms a basis for the integrity of "our group." In America, on the other hand, the focus is on the feelings of two individuals. From the potential teller's viewpoint, the primary concern is how to maintain social politeness, whereas from the target person's viewpoint, the primary concern is how to maintain self-esteem. Indeed, these two diametrically opposed frames of reference—self-discipline and self-esteem—make one culture collective and the other individualistic.

It is rather amazing that for all the mistakes I must have made in the past twenty years, only one non-Korean American friend gave me such an "honest" criticism. In a sense, this concern for interpersonal politeness conceals their disapproval of my undesirable behavior for a time and ultimately delays the adjustment or realignment of my behavior, since it is likely to take quite a while for the collective judgment to reach me through the "publicized" channels of communication. So many Korean immigrants express their indignation about their American colleagues who smile at them but who criticize them behind their backs. If you ever become a victim of such a perception, MK, please take heart that you are not the only one who feels that pain.

MK—The last facet of the individualism–collectivism continuum likely to cause a great amount of cognitive dissonance in the process of your assimilation to American life is the extent to which you have to assert your individuality to other people. You probably have no difficulty remembering our high school principal, K. W. Park, for whom we had a respect–contempt complex. He used to lecture, almost daily at morning assemblies, on the virtue of being modest. As he preached it, it was a form of the Confucian virtue of self-denial. Our existence or presence among other people, he told us, should not be overly felt through communicated messages (regardless of whether they are done with a tongue or pen). . . . One's existence, we were told, should be noticed by others in the form of our acts and conduct. One is obligated to provide opportunities for others to experience one's existence through what he or she does. Self-initiated effort for public recognition or self-aggrandizement was the most shameful conduct for a person of virtue.

This idea is interesting and noble as a philosophical posture, but when it is practiced in America, it will not get you anywhere in most circumstances. The lack of self-assertion is translated directly into timidity and lack of self-confidence. This is a culture where you must exert your individuality to the extent that it would make our high school principal turn in his grave out of shame and disgust. Blame the size of the territory or the population of this country. You may even blame the fast-paced cadence of life or the social mobility that moves people around at a dizzying speed. Whatever the specific reason might be, Americans are not waiting to experience you or your behaviors as they exist. They want a "documented" version of you that is eloquently summarized, decorated, and certified. What they are looking for is not your raw, unprocessed being with rich texture; rather, it is a slickly processed self, neatly packaged and, most important, conveniently delivered to them. Self-advertising is encouraged almost to the point of pretentiousness. Years ago in Syracuse, I had an occasion to introduce a visiting Korean monk-scholar to a gathering of people who wanted to hear something about Oriental philosophies. After taking an elegantly practiced bow to the crowd, this humble monk declared, "My name is . . . Please teach me, as I do not know anything." It took quite a bit of probing and questioning for us to extract something to chew on from that monk with the mysterious smile. Contrast this with an American colleague of mine applying for a promotion several years ago, who literally hauled in two cabinets full of documented evidence of his scholarly achievements.

The curious journey toward the American end of the individualism–collectivism continuum will be inevitable, I assure you. The real question is whether it will be in your generation, your children's, or their children's. Whenever it happens, it will be a bittersweet revenge for me, since only then will you realize how it feels to be called an American by your best high school chum.

SOURCE: EXCERPTED FROM A LETTER BY DR. JIN K. KIM, STATE UNIVERSITY OF NEW YORK AT PLATTSBURGH. COPYRIGHT © 2001 BY DR. JIN K. KIM. USED WITH PERMISSION OF DR. KIM.

CULTURE AND MANAGEMENT STYLES AROUND THE WORLD

As an international manager, once you have researched the culture of a country in which you may be going to work or do business, and developed a cultural profile, it is useful then to apply that information to develop an understanding of the expected management styles and ways of doing business that predominate in that region, or within that type of business setting. Two examples follow for Saudi Arabia and for Chinese Small Family Businesses.

Saudi Arabia

Understanding how business is conducted in the modern Middle East requires an understanding of the Arab culture, since the Arab peoples are the majority there and most of them are Muslim. The Arab culture is intertwined with the pervasive influence of Islam. Even though not all Middle Easterners are Arab, the Arab culture and management style predominates in the Gulf region. Shared culture, religion, and language underlie behavioral similarities throughout the Arab world. Islam "permeates Saudi life—Allah is always present, controls everything, and is frequently referred to in conversation."[42] Employees may spend over two hours a day in prayer, part of the life patterns that intertwine work with religion, politics, and social life.

Arab history and culture is based on tribalism, with its norms of reciprocity of favors, support, obligation, and identity passed on to the family unit, which is the primary structural model. Family life is based on closer personal ties than in the West. Arabs value personal relationships, honor, and saving face for all concerned; these values take precedence over the work at hand or verbal accuracy. "Outsiders" must realize that establishing a trusting relationship and respect for the Arab social norms have to precede any attempts at business discussions. Honor, pride, and dignity are at the core of "shame" societies such as the Arabs. As such, shame and honor provide the basis for social control and motivation. Circumstances dictate what is right or wrong and what is acceptable behavior.[43]

Open admission of error is avoided by Arabs at all costs because weakness (muruwwa) is a failure to be manly. It is sometimes difficult for westerners to get at the truth because of the Arab need to avoid showing weakness; instead a desired, or idealized situation is painted by Arabs. Shame is also brought on someone who declines to fulfil a request or a favor; therefore, a business arrangement is left open if something has yet to be completed.

The communication style of Middle Eastern societies is high context (that is, implicit and indirect) and their use of time is polychronic—many things can be going on at the same time, with constant interruptions commonplace. The imposition of deadlines is considered rude, and business schedules take a back seat to the perspective that events will occur "sometime" when Allah wills (bukra insha Allah). Arabs give primary importance to hospitality; they are cordial to business associates and lavish in their entertainment, constantly offering strong black coffee (which you should not refuse) and banquets before considering business trans-

Exhibit 3-9

Behaviors That Will Likely Cause Offense in Saudi Arabia

- Bringing up business subjects before you get to know your host is considered rude.
- Commenting on a man's wife or female children over 12 years of age.
- Raising colloquial questions that may be common in your country, but possibly misunderstood in Saudi Arabia as an invasion of privacy.
- Using disparaging or swear words and off-color or obscene attempts at humor.
- Engaging in conversations about religion, politics, or Israel.
- Bringing gifts of alcohol or using alcohol, which is prohibited in Saudi Arabia.
- Requesting favors from those in authority or esteem, for it is considered impolite for Arabs to say no.
- Shaking hands too firmly or pumping—gentle or limp handshakes are preferred.
- Pointing your finger at someone or showing the soles of your feet when seated.

Source: P. R. Harris and R. T. Moran, *Managing Cultural Differences*, 5th ed. (Houston: Gulf Publishing, 2000).

actions. Westerners must realize the importance of personal contacts and networking, socializing, and building close relationships and trust, practicing patience regarding schedules, and doing business in person. Exhibit 3-9 gives some selected actions and nonverbal behaviors which may offend Arabs. The relationship between cultural values and norms in Saudi Arabia and managerial behaviors is illustrated in Exhibit 3-10.

Exhibit 3-10

The Relationship Between Culture and Managerial Behaviors in Saudi Arabia

CULTURAL VALUES	MANAGERIAL BEHAVIORS
Tribal and family loyalty	Work group loyalty Paternal sociability Stable employment and a sense of belonging A pleasant workplace Careful selection of employees Nepotism
Arabic language	Business as an intellectual activity Access to employees and peers Management by walking around Conversation as recreation
Close and warm friendships	A person rather than task and money orientation Theory Y management Avoidance of judgment
Islam	Sensitivity to Islamic virtues Observance of the Qur'an and Sharia Work as personal or spiritual growth
Majlis	Consultative management A full and fair hearing Adherence to norms
Honor and shame	Clear guidelines and conflict avoidance Positive reinforcement Training and defined job duties Private correction of mistakes Avoidance of competition
An idealized self	Centralized decision making Assumption of responsibility appropriate to position Empathy and respect for the self-image of others
Polychronic use of time	Right- and left-brain facility A bias for action Patience and flexibility
Independence	Sensitivity to control Interest in the individual
Male domination	Separation of sexes Open work life; closed family life

Source: P. R. Harris and R. T. Moran, *Managing Cultural Differences*, 4th ed. (Houston: Gulf Publishing, 1996).

Chinese Small Businesses

The predominance of small businesses in China and the region highlights the need for managers from around the world to gain an understanding of how such businesses operate. Many small businesses—most of which are family or extended-family businesses—become part of the value chain (suppliers, buyers, retailers, etc.) within industries in which "foreign" firms may compete.

Exhibit 3-11 gives a general framework for comparing Western and Chinese cultures; shown are the resulting differences in Chinese attitudes and behavior,

Exhibit 3-11
A Summary of Western and Chinese Cultural Differences and the Implications for Management

Comparing pertinent features of the history of the West with that of China, we can make the following distinctions:

THE WEST	CHINA
Individual rights	Individual duty and collective obligations
Rule by law	Rule by personality and imperial authority
The collective right to grant, question, and reject political authority	Unquestioning submission to hereditary authority backed by force
Political and ethnic pluralism	Monolithic power and homogeneity
Cultural interaction	Cultural isolation
Sufficient resources to support early urbanization, specialization of labor, and large-scale trade	An agrarian, subsistence economy and endless hardship, both natural and imposed
An external orientation	An internal orientation
Physical and social mobility	Permanence *in situ*
Reliance on reason and the scientific method	Reliance on precedent, intuition, and wisdom
An aggressive, active approach to nature, technology, and progress	Passive, fatalistic submission

Resulting differences in Chinese values, attitudes, and behavior with managerial implications:

1. Larger power distance—a greater willingness to accept the authority of others
2. Collectivism
   a. Deriving satisfaction less from task competence and achievement and more from a sense of contribution to a group effort
   b. More value placed on the comfort and availability of mutual support and affiliation with a group than on independence, self-reliance, privacy and personal space
   c. More cooperativeness and less competitiveness as individuals
   d. Harmony and humility rather than aggressiveness
   e. High-content communication rather than directness and forthrightness
   f. Recognition of group, rather than individual, performance
   g. More relativistic, particularistic ethical standards
3. An external locus of control
4. More reliance on accumulated wisdom than upon reason and objectivity
5. Holistic thinking and synthesis rather than linear thinking and analysis

Source: J. Scarborough, "Comparing Chinese and Western Cultural Roots: Why East Is East and . . . ," *Business Horizons*, November–December 1998, 15–24.

along with the implications for managers. Further discussion of the Chinese culture continues in Chapter 5 in the context of negotiation. Here we will point out some specifics of Chinese management style and practices in particular as they apply to small businesses. It is important to point out that no matter what size company, but especially in small businesses, it is the all-pervasive presence and use of *guanxi* which provides the little red engine of business transactions in China. *Guanxi* means "connections"—the network of relationships the Chinese cultivate through friendship and affection; it entails the exchange of favors and gifts to provide an obligation to reciprocate favors. There is an unwritten code among those who share a guanxi network.[44] The philosophy and structure

Exhibit 3-12
Chinese Management Philosophies: The Old and the New

OLD GENERATION	YOUNG GENERATION
Claim that they have more experiences	Claim that they have more education
Perceive that their role is to intervene for the workers and help them	Perceive that their role is to hire competent workers and expect them to perform
Believe that it is the boss's responsibility to solve problems	Believe that it is the individual's responsibility to solve problems
Stress that a boss has the obligation to take care of the workers	Stress that workers have responsibility to perform the job well
Emphasize that individuals should conform to majority	Emphasize that individuals should maximize their talents and potentials
Believe that work cannot be divided clearly and like to be involved in everything	Believe that a boss should mind his or her own work and leave the workers to do their job
Perceive that work is more important than designation and organizational structure	Perceive that designation and organizational structure are important in order to get the work done
Believe that managers should help the workers solve their problems	Believe that managers should set objectives and achieve them
Complain that the young generation likes to use complicated management methods	Complain that the old generation does things on ad hoc basic
Perceive that the young generation likes to change and expects immediate results	Perceive that the old generation is static and resistant to change
Worry that the young generation is not experienced in running the business	Frustrated that the old generation still holds on strongly to their power
Emphasize that they have to take care of the old workers in the process of the company's growth	Emphasize that they have to gain acceptance from their peers
Emphasize that ethics are important in business	Emphasize that strategy is important in business
Anticipate that the young generation is going to have many difficulties if they adopt Western concepts of management	Frustrated that the old generation does not let them test out their concepts of management
Believe that one's ability is limited and one should be contented with what one has	Believe that there are a lot of opportunities for achievement and growth

Source: Dr. Jean Lee, "Culture and Management—A Study of Small Chinese Family Business in Singapore," *Journal of Small Business Management* (July 1996).

of Chinese businesses comprises paternalism, mutual obligation, responsibility, hierarchy, familialism, personalism, and connections.[45] Autocratic leadership is the norm, with the owner using his or her power, but also with a caring about other people which may predominate over efficiency.[46]

According to Lee major differences between Chinese management styles and those of their Western counterparts are human-centeredness, family-centeredness, centralization of power, and small size.[47] Their human-centered management style puts people ahead of a business relationship and focuses on friendship, loyalty, and trustworthiness.[48] The family is extremely important in Chinese culture, and small businesses tend to be run like a family.

The centralized power structure in Chinese organizations, unlike those in the West, splits into two distinct levels—at the top is the boss and a few family members, and at the bottom are the employees, with no ranking among the workers.[49]

As Chinese firms in many modern regions in the Pacific Rim seek to modernize and compete locally and globally, there is a tug of war between the old and the new—the traditional Chinese management practices, and the increasingly "imported" Western management styles. As discussed by Lee, this struggle is encapsulated in the different management perspectives of the old and young generations, as shown in Exhibit 3-12. A two-generational study of Chinese managers by Raltson et al. also found generational shifts in work values in China. They concluded that the new generation manager is more individualistic, independent, and risk-taking in the pursuit of profits. However, they also found the new generation holding on to their Confucian values, concluding that the new generation may be viewed as "crossverging their Eastern and Western influences, while on the road of modernization."[50]

Conclusion

We have examined various cultural values and how managers can understand them with the help of cultural profiles. Now we will turn our attention to the applications of this cultural knowledge to management in an international environment (or, alternatively in a domestic multicultural environment)—especially as relevant to cross-cultural communication (Chapter 4), negotiation and decision making (Chapter 5), and motivating and leading (Chapter 10). Culture and communication are essentially synonymous; what happens when people from different cultures communicate and how can the international manager understand the underlying process and adapt her or his style and expectations accordingly? For the answers read the next chapter.

INTERNET RESOURCES

Visit the Deresky companion Web site at http://prenhall.com/Deresky for this chapter's Internet resources.

SUMMARY OF KEY POINTS

1. The culture of a society comprises the shared values, understandings, assumptions, and goals that are passed down through generations and imposed by members of the society.

2. Cultural and national differences strongly influence the attitudes and expectations and therefore the on-the-job behavior of individuals and groups.

3. Managers must develop cultural sensitivity to anticipate and accommodate behavioral differences in different societies.

4. Managers must avoid parochialism, an attitude that assumes one's own management techniques are best in any situation or location and that other people should follow one's patterns of behavior.

5. Harris and Moran take a systems approach to understanding cultural and national variables and their effects on work behavior. They identify eight subsystems of variables: kinship, education, economy, politics, religion, associations, health, and recreation.

6. From his research in 50 countries, Hofstede proposes four underlying value dimensions that help to identify and describe the cultural profile of a country and affect organizational processes. These are power distance, uncertainty avoidance, individualism, and masculinity. Through the research of Hofstede and others, we can cluster countries based on intercultural similarities.

7. On-the-job conflicts in international management frequently arise out of conflicting values and orientations regarding time, change, material factors, and individualism.

8. Managers can use research results and personal observations to develop a character sketch, or cultural profile, of a country. This profile can help managers anticipate how to motivate people and coordinate work processes in a particular international context.

Chapter 4

Communicating Across Cultures

Opening Profile: Oriental Poker Face: Eastern Deception or Western Inscrutability?

Among many English expressions that are likely to offend those of us whose ancestry may be traced to the Far East, two stand out quite menacingly for me: "Oriental poker face" and "idiotic Asian smile." The former refers to the supposedly inscrutable nature of a facial expression that apparently reflects no particular state of mind, while the latter pokes fun at a face fixed with a perpetually friendly smile. Westerners' perplexity, when faced with either, arises from the impression that these two diametrically opposed masquerading strategies prevent them from extracting useful information—the type of information which at least they could process with a reasonable measure of confidence—about the feelings of the person before them. An Asian face that projects no signs of emotion, then, seems to most westerners nothing but a facade. It does not matter whether that face wears an unsightly scowl or a shining ray; a facial expression they cannot interpret poses a genuine threat.

Compassionate and sympathetic to their perplexity as I may be, I am also insulted by the Western insensitivity to the significant roles that subtle signs play in Asian cultures. Every culture has its unique set of modus operandi for communication. Western culture, for example, apparently emphasizes the importance of direct communication. Not only are the communicators taught to look directly at each other when they convey a message, but they are also encouraged to come right to the point of the message. Making bold statements or asking frank questions in a less than diplomatic manner (i.e.: "That was really a very stupid thing to do!" or "Are you interested in me?") is rarely construed as rude or indiscreet. Even embarrassingly blunt questions such as "Senator Hart, have you ever had sexual intercourse with anyone other than your wife?" are tolerated most of the time. Asians, on the other hand, find this direct communicative style quite unnerving. In many social interaction situations, they avoid direct eye contact. They "see" each other without necessarily looking directly at each other, and they gather information about inner states of mind without asking even the most discreet or understated questions. Many times they talk around the main topic and, yet, succeed remarkably well in understanding one another's position. (At least they believe they have developed a reasonably clear understanding.)

To a great extent, Asian communication is listening-centered; the ability to listen (and a special talent for detecting various communicative cues) is treated as equally important as, if not more important than, the ability to speak. This contrasts clearly with the American style of communication that puts the utmost emphasis on verbal expression; the speaker carries most of the burden for ensuring that everyone understands his or her message. An Asian listener, however, is prone to blame himself or herself for failing to reach a comprehensive understanding from the few words and gestures performed by the speaker. With this heavier burden placed on the listener, an Asian speaker does not feel obliged to send clearly discernible message cues (at least not nearly so much as he or she is obliged to do in American cultural contexts). Not obligated to express themselves without interruption, Asians use silence as a tool in communication. Silence, by most Western conventions, represents discontinuity of communication, and creates a feeling of discomfort and anxiety. In the Orient, however, silence is not only comfortably tolerated but is considered a desirable form of expression. Far from being a sign of displeasure or animosity, it serves as an integral part of the communication process, used for reflecting upon messages previously exchanged and for carefully crafting thoughts before uttering them.

It is not outlandish at all, then, for Asians to view Americans as unnecessarily talkative and lacking in the ability to simply listen. For the Asian, it is the American who projects a mask of confidence by being overly expressive both verbally and nonverbally. Since the American style of communication places less emphasis on the act of listening than on speaking, Asians suspect that their American counterparts fail to pick up subtle and astute communicative signs in conversation. To a cultural outlook untrained in reading those signs, an inscrutable face represents no more than a menacing or amusing mask.

SOURCE: Dr. Jin Kim, State University of New York–Plattsburgh.
Copyright © 1995 by Dr. Jin Kim. Used with permission of Dr. Kim.

Cultural communications are deeper and more complex than spoken or written messages. The essence of effective cross-cultural communication has more to do with releasing the right responses than with sending the "right" messages.

HALL AND HALL[1]

Multi-local online strategy . . . is about meeting global business objectives by tuning into the cultural dynamics of their local markets.

WILMOTT[2]

As the opening profile suggests, communication is a critical factor in the cross-cultural management issues discussed in this book, particularly those of an interpersonal nature, involving motivation, leadership, group interactions, and negotiation. Culture is conveyed and perpetuated through communication in one form or another. Culture and communication are so intricately intertwined that they are, essentially, synonymous.[3] By understanding this relationship, managers can move toward constructive intercultural management.

Communication, whether in the form of writing, talking, listening, or through the Internet, is an inherent part of a manager's role and takes up the majority of the manager's time on the job. Studies by Mintzberg demonstrate the importance of oral communication; he found that most managers spend between 50 and 90 percent of their time talking to people.[4] The ability of a manager to communicate effectively across cultural boundaries will largely determine the success of international business transactions or the output of a culturally diverse workforce. It is useful, then, to break down the elements involved in the communication process, both to understand the cross-cultural issues at stake and to maximize the process.

THE COMMUNICATION PROCESS

The term **communication** describes the process of sharing meaning by transmitting messages through media such as words, behavior, or material artifacts. Managers communicate to coordinate activities, to disseminate information, to motivate people, and to negotiate future plans. It is of vital importance, then, that the meaning of a particular communication is interpreted by the receiver the way the sender intended. Unfortunately, the communication process, as shown in Exhibit 4-1, involves stages during which the meaning can be distorted. Anything that serves to undermine the communication of the intended meaning is typically referred to as **noise**.

The primary cause of noise stems from the fact that the sender and the receiver each exist in a unique, private world called her or his life space. The context of that private world, based largely on culture, experience, relations, values, and so forth, determines the interpretation of meaning in communication. People filter, or selectively understand, messages according to what is consistent with their own expectations and perceptions of reality and their values and norms of behavior. The more dissimilar the cultures of those involved, the more likelihood for misinterpretation. In this way, as Samovar, Porter, and Jain state, cultural factors pervade the communication process:

> Culture not only dictates who talks with whom, about what, and how the communication proceeds, it also helps to determine how people encode messages, the meanings they have for messages, and the conditions

Exhibit 4-1
The Communication Process

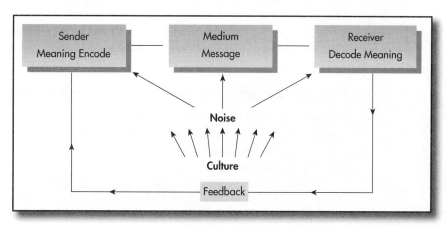

and circumstances under which various messages may or may not be sent, noticed, or interpreted. In fact, our entire repertory of communicative behaviors is dependent largely on the culture in which we have been raised. Culture, consequently, is the foundation of communication. And, when cultures vary, communication practices also vary.[5]

Communication, therefore, is a complex process of linking up or sharing the perceptual fields of sender and receiver; the perceptive sender builds a bridge to the life space of the receiver.[6] After the receiver interprets the message and draws a conclusion about what the sender meant, he or she will, in most cases, encode and send back a response, making communication a circular process.

The communication process is rapidly changing, however, as a result of technological developments, therefore propelling global business forward at a phenomenal growth rate; these changes are discussed later in this chapter.

CULTURAL NOISE IN THE COMMUNICATION PROCESS

Because our focus here is on effective cross-cultural communication, we need to understand what cultural variables cause noise in the communication process. This knowledge of **cultural noise** will enable us to take steps to minimize that noise and so improve communication.

When a member of one culture sends a message to a member of another culture, **intercultural communication** takes place. The message contains the meaning intended by the encoder. When it reaches the receiver, however, it undergoes a transformation in which the influence of the decoder's culture becomes part of the meaning.[7] Let's take a look at an example (Exhibit 4-2) of intercultural communication in which the meaning got all mixed up. Note how the attribution of behavior differs for each participant. **Attribution** is the process in which people look for the explanation of another person's behavior. When they realize that they do not understand another, they tend, say Hall and Hall, to blame their confusion on the other's "stupidity, deceit, or craziness."[8]

In the situation depicted in Exhibit 4-2, the Greek employee gets frustrated and resigns after experiencing communication problems with his American boss. How could this outcome have been avoided? We do not have much information about the people or the context of the situation, but we can look at some of the variables that might have been involved and use them as a basis for analysis.

Cultural Variables in the Communication Process

Cultural variables that can affect the communication process by influencing a person's perceptions have been identified by Samovar and Porter and discussed by Harris and Moran, Ronen, and others.[9,10,11] These variables are as follows: attitudes, social organization, thought patterns, roles, language (spoken or written), nonverbal communication (including kinesic behavior, proxemics, paralanguage, and object language), and time. Although we discuss these variables separately, their effects are interdependent and inseparable, or, as Hecht, Andersen, and

Exhibit 4-2
Cultural Noise in International Communication

BEHAVIOR		ATTRIBUTION	
American:	"How long will it take you to finish this report?"	*American*: *Greek*:	I asked him to participate. His behavior makes no sense. He is the boss. Why doesn't he tell me?
Greek:	"I don't know. How long should it take?"	*American*: *Greek*:	He refuses to take responsibility. I asked him for an order.
American:	"You are in the best position to analyze time requirements."	*American*: *Greek*:	I press him to take responsibility for his actions. What nonsense: I'd better give him an answer.
Greek:	"10 days."	*American*:	He lacks the ability to estimate time; this time estimate is totally inadequate.
American:	"Take 15. Is it agreed? You will do it in 15 days?"	*American*: *Greek*:	I offer a contract. These are my orders: 15 days.

In fact, the report needed 30 days of regular work. So the Greek worked day and night, but at the end of the 15th day, he still needed to do one more day's work.

American:	"Where is the report?"	*American*: *Greek*:	I am making sure he fulfills his contract. He is asking for the report.
Greek:	"It will be ready tomorrow."	(Both attribute that it is not ready.)	
American:	"But we agreed it would be ready today."	*American*: *Greek*:	I must teach him to fulfill a contract. The stupid, incompetent boss! Not only did he give me the wrong orders, but he doesn't even appreciate that I did a 30-day job in 16 days.
The Greek hands in his resignation.		The American is surprised.	
		Greek:	I can't work for such a man.

Source: Adapted from H. C. Triandis, *Interpersonal Behavior* (Monterey, CA: Brooks/Cole, 1977): 248; reported in Simcha Ronen, *Comparative and Multinational Management* (New York: John Wiley and Sons, 1986): 101–102.

Ribeau put it: "Encoders and decoders process nonverbal cues as a conceptual, multichanneled gestalt."[12]

Attitudes

We all know that our attitudes underlie the way we behave and communicate and the way we interpret messages from other people. Ethnocentric attitudes are a particular source of noise in cross-cultural communication. In the incident described in Exhibit 4-2, both the American and the Greek are clearly attempting to interpret and convey meaning based on their own experiences of that kind of transaction. The American is probably guilty of stereotyping the Greek employee by quickly jumping to the conclusion that he is unwilling to take responsibility for the task and the scheduling.

This problem, **stereotyping**, occurs when a person assumes that every member of a society or subculture has the same characteristics or traits. Stereotyping is a common cause of misunderstanding in intercultural communication. It is an arbitrary, lazy, and often destructive way to find out about people. A stereotype should be distinguished from a **sociotype**: a means of accurately describing members of a group by their traits, which is useful to provide some initial basis for understanding people in a new encounter.[13] Astute managers are aware of the dangers of cultural stereotyping and deal with each person as an individual with whom they may form a unique relationship.

Social Organization

Our perceptions can be influenced by differences in values, approach, or priorities relative to the kind of social organizations to which we belong. These organizations may be based on one's nation, tribe, or religious sect, or they may consist of the members of a certain profession. Examples of such organizations include the Academy of Management or the UAW (United Auto Workers).[14]

Thought Patterns

The logical progression of reasoning varies widely around the world and greatly affects the communication process. Managers cannot assume that others use the same reasoning processes, as illustrated by the experience of a Canadian expatriate in Thailand:

> While in Thailand a Canadian expatriate's car was hit by a Thai motorist who had crossed over the double line while passing another vehicle. After failing to establish that the fault lay with the Thai driver, the Canadian flagged down a policeman. After several minutes of seemingly futile discussion, the Canadian pointed out the double line in the middle of the road and asked the policeman directly, "What do these lines signify?" The policeman replied, "They indicate the center of the road and are there so I can establish just how far the accident is from that point." The Canadian was silent. It had never occurred to him that the double line might not mean "no passing allowed."[15]

In the Exhibit 4-2 scenario, perhaps the American did not realize that the Greek employee had a different rationale for his time estimate for the job. Because the Greek was not used to having to estimate schedules, he just took a guess, which he felt forced into.

Roles

Societies differ considerably in their perception of a manager's role. Much of the difference is attributable to their perception of who should make the decisions and who has responsibility for what. In our example, the American assumes that his role as manager is to delegate responsibility, to foster autonomy, and to practice participative management. He is prescribing the role of the employee without any consideration of whether the employee will understand that role. The Greek's frame of reference leads him to think that the manager is the boss and should give the order about when to have the job completed. He interprets the American's behavior as breaking that frame of reference, and therefore he feels that the boss is "stupid and incompetent" for giving him the wrong order and for not recognizing and appreciating his accomplishment. The manager should have considered what behaviors Greek workers would expect of him and then either played that role or discussed the situation carefully, in a training mode.

Language

Spoken or written language, of course, is a frequent cause of miscommunication, stemming from a person's inability to speak the local language, a poor or too-literal translation, a speaker's failure to explain idioms, or a person missing the meaning conveyed through body language or certain symbols. Even among countries that share the same language, there can be problems in the subtleties and nuances inherent in the use of the language, as noted by George Bernard Shaw: "Britain and America are two nations separated by a common language." This problem can exist even within the same country among subcultures or subgroups.[16]

Many international executives tell stories about lost business deals or lost sales because of communication blunders:

> When Pepsi Cola's slogan "Come Alive with Pepsi" was introduced in Germany, the company learned that the literal German translation of "come alive" is "come out of the grave."

> A U.S. airline found a lack of demand for its "rendezvous lounges" on its Boeing 747s. They later learned that "rendezvous" in Portuguese refers to a room that is rented for prostitution.[17]

More than just conveying objective information, language also conveys cultural and social understandings from one generation to the next.[18] Examples of how language reflects what is important in a society include the 6000 different Arabic words used to describe camels and their parts and the 50 or more classifications of snow used by the Inuit Eskimos.

Inasmuch as language conveys culture, technology, and priorities, it also serves to separate and perpetuate subcultures. In India, 14 official and many unofficial languages are used, and over 800 languages are spoken on the African continent.

Because of increasing workforce diversity around the world, the international business manager will have to deal with a medley of languages. For example, assembly-line workers at the Ford plant in Cologne speak Turkish and Spanish as well as German. In Malaysia, Indonesia, and Thailand, many of the buyers and traders are Chinese. Not all Arabs speak Arabic; in Tunisia and Lebanon, for example, French is the commercial language.[19]

International managers need either a good command of the local language or competent interpreters. The task of accurate translation to bridge cultural gaps is fraught with difficulties, as Schermerhorn discovered in his study of 153 Hong Kong Chinese bilinguals; he found a considerable difference in interpretation and response according to whether the medium used was Chinese or English, even after many experts were involved in the translation process.[20]

Even the direct translation of specific words does not guarantee the congruence of their meaning, as with the word "yes" used by Asians, which usually means only that they have heard you, and, often, that they are too polite to disagree. The Chinese, for example, through years of political control, have built into their communication culture a cautionary stance to avoid persecution by professing agreement with whatever opinion was held by the person questioning them.[21]

Politeness and a desire to say only what the listener wants to hear creates noise in the communication process in much of the world. Often, even a clear translation does not help a person to understand what is meant because the encoding process has obscured the true message. With the poetic Arab language—replete with exaggeration, elaboration, and repetition—meaning is attributed more to how something is said rather than what is said.

In our situation with the American supervisor and Greek employee, it is highly likely that the American could have picked up some cues from the employee's body language, which probably implied problems with the interpretation of meaning. Let's now look at how body language may have created noise in this case.

Nonverbal Communication

Behavior that communicates without words (although it often is accompanied by words) is called **nonverbal communication**. People will usually believe what they see over what they hear—hence the expression, "a picture is worth a thousand words." Studies show that these subtle messages account for between 65 and 93 percent of interpreted communication.[22] Even minor variations in body language, speech rhythms, and punctuality, for example, often cause mistrust and misperception of the situation among cross-national parties.[23] The media for such nonverbal communication can be categorized into four types: (1) kinesic behavior, (2) proxemics, (3) paralanguage, and (4) object language.

The term **kinesic behavior** refers to body movements—posture, gestures, facial expressions, and eye contact. While such actions may be universal, their meaning often is not. Because kinesic systems of meaning are culturally specific and learned, they cannot be generalized across cultures. Most people in the West would not correctly interpret many Chinese facial expressions; sticking out the tongue expresses surprise, a widening of the eyes shows anger, and scratching the ears and cheeks indicates happiness.[24] Research has shown for some time, however, that most people worldwide can recognize displays of the basic emotions of anger, disgust, fear, happiness, sadness, surprise, and contempt.[25,26]

Many businesspeople and visitors react negatively to what they feel are inappropriate facial expressions, without understanding the cultural meaning behind them. In his studies of cross-cultural negotiations, Graham observed that the Japanese feel uncomfortable when faced with the Americans' eye-to-eye posture. They are taught since childhood to bow their heads out of humility, whereas the automatic response of Americans is "look at me when I'm talking to you!"[27]

Subtle differences in eye behavior (called oculesics) can throw off a communication badly if they are not understood. Eye behavior includes differences not only in eye contact but also in the use of eyes to convey other messages, whether or not that involves mutual gaze. Edward T. Hall, author of the classic *The Silent*

Language, explains the differences in eye contact between the British and the Americans. During speech, Americans will look straight at you, while the British keep your attention by looking away. They will then look at you when they have finished speaking, which signals that it is your turn to talk. The implicit rationale for this is that you can't interrupt people when they are not looking at you.[28]

It is helpful for American managers to be aware of the many cultural expectations regarding posture and how they may be interpreted. In Europe or Asia, relaxed posture in business meetings may be taken as bad manners or the result of poor upbringing. In Korea you are expected to sit upright, with feet squarely on the floor, and to speak slowly, showing a blending of body and spirit.

Managers can also familiarize themselves with the many different interpretations of hand and finger signals around the world, some of which may even represent obscene gestures. Of course, we cannot expect to change all of our ingrained, natural kinesic behavior, but we can be aware of what it means to others. And we can learn to understand the kinesic behavior of others and the role it plays in their society, as well as how it can affect business transactions. Misunderstanding the meanings of body movements—or an ethnocentric attitude toward the "proper" behavior—can have negative repercussions, as illustrated in the opening profile in this chapter.

Proxemics deals with the influence of proximity and space on communication—both personal space and office space or layout. Americans expect office layout to provide private space for each person, usually a larger and more private space as one goes up the hierarchy. In much of Asia, the custom is open office space, with people at all levels working and talking in close proximity to one another. Space communicates power in both Germany and the United States, evidenced by the desire for a corner office or one on the top floor. The importance of French officials, however, is made clear by a position in the middle of subordinates, communicating that they have a central position in an information network, where they can stay informed and in control.[29]

Do you ever feel vaguely uncomfortable and start slowly moving backward when someone is speaking to you? This is because that person is invading your "bubble"—your personal space. Personal space is culturally patterned, and foreign spatial cues are a common source of misinterpretation. When someone seems aloof or pushy, it often means that she or he is operating under subtly different spacial rules.

Hall and Hall suggest that cultural differences affect the programming of the senses and that space, perceived by all the senses, is regarded as a form of territory to be protected.[30] South Americans, southern and eastern Europeans, Indonesians, and Arabs are **high-contact cultures**, preferring to stand close, touch a great deal, and experience a "close" sensory involvement. On the other hand, North Americans, Asians, and northern Europeans are **low-contact cultures** and prefer much less sensory involvement, standing further apart and touching far less. They have a "distant" style of body language.[31]

Interestingly, high-contact cultures are mostly located in warmer climates, and low-contact cultures in cooler climates. Americans are relatively nontouching, automatically standing at a distance so that an outstretched arm would touch the other person's ear.[32] Standing any closer than that is regarded as invading intimate space. However, Americans and Canadians certainly expect a warm handshake and maybe a pat on the back for closer friends, though not the very warm double handshake of the Spaniards (clasping the forearm with the left hand). The Japanese, considerably less haptic (touching), do not shake hands; an initial greeting between a Japanese and a Spanish businessperson would be uncomfortable for both parties if they were untrained in cultural haptics.

When considering high- and low-contact cultures, we can trace a correlation between Hofstede's cultural variables of individualism and collectivism and the types of kinesic and proxemic behaviors people display. Generally, people from individualistic cultures are more remote and distant, whereas those from collectivist cultures are interdependent—they tend to work, play, live, and sleep in close proximity.[33]

The term **paralanguage** refers to how something is said rather than the content—the rate of speech, the tone and inflection of voice, other noises, laughing, or yawning. The culturally aware manager learns how to interpret subtle differences in paralanguage, including silence. Silence is a powerful communicator. It may be a way of saying no, of being offended, or of waiting for more information to make a decision. There is considerable variation in the use of silence in meetings. While Americans get uncomfortable after 10 or 15 seconds of silence, Chinese prefer to think about the situation for over 30 seconds before speaking. The typical scenario between Americans and Chinese, then, is that the American gets impatient, says something to break the silence, and offends the Chinese by interrupting his chain of thought and comfort level with the subject.[34] Graham, a researcher on international negotiations, taped a bargaining session held at Toyota's U.S. headquarters in California. The American executive had made a proposal to open a new production facility in Brazil and was waiting for a response from the three Japanese executives, who sat with lowered eyes and hands folded on the table. After about 30 seconds—an eternity to Americans, accustomed to a conversational response time of a few tenths of a second—the American blurted out that they were getting nowhere, and the meeting ended in a stalemate. More sensitivity to cultural differences in communication might have led him to wait longer or perhaps to prompt some further response through another polite question.[35]

The term **object language**, or **material culture**, refers to how we communicate through material artifacts, whether architecture, office design and furniture, clothing, cars, or cosmetics. Material culture communicates what people hold as important. In Mexico, a visiting international executive or salesperson is advised to take time out, before negotiating business, to show appreciation for the surrounding architecture, which is prized by Mexicans.

Time

Another variable that communicates culture is the way people regard and use time (discussed in Chapter 3). To Brazilians, relative punctuality communicates the level of importance of those involved. To Middle Easterners, time is something controlled by the will of Allah.

To initiate effective cross-cultural business interactions, managers should know the difference between **monochronic time systems** and **polychronic time systems** and how they affect communications. Hall and Hall explain that in monochronic cultures (Switzerland, Germany, and the United States), time is experienced in a linear way, with a past, a present, and a future, and time is treated as something to be spent, saved, made up, or wasted. Classified and compartmentalized, time serves to order life. This attitude is a learned part of Western culture, probably starting with the industrial revolution. Monochronic people, found in individualistic cultures, generally concentrate on one thing at a time, adhere to time commitments, and are accustomed to short-term relationships.

In contrast, polychronic systems tolerate many things occurring simultaneously and emphasize involvement with people. Two Latin friends, for example, will put an important conversation ahead of being on time for a business meeting, thus communicating the priority of relationships over material systems. Polychronic people—Latin Americans, Arabs, and those from other collectivist cultures—may focus on several things at once, be highly distractible, and change plans often.[36]

The relationship between time and space also affects communication. Polychronic people, for example, are likely to hold open meetings, moving around and conducting transactions from one party to another, rather than compartmentalizing meeting topics, as do monochronic people.

We can discuss endless nuances and distinctions regarding cultural differences in nonverbal communication listed in Exhibit 4-3. Wise intercultural managers will take careful account of the role that such differences might play.

What aspects of nonverbal communication might have created noise in the interactions between the American supervisor and the Greek employee in Exhibit 4-2? Undoubtedly, there were some cues in the kinesic behavior of each person that could have been picked up. It was the responsibility of the manager, in particular, to notice any indications from the Greek that could have prompted him to change his communication pattern or assumptions. Face-to-face communication permits the sender of the message to get immediate feedback, verbal and nonverbal, and thus to have some idea as to how that message is being received and whether additional information is needed. What aspects of the Greek employee's kinesic behavior or paralanguage do you think might have been evident to a more culturally sensitive manager? Did both parties' sense of time affect the communication process?

Exhibit 4-3
Forms of
Nonverbal
Communication

- Facial expressions
- Body posture
- Gestures with hands, arms, head, etc.
- Interpersonal distance (proxemics)
- Touching, body contact
- Eye contact
- Clothing, cosmetics, hairstyles, jewelry
- Paralanguage (voice pitch and inflections, rate of speech, and silence)
- Color symbolism
- Attitude toward time and the use of time in business and social interactions
- Food symbolism and social use of meals

Context

A major differentiating factor that is a primary cause of noise in the communication process is that of **context**, which, as you will see, actually incorporates many of the variables just discussed. The context in which the communication takes place affects the meaning and interpretation of the interaction. Cultures are known to be high- or low-context cultures, with a relative range in between.[37] In **high-context cultures** (Asia, the Middle East, Africa, and the Mediterranean), feelings and thoughts are not explicitly expressed; instead, one has to read between the lines and interpret meaning from one's general understanding. Two such high-context cultures were just described—those of South Korea and Arab cultures. In such cultures, key information is embedded in the context rather than made explicit. People make assumptions about what the message means through their knowledge of the person or the surroundings. In these cultures, most communication takes place within a context of extensive information networks resulting from close personal relationships. In **low-context cultures** (Germany, Switzerland, Scandinavia, and North America), where personal and business relationships are more separated, communication media have to be more explicit. Feelings and thoughts are expressed in words, and information is more readily available.

In cross-cultural communication between high- and low-context people, a lack of understanding may preclude reaching a solution, and conflict may arise. Germans, for example, will expect considerable detailed information before making a business decision, whereas Arabs will base their decision more on knowledge of the people involved—the information is still there, but it is implicit.

People in high-context cultures expect others to understand unarticulated moods, subtle gestures, and environmental clues that people from low-context cultures simply do not process. Misinterpretation and misunderstanding often result.[38] People from high-context cultures perceive those from low-context cultures as too talkative, too obvious, and redundant. Those from low-context cultures perceive high-context people as nondisclosing, sneaky, and mysterious.[39] Research indicates, for example, that Americans find talkative people more attractive, whereas Koreans, high-context people, perceive less verbal people as more attractive. Finding the right balance between low- and high-context communication can be tricky, as Hall and Hall point out: "Too much information leads people to feel they are being talked down to; too little information can mystify them or make them feel left out."[40] Exhibit 4-4 shows the relative level of context in various countries.

The importance of understanding the role of context and nonverbal language to avoid misinterpretation is illustrated in the following section describing communication between Americans and Arabs.

Comparative Management in Focus

Communicating with Arabs

In the Middle East, the meaning of a communication is implicit and interwoven, and consequently much harder for Americans, accustomed to explicit and specific meanings, to understand.

Arabs are warm, emotional, and quick to explode: "sounding off" is regarded as a safety valve.[41] In fact, the Arabic language aptly communicates the Arabic culture, one of emotional extremes. The language contains the means for

Exhibit 4-4
Cultural Context
and Its Effects on
Communication

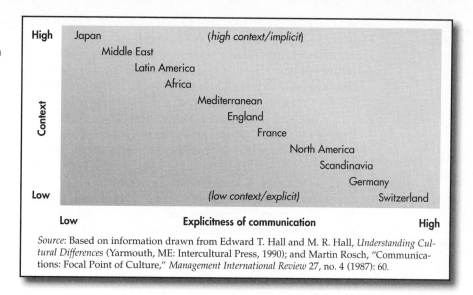

Source: Based on information drawn from Edward T. Hall and M. R. Hall, *Understanding Cultural Differences* (Yarmouth, ME: Intercultural Press, 1990); and Martin Rosch, "Communications: Focal Point of Culture," *Management International Review* 27, no. 4 (1987): 60.

overexpression, many adjectives, words that allow for exaggeration, and metaphors to emphasize a position. What is said is often not as important as how it is said.[42] Eloquence and flowery speech are admired for their own sake, regardless of the content. Loud speech is used for dramatic effect.

At the core of Middle Eastern culture are friendship, honor, religion, and traditional hospitality. Family, friends, and connections, very important on all levels in the Middle East, will take precedence over business transactions. Arabs do business with people, not companies, and they make commitments to people, not contracts. A phone call to the right person can help to get around seemingly insurmountable obstacles. An Arab expects loyalty from friends, and it is understood that giving and receiving favors is an inherent part of the relationship; no one says no to a request for a favor. A lack of follow through is assumed to be beyond the friend's control.[43]

Because hospitality is a way of life and highly symbolic, a visitor must be careful not to reject it by declining refreshment or rushing into business discussions. Part of that hospitality is the elaborate system of greetings and the long period of getting acquainted, perhaps the entire first meeting. While the handshake may seem limp, the rest of the greeting is not. Kissing on the cheeks is common among men, as is handholding between male friends. However, any public display of intimacy between men and women is strictly forbidden by the Arab social code.

Women, in fact, play little or no role in business or entertainment; the Middle East is a male-dominated society, and it is impolite to inquire about women. Other, nonverbal taboos include showing the soles of one's feet and using the left (unclean) hand to eat or pass something. In discussions, a lack of respect is communicated by slouching in a seat or leaning against a wall.

The Arab society also values honor. Harris and Moran explain: "Honor, social prestige, and a secure place in society are brought about when conformity is achieved. When one fails to conform, this is considered to be damning and leads to a degree of shame."[44] Shame results not from just doing something wrong, but from having others find out about that wrongdoing. Establishing a climate of honesty and trust is part of the sense of honor; therefore, considerable tact is needed to avoid conveying any concern or doubt. Arabs tend to be quite introverted until a mutual trust is built, which takes a long time.[45]

In their nonverbal communication, most Arab countries are high-contact cultures. Arabs stand and sit closer and touch people of the same sex more than westerners. They do not have the same concept of "public" and "private" space, or as Hall puts it: "Not only is the sheer noise level much higher, but the piercing look of the eyes, the touch of the hands, and the mutual bathing in the warm moist breath during conversation represent stepped-up sensory inputs to a level which many Europeans find unbearably intense."[46] On the other hand, the distance preferred by North Americans may leave an Arab suspicious of intentions because of the lack of olfactory contact.[47]

The Muslim expression *bukra insha Allah* ("tomorrow if Allah wills") explains much about the Arab culture and its approach to business transactions. A cultural clash typically occurs when an American tries to give an Arab a deadline. "'I am going to Damascus tomorrow morning and will have to have my car tonight,' is a sure way to get the mechanic to stop work," explains Hall, "because to give another person a deadline in this part of the world is to be rude, pushy, and demanding."[48] In such instances, the attitude toward time communicates as loudly as words.

In verbal interactions, managers need to be aware of different patterns of Arab thought and communication. Compared to the direct, linear fashion of American communication, Arabs tend to meander: they start with social talk, discuss business for a while, loop round to social and general issues, then back to business, and so on.[49] American impatience and insistence on sticking to the subject will "cut off their loops," triggering confusion and dysfunction.

Exhibit 4-5 illustrates some of the sources of noise that are likely to interfere in the communication process between Americans and Arabs. For people doing business in the Middle East, the following are some useful guidelines for effective communication:

- Be patient. Recognize the Arab attitude toward time and hospitality—take time to develop friendship and trust, as these are prerequisites for any social or business transactions.
- Recognize that people and relationships matter more to Arabs than the job, company, or contract—conduct business personally, not by correspondence or telephone.
- Avoid expressing doubts or criticism when others are present—recognize the importance of honor and dignity to Arabs.
- Adapt to the norms of body language, flowery speech, and circuitous verbal patterns in the Middle East, and don't be impatient to "get to the point."
- Expect many interruptions in meetings, delays in schedules, and changes in plans.[50]

Exhibit 4-5

Miscommunication Between Americans and Arabs Caused by Cross-Cultural Noise

Communication Channels

In addition to the variables related to the sender and the receiver of a message, the variables linked to the channel itself and the context of the message must be taken into consideration. These variables include fast or slow messages and information flows, and different types of media.

Information Systems

Communication in organizations varies according to where and how it originates, the channels and the speed at which it flows, whether it is formal or informal, and so forth. The type of organizational structure, the staffing policies, and the leadership style will affect the nature of an organization's information system.

As an international manager, it is useful to know where and how information originates and the speed at which it flows, both internally and externally. In centralized organizational structures, as in South America, most information originates from top managers. Workers take less responsibility to keep managers informed than in a typical company in the United States, where delegation results in information flowing from the staff to the managers. In a decision-making system where many people are involved, such as the *ringi* system (a consultative, bottom-up approval system) in Japan there is a systematic pattern for information flow that the expatriate needs to understand.[51]

Context also affects information flow. In high-context cultures (such as in the Middle East), information spreads rapidly and freely because of the constant close contact and the implicit ties among people and organizations. Information flow is often informal. In low-context cultures (such as Germany or the United States), information is controlled and focused, and thus it does not flow so freely.[52] Compartmentalized roles and office layouts stifle information channels; information sources tend to be more formal.

It is crucial for an expatriate manager to find out how to tap into a firm's informal sources of information. In Japan, employees usually have a drink together on the way home from work, and this becomes an essential source of information. However, such communication networks are based on long-term relationships in Japan (and in other high-context cultures). The same information may not be readily available to "outsiders." A considerable barrier in Japan separates strangers from familiar friends, a situation that discourages communication.

Americans are more open and talk freely about almost anything, whereas Japanese will disclose little about their inner thoughts or private issues. Americans are willing to have a wide "public self," disclosing their inner reactions verbally and physically. In contrast, the Japanese prefer to keep their responses largely to their "private self." The Japanese expose only a small portion of their thoughts; they reduce, according to Barnlund, "the unpredictability and emotional intensity of personal encounters."[53] Barnlund depicts this difference diagrammatically, as shown in Exhibit 4-6, which illustrates the cultural clash between the public and private selves in intercultural communication between Americans and Japanese. The plus and minus signs indicate the areas of agreement or disagreement (respectively) resulting when each party forces its cultural norms of communication on the other. In the American style, the American's cultural norms of explicit communication impose on the Japanese by invading the person's private self. The Japanese style of implicit communication causes a negative reaction from the American because of what is perceived as too much formality and ambiguity, which wastes time.[54]

Cultural variables in information systems and context underlie the many differences in communication style between Japanese and Americans. Exhibit 4-7 shows some specific differences. The Japanese *ningensei* ("human beingness") style of communication refers to their preference for humanity, reciprocity, a receiver orientation, and an underlying distrust of words and analytic logic.[55] The Japanese believe that true intentions are not readily revealed in words or contracts, but are in fact masked by them. In contrast to the typical American's verbal agility and explicitness, Japanese behaviors and communications are directed to defend and give face for everyone concerned; to do so they avoid public disagreements at all costs. In cross-cultural negotiations this last point is essential.

The speed with which we try to use information systems is another key variable that needs attention to avoid misinterpretation and conflict. Americans expect to give and receive information very quickly and clearly, moving through

Exhibit 4-6
Intercultural
Communication
Conflicts Between
Americans and
Japanese

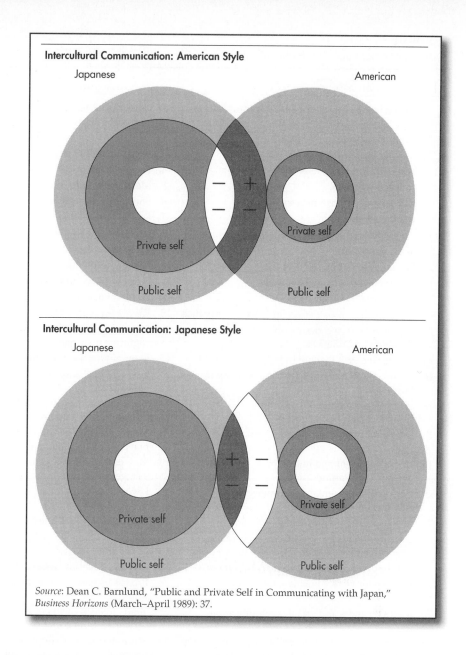

Intercultural Communication: American Style

Japanese   American

Private self

Private self

Public self   Public self

Intercultural Communication: Japanese Style

Japanese   American

Private self

Private self

Public self   Public self

Source: Dean C. Barnlund, "Public and Private Self in Communicating with Japan," *Business Horizons* (March–April 1989): 37.

details and stages in a linear fashion to the conclusion. They usually use various media for fast messages—letters giving all the facts and plans up front, faxes, and familiar relationships. In contrast, the French use the slower message channels of deep relationships, culture, and sometimes mediators to exchange information. A French written communication will be tentative, with subsequent letters slowly building up to a new proposal. In fact, the French preference for written communication, even for informal interactions, echoes the formality of their relationships—and results in a slowing down of message transmission that often

Exhibit 4-7
Differences Between Japanese and American Communication Styles

JAPANESE *NINGENSEI* STYLE OF COMMUNICATION	U.S. ADVERSARIAL STYLE OF COMMUNICATION
1. Indirect verbal and nonverbal communication	1. More direct verbal and nonverbal communication
2. Relationship communication	2. More task communication
3. Discourages confrontational strategies	3. Confrontational strategies more acceptable
4. Strategically ambiguous communication	4. Prefers more to-the-point communication
5. Delayed feedback	5. More immediate feedback
6. Patient, longer term negotiators	6. Shorter term negotiators
7. Uses fewer words	7. Favors verbosity
8. Distrustful of skillful verbal communicators	8. Exalts verbal eloquence
9. Group orientation	9. More individualistic orientation
10. Cautious, tentative	10. More assertive, self-assured
11. Complementary communicators	11. More publicly critical communicators
12. Softer, heartlike logic	12. Harder, analytic logic preferred
13. Sympathetic, empathetic, complex use of pathos	13. Favors logos, reason
14. Expresses and decodes complex relational strategies and nuances	14. Expresses and decodes complex logos, cognitive nuances
15. Avoids decision making in public	15. Frequent decision making in public
16. Makes decisions in private venues, away from public eye	16. Frequent decisions in public at negotiating tables
17. Decision via *ringi* and *nemawashi* (complete consensus process)	17. Decisions by majority rule and public compromise is more commonplace
18. Uses go-betweens for decision making	18. More extensive use of direct person-to-person, player-to-player interaction for decisions
19. Understatement and hesitation in verbal and nonverbal communication	19. May publicly speak in superlatives, exaggerations, nonverbal projection
20. Uses qualifiers, tentative, humility as communicator	20. Favors fewer qualifiers, more ego-centered
21. Receiver/listening-centered	21. More speaker- and message-centered
22. Inferred meanings, looks beyond words to nuances, nonverbal communication	22. More face-value meaning, more denotative
23. Shy, reserved communicators	23. More publicly self-assertive
24. Distaste for purely business transactions	24. Prefers to "get down to business" or "nitty gritty"
25. Mixes business and social communication	25. Tends to keep business negotiating more separated from social communication
26. Utilizes *matomari* or "hints" for achieving group adjustment and saving face in negotiating	26. More directly verbalizes management's preference at negotiating tables
27. Practices *haragei* or belly logic and communication	27. Practices more linear, discursive, analytical logic; greater reverence for cognitive than for affective

Source: A. Goldman, "The Centrality of 'Ningensei' to Japanese Negotiating and Interpersonal Relationships: Implications for U.S. Japanese Communication," *International Journal of Intercultural Relations* 18, no. 1 (Winter 1994).

seems unnecessary to Americans. Jean-Louis Reynal, a plant manager at Citroen, explains that "it wouldn't be too much of an exaggeration to say that, until they are written, until they are entrusted to the blackboard, the notepad, or the flip chart, ideas have no reality for the French manager. You could even say that writing is an indispensable aid to 'being' for us."[56]

In short, it behooves Americans to realize that, because most of the world exchanges information through slower message media, it is wise to schedule more time for transactions, develop patience, and learn to get at needed information in more subtle ways—after building rapport and taking time to observe the local system for exchanging information.

We have seen that cross-cultural misinterpretation can result from noise in the actual transmission of the message—the choice or speed of media. Interpreting the meaning of a message can thus be as much a function of the transmission channel (or medium) as it is of examining the message itself.

INFORMATION TECHNOLOGY—GOING GLOBAL AND ACTING LOCAL

> All information is local; IT systems can connect every corner of the globe, but IT managers are learning they have to pay attention to regional differences.[57]
>
> *COMPUTERWORLD*, APRIL 10, 2000

> Deploying B2B e-commerce technology [globally] . . . becomes exponentially more difficult because systems must address concerns not germain to domestic networks, such as language translation, currency conversion and even cultural differences.[58]
>
> *INTERNET WEEK*, OCTOBER 9, 2000

Using the Internet as a global medium for communication has enabled companies of all sizes to quickly develop a presence in many markets around the world; in fact, it has enabled them to "go global." However, their global reach cannot alone translate into global business. Those companies are learning that they have to adapt their e-commerce and their enterprise resource planning (ERP) applications to regional idiosyncrasies beyond translation or content management issues: Even asking for a name or e-mail address can incur resistance in many countries where people do not like to give out personal information.[59] While communication over the Internet is clearly not as personal as face-to-face cross-cultural communication, those transactions must still be regionalized and personalized to adjust to differences in language, culture, local laws, and business models, as well as differences in the level of development in the local telecommunications infrastructure. And yet, if the Internet is a global medium for communication, why do so many U.S. companies treat the Web as a U.S.-centric phenomenon? Giving preference to some geographic regions, languages, and cultures is "a short-sighted business decision that will result in diminished brand equity, market share, profits and

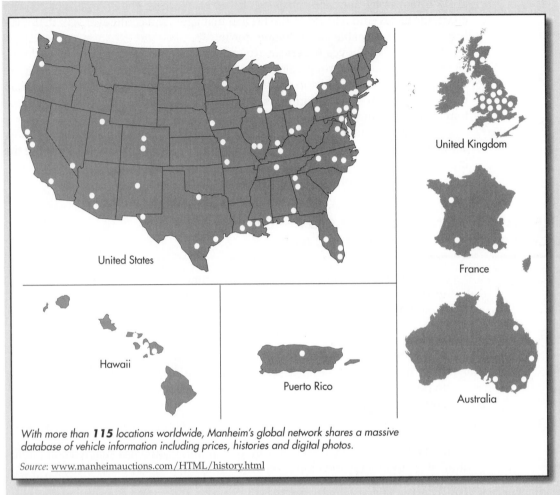

With more than **115** locations worldwide, Manheim's global network shares a massive database of vehicle information including prices, histories and digital photos.

Source: www.manheimauctions.com/HTML/history.html

Exhibit 4-8
Manheimauctions.com Logo Map

With headquarters in Atlanta, Georgia, Manheim Auctions is the largest and highest volume wholesale automobile auction company in the world. The company operates more than 115 auction facilities worldwide, and employs over 30,000 people. Manheim remarkets vehicles for wholesale consignors. These sellers include car dealers, manufacturers, rental car operators, fleet/lease companies and financial institutions. The buyers of the vehicles are licensed franchise and independent auto dealers. Thousands of dealers conduct business using Manheim's global network, which shares a massive database of vehicle information, including prices, histories and digital photos through www.Manheimauctions.com and www.Autotrader.com, as well as localized addresses.[63]

Mainheim has had its share of challenges as it attempts to localize its "cyberlots" while expanding globally. New partners in the U.K. and Australia, for example, unknown to Manheim, had lines of business that Manheim's on-line site did not support. The company also had to make adjustments for different measurement standards, such as kilometers, and different terminology for car parts, such as a "boot" in the U.K. instead of "trunk."[64] In addition, with feedback from its Australian acquisition partner, Manheim made changes to its corporate logo, shown in Exhibit 4-8. Those partners "down under" naturally felt left out when seeing that the original logo showed only North and South America.[65]

global leadership."[60] In fact, with an annual predicted growth rate of 70 percent in non-English language sites and usage, this would put English-language sites in the minority somewhere around 2002–2003.[61]

It seems essential, then, that a global online strategy must also be multilocal. The impersonal nature of the Web must somehow be adapted to local cultures in order to establish relationships and create customer loyalty. Effective technological communication requires even more cultural sensitivity than face-to-face communication, because of the inability to assess reactions and get feedback, or even to retain contact in many cases. It is still people, after all, who respond to and interact with other people through the medium of the Internet, and those people interpret and respond according to their own languages and cultures as well as local business practices and expectations. In Europe, for example, there are significant differences in business cultures and e-business technology, which have slowed e-business progress there. However, some companies are making progress in pan-European integration services, such as *leEurope*, which aims to cross language, currency and cultural barriers. *leEurope* is building a set of services "to help companies tie their back-end e-business systems together across European boundaries through a series of mergers involving regional e-business integrators in more than a dozen countries."[62]

One global company which has successfully added a multilocal on-line strategy to its long-established bricks and mortar facilities is Manheim Auctions, Inc., featured in the accompanying *E-Biz Box*.

MANAGING CROSS-CULTURAL COMMUNICATION

Steps toward effective intercultural communication include the development of cultural sensitivity, careful encoding, selective transmission, careful decoding, and appropriate follow-up actions.

Developing Cultural Sensitivity

When acting as a sender, a manager must make it a point to know the receiver and to encode the message in a form that will most likely be understood as intended. On the manager's part, this requires an awareness of his or her own cultural baggage and how it affects the communication process. In other words, what kinds of behaviors does the message imply, and how will they be perceived by the receiver? The way to anticipate the most likely meaning that the receiver will attach to the message is to internalize honest cultural empathy with that person. What is the cultural background—the societal, economic, and organizational context—in which this communication is taking place? What are this person's expectations regarding the situation, what are the two parties' relative positions, and what might develop from this communication? What kinds of transactions and behaviors is this person used to? Cultural sensitivity (discussed in Chapter 3) is really just a matter of understanding the other person, the context, and how the person will respond to the context.

Careful Encoding

In translating his or her intended meaning into symbols for cross-cultural communication, the sender must use words, pictures, or gestures that are appropriate to the receiver's frame of reference. Of course, language training is invaluable, but senders should also avoid idioms and regional sayings (such as "go fly a kite" or "foot the bill") in a translation, or even in English when speaking to a non-American who knows little English.

Literal translation, then, is a limited answer to language differences. Even among English-speaking countries, words may have different meanings—as experienced by a U.S. banker in Australia after a business dinner. To show appreciation, he said he was "full" (interpreted by his hosts as drunk); as the silence spread at the table, he tried to correct himself by saying he was "stuffed" (a word used locally only in a sexual context).[66] Ways to avoid such problems are to speak slowly and clearly, avoid long sentences and colloquial expressions, and explain things in several different ways and through several media, if possible.[67] However, even though English is in common use around the world for business transactions, the manager's efforts to speak the local language will greatly improve the climate. Sometimes people from other cultures resent the assumption by English-speaking executives that everyone else will speak English.

Language translation is only part of the encoding process; the message also is expressed in nonverbal language. In the encoding process, the sender must ensure congruence between the nonverbal and the verbal message. In encoding a message, therefore, it is useful to be as objective as possible and not to rely on personal interpretations. To further clarify their message, managers can hand out written summaries of verbal presentations and use visual aids—graphs or pictures. A good general guide is to move slowly, wait, and take cues from the receivers.

Selective Transmission

The type of medium chosen for the message depends on the nature of the message, its level of importance, the context and expectations of the receiver, the timing involved, and the need for personal interaction, among other factors. Typical media include e-mail, letters or memos, reports, meetings, telephone calls, teleconferences, videoconferences, or face-to-face conversations. The secret is to find out how communication is transmitted in the local organization—how much is downward versus upward or vertical versus horizontal, how the grapevine works, and so on. In addition, cultural variables discussed earlier need to be considered: whether the receiver is from a high- or low-context culture, whether he or she is used to explicit or implicit communication, and what speed and routing of messages will be most effective.

For the most part, it is best to use face-to-face interaction for relationship building or for other important transactions, particularly in intercultural communications, because of the lack of familiarity between parties. Personal interactions give the manager the opportunity to get immediate verbal and visual feedback and to make rapid adjustments in the communication process.

International dealings are often long-distance, of course, limiting the opportunity for face-to-face communication. However, personal rapport can be established or enhanced through telephone calls or videoconferencing and through trusted contacts. Modern electronic media can be used to break down communication barriers by reducing waiting periods for information, clarifying issues, and allowing instant consultation. Global telecommunications and computer networks are changing the face of cross-cultural communication through the faster dissemination of information within the receiving organization. Ford of Europe uses videoconferencing for engineers in Britain and Germany to consult about quality problems. Through the television screen, they examine one another's engineering diagrams and usually find a solution that gets the factory moving again in a short time.[68]

Careful Decoding of Feedback

Timely and effective feedback channels can also be set up to assess a firm's general communication about the progression of its business and its general management principles. The best means to get accurate feedback is through face-to-face interaction because this allows the manager to hear, see, and sense immediately how a message is being interpreted. When visual feedback on important issues is not possible or appropriate, it is a good idea to use several means of attaining feedback, in particular, employing third parties.

Decoding is the process of translating the received symbols into the interpreted message. The main causes of incongruence are (1) the receiver misinterprets the message, (2) the receiver encodes his or her return message incorrectly, or (3) the sender misinterprets the feedback. Two-way communication is thus essential for important issues so that successive efforts can be made until an understanding has been achieved. Asking other colleagues to help interpret what is going on is often a good way to break a cycle of miscommunication.

Perhaps the most important means to avoiding miscommunication is to practice careful decoding by improving one's listening and observation skills. A good listener practices projective listening, or empathetic listening—listening without interruption or evaluation to the full message of the speaker, attempting to recognize the feelings behind the words and nonverbal cues, and understanding the speaker's perspective.

At the MNC level, avenues of communication and feedback among parent companies and subsidiaries can be kept open through telephone calls, regular meetings and visits, reports, and plans—all of which facilitate cooperation, performance control, and the smooth running of the company. Communication among far-flung operations can be best managed by setting up feedback systems and liaison people. The headquarters people should maintain considerable flexibility in cooperating with local managers and allowing them to deal with the local context as they see fit.

Follow-up Actions

Managers communicate both through action and inaction. Therefore, to keep open the lines of communication, feedback, and trust, managers must follow through with action on what has been discussed and then agreed upon—typically a contract, which is probably the most important formal business communication. Unfortunately, the issue of contract follow-through is a particularly sensitive one across cultures because of the different interpretations regarding what constitutes a contract (perhaps a handshake, perhaps a full legal document) and what actions should result. Trust, future communications, and future business are based on such interpretations, and it is up to the manager to understand them and to follow through on them.

The management of cross-cultural communication depends largely on a manager's personal abilities and behavior. Those behaviors that researchers indicate to be most important to **intercultural communication effectiveness** (ICE) are listed here, as reviewed by Ruben:

1. Respect (conveyed through eye contact, body posture, voice tone, and pitch)
2. Interaction posture (the ability to respond to others in a descriptive, nonevaluative, and nonjudgmental way)
3. Orientation to knowledge (recognizing that one's knowledge, perception, and beliefs are valid only for oneself and not for everyone else)
4. Empathy
5. Interaction management
6. Tolerance for ambiguity
7. Other-oriented role behavior (one's capacity to be flexible and to adopt different roles for the sake of greater group cohesion and group communication)[69]

Whether at home or abroad, certain personal capabilities facilitate effective intercultural communication; these abilities can help the expatriate to adapt to the host country and enable productive working relations to develop in the long term. Researchers have established a relationship between personality traits and behaviors and the ability to adapt to the host-country's cultural environment.[70] What is seldom pointed out, however, is that communication is the mediating factor between those behaviors and the relative level of adaptation the expatriate achieves. The communication process facilitates cross-cultural adaptation—through this process, expatriates learn the dominant communication patterns of the host society. Therefore, we can link those personality factors shown by research to ease adaptation with those necessary for effective intercultural communication.

Kim has consolidated the research findings of these characteristics into two categories: (1) **openness**—traits such as open-mindedness, tolerance for ambiguity, and extrovertedness; and (2) **resilience**—traits such as having an internal locus of control, persistence, a tolerance of ambiguity, and resourcefulness.[71] These personality factors, along with the expatriate's cultural and racial identity and the level of preparedness for change, comprise that person's potential for adaptation. The level of preparedness can be improved by the manager before his or her assignment by gathering information about the host country's verbal and nonverbal communication patterns and norms of behavior. Kim incorporates these factors in a communication model of cross-cultural adaptation. Exhibit 4-9 shows the major variables affecting the level of communication competence achieved between the host and the expatriate. These are the adaptive predisposition of the expatriate and the conditions of receptivity and conformity to pressure in the host environment. These factors affect the process of personal and social communication, and, ultimately, the adaptation outcome. Explains Kim: "Three aspects of strangers' adaptive change—increased functional fitness, psychological health, and intercultural identity—have been identified as direct consequences of prolonged communication-adaptation experiences in the host society."[72] In Chapter 10, we will point out areas where the firm has responsibility to improve the employee and managerial ability to adapt.

In identifying personal and behavioral specifics that facilitate ICE, however, we cannot lose sight of the whole picture. We must remember the basic principle of contingency management, that is, that managers operate in a system of many interacting variables in a dynamic context. Studies show that situational factors—such as the physical environment, time constraints, degree of structure, feelings of boredom or overwork, anonymity, and so forth—are strong influences on intercultural communication competence.[73]

It is this interdependence of many variables, in fact, that makes it difficult for intercultural researchers to isolate and identify factors for success. Although managers try to understand and control up front as many factors as possible that will lead to management effectiveness, often they only find out what works from the results of their decisions.

Conclusion

Effective intercultural communication is a vital skill for international managers and domestic managers of multicultural work forces. Because we have learned that miscommunication is much more likely to occur among people from different countries or racial backgrounds than among those from similar backgrounds, we try to be alert to how culture is reflected in communication—in particular by developing cultural sensitivity and an awareness of potential sources of cultural noise in the communication process. A successful international manager is thus attuned to these variables and is flexible enough to adjust his or her communication style to best address the intended receivers: that is, to do it "their way."

Cultural variables and the manner in which culture is communicated underlie the processes of negotiation and decision making. How do people around the world negotiate—what are their expectations and their approach to negotiations? What is the importance of understanding negotiation and decision-making processes in other countries? Chapter 5 will address these questions and make suggestions for the international manager to handle these important tasks.

Exhibit 4-9
A Communication Model of Cross-Cultural Adaptation

Adaptive Predisposition
Cultural/racial background
Open/resilient personality
Preparedness for change

Host Environmental Conditions
Receptivity
Conformity pressure

Adaptation Outcome
Functional fitness
Psychological health
Intercultural identity

Host IC
Host MC

Host communication competence

Expatriate IC
Expatriate MC

Personal communication

Social communication

IC = Interpersonal communication
MC = Mass communication

Source: Adapted from Young Yun Kim, *Communication and Cross-Cultural Adaptation* (Clevedon, England: Multilingual Matters, 1988): 79.

INTERNET RESOURCES

 Visit the Deresky companion Web site at http://prenhall.com/Deresky for this chapter's Internet resources.

SUMMARY OF KEY POINTS

1. Communication is an inherent part of a manager's role, taking up the majority of the manager's time on the job. Effective intercultural communication largely determines the success of international transactions or the output of a culturally diverse workforce.

2. Culture is the foundation of communication, and communication transmits culture. Cultural variables that can affect the communication process by influencing a person's perceptions include attitudes, social organizations, thought patterns, roles, language, nonverbal language, and time.

3. Language conveys cultural understandings and social norms from one generation to the next. Body language, or nonverbal communication, is behavior that communicates without words. It accounts for 65 to 93 percent of interpreted communication.

4. Types of nonverbal communication around the world are kinesic behavior, proxemics, paralanguage, and object language.

5. Effective cross-cultural communication must take account of whether the receiver is from a country with a monochronic or a polychronic time system.

6. Variables related to channels of communication include high- and low-context cultures, fast or slow messages and information flows, and various types of media.

7. In high-context cultures, feelings and messages are implicit and must be accessed through an understanding of the person and the system. In low-context cultures, feelings and thoughts are expressed, and information is more readily available.

8. The effective management of intercultural communication necessitates the development of cultural sensitivity, careful encoding, selective transmission, careful decoding, and follow-up actions.

9. Certain personal abilities and behaviors facilitate adaptation to the host country through skilled intercultural communication.

10. Communication over the Internet must still be localized to adjust to differences in language, culture, local laws, and business models.

Chapter 5

Cross-Cultural Negotiation and Decision Making

Opening Profile: Sparks Fly at Enron's Power Plant in India

We faced a lot of naysayers throughout the entire process, and people who thought we could never pull it off.

—REBECCA MARK, CHAIRPERSON ENRON'S INTERNATIONAL UNIT, *WALL STREET JOURNAL*, FEBRUARY 1999.

On April 9, 2001, Enron issued a "political force majeure" notice to the Maharashtra State Electricity Board (MSEB), a standard contractual clause that aggrieved parties use as a first step towards possible quitting. Companies issue the notice if they believe circumstances on the ground have undermined a contract.

—ENRON'S THREAT TO WITHDRAW FROM INDIA, *FINANCIAL TIMES*, APRIL 10, 2001.

It took three years, to February 1999, for Rebecca Mark and her team at Enron's International Unit to bring its Dabhol power plant in India back into operation. In 1996, the Indian government had canceled the partially built plant because of pressure from environmentalists and a derailed economic reform plan that had placed the Dabhol plant as the first foreign-owned power project. But both sides learned from their mistakes, and Ms. Mark's patient and skillful negotiations eventually brought about consensus to reignite economic reform and to get the Dabhol plant going again. Enron submitted a proposal in 1997 to build five-to-seven additional power plants in India. The first phase, the Dabhol plant, was completed in December 1998.

Ms. Mark had worked on the relationship between Enron International and India, with an on-again, off-again relationship, since the early 1990s, when the Indian government began to be more open toward foreign investment. Prior to that Gandhi's philosophy of *swadeshi*, meaning self-reliance, had perpetuated protectionism for its domestic industries. Ms. Mark had an ambitious plan to construct a $3 billion power plant in Dabhol, in Maharashtra state. She negotiated extensively with the Maharashtra state government and members of India's civil service. She needed 170 different state and federal permits, along with layers of legal and tax paperwork. She commented on this process:

I've had tea with every bureaucrat in India. . . . People don't understand how to get things done in India. Politicians lay out a plan, but that's different from working through the system.

—C. HILL, *INSTITUTIONAL INVESTOR*, JANUARY 1998.

Today, (as of April 2001), Enron's 2,364-megawatt plant at Dabhol is the biggest foreign investment in India. However, officials at Enron, the Houston-based company, announced on April 9, 2001, that it had lost confidence in the state company that is contractually obliged to buy the output of its Maharashtra plant. The problem was that the energy Enron sold to local utilities cost four times the going rate. While there had been an agreement for the Maharashtra officials to pay partly in U.S. dollars, no one foresaw the decline of the rupee or the surge in oil prices. The bill ran up to Rs.2.25 billion (Pounds 33 million), and a Maharashtra government plea to the federal government to bail out the state fell on deaf ears. Enron Dabhol noted that it had been subjected to the politically motivated agenda of both the Maharashtra government and the government of India, resulting in an adverse effect on the company's ability to perform obligations under the Purchase Power Agreement. This situation resulted in Enron Dabhol issuing a "political force majeure" notice to the Maharashtra State Electricity Board. This is a standard contractual clause in which a company can give warning of withdrawing when their contract has been undermined—in this case where it is locked in a payment dispute. While India's federal power minister, Suresh Prabhu states that the bill will be paid, there are broader ramifications of this situation for foreign investors and for India itself. Although it has been over ten years since India started dismantling its socialist economy and encouraging foreign investors, only a few of the two dozen foreign power players who invested there remain.

It seems that Ms. Mark's tireless negotiations may not have been enough to contend with India's political volatility and bureaucracy. Enron has decided not to build more plants in India, and instead, as part of its worldwide strategy, move out of the ownership of assets into the trading of power as a commodity.

SOURCES: "India: 'Force Majeure' Clause Invoked in Enron Power Case," report by Indian New Agency PTI, BBC Monitoring Service, U.K., April 9, 2001; "Enron Threat to Withdraw from India," www.FT.com, April 10, 2001; "Who Benefited from 'Sweetheart' Deal with Enron?" *Hindustan Times*, India, January 22, 2001; "A Power Play India Can't Afford to Lose," www.businessweek.com, January 31, 2001; *Business Week*, January 8, 2001; "Enron's Plant in India Was Dead; This Month, It Will Go on Stream," *Wall Street Journal*, February 5, 1999; C. Hill, "How Rebecca Mark Solved India," *Institutional Investor*, January 1998.

Global managers negotiate with parties in other countries to make specific plans for strategies (exporting, joint ventures, and so forth), and for continuing operations. While the complexities of cross-cultural negotiations among firms around the world is challenge enough, managers also sometimes are faced with negotiating with various governmental agencies; this kind of situation is illustrated in the opening profile of Enron's Dabhol plant, where negotiators were faced with shifting political agendas over time, internal political conflicts between state and national governments, and multiple layers of bureaucratic hurdles. The high-level political negotiations between the United States and China to gain the return of the U.S. military crew from the plane that was forced to land there in April 2001 is another example of complex situations fraught with both political agenda and cultural nuances, such as the need for the Chinese to "save face" by demanding an apology.

Managers must prepare for strategic negotiations; next the operational details must be negotiated—the staffing of key positions, the sourcing of raw materials or component parts, the repatriating of profits, to name a few. As globalism burgeons, the ability to conduct successful cross-cultural negotiations cannot be overemphasized. Failure to negotiate productively will result in lost potential alliances and lost business at worst; confusion and delays at best.

During the process of negotiation—whether before, during, or after negotiating sessions—all kinds of decisions are made, both explicitly or implicitly. A consideration of cross-cultural negotiations must therefore include the various decision-making processes that occur around the world. Negotiations cannot be conducted without decisions being made.

This chapter will examine the processes of negotiation and decision making as they apply to international and domestic cross-cultural contexts. Our objective is a better understanding of successful management.

NEGOTIATION

Effecting strategy depends on management's ability to negotiate productively: a skill widely considered one of the most important in international business. In the global arena, cultural differences produce great difficulties in the negotiation process. In fact, ignorance of native bargaining rituals, more than any other single factor, accounts for our unimpressive sales efforts with the Japanese and others.[1] Important differences in the negotiation process from country to country include (1) the amount and type of preparation for a negotiation, (2) the relative emphasis on tasks versus interpersonal relationships, (3) the reliance on general principles rather than specific issues, and (4) the number of people present and the extent of their influence.[2] In every instance, managers need to familiarize themselves with the cultural background and underlying motivations of the negotiators—and the tactics and procedures they use—to control the process, make progress, and therefore maximize company goals.

The word **negotiation** describes the process of discussion between two or more parties aimed at reaching a mutually acceptable agreement. For long-term positive relations, the goal should be to set up a **win-win situation**: that is, to bring about a settlement beneficial to all parties concerned. This process, difficult enough when it takes place among people of similar backgrounds, is even more complex in international negotiations because of differences in cultural values, lifestyles, expectations, verbal and nonverbal language, approaches to formal procedures, and

Exhibit 5-1

Stakeholders in Cross-Cultural Negotiations

problem-solving techniques. The complexity is heightened when negotiating across borders because of the greater number of stakeholders involved. These stakeholders are illustrated in Exhibit 5-1. In preparing for negotiations, it is critical to avoid **projective cognitive similarity**—that is, the assumption that others perceive, judge, think, and reason in the same way when, in fact, they do not, because of differential cultural and practical influences. Instead, astute negotiators empathetically enter into the private world or cultural space of their counterparts while willingly sharing their own view of the situation.[3]

THE NEGOTIATION PROCESS

The negotiation process comprises five stages, the ordering of which may vary according to the cultural norms; for most people relationship building is part of a continuous process of preparation in any event: (1) preparation, (2) relationship building, (3) the exchange of task-related information, (4) persuasion, and (5) concessions and agreement.[4,5,6] Of course, in reality these are seldom distinct stages, but rather they tend to overlap; negotiators may also revert to an earlier stage temporarily. With that in mind, it is useful to break down the negotiation process into stages to discuss the issues relevant to each stage and what international managers might expect, so that they might more successfully manage this process. These stages are shown in Exhibit 5-2 and discussed in the following sections.

Stage One: Preparation

The importance of careful preparation for cross-cultural negotiations cannot be overstated. To the extent that time permits, a distinct advantage can be gained if negotiators familiarize themselves with the entire context and background of their counterparts (no matter where the meetings will take place) in addition to the specific subjects to be negotiated. Because most negotiation problems are caused by differences in culture, language, and environment, hours or days of

Exhibit 5-2
The Negotiation Process

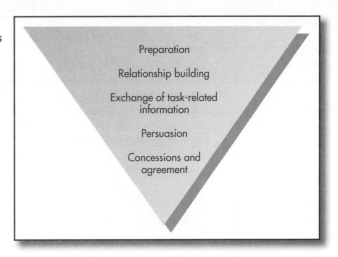

Preparation

Relationship building

Exchange of task-related
information

Persuasion

Concessions and
agreement

tactical preparation for negotiation can be wasted if these factors are not carefully considered.[7]

To understand cultural differences in negotiating styles, managers first need to understand their own styles and then determine how their style differs from the norm in other countries. They can do this by comparing profiles of those perceived to be successful negotiators in different countries. Such profiles reflect the value system, attitudes, and expected behaviors inherent in a given society. Later sections in this chapter will describe and compare negotiating styles around the world.

Variables in the Negotiating Process

Adept negotiators do some research to develop a profile of their counterparts so that they know, in most situations, what to expect, how to prepare, and how to react. Exhibit 5-3 shows 12 variables to consider when preparing to negotiate. These variables can, to a great degree, help managers understand the deep-rooted cultural and national motivations and traditional processes underlying negotiations with people from other countries.

After developing thoughtful profiles of the other party or parties, managers can plan for the actual negotiation meetings. Prior to the meetings, they should find out as much as possible about (1) the kinds of demands that might be made, (2) the composition of the "opposing" team, and (3) the relative authority that the members possess. After this, the managers can gear their negotiation strategy specifically to the other side's firm, allocate roles to different team members, decide on concessions, and prepare an alternative action plan in case a negotiated solution cannot be found.[8]

In some situations, however, the entire negotiation process is something people have to learn from scratch. After the splintering of the Soviet Union into fifteen independent republics, managers from the Newmont Mining Corporation of Denver, wishing to form a joint venture to refine gold deposits in Uzbekistan,

Exhibit 5-3

Variables in the Negotiation Process

1. *Basic conception of negotiation process:* Is it a competitive process or a problem-solving approach?
2. *Negotiator selection criteria:* Is selection based on experience, status, expertise, personal attributes, or some other characteristic?
3. *Significance of type of issues:* Is it specific, such as price, or is the focus on relationships or the format of talks?
4. *Concern with protocol:* What is the importance of procedures, social behaviors, and so forth in the negotiation process?
5. *Complexity of communicative context:* What degree of reliance is placed on nonverbal cues to interpret information?
6. *Nature of persuasive arguments:* How do the parties attempt to influence each other? Do they rely on rational arguments, on accepted tradition, or on emotion?
7. *Role of individuals' aspirations:* Are motivations based on individual, company, or community goals?
8. *Bases of trust:* Is trust based on past experience, intuition, or rules?
9. *Risk-taking propensity:* How much do the parties try to avoid uncertainty in trading information or making a contract?
10. *Value of time:* What is each party's attitude toward time? How fast should negotiations proceed, and what degree of flexibility is there?
11. *Decision-making system:* How does each team reach decisions—by individual determination, by majority opinion, or by group consensus?
12. *Form of satisfactory agreement:* Is agreement based on trust (perhaps just a handshake), the credibility of the parties, commitment, or a legally binding contract?

Source: Adapted from S. E. Weiss and W. Stripp, *Negotiation with Foreign Business Persons: An Introduction for Americans with Propositions on Six Cultures* (New York University Faculty of Business Administration, February 1985).

found themselves at a standstill. Officials in Uzbekistan had never negotiated a business contract and had no one to tell them how to proceed.[9]

Following the preparation and planning stage, usually done at the home office, the core of the actual negotiation takes place on-site in the foreign location (or at the manager's home office if the other team has decided to travel there). In some cases a compromise on the location for negotiations can signal a cooperative strategy, which Weiss calls "Improvise an approach: Effect Symphony"—a strategy available to negotiators familiar with each others' culture and willing to put negotiation on an equal footing.[10] Weiss gives the following example of this negotiation strategy:

> For their negotiations over construction of the tunnel under the English Channel, British and French representatives agreed to partition talks and alternate the site between Paris and London. At each site, the negotiators were to use established, local ways, including the language, . . . thus punctuating approaches by time and space.

In this way, each side was put into the context and the script of the other culture about half the time.

The next stage of negotiation—often given short shrift by westerners—is that of relationship building; this stage, in fact, usually has either taken place already or is concurrent with other preparations in most parts of the world.

Stage Two: Relationship Building

The process of relationship building is regarded with much more significance in most parts of the world than it is in America. American negotiators are, generally speaking, objective about the specific matter at hand and usually want to waste no time in getting down to business and making progress. This approach, well understood in the United States, can be disastrous if the foreign negotiators want to take enough time to build trust and respect as a basis for negotiating contracts. In such cases, American efficiency interferes with the patient development of a mutually trusting relationship, which is the very cornerstone of an Asian business agreement.[11]

In many countries, such as Mexico and China, personal commitments to individuals, rather than the legal system, form the basis for the enforcement of contracts. Effective negotiators allow plenty of time in their schedule for such relationship building with bargaining partners; this process usually takes the form of social events, tours, and ceremonies, along with much light conversation, or nontask sounding, while both sides get to know one another. In such cultures, one patiently waits for the other party to start actual business negotiations, aware that relationship building is, in fact, the first phase of negotiations.[12] It is usually recommended that managers new to such scenarios use an intermediary—someone who already has the trust and respect of the foreign managers and who therefore acts as a "relationship bridge." Middle easterners, in particular, prefer to negotiate through a trusted intermediary, and for them as well, initial meetings are only for the purpose of getting acquainted. Arabs do business with the person, not the company, and therefore mutual trust must be established.

In their best-seller on negotiation, Getting to Yes, Fischer and Ury point out the dangers of not preparing well for negotiations:

> In Persian, the word "compromise" does not have the English meaning of a midway solution which both sides can accept, but only the negative meaning of surrendering one's principles. Also, a "mediator" is a meddler, someone who is barging in uninvited. In 1980, United Nations Secretary-General Kurt Waldheim flew to Iran to deal with the hostage situation. National Iranian radio and television broadcast in Persian a comment he was to have made upon his arrival in Tehran: "I have come as a mediator to work out a compromise." Less than an hour later, his car was being stoned by angry Iranians.[13]

As a bridge to the more formal stages of negotiations, such relationship building is followed by posturing—that is, general discussion that sets the tone for the meetings. This phase should result in a spirit of cooperation; to help ensure this result, negotiators must use words like respect and mutual benefit rather than language that would suggest arrogance, superiority, or urgency.[14]

Stage Three: Exchanging Task-Related Information

In the next stage, exchanging task-related information, each side typically makes a presentation and states its position; a question-and-answer session usually ensues, and alternatives are discussed. From an American perspective, this represents a straightforward, objective, efficient, and understandable stage. However, Copeland and Griggs point out that negotiators from other countries continue to take a more indirect approach at this stage. Mexican negotiators are usually suspicious and indirect, presenting little substantive material and more lengthy, evasive conversation. French negotiators enjoy debate and conflict and will often interrupt presentations to argue about an issue even if it has little relevance to the topic being presented. The Chinese also ask many questions of their counterparts, and they delve specifically and repeatedly into the details at hand; conversely, the Chinese presentations contain only vague and ambiguous material. For instance, after about twenty Boeing officials spent six weeks presenting masses of literature and technical demonstrations to the Chinese, the Chinese said, "Thank you for your introduction."[15]

The Russians also enter negotiations well prepared and well versed in the specific details of the matter being presented. To answer their (or any other side's) questions, it is generally a good idea to bring along someone with expertise to answer any grueling technical inquiries. Russians also put a lot of emphasis on protocol and expect to deal only with top executives.

Adler suggests that negotiators should focus not only on presenting their situation and needs but also on showing an understanding of their opponents' viewpoint. Focusing on the entire situation confronting each party encourages the negotiators to assess a wider range of alternatives for resolution, rather than limiting themselves to their preconceived, static positions. She suggests that to be most effective, negotiators should prepare for meetings by practicing role reversal.[16]

Stage Four: Persuasion

In the next phase of negotiations, persuasion, the hard bargaining starts. Typically, both parties try to persuade the other to accept more of their position and to give up some of their own. Often, some persuasion has already taken place beforehand in social settings and through mutual contacts. In the Far East, details are likely to be worked out ahead of time through the backdoor approach *(houmani)*. For the most part, however, the majority of the persuasion takes place over one or more negotiating sessions. International managers usually find that this process of bargaining and making concessions is fraught with difficulties because of the different uses and interpretations of verbal and nonverbal behaviors. While variations in such behaviors influence every stage of the negotiation process, they can play a particularly powerful role in persuasion, especially if they are not anticipated.

Studies of negotiating behavior have revealed the use of certain recognizable **tactics**, which skilled negotiators recognize and use. Exhibit 5-4 shows the results of a study comparing the use of various tactics (promises, threats, and so forth) among the Japanese, Americans, and Brazilians. The results indicate that the Japanese and the Americans tend to be more alike in the use of these behaviors,

Exhibit 5-4

Differences Among Japanese, American, and Brazilian Verbal Negotiations Behavior

BARGAINING BEHAVIORS AND DEFINITION	FREQUENCY PER HALF-HOUR BARGAINING SESSION		
	JAPANESE	AMERICAN	BRAZILIAN
Promise. A statement in which the source indicated his or her intention to provide the target with a reinforcing consequence that source anticipates target will evaluate as pleasant, positive, or rewarding.	7	8	3
Threat. Same as promise, except that the reinforcing consequences are thought to be noxious, unpleasant, or punishing.	4	4	2
Recommendation. A statement in which the source predicts that a pleasant environmental consequence will occur to the target. Its occurrence is not under the source's control.	7	4	5
Warning. Same as recommendation, except that the consequences are thought to be unpleasant.	2	1	1
Reward. A statement by the source that is thought to create pleasant consequences for the target.	1	2	2
Punishment. Same as reward, except that the consequences are thought to be unpleasant.	1	3	3
Positive normative appeal. A statement in which the source indicates that the target's past, present, or future behavior was or will be in conformity with social norms.	1	1	0
Negative normative appeal. Same as positive normative appeal, except that the target's behavior is in violation of social norms.	3	1	1
Commitment. A statement by the source to the effect that its future bids will not go below or above a certain level.	15	13	8
Self-disclosure. A statement in which the source reveals information about itself.	34	36	39
Question. A statement in which the source asks the target to reveal information about itself.	20	20	22
Command. A statement in which the source suggests that the target perform a certain behavior.	8	6	14

Source: From John L. Graham, "The Influence of Culture on the Process of Business Negotiations in an Exploratory Study," *Journal of International Business Studies* (Spring 1985): 88.

whereas the Japanese and the Brazilians are less alike. For example, the Brazilians use fewer promises and commitments than the Japanese or the Americans (only half as many), but they use commands far more often. The Japanese and the Americans use threats twice as often as the Brazilians, and they use commands only about half as often as the Brazilians. The Brazilians and the Japanese seldom behave similarly.

Other, less savory tactics are sometimes used in international negotiations. Often called **dirty tricks**, these tactics, according to Fisher and Ury, include efforts to mislead "opponents" deliberately.[17] Some negotiators may give wrong or distorted factual information or use the excuse of ambiguous authority—giving conflicting impressions about who in their party has the power to make a commitment. In the midst of hard bargaining, the prudent international manager will follow up on possibly misleading information before taking action based on trust.

Other rough tactics are designed to put opposing negotiators in a stressful situation physically or psychologically so that they are more likely to give in. These include uncomfortable room temperatures, too-bright lighting, rudeness, interruptions, and other irritations. Specific bargaining pressures include extreme or escalating demands, threats to stop negotiating, calculated delays, and a take-it-or-leave-it attitude. In a survey of 18 U.S.-Korean joint ventures, for example, U.S. executives reported that the behavior of the Koreans during the course of negotiations was often "abusive," resulting in "shouting matches, desk pounding, and chest beating."[18]

International negotiators must keep in mind, however, that what might seem like dirty tricks to Americans is simply the way other cultures conduct negotiations. In some South American countries, for example, it is common to start negotiations with misleading or false information.

The most subtle behaviors in the negotiation process, and often the most difficult to deal with, are usually the nonverbal messages—the use of voice intonation, facial and body expressions, eye contact, dress, and the timing of the discussions. **Nonverbal behaviors** are ingrained aspects of culture used by people in their daily lives; they are not specifically changed for the purposes of negotiation. In a comparative study of the nonverbal negotiating behaviors of Japanese, Americans, and Brazilians, Graham assessed the relative frequency of the use of silent periods, conversational overlaps, facial gazing (staring at people's faces), and touching. He found that the Brazilians interrupted conversation about twice as often as the Japanese and the Americans and used much more touching and facial gazing; needless to say, they scored low on silent periods. The Japanese tended to use more silent periods and interruptions than the Americans, but less facial gazing. The Japanese and the Americans evidenced no touching whatsoever, other than handshaking, during a 30-minute period.[19]

Although we have discussed persuasion as if it were always a distinct stage, it is really the primary purpose underlying all stages of the negotiation process. In particular, persuasion is clearly an integral part of the process of making concessions and arriving at an agreement.

Stage Five: Concessions and Agreement

In the last stage of negotiation, concessions and agreement, tactics vary greatly across cultures. Well-prepared negotiators are aware of various concession strategies and have decided ahead of time what their own concession strategy will be. Familiar with the typical initial positions that various parties are likely to take, they know that the Russians and the Chinese generally open their bargaining with extreme positions, asking for more than they hope to gain, whereas the Swedes usually start with what they are prepared to accept.

Research in the United States indicates that better end results are attained by starting with extreme positions. With this approach, the process of reaching an agreement involves careful timing of the disclosure information and of concessions. Most people who have studied negotiations believe that negotiators should disclose only the information that is necessary at a given point and that they should try to obtain information piece by piece to get the whole picture gradually without giving away their goals or concession strategy. These guidelines will not always work in intercultural negotiations because the American process of addressing issues one at a time, in a linear fashion, is not common in other countries or cultures. Negotiators in the Far East, for example, approach issues in a holistic manner, deciding on the whole deal at the end, rather than making incremental concessions.

Again, at the final stage of agreement and contract, cultural values determine how these agreements will be honored. Whereas Americans take contracts very seriously, Russians often renege on their contracts. The Japanese, on the other hand, consider a formal contract to be somewhat of an insult and a waste of time and money in legal costs, since they prefer to operate on the basis of understanding and social trust.[20]

UNDERSTANDING NEGOTIATION STYLES

Global managers can benefit from studying differences in negotiating behaviors (and the underlying reasons for them), which can help them recognize what is happening in the negotiating process. Exhibit 5-5 shows some examples of differences among North American, Japanese, and Latin American styles. Brazilians, for example, generally have a spontaneous, passionate, and dynamic style. They are very talkative and particularly use the word no extensively—in fact, more than 40 times per half hour, compared with 4.7 times for Americans and only 1.9 times for the Japanese. They also differ markedly from the Americans and Japanese by their use of extensive physical contact.[21]

The Japanese are typically skillful negotiators. They have spent a great deal more time and effort studying American culture and business practices than Americans have spent studying theirs. A typical example of this contrast was apparent at recent trade negotiations between Japan and the United States in 1994. Charlene Barshefsky—though a tough American international lawyer—had never visited Japan before being sent there as a trade negotiator, and she had little knowledge of her counterparts. But Mr. Okamatsu, as most Japanese negotiators, is very familiar with America. He lived in New York for three years with his family and had spent many years handling bilateral trade disputes between the two countries. The different styles of Mr. Okamatsu and Ms. Barshefsky were apparent in the negotiations. Ms. Barshefsky wanted specific import goals. Mr. Okamatsu wanted to talk more about the causes of trade problems rather than set specific targets, which he calls the "cooperative approach." Ms. Barshefsky snapped that the approach is nonsense and "would analyze the past to death, with no link to future change."[22] Such differences in philosophy and style between the two countries reflect ten years of anger and feelings of betrayal in trade negotiations. John Graham, a California professor who has studied international negotiating styles, says that the differences between American and Japanese styles are well illustrated by their respective proverbs: the American believes that "the squeaking wheel gets the grease," and the Japanese say that "the pheasant would not be shot but for its cry."[23] The Japanese are calm, quiet, patient negotiators; they are accustomed to long, detailed negotiating sessions. Whereas Americans often plunge straight to the matter at hand, the Japanese want instead to develop long-term, personal relationships. The Japanese want to get to know those on the other side and will spend some time in **nontask sounding**—general polite conversation and informal communication before meetings (*nemawashi*).

In negotiations, the Japanese culture of politeness and the hiding of emotions can be disconcerting to Americans when they are unable to make straightforward eye contact or when the Japanese maintain smiling faces in serious situations. It is important that Americans understand what is polite and what is offensive to the Japanese (and vice versa). Americans must avoid anything that resembles boasting because the Japanese value humility, and they must avoid physical contact or touch-

Exhibit 5-5
Comparison of Negotiation Styles—Japanese, North American, and Latin American

JAPANESE	NORTH AMERICAN	LATIN AMERICAN
Emotional sensitivity highly valued	Emotional sensitivity not highly valued	Emotional sensitivity valued
Hiding of emotions	Dealing straightforwardly or impersonally	Emotionally passionate
Subtle power plays; conciliation	Litigation not so much as conciliation	Great power plays; use of weakness
Loyalty to employer; employer takes care of employees	Lack of commitment to employer; breaking of ties by either if necessary	Loyalty to employer (who is often family)
Face-saving crucial; decisions often made on basis of saving someone from embarrassment	Decisions made on a cost benefit basis; face-saving does not always matter	Face-saving crucial in decision making to preserve honor, dignity
Decision makers openly influenced by special interests	Decision makers influenced by special interests but often not considered ethical	Execution of special interests of decision expected, condoned
Not argumentative; quiet when right	Argumentative when right or wrong, but impersonal	Argumentative when right or wrong; passionate
What is down in writing must be accurate, valid	Great importance given to documentation as evidential proof	Impatient with documentation as obstacle to understanding general principles
Step-by-step approach to decision making	Methodically organized decision making	Impulsive, spontaneous decision making
Good of group is the ultimate aim	Profit motive or good of individual ultimate aim	What is good for group is good for the individual
Cultivate a good emotional social setting for decision making; get to know decision makers	Decision making impersonal; avoid involvements, conflict of interest	Personalism necessary for good decision making

Source: From Pierre Casse, *Training for the Multicultural Manager: A Practical and Cross-Cultural Approach to the Management of People* (Washington, D.C.: Society for Intercultural Education, Training, and Research, 1982).

ing of any sort.[24] Consistent with the culture-based value of maintaining harmony, the Japanese are likely to be evasive or even leave the room rather than give a direct negative answer.[25,26] Fundamental to the Japanese culture is a concern for the welfare of the group; anything that affects one member or part of society affects the others. Thus, the Japanese view decisions carefully in light of long-term consequences; they use objective, analytic thought patterns; and they take time for reflection.[27]

Further insight into negotiating styles around the world can be gained by comparing the North American, Arab, and Russian styles. As shown in Exhibit 5-6, basic cultural values often shed light on the manner in which information is presented, whether and how concessions will be made, and the general nature and duration of the relationship.

For North Americans, negotiations are businesslike; their **factual appeals** are based on what they believe is objective information, presented with the assumption that it is understood by the other side on a logical basis. Arabs use **affective appeals** based on emotions and subjective feelings; Russians employ **axiomatic appeals**—that is, their appeals are based on the ideals generally accepted in their society. The Russians are tough negotiators; they stall for time until they unnerve Western negotiators by continuously delaying and haggling. Much of this is based on the Russians' different attitude toward time. Because Russians do not subscribe to the Western belief that "time is money," they are more patient, more determined, more dogged negotiators. They try to keep smiles and other expressions of emotion to a minimum to present a calm exterior.[28]

Exhibit 5-6

Comparison of Negotiation Styles—North Americans, Arabs, Russians

	NORTH AMERICANS	ARABS	RUSSIANS
Primary negotiating style and process	Factual: appeals made to logic	Affective: appeals made to emotions	Axiomatic: appeals made to ideals
Conflict: opponent's arguments countered with . . .	Objective facts	Subjective feelings	Asserted ideals
Making concessions	Small concessions made early to establish a relationship	Concessions made throughout as a part of the bargaining process	Few, if any, small concessions made
Response to opponent's concessions	Usually reciprocate opponent's concessions	Almost always reciprocate opponent's concessions	Opponent's concessions viewed as weakness and almost never reciprocated
Relationship	Short-term	Long-term	No continuing relationship
Authority	Broad	Broad	Limited
Initial position	Moderate	Extreme	Extreme
Deadline	Very important	Casual	Ignored

Source: Adapted from E. S. Glenn, D. Witmeyer, and K. A. Stevenson, "Cultural Styles of Persuasion," *International Journal of Intercultural Relations* 1 (1984).

In contrast to the Russians, Arabs are more interested in long-term relationships and therefore are more likely to make concessions. Compared with Westerners, Arabs have a casual approach to deadlines and frequently lack the authority to finalize a deal.[29]

Successful Negotiators Around the World

Following are selected profiles of what it takes to be a successful negotiator, as perceived by people in their home country. These are profiles of American, Indian, Arab, Swedish, and Italian negotiators, according to Pierre Casse, and give some insight into what to expect from the different negotiators and what they expect from others.[30]

American Negotiators

According to Casse, a successful American negotiator acts as follows:

1. Knows when to compromise
2. Takes a firm stand at the beginning of the negotiation
3. Refuses to make concessions beforehand
4. Keeps his or her cards close to his or her chest
5. Accepts compromises only when the negotiation is deadlocked
6. Sets up the general principles and delegates the detail work to associates
7. Keeps a maximum of options open before negotiation
8. Operates in good faith
9. Respects the "opponents"
10. States his or her position as clearly as possible
11. Knows when he or she wishes a negotiation to move on
12. Is fully briefed about the negotiated issues
13. Has a good sense of timing and is consistent
14. Makes the other party reveal his or her position while keeping his or her own position hidden as long as possible
15. Lets the other negotiator come forward first and looks for the best deal

Indian Negotiators

Indians, says Casse, often follow Gandhi's approach to negotiation, which he called *satyagraha*, "firmness in a good cause." This approach combines strength with the love of truth. The successful Indian negotiator thus acts as follows:

1. Looks for and says the truth
2. Is not afraid of speaking up and has no fears
3. Exercises self-control ("The weapons of the *satyagraha* are within him.")
4. Seeks solutions that will please all the parties involved ("*Satyagraha* aims to exalt both sides.")
5. Respects the other party ("The opponent must be weaned from error by patience and sympathy. Weaned, not crushed; converted, not annihilated.")
6. Neither uses violence nor insults
7. Is ready to change his or her mind and differ with himself or herself at the risk of being seen as inconsistent and unpredictable

8. Puts things into perspective and switches easily from the small picture to the big one
9. Is humble and trusts the opponent
10. Is able to withdraw, use silence, and learn from within
11. Relies on himself or herself, his or her own resources and strengths
12. Appeals to the other party's spiritual identity ("To communicate, the West moves or talks. The East sits, contemplates, suffers.")
13. Is tenacious, patient, and persistent
14. Learns from the opponent and avoids the use of secrets
15. Goes beyond logical reasoning and trusts his or her instinct as well as faith

Arab Negotiators

Many Arab negotiators, following Islamic tradition, use mediators to settle disputes. A successful Arab mediator acts in the following way:

1. Protects all the parties' honor, self-respect, and dignity
2. Avoids direct confrontations between opponents
3. Is respected and trusted by all
4. Does not put the parties involved in a situation where they have to show weakness or admit defeat
5. Has the necessary prestige to be listened to
6. Is creative enough to come up with honorable solutions for all parties
7. Is impartial and can understand the positions of the various parties without leaning toward one or the other
8. Is able to resist any kind of pressure that the opponents could try to exercise on him
9. Uses references to people who are highly respected by the opponents to persuade them to change their minds on some issues ("Do it for the sake of your father.")
10. Can keep secrets and in so doing gains the confidence of the negotiating parties
11. Controls his temper and emotions (or loses it when and where necessary)
12. Can use conferences as mediating devices
13. Knows that the opponents will have problems in carrying out the decisions made during the negotiation
14. Is able to cope with the Arab disregard for time
15. Understands the impact of Islam on the opponents who believe that they possess the truth, follow the Right Path and are going to "win" because their cause is just

Swedish Negotiators

Swedish negotiators, according to Casse, have the following traits:

1. Very quiet and thoughtful
2. Punctual (concerned with time)
3. Extremely polite
4. Straightforward (they get straight down to business)
5. Eager to be productive and efficient

6. Heavy-going
7. Down-to-earth and overcautious
8. Rather flexible
9. Able to and quite good at holding emotions and feelings
10. Slow at reacting to new (unexpected) proposals
11. Informal and familiar
12. Conceited
13. Perfectionist
14. Afraid of confrontations
15. Very private

Italian Negotiators

Italians, says Casse, value a negotiator who acts as follows:

1. Has a sense of drama (acting is a main part of the culture)
2. Does not hide his or her emotions (which are partly sincere and partly feigned)
3. Reads facial expressions and gestures very well
4. Has a feeling for history
5. Does not trust anybody
6. Is concerned about the *bella figura*, or the "good impression," he or she can create among those who watch his or her behavior
7. Believes in the individual's initiatives, not so much in teamwork
8. Is good at being obliging and simpatico at all times
9. Is always on the *qui vive*, the "lookout"
10. Never embraces definite opinions
11. Is able to come up with new ways to immobilize and eventually destroy his or her opponents
12. Handles confrontations of power with subtlety and tact
13. Has a flair for intrigue
14. Knows how to use flattery
15. Can involve other negotiators in complex combinations

Comparing such profiles is useful; Indian negotiators, for example, are humble, patient, respectful of the other parties, and very willing to compromise, compared with Americans, who are firmer about taking stands. An important difference between Arab negotiators and those from most other countries is that the negotiators are mediators, not the parties themselves; hence direct confrontation is made impossible. Successful Swedish negotiators are conservative and careful, dealing with factual and detailed information. This profile contrasts with Italian negotiators, who are expressive and exuberant but less straightforward than their Swedish counterparts.

MANAGING NEGOTIATION

Skillful global managers need to assess many factors when **managing negotiation**. They must understand the position of the other parties in regard to their goals—whether national or corporate—and whether these goals are represented by principles or specific details. They should have the ability to recognize the relative importance attached to completing the task versus developing interpersonal relationships. Managers also need to know the composition of the teams involved, the power allotted to the members, and the extent of the teams' preparation. In addition, they must grasp the significance of personal trust in the relationship. As said earlier, the culture of the parties involved affects their negotiating styles and behavior and thus the overall process of negotiation. However, whatever the culture, person-related conflicts have been found by research done by Tse, Francis, and Walls, to "invite negative, more relation-oriented (versus information-oriented) responses," leading them to conclude that:

> The **software of negotiation**—that is, the nature and the appearance of the relationship between the people pursuing common goals—needs to be carefully addressed in the negotiation process.[31]

This is particularly true when representatives of individual-focused cultures (such as Americans) and group-focused cultures (such as Chinese) are on opposite sides of the table. Many of these cultural-based differences in negotiations in fact came to light in a study by Husted of the perceptions of Mexican negotiators of the reasons for the failure of their negotiations with U.S. teams. The summary findings are shown in Exhibit 5-7. However, Husted interprets that "many of the perceived differences relate to the typical differences found between high-context and low-context cultures."[32] In other words, the interpretations by the Mexican managers were affected by their high-context culture, with the characteristics of an indirect approach, patience in discussing ideas, and maintenance of dignity. Instead, the low-context Americans conveyed an impatient, cold, blunt communicative style. To maintain the outward dignity of their Mexican counterparts, Americans need to approach negotiations with Mexicans with patience and tolerance, and by not attacking ideas because these attacks may be taken personally.

The relationships among the factors of cross-cultural negotiation that we have discussed in this chapter are illustrated in Exhibit 5-8.

The successful management of intercultural negotiations requires a manager to go beyond a generalized understanding of the issues and variables involved. She or he must (1) gain specific knowledge of the parties in the upcoming meeting, (2) prepare accordingly to adjust to and control the situation, and (3) be innovative.[33]

Research has shown that a problem-solving approach is essential to successful cross-cultural negotiations, whether abroad or in the home office, although the approach works differently in various countries.[34] This problem-solving approach requires that a negotiator treat everyone with respect, avoid making anyone feel uncomfortable, and not criticize or blame the other parties in a personal way that would make someone feel shame—that is, lose face.

Research by the Huthwaite Research Group reveals how successful negotiators, compared to average negotiators, manage the planning process and their face-to-face behavior. The group found that during the planning process,

Exhibit 5-7

Bargaining with the Gringos

Mexican Managers' Perceptions of Causes of Failure of Negotiations with Americans

	VERY IMPORTANT (%)	IMPORTANT (%)	MODERATELY IMPORTANT (%)	TOTAL (%)
Problems with U. S. team				
Lack of authority of U.S. team to make decisions	37.0	20.0	15.0	72.0
U.S. team's failure to resolve doubts of Mexican team	34.0	26.0	14.0	74.0
U.S. team's lack of sincerity	41.0	20.0	9.0	70.0
Eigenvalue: 2.9009/Percent of var.: 26.4/Cum. var.: 26.4				
Negotiation process				
Differences in negotiation styles	26.5	28.4	22.5	77.4
U.S. team quoting unreasonable prices	52.5	17.8	8.9	79.2
Mexican lack of knowledge of delivery system	42.0	19.0	11.0	72.0
Mexican lack of preparation	40.6	21.8	9.9	72.3
Eigenvalue: 2.3577/Percent of var.: 21.4/Cum. var.: 47.8				
Cultural barriers				
Differences in business practices	24.5	29.4	22.5	76.4
Communication barriers	37.3	17.6	12.7	67.6
Eigenvalue: 1.7976/Percent of var.: 16.3/Cum. var.: 64.1				
Language problems	41.2	21.6	5.9	68.7
Eigenvalue: 1.0763/Percent of var.: 9.8/Cum. var.: 73.9				
Price constraints				
Mexican team's inability to lower the price	32.0	22.0	18.0	72.0
Eigenvalue: 1.0433/Percent of var.: 9.5/Cum. var.: 83.4				

Source: Bryan W. Husted, "Bargaining with the Gringos: An Exploratory Study of Negotiations between Mexican and U.S. Firms," *International Executive* 36(5) (September–October 1994): 625–644.

successful negotiators consider a wider range of options and pay greater attention to areas of common ground. Skillful negotiators also tend to make twice as many comments regarding long-term issues and are more likely to set upper and lower limits regarding specific points. In their face-to-face behavior, skillful negotiators make fewer irritating comments—such as "we're making you a generous offer,"—make counterproposals less frequently, and use fewer reasons to back up arguments. In addition, skilled negotiators practice active listening—asking questions, clarifying their understanding of the issues, and summarizing the issues.[35]

Exhibit 5-8
Cross-Cultural
Negotiation Variables

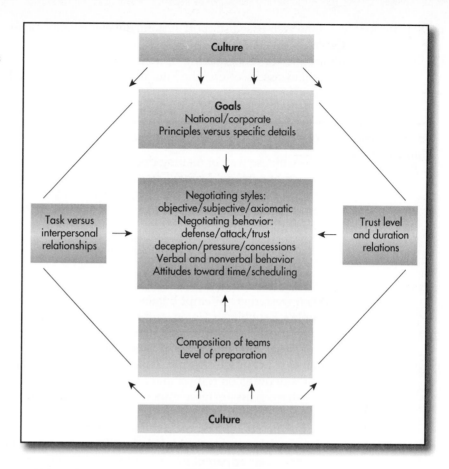

Using the Web to Support Negotiations

Modern technology can provide support for the negotiating process, though it can't take the place of the essential face-to-face ingredient in many instances. A growing component for electronic commerce are applications to support the negotiation of contracts and resolution of disputes. As web applications develop, they may provide support for various phases and dimensions, such as:

> Multiple issue, multiple party business transactions of a buy-sell nature, international dispute resolution (business disputes, political disputes), internal company negotiations and communications, among others.[36]

Negotiation Support Systems (NSS) can provide support for the negotiation process by:

- Increasing the likelihood that an agreement is reached when a zone of agreement exists (solutions that both parties would accept)
- Decreasing the direct and indirect costs of negotiations, such as costs caused by time delays (strikes, violence), and attorneys' fees, among others
- Maximizing the chances for optimal outcomes[37]

One Web-based support system, developed at Carleton University in Ottawa, Canada—called INSPIRE— provides applications to prepare and conduct negotiations and for renegotiating options after a settlement. Users can specify preferences and assess offers; the site also has graphical displays of the negotiation process.[38]

Comparative Management in Focus	## Negotiating with the Chinese The Chinese way of making decisions begins with socialization and initiation of personal guanxi [friendships] rather than business discussion. The focus is not market research, statistical analysis, facts, power-point presentations, or to-the-point business discussion. My focus must be on fostering guanxi. SUNNY ZHOU, GENERAL MANAGER OF KUNMING LIDA WOOD AND BAMBOO PRODUCTS.[39]

When westerners attempt business negotiations with representatives from the People's Republic of China, cultural barriers confront both sides. The negotiation process used by the Chinese—although there are variations among the Cantonese, Shanghainese, and northern Chinese—is dramatically different from that of Americans. For instance, the Chinese put much greater emphasis than Americans on respect and friendship, on saving face, and on group goals. Long-term goals are more important to the Chinese than the specific current objectives typical of Western negotiators.[40,41]

Businesspeople report two major areas of conflict in negotiating with the Chinese—the amount of detail the Chinese want about product characteristics, and their apparent insincerity about reaching an agreement. In addition, Chinese negotiators frequently have little authority, frustrating Americans who do have the authority and are ready to conclude a deal.[42] This situation arises because Chinese companies report to the government trade corporations, who are involved in the negotiations, often having a representative on the team. The goals of Chinese negotiators remain primarily within the framework of state planning and political ideals. Although China is tending to become more profit-oriented, most deals are still negotiated within the confines of the state budget allocation for that project, rather than assessment of profitability or value. It is crucial, then, to find out which officials—national, provincial, local—have the power to make, and keep, a deal. According to James Broering of Arthur Andersen, who does much business in China, "Companies have negotiated with government people for months, only to discover that they were dealing with the wrong people."[43]

Research shows that for the Chinese, the negotiation process is greatly affected by three cultural norms: their ingrained politeness and emotional restraint, their emphasis on social obligations, and their belief in the interconnection of work, family, and friendship. Because of the Chinese preference for emotional restraint and saving face, aggressive or emotional attempts at persuasion in negotiation are likely to fail. Instead, the Chinese tendency to avoid open conflict will more likely result in negative strategies such as discontinuing or withdrawing from negotiation."[44] At the heart of this kind of response is the concept of **face**—a concept so important that it is essential for foreigners to understand it to recognize the role that face behavior plays in negotiations. There are two components of face: *lien* and *mien-tzu*. *Lien* refers to a person's moral character, the most important thing defining that person, without which one cannot function in society. It can only be earned by fulfilling obligations to others. *Mien-tzu* refers to one's reputation or prestige, earned through accomplishments, bureaucratic or political power.[45] Giving others one's time, gifts, or praise enhances one's own face. In negotiations, it is vital that you do not make it obvious that you have "won" because that means that the other party has "lost" and will lose face. To avoid this, token concessions and other attempts to show respect must be made, and modesty and control must be maintained, otherwise anyone who feels he or she has "lost face" will not want to deal with you again. The Chinese will later ignore any dealings or incidents which caused them to lose face, maintaining the expected polite behavior out of social consciousness and concern for others. When faced with an embarrassing situation, they will typically smile or laugh in an attempt to save face, responses which are confusing to Western negotiators.[46]

The Chinese emphasis on social obligations underlies their strong orientation toward collective goals. Therefore, appeals to individual members of the Chinese negotiating team, rather than appeals to benefit the group as a whole, will probably backfire.[47] The Confucian emphasis on the kinship system and the hierarchy of work, family, and friends explains the Chinese preference for doing business with familiar, trusted people and trusted companies. "Foreign" negotiators, then, should focus on establishing long-term, trusting relationships, even at the expense of some immediate returns.

Deeply ingrained in the Chinese culture is the importance of harmony for the smooth functioning of society. Harmony is based primarily on personal relationships, trust, and ritual. After the Chinese establish a cordial relationship with foreign negotiators, they use this relationship as a basis for the give-and-take of business discussions. This implicit cultural norm is commonly known as *guanxi*, which refers to the intricate, pervasive network of personal relations which every Chinese carefully cultivates; it is the primary means of accomplishing things and getting ahead.[48] In other words, *guanxi* establishes obligations to exchange favors in future business activities.[49] Even within the Chinese bureaucracy, *guanxi* prevails over legal interpretations. Although networking is important anywhere to do business, the difference in China is that "*guanxi* networks are not just commercial, but also social, involving the exchange both of favor and affection".[50] Firms which have special *guanxi* connections and give preferential treatment to one another are known as members of a *guanxihu* network.[51] Says Sunny Zhou, general manager of Kumming Lida Wood and Bamboo Products, when he shops for lumber "the lumber price varies drastically, depending on whether one has strong *guanxi* with the local administrators."[52]

Western managers should thus anticipate extended preliminary visiting (relationship building), in which the Chinese expect to learn more about them and their trustworthiness. The Chinese also use this opportunity to convey their own deeply held principles. They attach considerable importance to mutual benefit.[53] The Chinese expect Western firms to sacrifice corporate goals and above-average profits to Chinese national goals and principles, such as meaningful friendship, Chinese national development, and the growth and enhancement of the Chinese people. Misunderstandings occur when Americans show polite acceptance of these general principles without understanding their significance, because they do not have any obvious relationship to American corporate goals, such as profit. Nor do such principles seem relevant to practical decisions on plant locations, employee practices, or sourcing.[54]

Americans often experience two negotiation stages with the Chinese—the technical and the commercial. During the long technical stage, the Chinese want to hammer out every detail of the proposed product specifications and technology. If there are two teams of negotiators, it may be several days before the commercial team is actually called in to deal with aspects of production, marketing, pricing, and so forth. However, the commercial team should sit in on the first stage to become familiar with the Chinese negotiating style.[55] The Chinese negotiating team is usually about twice as large as the Western team; about a third of the time is spent discussing technical specifications, and a third is spent on price negotiations.[56]

The Chinese are among the toughest negotiators in the world. American managers must anticipate various tactics, such as their delaying techniques and their avoidance of direct, specific answers: both ploys used to exploit the known impatience of Americans. The Chinese frequently try to put pressure on Americans by "shaming" them, thereby implying that the Americans are trying to renege on the friendship—the basis of the implicit contract. Whereas westerners come to negotiations with specific and segmented goals and find it easy to compromise, the Chinese are reluctant to negotiate details; they find it difficult to compromise and trade because they have entered negotiations with a broader vision of achieving development goals for China, and they are offended when westerners don't internalize those goals.[57] Under these circumstances, the Chinese will adopt a rigid posture, and no agreement or contract is final until the negotiated activities have actually been completed.

Patience, respect, and experience are necessary prerequisites for anyone negotiating in China. For the best outcomes, older, more experienced people are more acceptable to the Chinese in cross-cultural negotiations. The Chinese want to deal with the top executive of an American company, under the assumption that the highest officer has attained that position by establishing close personal relationships and trust with colleagues and others outside the organization. Western delegation practices are unfamiliar to them and they are reluctant to come to an agreement without the presence of the Chinese foreign negotiator.[58] From the Western perspective, confusing jurisdictions of government ministries hamper decisions in negotiations.[59] Americans tend to send specific technical personnel with experience on the task at hand; therefore, they have to take care in selecting the most suitable negotiators. In addition, visiting negotiating teams should realize that the Chinese are probably negotiating with other foreign teams, often at the same time, and will use that setup to play one company's offer against the others. On an interpersonal level, Western negotiators must also realize that, while a handshake is polite, physical contact is not acceptable in Chinese social behavior; nor are personal discussion topics such as one's family. However, it is customary to take small gifts as tokens of friendship. Pye offers the following additional tips to foreigners conducting business with the Chinese:[60]

- Practice patience
- Accept prolonged periods of stalemate
- Refrain from exaggerated expectations and discount Chinese rhetoric about future prospects
- Expect the Chinese will try to manipulate by shaming
- Resist the temptation to believe that difficulties may have been caused by one's own mistakes
- Try to understand Chinese cultural traits, but realize that a foreigner cannot practice them better than the Chinese.

Managing Conflict Resolution

Much of the negotiation process is fraught with conflict—explicit or implicit, and such conflict can often lead to a stand-off, or a lose–lose situation. This is regrettable, not only for the situation at hand, but because it probably will shut off future opportunities for deals between the parties. Much of the cause of such conflict can be found in cultural differences between the parties—in their expectations, in their behaviors, and particularly in their communication styles.

As discussed in Chapter 4, much of the difference in communication styles is attributable to whether you are part of a high-context or low-context culture (or somewhere in between), as shown in Exhibit 4-4.) In low-context cultures such as that in the United States, conflict is handled directly and explicitly. It is also regarded as separate from the person negotiating—that is, the negotiators draw a distinction between the people involved and the information or opinions they are representing. They also tend to deal on the basis of factual information and logical analysis. That approach to conflict is called **instrumental oriented.**[61] In high-context cultures, such as in the Middle East, the approach to conflict is **expressive oriented**—that is, the situation is handled indirectly and implicitly and there is no clear delineation of the situation from the person handling it. Those negotiators do not want to get in a confrontational situation because it is regarded as insulting and would cause a loss of "face," so they tend to use evasion and avoidance if they cannot reach agreement through emotional appeals. Their avoidance and inaction conflicts with the expectations of the low-context negotiators who are looking to move ahead with the business at hand and arrive at a solution.

Exhibit 5-9

Sources of Conflict Between Low-Context and High-Context Cultures

KEY QUESTIONS	LOW-CONTEXT CONFLICT	HIGH-CONTEXT CONFLICT
Why	Analytic, linear logic; instrumental oriented; dichotomy between conflict and conflict parties	Synthetic, spiral logic; expressive oriented; integration of conflict and conflict parties
When	Individualistic oriented; low collective normative expectations; violations of individual expectations create conflict potentials	Group oriented; high collective normative expectations; violations of collective expectations create conflict potentials
What	Revealment; direct, confrontational attitude; action and solution oriented	Concealment; indirect, nonconfrontational attitude; "face" and relationship oriented
How	Explicit communication codes; line-logic style: rational–factual rhetoric; open, direct strategies	Implicit communication codes; point-logic style: intuitive–effective rhetoric; ambiguous, indirect strategies

Source: W. Gudykunst, L. Stewart, and S. Ting-Toomey, *Communication, Culture, and Organizational Processes.* Copyright © 1985 by Sage Publications, Inc. Reprinted by permission of Sage Publications, Inc.

The differences between high- and low-context cultures which often lead to conflict situations are summarized in Exhibit 5-9. As you can see, most of these variables were discussed earlier in this chapter or in Chapter 4 on communication. The reason for the overlap is that the subjects and culture and communication are really inseparable, and negotiation differences and conflict situations arise from variables in culture and communication.

The point here is, how can a manager from France, from Japan, or from Brazil, for example, manage conflict situations? The solution, as discussed before, lies mainly in your ability to know and understand the people and the situation you will face. Be prepared by developing an understanding of the cultural context in which you will be operating: What are the expectations of the persons you will be negotiating with? What kinds of communication styles and negotiating tactics should you expect, and how will they differ from your own? It is important to bear in mind your own expectations and negotiating style and to be aware of the other parties' expectations about your behavior. Try to consider in advance what it will take to arrive at a win–win solution. Often it helps to use the services of a host-country adviser or mediator who may be able to help with early diffusion of a conflict situation.

One contemporary tool in negotiation and decision making which helps to avoid circumstances of conflict is the on-line B2B marketplace: exchanges, where buyers and sellers negotiate prices, speed up the decision-making and transaction process, as described in the accompanying *E-Biz Box.*

Over 80 percent of on-line downloads are business-to-business (B2B) transactions. B2B e-commerce, in which transactions between businesses are conducted on-line, offers a number of inherent advantages over traditional commerce. First, it's cheaper to process the nuts and bolts of transactions—purchase orders, proposals, billing statements, fund transfers—when customers are serving themselves on-line. Also, large buyers such as manufacturers can find better prices if they set up reverse-bidding systems on the Internet that pit suppliers against each other.

For sellers who participate in these markets, there's a lower comfort level with the customer, but there are opportunities for more flexible pricing—at least in theory. And the Internet helps everyone reach more potential trading partners.

The Internet adds new dynamics to the traditional one-to-one model for business transactions. Many vendors sell directly from their sites (virtually all computer-related companies now provide an on-line storefront), but more sophisticated virtual marketplaces seek to bring buyers and sellers together in one place. By doing this, they hope to increase pricing efficiencies. Some B2B marketplaces are vertically oriented, seeking to capture a large share of a single industry's transactions. Others are horizontal, offering, for instance, places where small businesses can purchase telephone service, office supplies, and insurance.

These on-line markets where buyers and sellers negotiate prices are called *exchanges*. They usually use some sort of bidding or reverse-bid system, and prices fluctuate based on demand. These types of exchanges work well with commodity-type goods that are easily definable. Other B2B sites make comparison shopping possible by aggregating catalogs from more than one vendor.

Typically, B2B sites are supported by membership, subscription, or transaction fees, along with revenue from advertisers. Like stock markets, on-line B2B markets seek to drive volume to their sites to create liquidity and thus efficient pricing.

SOURCE: Adapted from A. Palazzo, B2B Markets Basics, www.business.com and www.FT.com, January 28, 2001.

DECISION MAKING

Negotiation actually represents the outcome of a series of small and large decisions. The decisions include those made by each party before actual negotiations start—in determining, for example, the position of the company and what fallback proposals it may propose or accept. They also include incremental decisions, made during the negotiation process, on how to react and proceed, when to concede, and on what to agree or disagree. Negotiation can thus be seen as a series of explicit and implicit decisions, and the subjects of negotiation and decision making become interdependent.

For instance, sometimes just the way in which a decision is made during the negotiation process can have a profound influence on the outcome, as this example shows:

In his first loan negotiation, a banker new to Japan met with seven top Japanese bankers who were seeking a substantial amount of money. After hearing their presentation, the American agreed on the spot. The seven Japanese then conferred among themselves and told the American they would get back to him in a couple of days as to whether they would accept his offer or not. The American banker learned a lesson he never forgot.[62]

The Japanese bankers expected the American to negotiate, to take time to think it over, and to consult with colleagues before giving the final decision. His immediate decision made them suspicious, so they decided to reconsider the deal.

There is no doubt that the speed and manner of decision making affects the negotiation process. In addition, how well negotiated agreements are implemented is affected by the speed and manner of decision making. In that regard, it is clear that the effective use of technology is playing an important role, especially when dealing with complex cross-border agreements in which the hundreds of decision makers involved are separated by time and space.

The role of decision making in management, however, goes far beyond the finite occasions of negotiations. It is part of the manager's daily routine—from operational-level, programmed decisions requiring minimal time and effort to those nonprogrammed decisions of far broader scope and importance, such as the decision to enter into a joint venture in a foreign country.

The Influence of Culture on Decision Making

It is crucial for international managers to understand the influence of culture on decision-making styles and processes. Culture affects decision making both through the broader context of the nation's institutional culture, which produces collective patterns of decision making, and through culturally based value systems that affect each individual decision maker's perception or interpretation of a situation.[63]

The extent to which decision making is influenced by culture varies among countries. For example, Hitt, Tyler, and Park have found a "more culturally homogenizing influence on the Korean executives' cognitive models" than on those of U.S. executives, whose individualistic tendencies lead to different decision patterns.[64] The ways that culture influences an executive's decisions can be studied by looking at the variables involved in each stage of the rational **decision-making process**. These stages are (1) defining the problem, (2) gathering and analyzing relevant data, (3) considering alternative solutions, (4) deciding on the best solution, and (5) implementing the decision.

One of the major cultural variables affecting decision making is whether a country assumes an **objective approach** or a **subjective approach**. Whereas the Western approach is based on rationality (managers interpret a situation and consider alternative solutions based on objective information), this approach is not common throughout the world. Latin Americans, among others, are more subjective, basing decisions on emotions.

Another cultural variable that greatly influences the decision-making process is the **risk tolerance** of those making the decision. Research shows that people from Belgium, Germany, and Austria have a considerably lower tolerance for risk than people from Japan or the Netherlands, whereas American managers have the highest tolerance for risk.[65]

One important variable in the decision-making process is the manager's perception of the **locus of control** over outcomes—whether that locus is internal or external. Some managers feel that they can plan on certain outcomes because they are in control of events that will direct the future in the desired way. In contrast, other managers believe that such decisions are of no value because they have little control over the future, which lies in the hands of outside forces, such as fate, god, or nature. American managers believe strongly in self-determination and perceive problem situations as something they can control and that they should change. However, managers in many other countries, Indonesia and Malaysia among them, are resigned to problem situations and do not feel that they can change them. Obviously, these different value systems will result in a great difference in the stages of consideration of alternative actions and choice of solution, often because certain situations may or may not be viewed as problems in the first place.

Another variable that affects the consideration of alternative solutions is how managers feel about staying with familiar solutions or trying new ones. Many managers, particularly those in Europe, value decisions based on past experiences and tend to emphasize quality. Americans, on the other hand, are more future oriented and look toward new ideas to get them there.

Approaches to Decision Making

In addition to affecting different stages of the decision-making process, value systems influence the overall approach of decision makers from various cultures. The relative level of **utilitarianism** versus moral idealism in any society affects its overall approach to problems. Generally speaking, utilitarianism strongly guides behavior in the Western world. In fact, research has shown that Canadian executives are more influenced by a short-term, cost-benefit approach to decision making than their Hong Kong counterparts. Canadian managers are considerably more utilitarian than leaders from the People's Republic of China, who approach problems from a standpoint of moral idealism; they consider the problems, alternatives, and solutions from a long-term, societal perspective rather than an individual perspective.[66]

Another important variable in companies' overall approach to decision making is that of autocratic versus participative leadership. In other words, who has the authority to make what kinds of decisions? A country's orientation—whether it is **individualistic** or **collectivist** (as discussed in Chapter 3)—influences the level at which decisions are made. In many countries with hierarchical cultures—Germany, Turkey, and India, among others—the authorization for action has to be passed upward through echelons of management before final decisions can be made. Most employees in these countries simply expect the autocrat, the boss, to do most of the decision making and would not be comfortable otherwise. Even in China, which is a highly collectivist society, employees expect **autocratic leadership** because their value system presupposes the superior to be automatically the most wise. In comparison, in Sweden, decision-making authority is very decentralized. Americans talk a lot about the advisability of such **participative leadership**, but in practice they are probably around the middle between autocratic and participative management styles.

Arab managers have long traditions of consultative decision making, supported by the Koran and the sayings of Mohamed. However, such consultation occurs more on a person-to-person basis than in group meetings, and thus diffuses potential opposition.[67] While business in the Middle East tends to be transacted in a highly personalized manner, the final decisions are made by the top leaders, who feel that they must impose their will for the company to be successful. In comparison, in cultures like Japan's that emphasize collective harmony, participatory or group decision making predominates, and consensus is important. The best-known example is the bottom-up (rather than top-down) decision-making process used in most Japanese companies, described in more detail in the Comparative Management in Focus.

One final area of frequent incongruence concerns the relative speed of decision making. A country's culture affects how fast or slow decisions tend to be made. The relative speed may be closely associated with the level of delegation, as just discussed, but not always. The pace at which decisions are made can be very disconcerting for outsiders. North Americans and Europeans pride themselves on being decisive; managers in the Middle East, with a different sense of temporal urgency, associate the importance of the matter at hand with the length of time needed to make a decision. Without knowing this cultural attitude, a hasty American would insult an Egyptian; a quick decision, to the Egyptian, would reflect a low regard for the relationship and the deal.

As a summary, Exhibit 5-10 illustrates how all the variables just discussed can affect the steps in the decision-making process.

Exhibit 5-10
Cultural Variables in the Decision-Making Process

Comparative Management in Focus

Decision Making in Japanese Companies

Japanese companies are involved in joint ventures throughout the world, especially with American companies. The GM–Toyota joint venture agreement process was the result of over two years of negotiation and decision making. In this new company and in similar companies, Americans and Japanese are involved in decision making at all levels on a daily basis. The Japanese decision-making process greatly differs not only from the American process but from that of many other countries—especially at the higher levels of their organizations.

An understanding of the Japanese decision-making process, and indeed of many of their management practices, requires an understanding of their national culture. As previously discussed, much of the Japanese culture, and therefore the basis of Japanese working relationships, can be explained by the principle of *wa*, meaning "peace and harmony." This principle is one aspect of the value they attribute to *amae*, meaning "indulgent love," a concept probably originating in the Shinto religion, which focuses on spiritual and physical harmony. *Amae* results in *shinyo*, which refers to the mutual confidence, faith, and honor required for successful business relationships. The principle of *wa* influences the work group, the basic building block of Japanese work and management. The Japanese identify strongly with their work groups, where the emphasis is on cooperation, participative management, consensus problem solving, and decision making based on a patient, long-term perspective. Open expression or conflict is discouraged, and it is of utmost importance to avoid embarrassment or shame—to lose face—as a result of not fulfilling one's obligations. These elements of work culture generally result in a devotion to work, a collective responsibility for decisions and actions, and a high degree of employee productivity. It is this culture of collectivism and shared responsibility that underlies the Japanese *ringi* system of decision making.

In the *ringi* system, the process works from the bottom up. Americans are used to a centralized system, where major decisions are made by upper-level managers in a top-down approach typical of individualistic societies. The Japanese process, however, is dispersed throughout the organization, relying on group consensus.

The *ringi* process is one of gaining approval on a proposal by circulating documents to those concerned throughout the company. It usually comprises four steps: proposal, circulation, approval, and record.[68] Usually, the person who originates the written proposal, which is called a *ringi-sho*, has already worked for some time to gain informal consensus and support for the proposal within the section and then from the department head.[69] The next step is to attain a general consensus in the company from those who would be involved in implementation. To this end, department meetings are held, and if necessary, expert opinion is sought. If more information is needed, the proposal goes back to the originator, who finds and adds the required data. In this way, much time and effort—and the input of many people—go into the proposal before it actually becomes formal.[70,71]

Up to this point, the process has been an informal one to gain consensus, called the *nemawashi* process. Then the more formal authorization procedure begins, called the *ringi* process. The *ringi-sho* is passed up through successive layers of management for approval—the approval made official by seals. In the end, many such seals of approval are gathered, thereby ensuring collective agreement and responsibility and giving the proposal a greater chance of final approval by the president. The whole process is depicted in Exhibit 5-11.

The *ringi* system is cumbersome and very time-consuming prior to the implementation stage, although implementation is facilitated because of the widespread awareness of and support for the proposal already gained throughout the organization. But its slow progress is problematic when decisions are time-sensitive. This process is the opposite of the top-down decisions made by Americans, which are made quite rapidly and without consultation, but which then take some time to implement because unforeseen practical or support problems often arise.

In addition, another interesting comparison is often made regarding the planning horizon (aimed at short- or long-term goals) in decision making between the American and Japanese systems. The Japanese spend considerable time in the early stages of the process defining the issue, considering what the

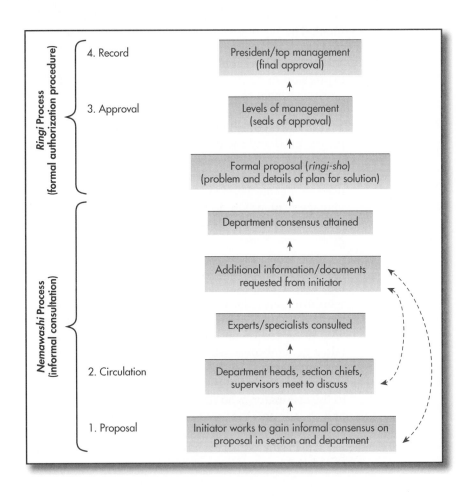

Exhibit 5-11
Decision-Making Procedure in Japanese Companies

issue is all about, and determining whether there is in fact a need for a decision. They are more likely than Americans to consider an issue in relation to the overall goals and strategy of the company. In this manner, they prudently look at the "big picture" and consider alternative solutions, instead of rushing into quick decisions for immediate solutions, as Americans tend to do.[72]

Of course, in a rapidly changing environment, quick decisions are often necessary—to respond to competitors' actions, a political uprising, and so forth—and it is in such contexts that the *ringi* system sometimes falls short because of its slow response rate. The system is, in fact, designed to manage continuity and to avoid uncertainty, which is considered a threat to group cohesiveness.[73]

Conclusion

It is clear that competitive positioning and long-term successful operations in a global market require a working knowledge of the decision-making and negotiating process of managers from different countries. These processes are complex and often interdependent. While managers may make decisions that do not involve negotiating, they cannot negotiate without making decisions, however small, or they would not be negotiating. In addition, managers must understand the behavioral aspects of these processes to work effectively with people in other countries or with a culturally diverse workforce in their own country.

With an understanding of the environment and cultural context of international management as background, we move next in Part 3 to planning and implementing strategy for international operations.

INTERNET RESOURCES

Visit the Deresky companion Web site at http://prenhall.com/Deresky for this chapter's Internet resources.

1. The ability to successfully negotiate is one of the most important in international business. Managers must prepare for certain cultural variables that influence negotiations, including the relative emphasis on task versus interpersonal relationships, the use of general principles versus specific details, the number of people present, and the extent of their influence.

2. The negotiation process typically progresses through the stages of preparation, relationship building, the exchange of task-related information, persuasion, and concessions and agreement. The process of building trusting relationships is a prerequisite to doing business in many parts of the world.

3. Culturally based differences in verbal and nonverbal negotiation behavior influence the negotiation process at every stage. Such tactics and actions include promises, threats, initial concessions, silent periods, interruptions, facial gaz-ing, and touching; some parties resort to various dirty tricks.

4. The effective management of negotiation requires an understanding of the perspectives, values, and agenda of the other parties and the use of a problem-solving approach.

5. Decision making is an important part of the negotiation process as well as an integral part of a manager's daily routine. Culture affects the decision-making process both through a society's institutions and through individuals' risk tolerance, their objective versus subjective perspective, their perception of the locus of control, and their past versus future orientation.

6. The Internet is increasingly being used to support the negotiation of contracts and resolution of disputes. Web sites, which provide open auctions take away the personal apsects of negotiations, although those aspects are still essential in many instances.

Chapter

6

Formulating Strategy

As the Opening Profile on FedEx illustrates, companies around the world are spending increasing amounts of money and time on global expansion in search of profitable new markets, acquisitions, and alliances—but often spending those resources on very different strategies. Experts predict that those companies with operations in major overseas markets (North America, Europe, and Asia) are far more likely to prosper in the twenty-first century than those without such operations.[5] Because these new international opportunities are far more complex than those in domestic markets, managers must plan carefully—that is, strategically—to benefit from them.

The process by which a firm's managers evaluate the future prospects of the firm and decide on appropriate strategies to achieve long-term objectives is called *strategic planning*. The basic means by which the company competes—its choice of business or businesses in which to operate and the ways in which it differentiates itself from its competitors—is its *strategy*. Almost all successful companies engage in long-range strategic planning, and those with a global orientation position themselves to take full advantage of worldwide trends and opportunities. MNCs, in particular, report that strategic planning is essential to contend with increasing global competition and to coordinate their far-flung operations.

In reality, though, that rational strategic planning is often tempered, or changed at some point, by a more incremental, sometimes messy, process of strategic decision making by some managers. When a new CEO is hired, for example, she will often call for a radical change in strategy. That is why new leaders are very carefully chosen, on the basis of what they are expected to do. So, while we discuss the rational strategic planning process here, because it is usually the ideal, inclusive, method of determining long-term plans, we need to remember that, throughout, there are people making decisions, and their own personal judgment, experiences, and motivations, will shape the ultimate strategic direction.

REASONS FOR GOING INTERNATIONAL

Companies "go international" for different reasons, some reactive (or defensive) and some proactive (or aggressive). The threat of their own decreased competitiveness is the overriding reason many large companies adopt a strategy of aggressive globalization. To remain competitive, these companies want to move fast to build strong positions in key world markets with products tailored to the common needs of 650 million customers in Europe, Latin America, and Japan.[6] Building on their past success, companies such as IBM and Digital Equipment are plowing profits back into operations overseas. Europe is now attracting much new investment capital because of both the European Union (EU) and the opening of extensive new markets in Eastern Europe.

Reactive Reasons

Globalization of Competitors
One of the most common reactive reasons that prompt a company to go overseas is global competition. If left unchallenged, competitors who already have overseas operations or investments may get so entrenched in foreign markets that it becomes difficult for other companies to enter at a later time. In addition, the lower costs and market power available to these competitors operating globally may also give them an advantage domestically.

Trade Barriers

Restrictive trade barriers are another reactive reason why companies often switch from exporting to overseas manufacturing. Barriers such as tariffs, quotas, buy-local policies, and other restrictive trade practices can make exports to foreign markets too expensive and too impractical to be competitive. Many firms, for example, want to gain a foothold in Europe—to be regarded as an insider—to counteract trade barriers and restrictions on non-EU firms (discussed further in the Comparative Management in Focus at the end of this chapter). In part, this fear of "Fortress Europe" is caused by actions such as the EU's block exemption for the franchise industry. This exemption prohibits a franchisor, say McDonald's, from contracting with a single company, say Coca-Cola, to supply all its franchisees, as it does in the United States.

Regulations and Restrictions

Similarly, regulations and restrictions by a firm's home government may become so expensive that companies will seek out less restrictive foreign operating environments. Avoiding such regulations prompted U.S. pharmaceutical maker SmithKline and Britain's Beecham to merge. Both thereby guaranteed that they would avoid licensing and regulatory hassles in their largest markets—Western Europe and the United States. The merged company is now an insider in both Europe and America.[7]

Customer Demands

Operations in foreign countries frequently start as a response to customer demands or as a solution to logistical problems. Certain foreign customers, for example, may demand that their supplying company operate in their local region so that they have better control over their supplies, forcing the supplier to comply or lose the business. McDonald's is one company that asks its domestic suppliers to follow it to foreign ventures. Meat supplier OSI Industries does just that, with joint ventures in 17 countries, such as Bavaria, so that it can work with local companies making McDonald's hamburgers.[8]

Proactive Reasons

> From rain forests to remote chinese villages, the queen of cosmetics (Avon) is cleaning up across the globe.[9]

Economies of Scale

Careful, long-term strategic planning encourages firms to go international for proactive reasons. One pressing reason for many large firms to expand overseas is to seek economies of scale—that is, to achieve world-scale volume to make the fullest use of modern capital-intensive manufacturing equipment and to amortize staggering research and development costs when facing brief product life cycles.[10] Otis Elevator, for example, developed the Elevonic 411 by means of six research centers in five countries; this international cooperation saved over $10 million in design costs and cut the development cycle from four years to two.

Economies of scale in production are achieved when higher levels of output spread fixed costs over more units, thus lowering the per-unit cost. Gerrit Jeelof, of Holland's Philips Group, contends that "only with a global market can a company afford the large development costs necessary to keep up with advancing technology."[11]

Growth Opportunities

Companies in mature markets in developed countries experience a growth imperative to look for new opportunities in emerging markets. When expansion opportunities become limited at home, firms such as McDonald's are often driven to seek expansion through new international markets. A mature product or service with restricted growth in its domestic market often has "new life" in another country, where it will be at an earlier stage of its life cycle. Avon Products Inc., for example, has seen a decline in its U.S. market since its traditional sales and marketing strategy of "Avon calling" (house-to-house sales) now meets with empty houses, due to the spiralling number of women who now work outside the home. To make up for this loss, Avon pushed overseas to 26 emerging markets, such as Mexico, Poland, China, India, South Africa, and Vietnam. In Brazil, for instance, Josina Reis Teixeira carries her sample kit to the wooden shacks in the tiny village of Registro, just outside of São Paulo. In some markets Avon adapts to cultural influences, such as in China, where consumers are suspicious of door-to-door salespeople. There, Avon sets up showrooms in its branch offices in major cities so that women can consult cosmeticians and sample products.[13]

In addition, new markets abroad provide a place to invest surplus profits as well as employ underutilized resources in management, technology, and machinery. When entirely new markets open up, such as in Eastern Europe, both experienced firms and those new to international competition usually rush to take advantage of awaiting opportunities. Such was the case with the proactive stance that Unisys took in preparing for and jumping on the newly opened market opportunity in Vietnam.

Resource Access and Cost Savings

Further, resource access and cost savings entice many companies to operate from overseas bases. The availability of raw materials and other resources offers both greater control over inputs and lower transportation costs. Lower labor costs (for production, service, and technical personnel), another major consideration, enable lower unit costs and have proved a vital ingredient to competitiveness for many companies.

Sometimes just the prospect of shifting production overseas improves competitiveness at home. When Xerox Corporation started moving copier rebuilding operations to Mexico, the union agreed to needed changes in work style and productivity to keep the jobs at home.[14] Lower operational costs in other areas—power, transportation, and financing—frequently prove attractive. Trinidad, for example, offers abundant inexpensive energy, a skilled and well-educated workforce with labor rates at about one-fourth of U.S. levels, and government incentives for export-oriented ventures that generate foreign exchange.[15]

Incentives

Governments in countries such as Poland seeking new infusions of capital, technology, and know-how willingly provide incentives: tax exemptions, tax holidays, subsidies, loans, and the use of property.[16] Because they both decrease risk and increase profits, these incentives are attractive to foreign companies. One study surveyed 103 experienced managers concerning the relative attractiveness of various incentives for expansion into the Caribbean region (primarily Mexico, Venezuela, Colombia, Dominican Republic, and Guatemala). The results indicate the opinion of those managers about which incentives are most important; however, the most desirable mix would depend on the nature of the particular company and its operations. The first two issues reflect managers' concerns about limiting foreign exchange risk, where restrictions often change overnight and limit the ability of the firm to repatriate profits. Other concerns are those of political instability in countries such as Haiti and Nicaragua, the possibility of expropriation, and those of tax concessions.[17]

STRATEGIC FORMULATION PROCESS

Typically, the strategic formulation process is necessary both at the headquarters of the corporation and at each of the subsidiaries. One study reported, for example, that 70 percent of 56 American MNC subsidiaries in Latin America and the Far East operated on planning cycles of five or more years.[18]

The global strategic formulation process, as part of overall corporate strategic management, parallels the process followed in domestic companies. However, the variables, and therefore the process itself, are far more complex because of the greater difficulty in gaining accurate and timely information, the diversity of geographic locations, and the differences in political, legal, cultural, market, and financial processes. These factors introduce a greater level of risk in strategic decisions. However, for firms that have not yet engaged in international operations (as well as for those that do), an ongoing strategic planning process with a global orientation identifies potential opportunities for (1) appropriate market expansion, (2) increased profitability, and (3) new ventures by which the firm can exploit its strategic advantages. Even in the absence of immediate opportunities, monitoring the global environment for trends and competition is important for domestic planning.

The strategic formulation process is part of the strategic management process in which most firms engage, either formally or informally. The planning modes range from a proactive, long-range format to a reactive, more seat-of-the-pants method, whereby the day-by-day decisions of key managers, in particular owner-managers, accumulate to what can be discerned retroactively as the new strategic direction.[19] The stages in the strategic management process described here are shown in Exhibit 6-1. In reality, these stages seldom follow such a linear format. Rather, the process is continuous and intertwined, with data and results from earlier stages providing information for the next stage.

The first phase of the strategic management process—the planning phase— starts with the company establishing (or clarifying) its mission and its overall

Exhibit 6-1
The Strategic Management Process

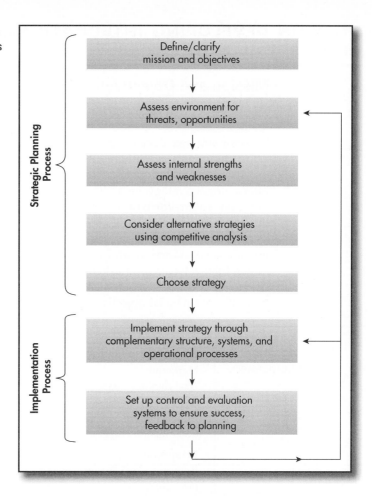

objectives. The next two steps comprise an assessment of the external environment that the firm faces in the future and an analysis of the firm's relative capabilities to deal successfully with that environment. Strategic alternatives are then considered, and plans are made based on the strategic choice. These five steps constitute the planning phase, which will be further detailed in this chapter.

The second part of the strategic management process is the implementation phase. Successful implementation requires the establishment of the structure, systems, and processes suitable to make the strategy work. These variables, as well as functional-level strategies will be explored in detail in the remaining chapters on organizing, leading, and controlling. At this point, however, note that the strategic planning process by itself does not change the posture of the firm until the plans are implemented. In addition, feedback from the interim and long-term results of such implementation, along with continuous environmental monitoring, flows directly back into the planning process.

Mission and Objectives

The mission of an organization is its overall raison d'être or the function it performs in society. This mission charts the direction of the company and provides a basis for strategic decision making.

A company's overall objectives flow from its mission, and both guide the formulation of international corporate strategy. Because we are focusing on issues of international strategy, we will assume that one of the overall objectives of the corporation is some form of international operation (or expansion). The objectives of the firm's international affiliates should also be part of the global corporate objectives. A firm's global objectives usually fall into the areas of marketing, profitability, finance, production, and research and development, among others, as shown in Exhibit 6-2. Goals for market volume and for profitability are usually set higher for international than for domestic operations because of the greater risk involved. In addition, financial objectives on the global level must take into account differ-

Exhibit 6-2

Global Corporate Objectives

Marketing
Total company market share—worldwide, regional, national
Annual percentage sales growth
Annual percentage market share growth
Coordination of regional markets for economies of scale

Production
Relative foreign versus domestic production volume
Economies of scale through global production integration
Quality and cost control
Introduction of cost-efficient production methods

Finance
Effective financing of overseas subsidiaries or allies
Taxation—minimizing tax burden globally
Optimum capital structure
Foreign-exchange management

Profitability
Long-term profit growth
Return on investment, equity, and assets
Annual rate of profit growth

Research and Development
Develop new products with global patents
Develop proprietary production technologies
Worldwide research and development labs

ing tax regulations in various countries and how to minimize overall losses from exchange rate fluctuations.

Environmental Assessment

After clarifying the corporate mission and objectives, the first major step in weighing international strategic options is the environmental assessment. This assessment includes environmental scanning and continuous monitoring to keep abreast of variables around the world that are pertinent to the firm and that have the potential to shape its future by posing new opportunities (or threats). Firms must adapt to their environment to survive. How to adapt is the focus of strategic planning.

The process of gathering information and forecasting relevant trends, competitive actions, and circumstances that will affect operations in geographic areas of potential interest is called *environmental scanning*. This activity should be conducted on three levels—multinational, regional, and national—which are discussed in detail later in this chapter. Scanning should focus on the future interests of the firm and should cover the following major variables (as discussed by Phatak and others).[20]

- *Political instability.* This variable represents a volatile and uncontrollable risk to the multinational corporation, as illustrated by the upheaval in the Middle East in recent years. MNCs must carefully assess such risk because it may result in a loss of profitability or even ownership.[21,22]
- *Currency instability.* This variable represents another risk; inflation and fluctuations in the exchange rates of currencies can dramatically affect profitability when operating overseas. In early 1995, for example, both foreign and local firms got a painful reminder of this risk when Mexico devalued its peso, and in 1998 currency collapse in Indonesia forced President Suharto to resign.
- *Nationalism.* This variable, representing the home government's goals for independence and economic improvement, often influences foreign companies. The home government may impose restrictive policies—import controls, equity requirements, local content requirements, limitations on the repatriation of profits, and so forth. Japan, for example, protects its home markets with these kinds of restrictive policies. Other forms of nationalism may be exerted through the following: (1) pressure from national governments—exemplified by the United States putting pressure on Japan to curtail unfair competition; (2) lax patent and trademark protection laws, such as those in China in recent years, which erode a firm's proprietary technology through insufficient protection; and (3) the suitability of infrastructure, such as roads and telecommunications.
- *International competition.* Conducting a global competitor analysis is perhaps the most important task in environmental assessment and strategy formulation. The first step in analyzing the competition is to assess the relevant industry structures as they influence the competitive arena in the particular country (or region) being considered. For example, will the infrastructure support new companies in that industry? Is there room for

additional competition? What is the relative supply and demand for the proposed product or service? The ultimate profit potential in the industry in that location will be determined by these kinds of factors.[23]

- *Environmental Scanning.*   Managers must also specifically assess their current competitors—global and local—for the proposed market. They must ask, what are our competitors' positions, their goals and strategies, their strengths and weaknesses, relative to our firm's? What are the likely competitor reactions to our strategic moves? Managers should compare their company with potential international competitors; in fact, it is useful to draw up a competitive position matrix for each potential international market. For example, Exhibit 6-3 analyzes a U.S. specialty seafood firm's competitive profile in Malaysia.[24]

The U.S. firm in Exhibit 6-3 has advantages in financial capability, future growth of resources, and sustainability, but a disadvantage in quickness. It also is at a disadvantage compared to the Korean MNC in important factors such as manufacturing capability and flexibility and adaptability. Because the other firms seem to have little comparative advantage, the major competitor is likely to be the Korean firm. At this point, then, the U.S. firm can focus in more detail on assessing the Korean firm's relative strengths and weaknesses.

The firm can also choose varying levels of environmental scanning. To reduce risk and investment, many firms take on the role of the "follower," meaning that

Exhibit 6-3

Global Competitor Analysis: A U.S. Firm Compared with Its International Competitors in Malaysian Market

COMPARISON CRITERIA	A (U.S. MNC)	B (KOREAN MNC)	C (LOCAL MALAYSIAN FIRM)	D (JAPANESE MNC)	E (LOCAL MALAYSIAN FIRM)
Marketing capability	0	0	0	0	−
Manufacturing capability	0	+	0	0	0
R&D capability	0	0	0	−	0
HRM capability	0	0	0	0	0
Financial capability	+	−	0	0	−
Future growth of resources	+	0	−	0	−
Quickness	−	0	+	−	0
Flexibility/adaptability	0	+	+	0	0
Sustainability	+	0	0	0	−

Key:
+ = firm is better relative to competition.
0 = firm is same as competition.
− = firm is poorer relative to competition.

Source: Diane J. Garsombke, "International Competitor Analysis," *Planning Review* 17, no. 3 (May–June 1989): 42–47.

they limit their own investigations; instead, they simply watch their competitors' moves and go where they go, assuming that the competitors have done their homework. Other firms go to considerable lengths to gather data carefully and examine options in the global arena.

Ideally, the firm should conduct global environmental analysis on three different levels: the multinational, regional, and national levels. Analysis on the multinational level provides a broad assessment of significant worldwide trends—through identification, forecasting, and monitoring activities. These trends would include the political and economic developments of nations around the world as well as global technological progress. From this information, managers can choose certain appropriate regions of the world to consider further.

Next, at the regional level, the analysis focuses in more detail on critical environmental factors to identify opportunities (and risks) for marketing the company's products, services, or technology. For example, one such regional location ripe for investigation by a firm seeking new markets is the European Union.

Having zeroed in on one or more regions, the firm must, as its next step, analyze at the national level. Such an analysis explores in depth specific countries within the desired region for economic, legal, political, and cultural factors significant to the company. For example, the analysis could focus on the size and nature of the market, along with any possible operational problems, to consider how best to enter the market. In fact, in many volatile countries, continuous monitoring of such environmental factors is a vital part of ongoing strategic planning. In Peru in 1988, inflation had soared to 2000 percent, and leftist terrorists were kidnapping or murdering business leaders. Though key managers fled and many multinational companies pulled out of Peru, Procter & Gamble remained to take advantage of a potentially large market share when competitors left. "Everybody should be dying to come here—you couldn't go to a better business school [than what you learn by managing here]," said Susana Elesperu de Freitas, the 34-year-old Peruvian manager of Procter & Gamble's subsidiary, who was flanked by armed bodyguards wherever she went.[25] Since then, Procter & Gamble, a consumer-products company, has expanded and is now a major force in Peru.

This process of environmental scanning, from the broad global level down to the local specifics of entry planning, is illustrated in Exhibit 6-4. The first broad scan of all potential world markets results in the firm being able to eliminate from its list those markets that are closed or insignificant or do not have reasonable entry conditions. The second scan of remaining regions, and then countries, is done in greater detail—perhaps eliminating some based on political instability, for example. Remaining countries are then assessed for competitor strengths, suitability of products, and so on. This analysis leads to serious entry planning in selected countries; managers start to work on operational plans, such as negotiations and legal arrangements.

Sources of Environmental Information

The success of environmental scanning depends on the ability of managers to take a global perspective and to ensure that their sources of information and business intelligence are global. A variety of public resources are available to provide information. In the United States alone, over two thousand business information

Exhibit 6-4
Global Environmental Scanning Process

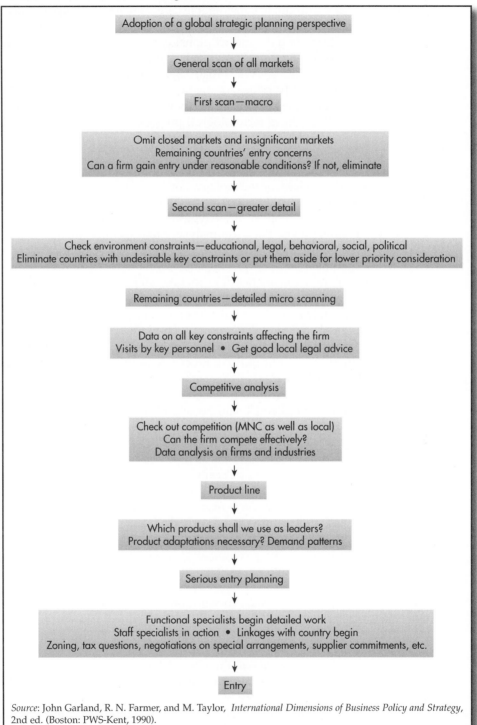

Adoption of a global strategic planning perspective

↓

General scan of all markets

↓

First scan—macro

↓

Omit closed markets and insignificant markets
Remaining countries' entry concerns
Can a firm gain entry under reasonable conditions? If not, eliminate

↓

Second scan—greater detail

↓

Check environment constraints—educational, legal, behavioral, social, political
Eliminate countries with undesirable key constraints or put them aside for lower priority consideration

↓

Remaining countries—detailed micro scanning

↓

Data on all key constraints affecting the firm
Visits by key personnel • Get good local legal advice

↓

Competitive analysis

↓

Check out competition (MNC as well as local)
Can the firm compete effectively?
Data analysis on firms and industries

↓

Product line

↓

Which products shall we use as leaders?
Product adaptations necessary? Demand patterns

↓

Serious entry planning

↓

Functional specialists begin detailed work
Staff specialists in action • Linkages with country begin
Zoning, tax questions, negotiations on special arrangements, supplier commitments, etc.

↓

Entry

Source: John Garland, R. N. Farmer, and M. Taylor, *International Dimensions of Business Policy and Strategy*, 2nd ed. (Boston: PWS-Kent, 1990).

services are available on computer database, tailored to specific industries and regions; other resources include corporate "clipping" services and information packages. However, internal sources of information are usually preferable—especially alert field personnel who, with firsthand observations, can provide up-to-date and relevant information for the firm. Using its own internal resources extensively, Mitsubishi Trading Company employs over sixty thousand market analysts worldwide, whose job it is to gather, analyze, and feed market information to the parent company.[26] Internal sources of information help to eliminate unreliable information from secondary sources, particularly in developing countries. As Garsombke points out, the "official" data from such countries can be misleading: "Census data can be tampered with by government officials for propaganda purposes or it may be restricted. . . . In South Korea, for instance, even official figures can be conflicting depending on the source."[27]

Internal Analysis

After the environmental assessment, the second major step in weighing international strategic options is the internal analysis. This analysis determines which areas of the firm's operations represent strengths or weaknesses (currently or potentially) compared to competitors, so that the firm may use that information to its strategic advantage.

The internal analysis focuses on the company's resources and operations, and global synergies. The strengths and weaknesses of the firm's financial and managerial expertise and functional capabilities are evaluated to determine what key success factors (KSFs) the company has and how well they can help the firm exploit foreign opportunities. Those factors increasingly involve superior technological capability (as with Microsoft and Intel); they also involve other strategic advantages such as effective distribution channels (as with Wal-Mart), superior promotion capabilities (Disney), low-cost production and sourcing position, superior patent and new product pipeline (Merck), and so on.

Using such operational strengths to advantage is exemplified by Japanese car manufacturers: their production quality and efficiency has catapulted them into world markets. As to their global strategy, they have recognized that their sales and marketing functions have proven a competitive weakness in the European car wars, and the Japanese are working on these shortcomings. Japanese automakers—Toyota, Honda, Mazda, and so on—are following Ford and GM in seeking to become more sophisticated marketers throughout Europe.[28]

All companies have strengths and weaknesses. Management's challenge is to identify both and take appropriate action. Many diagnostic tools are available for conducting an internal resource audit. Financial ratios, for example, may reveal an inefficient use of assets that is restricting profitability; a sales-force analysis may reveal that the sales force is an area of distinct competence for the firm. If a company is conducting this audit to determine whether to start international ventures or to improve its ongoing operations abroad, certain operational issues must be taken into account. These issues include (1) the difficulty of obtaining marketing information in many countries, (2) the often poorly developed financial markets, and (3) the complexities of exchange rates and government controls.

Competitive Analysis

At this point, the firm's managers assess its capabilities and key success factors compared to those of its competitors. They must judge the relative current and potential competitive position of firms in that market and location—whether that be a global position or that for a specific country or region. Like a chess game, the firm's managers need also to consider the strategic intent of competing firms and what might be their future moves (strategies). This process enables the strategic planners to determine where the firm has distinctive competencies that will give it strategic advantage as well as what direction might lead the firm into a sustainable competitive advantage—that is, one that will not be immediately eroded by emulation. The result of this process will also help to identify potential problems that can be corrected or that may be significant enough to eliminate further consideration of certain strategies.[29]

This stage of strategic formulation is often called a SWOT analysis (an acronym for Strengths, Weaknesses, Opportunities and Threats), in which the firms capabilities relative to its competitors is assessed as pertinent to the opportunities and threats in the environment for those firms. For example, Philip Morris (PM) considered entry into the Commonwealth of Independent States (CIS) in the early 1990s. The attraction, of course, was the newly opened market of 290 million consumers. Of these, 70 million were smokers and would provide an immediate target market for Philip Morris's cigarette brands. In addition, all 290 million would be a vast potential market for PM's Kraft and General Foods subsidiaries. The next step would be an in-depth assessment of the local and foreign competitors in the region, such as RJR Nabisco.

After its analysis, Philip Morris concluded that the Russian commonwealth presented an attractive opportunity, particularly if the firm could establish a market foothold before RJR Nabisco followed suit. In hindsight, however, Philip Morris might have done some more homework and added other threats to this matrix. After the company set up kiosks to sell packs of Marlboros to people in St. Petersburg in 1992, those booths were blown up overnight—a signal that Russian cigarette distributors didn't want any outside competitors on their turf. Philip Morris subsequently got out of the distribution business. It is also worth noting, that, in September 1998, RJR withdrew all operations from Russia as a result of that country's economic problems, after investing about $520 million. The company was among many suffering major losses in Russia's economic collapse in 1998, when the inflation rate reached 84.3 percent by the end of 1999.[30]

Most companies develop their strategy around key strengths, or core competencies. Core competencies represent important corporate resources because, as Prahalad and Hamel explain, they are the "collective learning in the organization, especially how to coordinate diverse production skills and integrate multiple streams of technologies."[31] Core competencies—like Sony's capacity to miniaturize and Philips's optical-media expertise—are usually difficult for competitors to imitate and represent a major focus for strategic development at the corporate level.[32] Canon, for example, has used its core competence in optics to its competitive advantage throughout its diverse businesses—cameras, copiers, and semiconductor lithographic equipment.

Managers must also assess their firm's weaknesses. A company already on shaky ground financially, for example, will not be able to consider an acquisition strategy, or perhaps any growth strategy. Of course, the subjective perceptions, motivations, capabilities, and goals of the managers involved in such diagnoses frequently cloud the decision-making process. The result is that sometimes firms embark on strategies that were contraindicated by objective information because of poor judgment by key players.

Global and International Strategic Alternatives

The fourth major step in the strategic planning process involves considering the advantages (and disadvantages) of various strategic alternatives in light of the competitive analysis. While weighing alternatives, managers need to take into account the goals of their firm and also the competitive status of other firms in the industry.

Depending on the size of the firm, there are two levels of strategic alternatives that a firm must consider. The first level, global strategic alternatives (applicable primarily to MNCs), determines what overall approach to the global marketplace a firm wishes to take. The second level, entry strategy alternatives, applies to firms of any size; these alternatives determine what specific entry strategy is appropriate for each country in which the firm plans to operate. Entry strategy alternatives will be discussed in a later section. We now turn to the two main global strategic approaches to world markets—globalization and regionalization.

Approaches to World Markets

Globalization

In the last decade, increasing competitive pressures have forced businesses to consider global strategies—to treat the world as an undifferentiated worldwide marketplace. Such strategies are now loosely referred to as *globalization*—a term that refers to the establishment of worldwide operations and the development of standardized products and marketing. Many, like Porter, have argued that globalization is a competitive imperative for firms in global industries: "In a global industry a firm must in some way integrate its activities on a worldwide basis to capture the linkages among countries. This includes, but requires more than, transferring intangible assets among countries."[33] The rationale behind globalization is to compete by establishing worldwide economies of scale, offshore manufacturing, and international cash flows. The term globalization, therefore, is as applicable to organizational structure as it is to strategy. (Organizational structure is discussed further in Chapter 8.)

The pressures to globalize include (1) increasing competitive clout resulting from regional trading blocs; (2) declining tariffs, which encourage trading across borders and open up new markets; and (3) the information technology explosion, which makes the coordination of far-flung operations easier and also increases the commonality of consumer tastes.[34] Use of Websites has allowed entrepreneurs, as well as established companies, to go global almost instantaneously through e-commerce—either B2B or B2C.[35] Examples are Yahoo!, Lands' End, and the ill-fated E-Toys, which met its demise in 2001. In addition, the success of

Japanese companies with global strategies has set the competitive standard in many industries—most visibly in the automobile industry. Other companies, such as Caterpillar, ICI, and Sony, have fared well with global strategies.

One of the quickest and cheapest ways to develop a global strategy is through strategic alliances. Many firms are trying to go global faster by forming alliances with rivals, suppliers, and customers. In fact, the rapidly developing information technologies are spawning cross-national business alliances from short-term virtual corporations to long-term strategic partnerships.[36] (Strategic alliances are discussed further in Chapter 7.)

Globalization is inherently more vulnerable to environmental risk, however, than a regionalization strategy. Global organizations are difficult to manage because doing so requires the coordination of broadly divergent national cultures. It also means, say Morrison, Ricks, and Roth, that firms must lose some of their original identity—they must "denationalize operations and replace home-country loyalties with a system of common corporate values and loyalties."[37] In other words, the globalization strategy necessarily treats all countries similarly, regardless of their differences in cultures and systems. Problems often result, such as a lack of local flexibility and responsiveness and a neglect of the need for differentiated products. In some recent research into how U.S. companies compete, Morrison et al. discovered that many companies are finding that "globalization is no panacea, and, in fact, global imperatives are being eclipsed by an upsurge in regional pressures."[38] These researchers claim that many companies now feel that regionalization is a more manageable and less risky approach, one that allows them to capitalize on local competencies as long as the parent organization and each subsidiary retain a flexible approach to each other.

Regionalization

For those firms in multidomestic industries—those industries in which competitiveness is determined on a country-by-country basis rather than a global basis—regional strategies are more appropriate than globalization.[39] The regionalization (or multilocal) strategy is one in which local markets are linked together within a region, allowing more local responsiveness and specialization. Top managers within each region decide on their own investment locations, product mixes, and competitive positioning; in other words, they run their subsidiaries as quasi-independent organizations.

As there are pressures to globalize—such as the need for economies of scale to compete on cost—there are opposing pressures to regionalize, especially for Newly Developed Economies (NDEs) and LDCs. These localization pressures include unique consumer preferences resulting from cultural or national differences (perhaps something as simple as right-hand-drive cars for Japan), domestic subsidies, and new production technologies that facilitate product variation for less cost than before.[40] By "acting local" firms can focus individually in each country or region on the local market needs for product or service characteristics, distribution, customer support, and so on.

As with any management function, the strategic choice as to where a company should position itself along the globalization–regionalization continuum is contingent on the nature of the industry, the type of company, the company's goals and strengths (or weaknesses), and the nature of its subsidiaries, among many factors. In addition, each company's strategic approach should be unique in adapting to its own environment. Many firms may try to "go global, act local" to trade off the best advantages of each strategy. Matsushita is one firm with considerable expertise at being a "GLOCAL" firm (*glo*bal, lo*cal*). Matsushita has over 150 production and R&D bases in 38 countries. In Malaysia, for example, where Matsushita employs 23,500 people in its 13 subsidiaries, the company diligently follows its policy of trying to keep the expatriate headcount down and train local managers; only 230 employees there are Japanese. Other Matsushita local policies are to develop local R&D to tailor products to markets, to let plants set their own rules, and to be a good corporate citizen in every country.[41]

Global Integrative Strategies

Many MNCs have developed their global operations to the point of being fully integrated—often both vertically and horizontally, including suppliers, productive facilities, marketing and distribution outlets, and contractors around the world. Dell, for example, is a globally integrated company, with worldwide sourcing and a fully integrated production and marketing system. It has factories in Ireland, Malaysia, and Texas, and has an assembly and delivery system from 47 locations around the world. At the same time, it has extreme flexibility; since Dell builds computers to each order, it carries very little inventory and therefore can change its operations at a moment's notice.

While some companies move very quickly to the stage of global integration—often through merger or acquisition—many companies evolve into multinational corporations by going through the entry strategies in stages, taking varying lengths of time between stages. Typically, a company starts with simple exporting, moves to large-scale exporting with sales branches abroad (or perhaps begins licensing), then proceeds to assembly abroad (either by itself or through contract manufacturing), and eventually evolves to full production abroad with its own subsidiaries. Finally, the MNC will undertake the global integration of its foreign subsidiaries, setting up cooperative activities among them to achieve economies of scale. By this point, the MNC has usually adopted a geocentric orientation, viewing opportunities and entry strategies in the context of an interrelated global market instead of regional or national markets. In this way, alternative entry strategies are viewed on an overall portfolio basis to take maximum advantage of potential synergies and leverage arising from operations in multicountry markets.[42]

Exhibit 6-5 illustrates the integrated, concurrent strategies used in the global network of the Helicopter Division of France's Société Nationale Industrielle Aerospatîale. The corporation employs a complex pattern of entry strategies and alliances among plants around the world, involving exporting, licensing, joint ventures, importing, and subassembly and maintenance facilities.[43] For example, the company has joint ventures with Brazil and Singapore and also exports parts to those countries for assembly; it licenses certain models to India and Yugoslavia and also exports to them; and it exports rotors and airframes to the United States, which, in turn, direct markets to Canada and Mexico and maintains spares and maintenance facilities for operations in those countries.

Exhibit 6-5
Network of Entry
Strategies and Alliances
at Société Nationale
Industrielle Aerospatîale:
Helicopter Division

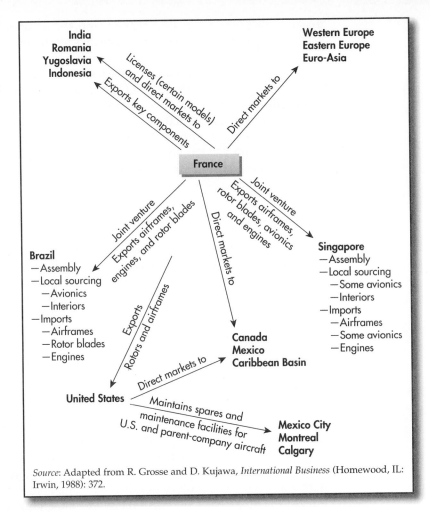

Source: Adapted from R. Grosse and D. Kujawa, *International Business* (Homewood, IL: Irwin, 1988): 372.

Using E-Business to Go Global

Companies of all sizes are increasingly looking to the Internet as a means to expand their global operations. However, the Internet is not just about e-commerce:

> The real story is the profound impact this medium will have on corporate strategy, organization and business models. Our research reveals that the Internet is driving global marketplace transformation and paradigm shift in how companies get things done, how they compete and how they serve their customers.
>
> www.IBM.com

While the benefits of B2B are many, including rapid entrance into new geographic markets, as shown in Exhibit 6-6, less touted are the many challenges inherent in a global B2B strategy. These include cultural differences and varying business models, governmental wrangling and border conflicts, in particular the question over which country has jurisdiction and responsibility over disputes regarding cross-border electronic transaction.[44] Potential problem areas that managers must assess in their global environmental analysis include conflicting consumer protection, intellectual property and tax laws, increasing isolationism even among democracies, language barriers, and a lack of tech-savvy legislators worldwide.[45]

Savvy global managers will realize that e-business cannot be regarded as just an extension of current businesses. It is a whole new industry in itself, complete with a different pool of competitors, and whole new sets of environmental issues. A reassessment of the environment forces in the newly configured industry, using Michael Porter's five forces analytical model, should take account of shifts in relative bargaining power of buyers and suppliers, the level of threat of new competitors, existing and potential substitutes, as well as a present and anticipated competitor analysis.[46]

It is clear that a competitive global B2B strategy must offer a technology solution that goes beyond basic transaction or listing service capabilities.[47] To assess the potential competitive position of the company, managers must ask themselves the following:

- Does the exchange provide a technology solution that helps industry-trading partners to do business more efficiently?
- Is the exchange known to be among the top three to five within its vertical industry?
- Does the exchange offer industry-specific technology and expertise that gives it an advantage over generic exchange-builders?[48]

There is no doubt that the global B2B competitive arena is a challenging one, both strategically and technologically. But many companies around the world are

Exhibit 6-6

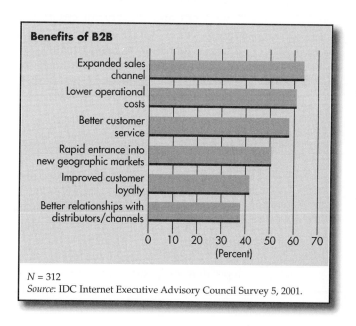

plunging in, fearing that they will be left behind in this fast developing global e-marketplace. Included are Fuji Xerox, which has formed a new e-marketplace with NEC and other leading e-commerce players, including Simitomo Corporation, Hewlett Packard Japan, Ltd., Sumisho Computer Systems, and U.S. software developer Ariba, Inc. Their site, PLEOMART (plenty of markets) is a B2B marketplace for companies to buy and sell office equipment and supplies, parts, and related solutions services such as consultation, finance, and logistics services on the web.[49] In Melbourne, Australia, the Broken Hill Proprietary Company, Ltd. (BHP), which specializes in natural resources and regional steel for the global market, has launched its own one-stop global e-marketplace. The site provides logistics, sample products, and supply procurements to e-business producer marketplaces. Recently BHP has conducted a series of Internet-based "reverse" auctions, where suppliers agree on a starting price then bid against each other to lower prices for ferro-alloys. BHP's Francis Egan, vice president global supply, says that BHP already spends about A$10 billion annually on goods and services on-line; he says that "online auctions allow us to move readily, aggregate out buying power and leverage greater savings. . . . They also provide economies of scale and promote greater efficiency in the supply function itself.".[50]

Far from Melbourne, but in a world made smaller by the Internet, Germany's Siemens AG has embarked on a global e-strategy, as described in the accompanying *E-Biz Box*.

Entry Strategy Alternatives

For a multinational corporation (or a company considering entry into the international arena), a more specific set of strategic alternatives, often varying by targeted country, focuses on different ways to enter a foreign market. Managers need to consider how potential new markets may best be served by their company in light of the risks and the critical environmental factors associated with their entry strategies. The following sections examine the various entry and ownership strategies available to firms, including exporting, licensing, franchising, contract manufacturing, turnkey operations, management contracts, joint ventures, and fully owned subsidiaries set up by the firm. These alternatives are not mutually exclusive; several may be employed at the same time. They are addressed in order of ascending risk.

Exporting

Exporting is a relatively low-risk way to begin international expansion or to test out an overseas market. Little investment is involved, and fast withdrawal is relatively easy. Small firms seldom go beyond this stage, and large firms use this avenue for many of their products. Because of their comparative lack of capital resources and marketing clout, exporting is the primary entry strategy used by small businesses to compete on an international level. Jordan Toothbrush, for example, a small company with one plant in Norway and with limited resources is dependent on good distributors; as Jordan exports around the world, the company recognizes the importance of maintaining good distributor relations. A re-

Siemens AG, the Munich-based electronics and electrical engineering giant, announced in October 2000 that the company was undergoing radical change and transforming itself into a company whose entire value chain will be characterized by e-business. All aspects of Siemens' global value chain—from purchasing, sales, and after-sales service, to internal business and production processes, from research and development to training, and the worldwide management of knowledge and expertise—will be networked and handled electronically. In short, Siemens is becoming "one of the world's largest e-business building sites." This was how President and CEO Heinrich v. Pierer described the process at the October 10, 2000, opening of the first Center of E-Excellence. The goal of the centers is to coordinate and control Siemens' transformation into an e-company. The first was founded at a location near Munich Airport, and others will follow in the United States (Atlanta) and Asia (Singapore). In his opening speech, Heinrich v. Pierer stated that "E-business will transform Siemens into a new company. We will base our entire business on a new foundation, thereby changing all processes, both internal and external ones." He added that

an initial investment of 1 billion euros has been earmarked for this purpose. It will be the lever for considerable productivity increases and a corresponding improvement in Siemens' cost position.

Siemens and IBM announced that Siemens will use IBM's WebSphere Commerce Suite, with features including support for dynamic retail models—like on-line catalogs, content management, and modern search engine technologies. Sellers and buyers are able to maintain control in the kind of transaction involving goods or services. Business analysis and personalization tools assist in the creation of individual customer profiles. The Siemens global e-business applications will be jointly developed and implemented by an alliance composed of Siemens' own Siemens Business Services (SBS), i2 Technologies, CommerceOne and IBM. Benefits expected include faster development of new markets, closer customer relationships and significant reduction of operational costs.

The Siemens program is expected to take around three years to complete. It is based on the concept of a global "e-community" embracing 447,000 Siemens employees as well as all the company's customers.

SOURCES: www.cyberlabsresearch.com/profile/Siemens.html, October 10, 2000; www.ibm.com/press, January 26, 2000.

cent survey by Dun and Bradstreet showed that more than half of small- to medium-sized businesses anticipate growth in their export sales in the next few years.[51]

An experienced firm may want to handle its exporting functions by appointing a manager or establishing an export department. Alternatively, an export management company (EMC) may be retained to take over some or all exporting functions, including dealing with host-country regulations, tariffs, duties, documentation, letters of credit, currency conversion, and so forth. Frequently, it pays to hire a specialist for a given host country.

Certain decisions need special care when managers are setting up an exporting system, particularly the choice of distributor. Many countries have regulations that make it very hard to remove a distributor who proves inefficient. Other critical environmental factors include export–import tariffs and quotas, freight costs, and distance from supplier countries.

Licensing

An international licensing agreement grants the rights to a firm in the host country to either produce or sell a product, or both. This agreement involves the transfer of rights to patents, trademarks, or technology for a specified period of time in return for a fee paid by the licensee. Anheuser-Busch, for instance, has granted licenses to produce and market Budweiser beer in England, Japan, Australia, and Israel, among other countries. Many food manufacturing MNCs license their products overseas, often under the names of local firms, and products like those of Nike and Disney can be seen around the world under various licensing agreements. Like exporting, licensing is also a relatively low-risk strategy because it requires little investment, and it can be a very useful option in countries where market entry by other means is constrained by regulations or profit-repatriation restrictions.

Licensing is especially suitable for the mature phase of a product's life cycle, when competition is intense, margins decline, and production is relatively standardized.[52] It is also useful for firms with rapidly changing technologies, for those with many diverse product lines, and for small firms with few financial and managerial resources for direct investment abroad. A clear advantage of licensing is that it avoids the tariffs and quotas usually imposed on exports. The most common disadvantage is the licensor's lack of control over the licensee's activities and performance.

Critical environmental factors to consider in licensing are whether sufficient patent and trademark protection is available in the host country, the track record and quality of the licensee, the risk that the licensee may develop its competence to become a direct competitor, the licensee's market territory, and legal limits on the royalty rate structure in the host country.[53]

Franchising

Similar to licensing, franchising involves relatively little risk. The franchisor licenses its trademark, products and services, and operating principles to the franchisee for an initial fee and ongoing royalties. Franchises are well known in the domestic fast-food industry; McDonald's, for example, operates primarily on this basis. For a large up-front fee and considerable royalty payments, the franchisee gets the benefit of McDonald's reputation, existing clientele, marketing clout, and management expertise. The "Big M" is well recognized internationally, as are many other fast-food and hotel franchises, such as Holiday Inn. A critical consideration for the franchisor's management is quality control, which becomes more difficult with greater geographic dispersion.

Franchising can be an ideal strategy for small businesses because outlets require little investment in capital or human resources. In fact, through franchising, an entrepreneur can use the resources of franchisees to expand; most of today's large franchises started out with this strategy. An entrepreneur can also use franchisees to enter a new business. Higher costs in entry fees and royalties are offset by the lower risk of an established product, trademark, and customer base, as well as the benefit of the franchisor's experience and techniques.[54]

Contract Manufacturing

A common means of using cheaper labor overseas is contract manufacturing, which involves contracting for the production of finished goods or component parts. These goods or components are then imported to the home country, or to other countries, for assembly or sale. Alternatively, they may be sold in the host country. If managers can ensure the reliability and quality of the local contractor and work out adequate means of capital repatriation, this strategy can be a desirable means of quick entry into a country with a low capital investment and none of the problems of local ownership. Firms like Nike use contract manufacturing around the world.

Turnkey Operations

In a so-called turnkey operation, a company designs and constructs a facility abroad (such as a dam or chemical plant), trains local personnel, and then turns the key over to local management—for a fee, of course. The Italian company Fiat, for example, constructed an automobile plant in the former Soviet Union under a turnkey agreement. Critical factors for success are the availability of local supplies and labor, reliable infrastructure, and an acceptable means of repatriating profits. There may also be a critical risk exposure if the turnkey contract is with the host government, which is often the case. This situation exposes the company to risks such as contract revocation and the rescission of bank guarantees.

Management Contracts

A management contract gives a foreign company the rights to manage the daily operations of a business, but not to make decisions regarding ownership, financing, or strategic and policy changes.[55] Usually, management contracts are enacted in combination with other agreements, such as joint ventures. By itself, a management contract is a relatively low-risk entry strategy, but it is likely to be short-term and to provide limited income unless it leads to another more permanent position in the market.[56]

International Joint Ventures (IJVs)

At a much higher level of investment and risk (though usually less risk than a wholly owned plant), joint ventures present considerable opportunities unattainable through other strategies. A joint venture involves an agreement by two or more companies to produce a product or service together. In an IJV ownership is shared, typically by an MNC and a local partner, through agreed-upon proportions of equity. This strategy facilitates an MNC's rapid entry into new markets by means of an already established partner who has local contacts and familiarity with local operations. IJVs are a common strategy for corporate growth around the world; they also are a means to overcome trade barriers, to achieve significant economies of scale for development of a strong competitive position, to secure access to additional raw materials, to acquire managerial and technological skills, and to spread the risk associated with operating in a foreign environment.[57] Not surprisingly, larger companies are more inclined to take a high equity stake in the IJV, engage in global industries, and are less vulnerable to the risk conditions in the host country.[58] The joint venture reduces the risks of expropriation and harassment by the host country; indeed, it may be the only means of entry into certain countries, like Mexico and Japan, that stipulate proportions of local ownership and local participation.

In recent years, IJVs have made up about 20 percent of direct investments by MNCs in other countries, including such deals as the robotics venture between Fujitsu and General Electric and the fiber-optic venture between Siemens A.G. and Corning Glass Works. Many companies have set up joint ventures with European companies to gain the status of an "insider" in the European Common Market. Most of these alliances are not just tools of convenience but are important—perhaps critical—means to compete in the global arena.[59] To compete globally, firms have to incur, and defray, immense fixed costs, and they need partners to help them in this.[60]

Sometimes countries themselves need such alliances to improve economic conditions: the Commonwealth of Independent States (CIS) has recently opened its doors to joint ventures, seeking an infusion of capital and management expertise. Philip Morris, discussed earlier, entered a joint venture with Artovaz, a Russian auto manufacturer, to produce Marlboro cigarettes at a converted plant in Samara.

International joint ventures are one of many forms of strategic global alliances that are further discussed in the next chapter.

In a joint venture, the level of relative ownership and specific contributions must be worked out by the partners. The partners must share management and decision making for a successful alliance. The company seeking such a venture must maintain sufficient control, however, because without adequate control, the company's managers may be unable to implement their desired strategies. Initial partner selection and the development of a mutually beneficial working agreement are therefore critical to the success of a joint venture. In addition, managers must ascertain that there will be enough of a "fit" between the partners' objectives, strategies, and resources—financial, human, and technological—to make the venture work. Unfortunately, too often the need for preparation and cooperation is given insufficient attention, resulting in many such marriages ending in divorce. In fact, about 60 percent of IJVs fail, usually because of ineffective managerial decisions regarding the type of IJV, its scope, duration and administration, as well as careless partner selection.[61] The list of cross-cultural disappointments is getting longer—Chrysler-Mitsubishi and Fiat-Nissan have, according to Business Week, "produced as much rancor as rewards."[62] After years of arguments, GM pulled out of its operations with Korea's Daewoo Motors, citing insufficient care given to their relationship.

Fully Owned Subsidiaries

In countries where a fully owned subsidiary is permitted, an MNC wishing total control of its operations can start its own product or service business from scratch, or it may acquire an existing firm in the host country. Philip Morris acquired the Swiss food firm Jacobs Suchard to gain an early inside track in the European Common Market and to continue its diversification away from its aging tobacco business. With this move, PM became the second U.S. company, after Mars, to assure itself a place in Europe's food industry.[63] Such acquisitions by MNCs allow rapid entry into a market with established products and distribution networks and provide a level of acceptability not likely to be given to a "foreign" firm. These advantages offset, somewhat, the greater level of risk stemming from the larger capital investments, compared with other entry strategies.

At the highest level of risk is the strategy of starting a business from scratch in the host country—that is, establishing a new wholly owned foreign manufacturing or service company or subsidiary, with products aimed at the local market or targeted for export. Japanese automobile manufacturers—Honda, Nissan, and Toyota—have successfully used this strategy in the United States to get around American import quotas.

This strategy exposes the company to the full range of risk, to the extent of its investment in the host country. As evidenced by events in South Africa and China, political instability can be devastating to a wholly owned foreign subsidiary. Add to this risk a number of other critical environmental factors—local attitudes toward foreign ownership, currency stability and repatriation, the threat of expropriation and nationalism—and you have a high-risk entry strategy that must be carefully evaluated and monitored. There are advantages to this strategy, however, such as full control over decision making and efficiency as well as the ability to integrate operations with overall companywide strategy.

Exhibit 6-7 summarizes the advantages and critical success factors of these entry strategies which must be taken into account when selecting one or a combination of strategies depending on the location, the environmental factors and competitive analysis discussed here, and the overall strategy in which the company approaches world markets.

Complex situational factors face the international manager as she or he considers strategic approaches to world markets, along with which entry strategies might be appropriate, as illustrated in the accompanying Comparative Management in Focus: Strategic Formulation for the EU Market.

Comparative Management in Focus

Strategic Planning for the EU Market[64]

> Business units [in Europe] still tend to focus on individual countries and managerial practices still follow long-standing national patterns.

FRANCESCO CAIO, CEO MERLONI ELETTRODOMESTICI, FABRIANO, ITALY.[65]

For firms within Europe, the euro eliminates currency risk, and so "Pan European thinking becomes not only practicable but essential."[66] The success of companies within Europe, then, will depend on their efficiency in streamlining and consolidating its processes and in integrating product and marketing plans across Europe. The challenge is to balance the national and the continental view, because a common currency does not bring about cultural or linguistic union.[67]

Clearly, both European and non-European companies will need to reconsider their European, and indeed global strategies, now that the EU has become a reality, complete with common currency, the euro. "Foreign" managers, for example, need to develop an action program to ensure that their products have continued access to the EU and to adapt their marketing efforts to encompass the whole EU. The latter task is difficult, if not impossible, however, because the

Exhibit 6-7

International Entry Strategies: Advantages and Critical Success Factors

STRATEGY	ADVANTAGES	CRITICAL SUCCESS FACTORS
Exporting	Low risk No long-term assets Easy market access and exit	Choice of distributor Transportation costs Tariffs and quotas
Licensing	No asset ownership risk Fast market access Avoids regulations and tariffs	Quality and trustworthiness of licensee Appropriability of intellectual property Host-country royalty limits
Franchising	Little investment or risk Fast market access Small business expansion	Quality control of franchisee and franchise operations
Contract manufacturing	Limited cost and risk Short-term commitment	Reliability and quality of local contractor Operational control and human rights issues
Turnkey operations	Revenue from skills and technology where FDI restricted	Reliable infrastructure Sufficient local supplies and labor Repatriable profits Reliability of any government partner
Management contracts	Low-risk access to further strategies	Opportunity gain longer-term position

Joint ventures	Insider access to markets
	Share costs and risk
	Leverage partner's skill base
	   technology, local contacts
		Strategic fit and complementarity of
		   partner, markets, products
		Ability to protect technology
		Competitive advantage
		Ability to share control
		Cultural adaptability of partners

Wholly owned subsidiaries	Realize all revenues and control
	Global economies of scale
	Strategic coordination
	Protect technology and skill base
	Acquisition provides rapid market
	   entry into established market
		Ability to assess and control economic,
		   political and currency risk
		Ability to get local acceptance
		Repatriability of profits

"citizen of Europe" is a myth; national cultures and tastes cannot be homogenized. With many different languages and distinctive national customs and cultures, companies trying to sell in Europe must thread their way through a maze of varying national preferences. These and other challenges lie ahead, along with numerous opportunities.

UPS is one of many firms experiencing this double-edged sword. Its managers realize that Europe is still virgin territory for service companies, and they expect revenue to grow by 15 percent a year there. However, it has run into many conflicts, both practical and cultural. Some of the surprises "Big Brown" had as it put its brown uniforms on 25,000 Europeans and sprayed brown paint on 10,000 delivery trucks around Europe were:

indignation in France, when drivers were told they couldn't have wine with lunch; protests in Britain, when drivers' dogs were banned from delivery trucks; dismay in Spain, when it was found that the brown UPS trucks resembled the local hearses; and shock in Germany, when brown shirts were required for the first time since 1945.[68]

Meanwhile, adventurous European businesses are spreading their wings across neighboring countries as they realize that open markets can offer as much growth and profitability as does protectionism—probably more. British Airways, for example, took the German market under its wing by buying 49 percent of a local airline and using a new Euroname, Deutsche BA. And, in one of Europe's biggest mergers, the Zeneca Group P.L.C., of Britain acquired Astra A.B., of Sweden. The resulting pharmaceutical giant was deemed necessary to fund new drug research and to compete in a market dominated by U.S. corporations. Early European mergers were dominated by British companies. But now that Continental European companies will have their shares denominated in euros, there will likely be more cross-border deals among those countries because they will be free of currency-exchange problems.[69]

Companies within the EU are gaining great advantages by competing in a continental-scale market and thereby avoiding duplication of administrative procedures, production, marketing, and distribution. The Italian company Benneton Group SPA is one such company—competing by being technologically efficient. For insiders, a single EU internal market means greater efficiencies and greater economic growth through economies of scale and the removal of barriers, with the consequent lowering of unit costs.

Stiffer competition, however, has resulted both within the market and outside of it, leading to a shakeout of firms; mergers and acquisitions will increase so that larger firms will be strong enough to survive. The twelve "Euroland" countries already have a combined 19 percent of world trade, compared to 17 percent for the United States and 8 percent for Japan, and continued strong growth is projected.

Companies based outside the EU enjoy the same advantages if they have a subsidiary in at least one member state. But they sometimes feel discrimination simply because they will be outside what for the member states is a domestic market. In other words, the EU may build a protectionist wall—of tariffs, quotas, and competitive tactics—to keep out the United States and Japan. However, the EU will also create opportunities for nonmembers—a market with a potential purchasing power of $2.5 trillion, for instance. Many companies, especially MNCs, will start from a better position than some firms based inside the community because of (1) their superior competitiveness and research and development, (2) an existing foothold in the market, and (3) reduced operating expenses (one subsidiary for the whole EU instead of several). But, European harmonized standards, while seeking to eliminate trade barriers within Europe, serve to limit access to EU markets by outside companies through the standardized specifications of products allowed to be sold in Europe. The harmonization laws set minimum standards for exports and imports that are EU-wide. However, those standards also frequently hinder European companies from efficient sourcing of raw materials or component parts from "foreign" companies. Opinions differ about the long-term impact on U.S. firms: the EU could unify its markets, adversely affecting some U.S. industries; market access could be reduced; and demands for reciprocal market access in the United States may ensue.

Others feel that the new single market provides little threat to and considerable opportunity for Americans. Many U.S. firms (in anticipation of protectionism) have invested in Europe since the beginning of the Common Market in 1958, and they now feel satisfied with their current positions. Indeed, U.S. companies (GE, Dow, 3M, Hewlett-Packard) who already have well-established European presences enjoy the same free flow of goods, services, capital, and people as Europeans.

Those U.S. companies not yet established in Europe must examine the EU internal market to decide on their most effective "European strategy." Many firms are opting for joint ventures with European partners, sacrificing their usual preference of 100 percent ownership (or majority control) to extend operations around Europe; this strategy also opens doors to markets dominated by public procurement, as with the AT&T–Philips venture to produce telecommunications equipment. But for a number of firms—both foreign and European—operating in Europe has become cost prohibitive. The average Western European earns more, works fewer hours, takes longer vacations, and receives more social entitlements and job protection than those in Asia and North America. European MNCs have the highest labor and taxation costs among the TRIAD nations.[70] Siemens AG of Germany, for example, shifted almost all its semiconductor assembly work from its plants in Germany—where it was not permitted to operate around the clock or on weekends—to a plant in Singapore, where it operates 24 hours a day, 365 days a year, and pays $4.40 an hour for workers.[71]

Suzuki, Toyota, Nissan, and other Japanese companies are also experiencing the dilemma of operating in Europe. They are reluctant to freely pour yen into Europe, but they want to keep a foothold in the market. Suzuki, for example, found that in its Spanish plant it took five times the number of workers and cost 46 percent more to produce a Suzuki Samurai than in Japan.

Strategic Choice

The strategic choice of one or more of the entry strategies will depend on (1) a critical evaluation of the advantages (and disadvantages) of each in relation to the firm's capabilities, (2) the critical environmental factors, and (3) the contribution that each choice would make to the overall mission and objectives of the company. Exhibit 6-7 summarized the advantages and the critical success factors for each entry strategy discussed. However, when it comes down to a choice of entry strategy or strategies for a particular company, there are more specific factors relating to that firm's situation that must be taken into account. These include factors relating to the firm itself, the industry in which it operates, location factors, and venture-specific factors, as summarized in Exhibit 6-8.

After consideration of the factors for the firm as shown in Exhibit 6-8, as well as what is available and legal in the desired location, some entry strategies will no

Exhibit 6-8

Factors Affecting Choice of Entry Mode in Global Markets

DIMENSIONS	VARIABLES
Firm factors	Firm size and global experience
	Core competencies
	Core capabilities
	Global strategic goals
Industry factors	Industry globalization
	Industry growth rate
	Technical intensity
Location factors	Country risk
	Cultural distance
	Market knowledge
	Potential of local market
	Local and global competition
Venture-specific factors	Value of firm assets
	Extent to which know-how involved in venture is informal (tacit)
	Contractual risk with local partners
	Venture size
	Intent to conduct research and development with local partners

Source: Excerpted and adapted from *International Management—Concepts and Cases* by A. V. Phatak. Copyright © 1997 South-Western College Publishing, Cincinnati, Ohio, a division of International Thomson Publishing Inc., pp. 270–275.

doubt fall out of the feasibility zone. With those options remaining, then, strategic planners need to decide which factors are more important to the firm than others. One method is to develop a weighted assessment to compare the overall impact of factors such as those in Exhibit 6-7, relative to the industry, the location, and the specific venture on each entry strategy. Specific evaluation ratings, of course, would depend on the country conditions at a given point in time, the nature of the industry, and the focal company.

Based on a study of over 10,000 foreign entry activities into China between 1979 and 1998, Pan and Tse concluded that managers tend to follow a hierarchy of decision-sequence in choosing an entry mode. As depicted in Exhibit 6-9, managers first decide between equity-based and non-equity based. Then, equity modes are split into wholly owned operations and equity joint ventures (EJVs); nonequity modes are divided into contractual agreements and export. Pan and Tse found that the location choice—specifically the level of country risk—was the primary influence factor at the level of deciding between equity and nonequity modes. Host-country government incentives also encouraged the choice of equity mode.[72]

Gupta and Govindarajan also propose a hierarchy of decision factors but consider two initial choice levels. The first is the extent to which the firm will export or produce locally; the second is the extent of ownership control over activities that will be performed locally in the target market.[73] As shown in

Exhibit 6-9

A Hierarchical Model of Choice of Entry Modes

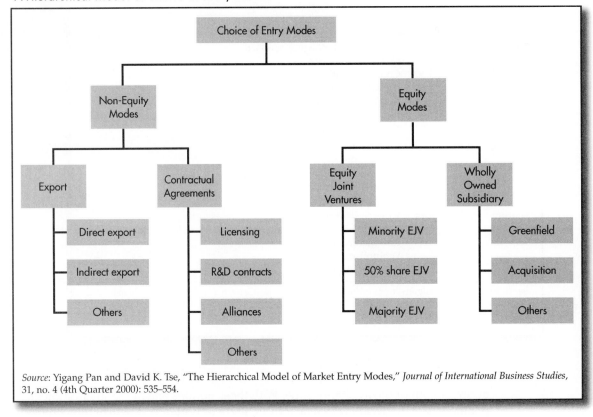

Source: Yigang Pan and David K. Tse, "The Hierarchical Model of Market Entry Modes," *Journal of International Business Studies*, 31, no. 4 (4th Quarter 2000): 535–554.

Exhibit 6-10, there is an array of choice combinations within those two dimensions. Gupta and Govindarajan point out that, among the many factors to take into account, alliance-based entry modes are more suitable under the following conditions:

- Physical, linguistic, and cultural distance between the home and host countries is high.
- The subsidiary would have low operational integration with the rest of the multinational operations
- The risk of asymmetric learning by the partner is low
- The company is short of capital
- Government regulations require local equity participation[74]

The choice of entry strategy for McDonald's, for example, varies around the world according to the prevailing conditions in each country. With its 4,700 foreign stores, McDonald's is, according to *Fortune*, "a virtual blueprint for taking a service organization global."[75] CEO Mike Quinlan notes that, in Europe, the company prefers wholly owned subsidiaries, since European markets are similar to those in the United States and can be run similarly. Those subsidiaries in the

Exhibit 6-10

Alternative Modes
of Entry

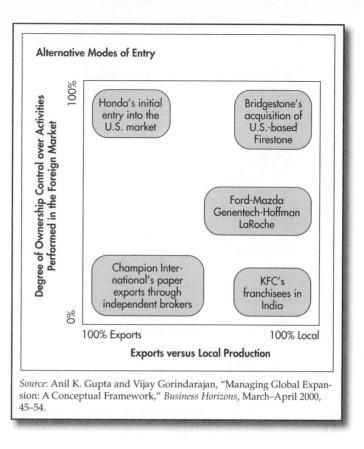

Alternative Modes of Entry

Degree of Ownership Control over Activities Performed in the Foreign Market

- 100%
- Honda's initial entry into the U.S. market
- Bridgestone's acquisition of U.S.-based Firestone
- Ford-Mazda Genentech-Hoffman LaRoche
- Champion International's paper exports through independent brokers
- KFC's franchisees in India
- 0%

100% Exports — 100% Local

Exports versus Local Production

Source: Anil K. Gupta and Vijay Gorindarajan, "Managing Global Expansion: A Conceptual Framework," *Business Horizons*, March–April 2000, 45–54.

United States both operate company-owned stores and license out franchises. Approximately 70 percent of McDonald's stores around the world are franchised. In Asia, joint ventures are preferred so as to take advantage of partners' contacts and local expertise and their ability to negotiate with bureaucracies such as the Chinese government. Headed by billionaire Den Fujita, McDonald's has over 1,000 stores in Japan; in China it had 23 stores in 1994, with more planned, in spite of conflicts with the Chinese government, such as when it made McDonald's move from its leased Tiananmen Square restaurant. In other markets, such as in Saudi Arabia, McDonald's prefers to limit its equity risk by licensing the name—adding strict quality standards—and keeping an option to buy later. Some of McDonald's implementation policies are given in the next chapter.[76]

Timing Entry and Scheduling Expansions

As with McDonald's, international strategic formulation requires a long-term perspective. Entry strategies, therefore, need to be conceived as part of a well-designed, overall plan. In the past, many companies have decided on a particular means of entry that seemed appropriate at the time, only to find later that it was shortsighted. For instance, if a company initially chooses to license a host-country company to produce a product, then later decides that the market is large enough to warrant its own production facility, this new strategy will no longer be feasible because the local host-country company already owns the rights.[77]

The Influence of Culture on Strategic Choice

In addition, strategic choices at various levels often are influenced by cultural factors, such as a long-term versus a short-term perspective. Hofstede found that most people in countries such as China and Japan generally had a longer-term horizon than those in Canada and the United States.[78] Whereas Americans, then, might make strategic choices with a heavy emphasis on short-term profits, the Japanese are known to be more patient in sacrificing short-term results in order to build for the future with investment, research and development, and market share.

Risk orientation was also found by Pan and Tse to explain the choice between equity and nonequity modes.[79] Risk orientation relates to Hofstede's uncertainty avoidance dimension.[80] Firms from countries where, generally speaking, people tend to avoid uncertainty (for example Latin American and African countries) tend to prefer nonequity entry modes in order to minimize exposure to risk. Managers from firms from low uncertainty avoidance countries are more willing to take risks and therefore are more likely to adopt equity entry modes.[81]

Choice of equity versus nonequity mode has been found also to be related to level of power distance. According to Hofstede, a high power distance country (such as Arab countries and Japan) is one where people observe interpersonal inequality and hierarchy.[82] Pan and Tse found that firms from countries tending toward high power distance are more likely to use equity modes of entry abroad.[83]

These are but a few of the examples of the relationships between culture and the choices that are made in the strategic planning and implementation phase. They serve to remind us that it is people who make those decisions and that the ways people think, feel, and act are based on their ingrained societal culture. People bring that context to work and it influences their propensity toward or against certain types of decisions.

Conclusion

The process of strategic formulation for global competitiveness is a daunting task in the volatile international arena and is further complicated by the difficulties involved in acquiring timely and credible information. However, early insight into global developments provides a critical advantage in positioning a firm for future success.

When an entry strategy is selected, the international manager focuses on translating strategic plans into actual operations. Often this involves strategic alliances; always it involves functional level activities for strategic implementation. These subjects are covered in the next chapter.

INTERNET RESOURCES

Visit the Deresky companion Web site at http://prenhall.com/Deresky for this chapter's Internet resources.

SUMMARY OF KEY POINTS

1. Companies "go international" for many reasons, including reactive ones, such as international competition, trade barriers, and customer demands. Proactive reasons include seeking economies of scale, new international markets, resource access, cost savings, and local incentives.

2. International expansion and the realization of a firm's strategy results from both rational planning and responding to emergent opportunities.

3. The steps in the rational planning process for developing an international corporate strategy comprise defining the mission and objectives of the firm, scanning the environment for threats and opportunities, assessing the internal strengths and weaknesses of the firm, considering alternative international entry strategies, and deciding on strategy. The strategic management process is completed by putting into place the operational plans necessary to implement the strategy and then setting up control and evaluation procedures.

4. Competitive analysis is an assessment of how a firm's strengths and weaknesses vis-à-vis those of its competitors affect the opportunities and threats in the international environment. Such assessment allows the firm to determine where the company has distinctive competences that will give it strategic advantage or where problem areas exist.

5. Corporate-level strategic approaches to international competitiveness include globalization and regionalization. Many MNCs have developed to the point of using an integrative global strategy. Entry and ownership strategies are exporting, licensing, franchising, contract manufacturing, turnkey operations, management contracts, joint ventures, and fully owned subsidiaries. Critical environmental and operational factors for implementation must be taken into account.

6. Companies of all sizes are increasingly looking to the Internet as a means to expand their global operations. However, localizing Internet operations is complex.

Chapter 7

Global Alliances and Strategy Implementation

Opening Profile: Backfire! The DaimlerChrysler AG Global Alliance Hits the Brakes

A financial turnaround plan that DaimlerChrysler AG laid out earlier this year appears to be in big trouble as losses accelerate. Chrysler's losses for 2001 are estimated at three billion euros ($2.74 billion).

WALL STREET JOURNAL, OCTOBER 11, 2001.

Juergen Schrempp, the German chairman and CEO of DaimlerChrysler had expected to make billions of dollars in cost savings and synergies from the merger of Daimler-Benz and Chrysler. In 1998, Schrempp pledged that the alliance would have the clout and profitability to take on everyone and be the most profitable automotive company in the world. Now, the company is taking extreme measures to get Chrysler back to profitability, a move expected to take two to four years, because of weak sales and spiraling costs; Chrysler's losses in the fourth quarter, for example, were $1.3 billion.

What went wrong? Much of the problem seems to stem from culture clashes, in particular the attitude of Schrempp toward the merger, Chrysler, and the Americans.

While Schrempp touted the alliance as a merger of equals in 1998, in 2000 he said that Daimler never intended to be an equal partner with Chrysler and that he had said that to gain shareholder approval. But DaimlerChrysler today is essentially a holding company run from Stuttgart that oversees separate business units, which share few products. From the beginning, the marriage was clearly not one made in heaven as Schrempp portrayed, because it was not long before it was clear that he did not view Chrysler as an equal, making it obvious that the American executives would have little more privilege in Stuttgart than the use of the men's room. Morale among the Americans was poor from beginning, with the Germans making it clear that it was a takeover not a merger, and holding meetings only in German, knowing that the Chrysler executives did not understand.

Part of the problem also has been that the synergies expected from the alliance have proved elusive. The macroeconomic forces which led to the alliance in the first place—intense competition, global industry overcapacity, and high need for capital—proved too much for the alliance. While Daimler needed to spread its R&D spending over a broader sales base, Chrysler's sales were already eroding. Then the Americans complained that the Germans were not allowing Chrysler to follow their own successful strategy to build cars inexpensively and sell at a good profit. So Schrempp, admitting that implementing the alliance was turning out to be

cont.

cont.

much harder than doing the deal in the first place, restructured to allow Chrysler more autonomy. Unfortunately, Chrysler ran into more competition than expected, and was forced to give massive incentive plans to move inventory, thus eroding profits.

Dieter Zetsche, a veteran Daimler executive has been made the new Chrysler's president and chief executive (Robert Eaton's successor); he plans to idle six plants over the next two years, slashing 26,000 U.S. jobs—about a fifth of the workforce. Wolfgang Bernhard has been assigned as chief operating officer. The other five on the seven-member rescue team are Americans. So, with 2001 losses for Chrysler estimated at $1.9 billion, perhaps the first cooperative German–American team, born out of necessity, will give Chrysler it's best chance at a turnaround. In spite of some Chrysler executives' griping that they don't want the Germans there, everyone recognized that there must be a team effort to save the company. Zetsche and Bernhard are making inroads at cultural integration by eating in the employee cafeteria rather than the executive dining room and mingling with Chrysler designers to learn about new products.

In the meantime, Schrempp concedes that the real value of the alliance won't be realized until there is joint production of cars by Daimler and Chrysler, which will take a couple of years. However, DaimlerChrysler's problems have made companies around the world cautious about global megamergers.

SOURCES: www.charlotte.com/observer January 30, 2001; www.businessweek.com January 15, 2001; *Wall Street Journal*, November 8, 2000; *Wall Street Journal*, October 27, 2000; www.FT.com (*Financial Times*, November 2, 2000); *Wall Street Journal*, September 20, 2000.

STRATEGIC ALLIANCES

It is no longer an era in which a single company can dominate any technology or business by itself. The technology has become so advanced, and the markets so complex, that you simply can't expect to be the best at the whole process any longer.

FUMIO SATO, CEO, TOSHIBA ELECTRONICS CO.[1]

Strategic alliances are partnerships between two or more firms which decide they can better pursue their mutual goals by combining their resources—financial, managerial, technological—as well as their existing distinctive competitive advantages. Alliances, often called cooperative strategies, are transition mechanisms that propel the partners' strategy forward in a turbulent environment faster than would be possible for each company alone.[2] Alliances typically fall under one of three categories:[3]

- **Joint ventures**—when two or more companies create an independent company; an example is the Nuumi corporation, created as a joint venture between Toyota and General Motors, which gave GM access to Toyota's manufacturing expertise and provided Toyota with a manufacturing base in the United States.
- **Equity strategic alliances**—in which two or more partners have different relative ownership shares (equity percentages) in the new venture. As with most global manufacturers, Toyota has equity alliances with suppliers, sub-assemblers, and distributors; most of these are part of their network of internal family and financial links.
- **Nonequity strategic alliances**—when agreements are carried out through contract rather than ownership sharing. Such contracts are often with a firm's suppliers, distributors, or manufacturers, or they may be for purposes of marketing and information sharing, such as with many airline partnerships.

Global strategic alliances are working partnerships between companies (often more than two) across national boundaries and increasingly across industries. A glance at the global airline industry, for example, tells us that global alliances have become a mainstay of competitive strategy:

> Not one airline is competing alone; each major U.S. carrier has established strategic links with non-U.S. companies. Delta is linked with Swissair, Sabena, and Austrian; American with British Airways, U.S. Airways, JAL, and Qantas; Northwest with Continental, KLM, and Alitalia; and United with SAS, Lufthansa, Air Canada, Thai, South African Airways, Varig, Singapore, Air New Zealand, and Ansett Australia.[4]

Alliances are also sometimes formed between a company and a foreign government, or among companies and governments. The European Airbus Industrie consortium comprises France's Aerospatiale and Germany's Daimler-Benz Aerospace, each with 37.9 percent of the business; British Aerospace has 20 percent, and Spain's Construcciones Aeronauticas has 4.2 percent.

Alliances may comprise full global partnerships, often joint ventures, in which two or more companies, while retaining their national identity, develop a common, long-term strategy aimed at world leadership. The intent of the Daimler-Chrysler global partnership was to achieve these kinds of objectives, though by 2001 it had run into problems (see the opening profile). Whereas such alliances have a broad agenda, others are formed for a narrow and specific function including production, marketing, research and development, and financing. More recently, these include electronic alliances, such as Covisint, which is redefining the entire system of car production and distribution through a common electronic marketplace (featured in the accompanying *E-Biz Box*).

Covisint is an e-business exchange developed by DaimlerChrysler AG, Ford, General Motors, Nissan, and Renault, to meet the needs of the automotive industry. It is a multimember joint venture with those companies and with Commerce One and Oracle as members. Covisint provides original equipment manufacturers (OEMs) and suppliers the ability to reduce costs and bring efficiencies to their business operations. Covisint has headquarters in Amsterdam, Tokyo, and Southfield, Michigan.

Covisint has more than 250 customers on two continents engaged in activities on the exchange including catalogs, auctions, quote management, and collaborative design. Its current product and service offering is focused on procurement, supply chain, and product development solutions. The purpose of Covisint is to harness the power of Internet technology to create visibility within a company's supply chain—transforming the linear chain into a far more productive and efficient networked model. Further, the company delivers build-to-order capability with proven, scalable, and secure technologies that reinforce our customers' individual competitiveness. Internet tech-

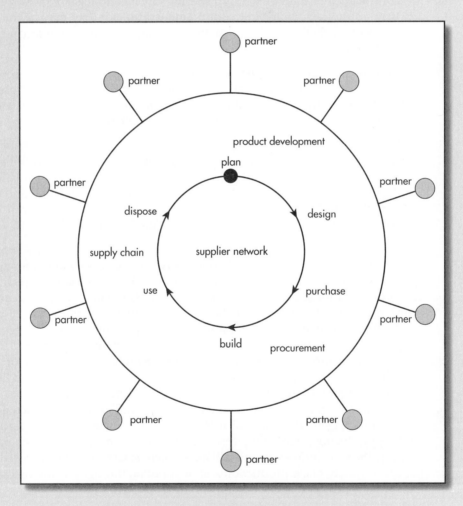

nology speeds the flow of material through the supply chain, increases response to consumer demand, and delivers new products to market faster than ever before. An overview is presented in the accompanying diagram.

Four Japanese car manufacturers—Toyota, Mazda, Honda, and Mitsubishi Motors—are also planning to join the Covisint global automotive on-line exchange, whereas European-owned firms have been more reluctant to commit to Covisint. PSA Peugeot later joined Covisint.[5] Covisint expects to generate $300 billion in car sales and save manufacturers up to $263 per car by 2005 as well as reduce delivery periods to a few days and give buyers the opportunity for customized car orders.[6]

SOURCE: www.covisint.com, September 28, 2001.

Global and Cross-Border Alliances: Motivations and Benefits

1. **To avoid import barriers, licensing requirements and other protectionist legislation**.   Japanese automotive manufacturers, for example, use alliances such as the GM–Toyota venture, or subsidiaries, to produce cars in the United States so as to avoid import quotas.

2. **To share the costs and risks of the research and development of new products and processes**.   In the semiconductor industry, for example, where each new generation of memory chips is estimated to cost over $1 billion to develop, those costs and the rapid technological evolution typically require the resources of more than one, or even two, firms. Intel, for example, has alliances with Samsung and NMB Semiconductor for DRAM technology development; Sun Microsystems has partners for its RISC technology, including N.V. Philips, Fujitsu, and Texas Instruments. Toshiba, Japan's third largest electronics company, has over two dozen major joint ventures and strategic alliances around the world, including partners such as Olivetti, Rhone-Poulenc, and GEC Alstholm in Europe, LSI Logic in Canada, and Samsung in Korea. Fumio Sato, Toshiba's CEO, recognized long ago that a global strategy for a high-tech electronics company such as his necessitated joint ventures and strategic alliances.

3. **To gain access to specific markets**, such as the EU, where regulations favor domestic companies, which was one of the enticements for Chrysler to ally with Daimler-Benz. Firms around the world are forming strategic alliances with European companies to bolster their chances of competing in the EU and to gain access to markets in Eastern European countries as they open up to world business. Chun Joo Bum, chief executive of the Daewoo Electronics unit, acknowledges that he is seeking local partners in Europe for two reasons: (1) to provide sorely needed capital (a problem amidst Asia's economic woes); (2) to help them navigate Europe's still disparate markets, saying, "I need to localize our management. It is not one market."[7]

   Market entry into some countries may only be attained through alliances—typically joint ventures. South Korea, for example has a limit of 18 percent on foreign investment in South Korean firms.

4. **To reduce political risk while making inroads into a new market.** Maytag Corporation, for example, determined to stay on the right side of the restrictive Chinese government while gaining market access, formed a joint venture with RSD, the Chinese appliance maker, to manufacture and market washing machines and refrigerators; Maytag also invested large amounts in jointly owned refrigeration products facilities to help RSD get into that market. Coca-Cola—a global player with large-scale alliances—is not beyond using some very small-scale alliances to be "political" in China. The company utilizes senior citizens in the party's neighborhood committees to sell coke locally.

Exhibit 7-1

AT&T's Alliance Strategy

PARTNER	TECHNOLOGY	INTENT
NEC	Customized chips, computer-design tools	Learn new core technologies from NEC; sales position in Japan
	Mobile phones	Penetrate cellular phone markets; compatible standards
Mitsubishi	SRAM and gallium-arsenide chips	Increase sales in Japan; learn new semiconductor technologies
Italtel	Telecommunications	Expand beachhead in Europe
N. V. Philips	Circuit boards	Market and technology access; purchased 1990
Lucky-Gold Star	Fibre optics, telecommunications, circuits	Entry into Asian markets; technology sharing agreement
Telefonics	Telecommunications and integrated circuits	Expand European production and marketing
Zenith Technology	High-definition television	Apply and learn digital compression
Intel	Personal computer networks and integrated (circuits)	Share manufacturing technology and capacity
		Develop UNIX computer operating system for local area net-works
Hoya	Photomasks and semiconductor equipment	Develop ion-beam masks and mask design software in Japan and the United States
Mannesmann	Microwave radio gear and cellular phone technology	Serve as OEM supplier to German firm
Go Corp.	Pen-based computers and wireless networks	Set industry standards for telecommunications power and range
Olivetti	Personal computers	Failed in 1988
Eo Corp.	Personal communicator devices	Create new handheld computers
Matsushita	Microprocessors	Encourage new technology standards for Hobbit-based systems
NEC & Toshiba McCaw Cellular	Cellular telephones	Secure downstream market in the United States

Source: D. Lei, "Offensive and Defensive Uses of Alliances," in *Strategic Management in a Global Economy*, 3rd ed., Heidi Vernon-Wortzel and L. H. Wortzel (eds.), (New York: John Wiley & Sons, 1997).

5. **To gain rapid entry into a new or consolidating industry and to take advantage of synergies**.   Technology is rapidly providing the means for overlapping and merging of traditional industries such as entertainment, computers, and telecommunications in new digital-based systems, creating an information superhighway. As evidenced by such partnerships as the MCI–WorldCom merger in August 1998, such developments are necessitating strategic alliances across industries in order for companies to gain rapid entry into areas in which they have no expertise or manufacturing capabilities; competition is so fierce that they cannot wait to develop those resources alone. Many of these objectives, such as access to new technology and to new markets, are evident in AT&T's network of alliances around the world, as shown in Exhibit 7-1. Agreements with Japan's NEC, for example, give AT&T access to new semiconductor and chip-making technologies in order to learn how to better integrate computers with communications. Another joint venture with Zenith Electronics will allow AT&T to codevelop the next generation of high-definition television (HDTV).[8]

Challenges in Implementing Global Alliances

Effective global alliances are usually tediously slow in the making but can be among the best mechanisms to implement strategies in global markets. In a highly competitive environment, alliances present a faster and less risky route to globalization. It is extremely complex to fashion such linkages, however, especially where many interconnecting systems are involved, forming intricate networks. Many alliances fail or end up in a takeover in which one partner swallows the other. McKinsey & Company, a consulting firm, surveyed 150 companies that had been in alliances and found that 75 percent of them had been taken over by Japanese partners.[9] Problems with shared ownership, the integration of vastly different structures and systems, the distribution of power between the companies involved, and conflicts in their relative locus of decision making and control are but a few of the organizational issues that must be worked out. But recent economic woes in Asia have turned the tables somewhat, with Western companies having to buy out their financially stressed allies in order to survive.

Often, the form of governance chosen for multinational firm alliances greatly influences their success, particularly in technologically intense fields—pharmaceuticals, computers, and semiconductors. In a study of 153 new alliances, researchers found that the choice of the means of governance—whether a contractual agreement or a joint venture—depended on a desire to control information about proprietary technology.[10] Thus, joint ventures are often the chosen form for such alliances because they provide greater control and coordination in high-technology industries.

Cross-border partnerships, in particular, often become a "race to learn"—with the faster learner later dominating the alliance and rewriting its terms. In a real sense, an alliance becomes a new form of competition. In fact, according to researcher David Lei,

> Perhaps the single greatest impediment managers face when seeking to learn or renew sources of competitive advantage is to realize that

co-operation can represent another form of unintended competition, particularly to shape and apply new skills to future products and businesses.[11]

All too often, cross-border allies have difficulty in collaborating effectively especially in competitively sensitive areas, creating mistrust and secrecy, which then undermine the purpose of the alliance. The difficulty that they are dealing with is the dual nature of strategic alliances—the benefits of cooperation versus the dangers of introducing new competition through sharing their knowledge and technological skills about their mutual product or the manufacturing process. Managers may fear that they will lose the competitive advantage of the firm's proprietary technology or the specific skills that their personnel possess. The cumulative learning that a partner attains through the alliance could potentially be applied to other products or even other industries that are beyond the scope of the alliance, and therefore would hold no benefit to the partner holding the original knowledge.[12] As noted by Lei, the Japanese, in fact have far outlearned their U.S. allies in developing and applying new technologies to other uses. Examples are in the power-equipment industry (e.g., Westinghouse–Mitsubishi), the office equipment industry (Kodak–Canon), and in the consumer electronics industry (General Electric–Samsung). Some of the trade-offs of the duality of cross-border ventures are shown in Exhibit 7-2.

The enticing benefits of cross-border alliances often mask the many pitfalls. In addition to potential loss of technology and knowledge or skill base, other areas of incompatibility often arise, such as conflicting strategic goals and objectives, cultural clashes, and disputes over management and control systems. Sometimes it takes a while for such problems to evidence themselves, particularly if insufficient homework has been done in meetings between the two sides to work out the implementation details. The alliance between KLM Royal Dutch Airlines and Northwest Airlines linking their hubs in Detroit and Amsterdam, for example, resulted in a bitter feud among the top officials of both companies over methods of running an airline business—the European way or the American way—and over cultural differences between the companies, as well as a power struggle at the top over who should call the shots.[13]

Guidelines for Successful Alliances

There is no doubt that many difficulties arise in cross-border alliances in melding both national and corporate cultures of the parties, in overcoming language and communication barriers, and in building trust between the parties over how to share proprietary assets and management processes. Some basic guidelines, given below, will serve to minimize potential problems. However, nothing is as important as having a long "courtship" with the potential partner to establish compatibility strategically and interpersonally and setting up a "prenuptial" plan with the prospective partner. Even setting up some pilot programs on a short-term basis for some of the planned combined activities can highlight areas that may become problematic.

1. Choose a partner with compatible strategic goals and objectives and one with whom the alliance will result in synergies through the combined markets, technologies, and management cadre.

Exhibit 7-2

The Dual Role of Strategic Alliances

COOPERATIVE	COMPETITIVE
Economies of scale in tangible assets (e.g., plant and equipment).	Opportunity to learn new intangible skills from partner, often tacit or organization embedded.
Upstream–downstream division of labor among partners.	Accelerate diffusion of industry standards and new technologies to erect barriers to entry.
Fill out product line with components or end products provided by supplier.	Deny technological and learning initiative to partner via out-sourcing and long-term supply arrangements.
Limit investment risk when entering new markets or uncertain technological fields via shared resources.	Encircle existing competitors and preempt the rise of new competitors with alliance partners in "proxy wars" to control market access, distribution, and access to new technologies.
Create a "critical mass" to learn and develop new technologies to protect domestic, strategic industries.	Form clusters of learning among suppliers and related firms to avoid or reduce foreign dependence for critical inputs and skills.
Assist short-term corporate restructurings by lowering exit barriers in mature or declining industries.	Alliances serve as experiential platforms to "demature" and transform existing mature industries via new components, technologies, or skills to enhance the value of future growth options.

Source: David Lei, "Offensive and Defensive Uses of Alliances," in *Strategic Management in Global Economy*, 3rd ed., Heidi Vernon-Wortzel and L. H. Wortzel (eds.), (New York: John Wiley & Sons, 1997).

2. Seek alliances where complementary skills, products, and markets will result. If each partner brings distinctive skills and assets to the venture, there will be reduced potential for direct competition in end products and markets; in addition, each partner will begin the alliance in a balanced relationship.[14]

3. Work out with the partner how you will each deal with proprietary technology or competitively sensitive information—what will be shared and what will not, and how shared technology will be handled. Trust is an essential ingredient of an alliance, particularly in these areas; but this needs to be backed up by contractual agreements.

4. Recognize that most alliances last only a few years and will probably break up once a partner feels that it has incorporated the skills and information it needs to go it alone. With this in mind, you need to "learn thoroughly and rapidly about a partner's technology and management: transfer valuable ideas and practices promptly into one's own operations."[15]

Some of the opportunities and complexities in cross-border alliances are illustrated in the following section on joint ventures in the Commonwealth of Independent States (CIS). Such alliances are further complicated by the different history of the two parties' economic systems and the resulting business practices.

Joint Ventures in the Commonwealth of Independent States

Invest early and move as fast as you can. . . . Benefit from the firesale prices in the largest market in the world.

I've seen too many westerners fall for the line, "Our license will be arriving any day," which usually means never.

VLADIMIR KVINT.[16]

These comments reflect both the opportunities and the threats involved in international joint ventures (IJVs) in the CIS. Those opportunities include abundant natural resources and cheap land, a highly educated and low-cost workforce with high quality basic research skills, and a huge, relatively untapped, market of people who have had little previous opportunity for quality consumer products. Those taking advantage of those opportunities include 35,000 Western companies that have set up shop in Moscow alone, and over 20,000 joint ventures in Russia. Of those IJVs, 2,800 are U.S.–Russian. They include Caterpillar, IBM, GE, Ford, Hewlett-Packard, Pepsi-Co., Eastman Kodak, and AT&T, as well as thousands of smaller IJVs—primarily in software, hotels, and heavy industrial production. Many, like Bell Labs, are involved in research and development, taking advantage of the high level of education and technical capabilities of the Russians.

The roadblocks to successful IJVs in the CIS are many. The overriding concern as of this writing in 2002 continues to be the possibility of a repeat of the 1998 economic collapse with the devalued ruble, the lack of debt and equity capital, and the nonconvertibility of currency. In fact, the barter system had taken over, with individuals, companies, and governments trading services and goods with no money changing hands. Russian teachers were being paid in vodka. Many foreign companies were losing large amounts of money, and some, such as RJR Nabisco, had withdrawn altogether. Most potential new alliances were put on hold by Western companies. In fact, as a result of the economic problems, many Russian companies benefited by reinforcing their market positions, with some strong local players gaining a foothold, such as Will-Bill-Dann, which produces dairy products, canned vegetables, and juices.[17]

Western companies had varied reactions to the financial problems. Pizza Hut and KFC (whose food was a luxury at that time) withdrew from Moscow, feeling that the market did not warrant their presence. Pizza Hut was in a joint venture with the city of Moscow, which held 51 percent. But when sales tumbled and at the same time its agreement with the City of Moscow was expiring and the city was demanding excessive increases in rent, the company decided to leave.[18] However, most large global companies—accustomed to economic upheavals in Russia—stuck to their long-term plans.[19] Gillette, for example, which has had a joint venture with Leninets, forming Petersburg Products International (PPI) since 1990, stayed and continues its commitment there. But it was not without its problems during the difficult 1998–99 period. The effective distribution systems it had painstakingly built up collapsed, as their wholesalers and retailers ran out of money and stopped their orders.

Overnight, the ability to invoice and receive payment disappeared. So Gillette had to rebuild the distribution system and develop financial support for its suppliers, offering them credit to be paid upon their next orders.[20]

Gillette now employs over 500 people throughout Russia and has built another $40 million razor blade manufacturing plant near St. Petersburg. Other Western companies are trying to move into locally based production in order to cut down on the expenses of a lot of expatriate staff:

Danone, the French dairy group, opened its second Russian factory in 2000; Merloni, the Italian fridge manufacturer, bought Stinol, a local competitor with which it already had links; and in 2001, the Greek-based Chipita acquired a bakery in St. Petersburg.[21]

In spite of continued economic progress since then, however, long-standing problems continue, including the lack of clear legal protection for investments, contracts, or rights to natural resources, and the lack of efficient infrastructure for sourcing materials, communication, transportation, and living arrangements. Problems involving organized crime—often referred to in the media as "the Mafia," and called "the racket" by Russians—add considerably to the cost of operating businesses such as hotels. When MNCs refuse to pay for "protection," they often suffer, as with the bazooka attack on the bottling plant that Coca-Cola was building in Moscow.

During 2001 and 2002, Russia's inflation rate continued to decline and consumer demand was growing again, especially for Western products. President Vladimir Putin continues to support free-market mechanisms, and Russia's stock market has performed very well.[22] In spite of the continuing political uncertainty and economic risk, joint ventures in the CIS offer great opportunities for both partners. Western companies willing to take the risk can pick up assets very cheaply because of the Russian need for hard currency, capital, new technology, and management skills.[23] Foreigners may now own 100 percent of a venture, although to get office space, supplies, and other essentials, it is often necessary to have the local partner own at least half. All registered citizens may now own and operate a business, and the governments in most parts of the CIS are encouraging the privatization of businesses, to move rapidly to a market economy—and to stave off economic disaster.

Exhibit 7-3 shows the joint venture relationship between a U.S. firm and a CIS firm, the different goals that they bring to the venture, and the barriers caused by their different operating environments.[24]

Success requires clearly defined goals, and any proposal must contain solutions to the systemic problems, such as the establishment of efficient supply channels and the repatriation of profits in hard currency. Most managers in the CIS are inexperienced in solving commercial problems based on a capitalist market economy, such as the sourcing of inputs and financing. Western managers still have to teach their joint venture partners about competition, advertising, pricing, distribution networks, and accountability.

Exhibit 7-3
U.S.–CIS Joint
Venture

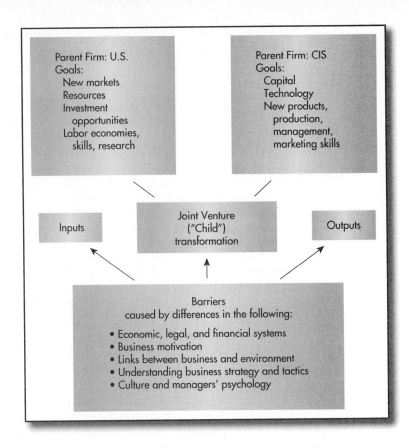

The following are some suggestions for foreign companies to minimize the risk of IJVs in the CIS:

Choose the Right Partner The primary reason for IJV failure is a poor match between partners—because of lack of compatible goals or strategy, because the CIS partner company is unreliable, or because it lacks the necessary licenses to either produce a product or to export it or be involved in development of natural resources. Check with regional government offices about whether the prospective partner has the requisite licenses, appropriate registrations, and reliable bank backing and history; also check on the status of future rights to assets which were previously under the control of the state, such as those for property, natural resources, or a reserve of shareholdings for future privatization voucher holders.

> The choice of a Russian partner can make or break a venture. A local partner may come with risks: you could end up inheriting his "krysha," or laundering money (krysha is the Russian term for paying for "protection").[25]

Businesspeople must realize that there are established procedures for getting out of disputes with partners and those procedures take place outside of the court system. In Russia a handshake is more binding than a 100-page legal document, so disputes are best solved quietly—"often through the mediation of kryshas." Paul Tatum, U.S. hotel developer, ignored those procedures to his peril. When he took on his fight for control of the Radisson Slavyanskaya Hotel in 1997, he was gunned down in front of his two bodyguards.

Find the Right Local General Manager   In a survey of 33 successful joint ventures, Lawrence and Vlachoutsicos found that delegating to the right Russian (or Ukrainian, etc.) executive is the secret to success for an IJV because that manager is familiar with the local networks and ministries, the suppliers and markets, and the maze of regulatory issues involved. In addition, local managers are part of the culture of the Russian *mir*, or collective; this involves direct bonds of loyalty between managers and employees, hands-on management practices and wide consultation but top-down final decision making.

Choose the Right Location   The political risk of investments in Russia decreases from south to north and west to east, according to the consultant Vladimir Kvint. Because most people in Siberia have stayed far away from communism and the centers of power and political turmoil in the European parts of Russia, investments there and along the Pacific coast are more reliable. These areas also have considerable natural resources available. Now that regional leaders have more autonomy, and some have set up economic zones with tax privileges, Kvint recommends that IJVs branch out, away from Moscow to those areas, and to the Russian Far East, where many Japanese IJVs have set up.

Control the IJV   To ensure that hard-currency cash flow will be available, it is best to set up the IJV to provide for more operational self-sufficiency than Western managers are used to. This would avoid world suppliers who require hard currency and local suppliers or distributors who provide poor-quality products or services. The venture's best chance of success is to be vertically integrated to retain control of supplies and access to customers. Not only does this avoid some problems of currency convertibility, but it also controls the high chance of shortages of critical materials and supplies. McDonald's, for example, controlled these elements and also the quality of its inputs for its Russian restaurants by setting up its own farms for potatoes and beef. Other ways to deal with the hard currency problem are (1) to sell products to other foreign businesses within the Commonwealth that hold hard currency; (2) to use IJV rubles to buy raw materials or other products that are marketable in the West—and for which hard currency is paid (as when PepsiCo bought vodka and ships); and (3) to export products. Of the 33 joint ventures studied by Lawrence and Vlachoutsicos, most had yet to repatriate profits to the West.

There is no doubt that the CIS needs more laws to control business; one less obvious area needing attention is that of cultural differences and how they affect operations.

While we refer to the new republics by one name—the Commonwealth of Independent States—it is easy to forget that they are separate republics, each with its own identity, culture, dominant language, ethnic and religious traditions, and economic and labor histories. Different terms are used to differentiate among native Russians (Great Russians), neighboring Ukrainians (Little Russians), and Byelorussians (White Russians). Foreigners need to learn about

Exhibit 7-4

Potential Problems and Solutions for U.S.–CIS IJVs

PROBLEMS	SOLUTIONS
Financial infrastructure: hard currency cash flow and repatriation; capital availability	Reinvest; vertical integration; avoid hard currency deals; get local bank guarantees
Organized crime	Local relationships
Access to materials and supplies; poor quality	Vertical integration, make or supply own
Infrastructure: transportation, communication, banking	Set up operational self-sufficiency where possible
Market access and distribution	Set up alliances; own systems where possible
Operational licenses; rights to assets and resources; liabilities under old system	Validate with central and local authorities before commitment
Political risk	Minimize by locating in New England or Far East if possible
Strategic and reliability conflicts	Explore compatibility and background of partner
Personnel and operational conflicts	Hire local executives and general manager
Motivation; compensation	Give respect; supply goods and services not accessible to employees

the particular people in the region where they plan to establish business. Westerners should take time to get to know Russians on a social basis, for example. According to Kvint, "many deals are hatched in saunas between talk of family and philosophy." In particular, it is a mistake to talk down to Russians; they are well educated and advanced in high-technology issues and they are sensitive to the apparent superiority and wealth of Americans.

Joint ventures in the CIS require a long-term financial and commercial commitment from the foreign partner, including the support of Western on-site personnel. Repatriable profits may not be realized for the first few years of the venture's existence.[26] (See Exhibit 7-4 for additional information.)

STRATEGIC IMPLEMENTATION

IMPLEMENTATION McDONALD'S STYLE
- *Form paradigm-busting arrangements with suppliers.*
- *Know a country's culture before you hit the beach.*
- *Hire locals whenever possible.*
- *Maximize autonomy.*
- *Tweak the standard menu only slightly from place to place.*
- *Keep pricing low to build market share. Profits will follow when economies of scale kick in.*[27]

Decisions regarding global alliances and entry strategies must now be put into motion with the next stage of planning—strategic implementation. Implementation plans are detailed and pervade the entire organization because they entail setting up overall policies, administrative responsibilities, and schedules throughout the organization to enact the selected strategy and to ensure it works. In the case of a merger or IJV, this process requires compromising and blending procedures among two or more companies and is extremely complex. The importance of the implementation phase of the strategic management process cannot be overemphasized. Until they are put into operation, strategic plans remain abstract ideas—verbal or printed proposals that have no effect on the organization.

Successful implementation requires the orchestration of many variables into a cohesive system that complements the desired strategy—that is, a system of fits that will facilitate the actual working of the strategic plan. In this way, the structure, systems, and processes of the firm are coordinated and set into motion by a system of management by objectives (MBO), with the primary objective being the fulfillment of strategy. Managers must review the organizational structure and, if necessary, change it to facilitate the administration of the strategy and to coordinate activities in a particular location with headquarters (as discussed further in Chapter 8). In addition to ensuring the strategy and structure fit, managers must allocate resources to make the strategy work: budgeting money, facilities, equipment, people, and other support. Increasingly, that support necessitates a unified technology infrastructure in order to coordinate diverse businesses around the world and to satisfy the need for current and reliable information. An efficient technology infrastructure can provide a strategic advantage in a globally competitive environment. Jack Welch, while CEO of General Electric (he retired in late 2001) used to refer to his e-commerce initiative, saying:

> It will change relationships with suppliers. Within 18 months, all our suppliers will supply us on the Internet, or they won't do business with us.

JACK WELCH, CEO, GENERAL ELECTRIC, *FORTUNE*, 1999.

An overarching factor affecting all the other variables necessary for successful implementation is that of leadership; it is people, after all, who make things happen. The firm's leaders must skillfully guide employees and processes in the desired direction. Managers with different combinations of experience, education, abilities, and personality tend to be more suited to implementing certain strategies.[28] In an equity-sharing alliance, sorting out which top managers in each company will be in which position is a sensitive matter. Who in which company will be CEO is usually worked out as part of the initial deal in alliance agreements. This problem seems to be frequently settled these days by setting up joint CEOs, one from each company. Setting monitoring systems into place to control activities and ensure success completes, but does not end, the strategic management process. Rather, it is a continuous process, using feedback to reevaluate strategy for needed modifications and for updating and recycling plans. Of particular note here we should consider what is involved in effective management of international joint ventures, since they are such a common form of global alliance, yet are fraught with implementation challenges.

Managing Performance in International Joint Ventures

Much of the world's international business activity involves IJVs, in which at least one parent is headquartered outside the venture's country of operation. IJVs require unique controls; ignoring these specific control requisites can limit the parent company's ability to efficiently use its resources, coordinate its activities, and implement its strategy.[29]

The term IJV control can be defined, according to Schaan, as "the process through which a parent company ensures that the way a joint venture is managed conforms to its own interest."[30] Most of a firm's objectives can be achieved by careful attention to control features at the outset of the joint venture, such as the choice of a partner, the establishment of a strategic fit, and the design of the IJV organization.

The most important single factor determining IJV success or failure is the choice of a partner. Most problems with IJVs involve the local partner, especially in less developed countries. In spite of this fact, many firms rush the process of partner selection because they are anxious to "get on the bandwagon" in an attractive market.[31] In this process, it is vital to establish whether the partners' strategic goals are compatible (discussed in the previous chapter). The strategic context and the competitive environment of the proposed IJV and the parent firm will determine the relative importance of the criteria used to select a partner.[32] IJV performance is also a function of the general fit between the international strategies of the parents, the IJV strategy, and the specific performance goals that the parents adopt.[33] Research has shown that, to facilitate this fit, the partner selection process must determine the specific task-related skills and resources needed from a partner as well as the relative priority of those needs.[34] To do this, managers must analyze their own firm and pinpoint any areas of weakness in task-related skills and resources that can be overcome with the help of the IJV partner.

Organizational design is another major mechanism for factoring in a means of control when an IJV is started. Beamish et al. discuss the important issue of the strategic freedom of an IJV. This refers to the relative amount of decision-making power that a joint venture will have, compared with the parents, in choosing suppliers, product lines, customers, and so on.[35] It is also crucial to consider beforehand the relative management roles each parent will play in the IJV because such decisions result in varying levels of control for different parties. An IJV is usually easier to manage if one parent plays a dominant role and has more decision-making responsibility than the other in daily operations; alternatively, it is easier to manage an IJV if the local general manager has considerable management control, keeping both parents out of most of the daily operations.[36]

International joint ventures are like a marriage—the more issues that can be settled before the merger, the less likely it will be to break up. Control over the stability and the success of the IJV can be largely built into the initial agreement between the partners. The contract can specify who has what responsibilities and rights in a variety of circumstances, such as the contractual links of the IJV with the parents, the capitalization, and the rights and obligations regarding intellectual property. Exhibit 7-5 lists some of the major areas of allocation of responsibility that can be delineated in the joint venture agreement to lessen the potential for strife later.

Exhibit 7-5

Control Elements in an IJV Agreement

- Definitions
- Scope of operations
- Management
  Shareholders and supervisory board
  Executive board
  Arrangements in event of deadlock
  Operating management
- Arbitration
- Representations and warranties of each partner

- Organization and capitalization
- Financial arrangements
- Contractual links with parents
- Rights and obligations regarding intellectual property
- Termination agreements
- Force majeur
- Covenants

Source: "Teaming Up for the Nineties—A Guide to International Joint Ventures and Strategic Alliances," Doorley and Collins, 1991, p. 230.

Of course, we cannot assume equal ownership of the IJV partners; where ownership is unequal, the partners will claim control and staffing choices proportionate to the ownership share. The choice of the IJV general manager, in particular, will influence the relative allocation of control because that person is responsible for running the IJV and for coordinating relationships with each of the parents.[37]

Where ownership is divided among several partners, the parents are more likely to delegate the daily operations of the IJV to the local IJV management—a move that resolves many potential disputes. In addition, the increased autonomy of the IJV tends to reduce many common human resource problems: staffing friction, blocked communication, and blurred organizational culture, to name a few, which all result from the conflicting goals and working practices of the parent companies.[38] Regardless of the number of parents, one way to avoid such potential problem situations is to provide special training to managers about the unique nature and problems of IJVs.[39]

Various studies reveal three complementary and interdependent dimensions of IJV control: (1) the focus of IJV control—the scope of activities over which parents exercise control; (2) the extent, or degree, of IJV control achieved by the parents; and (3) the mechanisms of IJV control used by the parents.[40]

We can conclude from two research studies—Geringer's study of 90 developed country IJVs and Schaan and Beamish's study of 10 IJVs in Mexico—that parent companies tend to focus their efforts on a selected set of activities that they consider important to their strategic goals, rather than attempting to monitor all activities.[41,42] Schaan also found a considerable range of mechanisms for control used by the parent firms in his study (detailed in Exhibit 7-6), including indirect mechanisms such as parent organizational and reporting structure, staffing policies, and close coordination with the IJV general manager (GM). Monitoring the GM typically includes indirect means, perhaps bonuses and career opportunities, and direct mechanisms, such as requiring executive

Exhibit 7-6

Control Mechanisms in International Joint Ventures

Ability to make specific decision	Ability to decide on future promotion of JVGM (and other JV managers)
Ability to design:	
1. Planning process	Feedback; strategy and plan budgets, appropriation requests
2. Appropriation requests	JVGM participation in parent's worldwide meetings
Policies and procedures	Relations with JVGM; phone calls, meetings, visits
Ability to set objectives for JVGM	Staffing parent with someone with experience with JV management
Contracts:	MNC level in Mexico
Management	Informal meetings with other parent
Technology transfer	Board
Marketing	Executive committee
Supplier	Approval required for:
Participation in planning or budgeting process	1. Specific decisions
Parent organization structure	2. Plans, budgets
Reporting structure	3. Appropriation requests
Staffing	4. Nomination of JVGM
Training programs	Screening/no objection of parent before ideas or projects are discussed with the other parent
Staff services	
Bonus of JVGM tied to parent results	

Source: J. L. Schaan, "Parent Control and Joint Venture Success: The Case of Mexico, 249," (doctoral dissertation, University of Western Ontario, 1983), reprinted in J. Michael Geringer and Louis Herbert, "Control and Performance of International Joint Ventures," *Journal of International Business Studies* 20, no. 2 (Summer 1989).

committee approval for specific decisions and budgets. These studies show that a variety of mechanisms are available to parent companies to monitor and guide IJV performance.

The extent of control exercised over an IJV by its parent companies seems to be primarily determined by the decision-making autonomy the parents delegate to the IJV management—which is largely dependent on staffing choices for the top IJV positions and thus on how much confidence the partners have in these managers. In addition, if top managers of the IJV are from the headquarters of each party, then the more similar are their national cultures, the more compatible their managers will be. This is because there are many areas of control decisions where agreement will be more likely between those of similar cultural backgrounds.[43]

The many activities and issues involved in strategic implementation—such as negotiating, organizing, staffing, leading, communicating, control, and so on—are the subjects of other chapters in this book. Elsewhere we include discussion of the many variables involved in strategic implementation which are specific to a particular country or region, such as goals, infrastructure, laws, technology, ways of doing business, people, and culture. Here, we take a look at three pervasive influences on strategy implementation: government policy, culture, and the Internet.

Government Influences on Strategic Implementation

There are many areas of influence by host governments on the strategic choice and implementation of foreign firms. The profitability of those firms is greatly influenced, for example, by the level of taxation in the host country and by any restrictions on profit repatriation. Also important influences are government policies on ownership by foreign firms, on labor union rules, on hiring and remuneration practices, on patent and copyright protection, and so on. For the most part, however, if the corporation's managers have done their homework, all these factors are known beforehand and are part of the location and entry strategy decisions. But what hurts is for managers to set up shop in a host country and then have major economic or governmental policy changes after they have made a considerable investment.

Unpredictable changes in governmental regulations can be a death knell to businesses operating abroad. While this problem occurs in many countries, one country which is often the subject of concern by foreign firms is that of China. In a survey of European investment in China, for example, 54 percent of companies questioned said their performance in China was worse than they had anticipated. Caterpillar, Inc., was one of the companies with rapid market growth in producing diesel engines in China in the early 1990s—construction was booming and foreign investment was flooding in. But in 1993, China, afraid that foreign investment was causing inflation, revoked tax breaks and restricted foreign investment. The tables turned on Caterpillar after that because there was not enough domestic demand for their products.[44] In addition, as reported in the *Wall Street Journal*, "the world's auto industry guessed wrong on China."[45] Certainly the market potential is there—only one Chinese out of every 110 has a car—but big problems are causing foreign car ventures to withdraw. Peugeot-Citroen SA of France abandoned their factory in China, and Daimler-Benz AG of Germany withdrew before it even started. Beijing is even worrying GM, which has invested millions in China, including 21 joint ventures and other projects. Out of concern that China cannot handle a surge in cars on its inadequate roads, with little parking and few service stations, the government has stopped an auto-loan program, and many cities can no longer issue license plates for private cars. Also Beijing has prohibited government officials below the rank of minister from buying big cars.[46]

Political change, in itself, can of course bring about sudden change in strategic implementation of alliances of foreign firms with host-country projects. This was evident in May of 1998 when President Suharto of Indonesia was ousted following economic problems and currency devaluation. The new government began reviewing and canceling some of the business deals linked with the Suharto family, including the cancellation of two water-supply privatization projects with foreign firms—Britain's Thames Water PLC and France's Suez Lyonnaise des Eaux SA. The Suharto family had developed a considerable fortune from licensing deals, monopolies, government "contracts," and protection from taxes.[47] Alliances with the family was often the only way to gain entry for foreign companies.

Cultural Influences on Strategic Implementation

Culture is one variable which is often overlooked when deciding on entry strategies and alliances, particularly when we perceive the target country to be familiar to us and similar to our own. However, cultural differences can have a subtle and often negative effect.

As many of Europe's largest MNCs—including Nestlé, Electrolux, Grand Metropolitan, Rhone-Poulenc—experience increasing proportions of their revenues from their positions in the United States, and employ over 2.9 million Americans, they have decided to shift headquarters of some product lines to the United States. As they have done so, however, there is growing evidence that managing in the United States is not as easy as they anticipated it would be because of their perceived familiarity with the culture. Rosenzweig documents some reflections of European managers on their experiences of managing U.S. affiliates. Generally, he has found that European managers appreciate that Americans are pragmatic, open, forthright, and innovative. But they also say that the tendency of Americans to be informal and individualistic means that their need for independence and autonomy on the job causes problems in their relationship with the head office Europeans; Americans simply do not take well to directives from a foreign-based headquarters. Resenzweig gives some comments from French managers below.[48]

FRENCH MANAGERS COMMENT ON THEIR ACTIVITIES IN THE UNITED STATES

- "Americans see themselves as the world's leading country, and it's not easy for them to accept having a European in charge."
- "It is difficult for Americans to develop a world perspective. It's hard for them to see that what may optimize the worldwide position may not optimize the U.S. activities."
- "The horizon of Americans often goes only as far as the U.S. border. As a result, Americans often don't give equal importance to a foreign customer. If a foreign customer has a special need, the response is sometimes: 'It works here, why do they need it to be different?'"
- "It might be said that Americans are the least international of all people, because their home market is so big."

Other European firms have had more successful strategic implementation in their U.S. plants by adapting to American culture and management styles. When Mercedes-Benz of Germany launched its plant in Tuscaloosa, Alabama, U.S. workers and German "trainers" had doubts. Lynn Snow, who works on the door line of the Alabama plant was skeptical whether the Germans and the Americans would mesh well. But now she proudly asserts that they work together determined to build a quality vehicle. Said Jurgen Schrempp, CEO of Mercedes' parent, Daimler Benz, "'Made in Germany'—we have to change that to 'Made by Mercedes,' and never mind where they are assembled."[49]

The German trainers recognized that the whole concept of building a Mercedes' quality car had to be taught to the American workers in a way that would appeal to them. They abandoned the typically German strict hierarchy and instead designed a plant in which any worker could stop the assembly line to correct manufacturing problems. In addition, taking their cue from Japanese rivals, they formed the workers into teams which met every day with the trainers to problem solve. Out the window went formal offices and uniforms, instead using casual shirts with personal names on the pocket. To add to the collegiality, gettogethers for a beer after work are common. "The most important thing is to bring together the two cultures," says Andreas Renschler, who has guided the M-Class since it began in 1993, "You have to generate a kind of ownership of the plant."[50] The local community has also embraced the mutual goals, often having beer fests, and including German-language stations on local cable TV.

The impact of cultural differences in management style and expectations is perhaps most noticeable and important when implementing international joint ventures. The complexity of a joint venture requires that managers from each party learn to compromise in order to create a compatible and productive working environment, particularly when operations are integrated.

Cultural impacts on strategic implementation are often even more pronounced in the service sector, because of many added variables, especially the direct contact with the consumer. Wal-Mart, for example, has not been immune to implementation problems overseas, particularly resulting from culture and lifestyle differences and from infrastructure problems. With its rapid global expansion efforts leading Wal-Mart to Indonesia, China, and South America, Wal-Mart has found that it cannot insist on doing everything "the Wal-Mart way." In Sao Paulo, for example, bumper-to-bumper traffic impedes timely delivery of merchandise. Also, because Wal-Mart doesn't own its distribution system, it loses its all-important logistic advantage. Often stores in Brazil process three hundred deliveries a day, compared with seven a day in the United States.[51] Add to the infrastructure problems, Wal-Mart's use of a bookkeeping system that failed to take into account Brazil's complicated tax system; failure to recognize postdated checks as the primary source of credit in Brazil since its currency problems; and merchandise errors such as American footballs instead of soccer balls, and you have an implementation plan that failed to take account of local culture and customs.[52]

In China, too, strategic implementation necessitates an understanding of the pervasive cultural practice of *guanxi* in business dealings. Discussed in previous chapters, *guanxi* refers to the relationship networks that "bind millions of Chinese firms into social and business webs, largely dictating their success."[53] Tapping into this system of reciprocal social obligation is essential to get permits, information, assistance to access material, and financial resources and tax considerations. Nothing gets done without these direct or indirect connections. In fact, a new term has arisen—*guanxihu*—which refers to a bond between specially connected firms that generates preferential treatment to members of the network. Without *guanxi*, implementing a strategy of withdrawal is even difficult. Joint ventures can get hard to dissolve and as bitter as an acrimonious divorce situation. Problems include the forfeiture of assets and the inability to gain market access through future joint venture partners—all experienced by Audi, Chrysler, and Daimler-Benz. For example,

> Audi's decision to terminate its joint venture prompted its Chinese partner, First Automobile Works, to expropriate its car design and manufacturing processes. The result was an enormously successful, unauthorized Audi clone, with a Chrysler engine and a First Automobile Works nameplate.[54]

E-Commerce Impact on Strategy Implementation

> With subsidiaries, suppliers, distributors, manufacturing facilities, carriers, brokers and customers all over the globe, global trade is complicated and fragmented. Shipments cross borders multiple times a day. Are they compliant with all the latest trade regulations? Are they consistently classified for each country? Can you give your buyers, customers and service providers the latest information, on demand?
>
> www.Nextlink.com 9.10.2001

As indicated in the quote above, global trade is extremely complicated. Deciding on a global strategy is one thing; implementing it through all the necessary parties and intermediaries around the world is a whole new level of complexity. Because of that complexity, many firms decide to implement their global e-commerce strategy by outsourcing the necessary tasks to companies that specialize in providing the technology to organize transactions and follow through with the regulatory requirements. These specialists are called **e-commerce enablers**; they can help companies sort through the maze of different taxes, duties, language translations, and so on, specific to each country. Such services allow small- and medium-sized companies to go global without the internal capabilities to carry out global e-commerce functions.

Conclusion

Cross-border strategic alliances are becoming increasingly common as innovative companies seek rapid entry into foreign markets and as they try to reduce the risks of going it alone in complex environments. Those companies which do well are those which do their homework and pick complementary strategic partners. Too many, however, get "divorced" because "the devil is in the details," which is what happens when "a marriage made in heaven" runs into unanticipated problems during actual strategic implementation.

INTERNET RESOURCES

Visit the Deresky companion Web site at http://prenhall.com/Deresky for this chapter's Internet resources.

SUMMARY OF KEY POINTS

1. Strategic alliances are partnerships with other companies for specific reasons. Cross-border, or global strategic alliances are working partnerships between companies (often more than two) across national boundaries, and increasingly across industries.

2. Cross-border alliances are formed for many reasons, including market expansion, cost- and technology-sharing, avoiding protectionist legislation, and taking advantage of synergies.

3. Technological advances and the resulting blending of industries, such as those in the telecommunications and entertainment industries, are factors prompting cross-industry alliances.

4. Alliances may be short- or long-term; they may be full global partnerships, or they may be for more narrow and specific functions such as research and development sharing.

5. Alliances often run into trouble in the strategic implementation phase. Problems include loss of technology and knowledge base to the other partner, conflicting strategic goals and objectives, cultural clashes, and disputes over management and control systems.

6. Successful alliances require compatible partners with complementary skills, products, and markets. Extensive preparation is necessary in order to work out how to share management control and technology and to understand each other's culture.

7. Strategic implementation—also called functional level strategies—entail setting up overall policies, administrative responsibilities, and schedules throughout the organization. Successful implementation results from setting up the structure, systems and processes of the firm, as well as the functional activities that create a "system of fits" with the desired strategy.

8. Differences in national culture and changes in the political arena or in government regulations often have unanticipated effects on strategic implementation.

9. Strategic implementation of global trade is increasingly being facilitated by e-commerce enablers—companies that specialize in providing the software and internet technology for complying with the specific regulations, taxes, shipping logistics, translations, and so on for each country with which their clients do business.

Chapter 8

Organizing Structure, Control Systems, and Labor Relations

Opening Profile: McDonald's in Moscow— A Decade of Control Challenges

We have proudly served millions of customers and are looking forward to working with our team of managers and crew to expand our operation to serve many more in communities across Russia.

KHAMZAT KHASBULATOV, PRESIDENT, MCDONALD'S IN RUSSIA, www.Mcdonalds.com, FEBRUARY 20, 2001.

As of 2001, McDonald's had 58 restaurants in the Moscow region, St. Petersburg, Nizhny Novgorod, Yaroslavl, Samara, and Kazan. The restaurants serve over 150,000 customers every day, and, since opening on January 31, 1990, they have served more than 250 million customers and more than 52 million Big Mac sandwiches.

It all started with a chance meeting between George Cohon, senior chairman, McDonald's Canada and a Soviet olympic delegation at the Olympic games in Montreal in 1976. It sparked 14 years of negotiations and culminated in the opening of the first McDonald's in Russia.

When the restaurant finally opened its doors in Moscow's busy Pushkin Square in January 1990, the largest agreement between the former Soviet Union and a food-service company became a reality. The 900-seat restaurant broke several of McDonald's previous records—30,000 Russians were served on opening day, and 1 million had been served by March. It took 12 years of negotiations by George A. Cohon, president and founder of McDonald's Restaurants of Canada, to open the doors in Pushkin Square. McDonald's has a 49 percent interest in the joint venture with the Moscow City Council Department of Food Service. In all, McDonald's Canada invested $50 million for construction and personnel training for the processing plant and the restaurant. They agreed to reinvest all their profits in Moscow for a chain of 20 restaurants.

The biggest control problem for McDonald's was that of quality control for its food products. Unlike its Western counterparts, this IJV has had to adopt a strategy of vertical

cont.

cont.

integration for its sourcing of raw materials. To control the quality, distribution, and reliability of its ingredients, McDonald's built a $40 million, 110,000-square-foot plant in a Moscow suburb to process the required beef, milk, buns, vegetables, sauces, and potatoes. The facility includes laboratories for testing to ensure compliance with quality and consistency standards. Peter Frings, an agronomist with McCain Foods Limited, was brought in to introduce the Russian farmers to the nonnative Russet Burbank potato used to make the famous McDonald's fries. Frings and other experts spent several months working on local farms to advise farmers on such aspects as increasing acreage yields and boosting overall quality.

Operational control was a considerable problem for McDonald's in this historic joint venture, specifically in regard to controlling the quality of food and service. The first challenge was the hiring and training of local employees; Craig Sopkowicz, McDonald's quality-control expert, was in charge of this. "We looked for applicants who lived close to the restaurant, among other things, in order to control the timeliness of employees," explains Sopkowicz. Most of the new hires were between 18 and 27 years old; this was usually their first job; teenagers seldom work in Russia because labor laws protect them from conflicts with school work. After selecting the 630-member crew, the all-important training and customer control began.

To be flexible when positions changed, the new crew was trained in all aspects of the restaurant's functions. Over 15,000 training hours were logged in by the new staff to ensure control similar to that in Western operations. In addition, Roy Ellis, the personnel specialist, had some concern about the employees' appearance and decided to construct an on-site laundry room. "It's more practical . . . and it means we can ensure our standards," explains Ellis. The four Russian managers (Khamzat Khazbulatov, Vladimir Zhurakovskij, Mikhail Sheleznov, and Georgij Smoleevskij) went through the same rigorous training that any other McDonald's manager would, enabling them to manage any of the 11,000 units worldwide. They went to McDonald's Institute of Hamburgerology in Toronto, Canada, for five months—a 1000-hour program; and from there they went to Hamburger University in Oakbrook, Illinois, for two weeks training along with 235 managers from around the world. The operating philosophy underlying the training can be summed up as QSC&V—quality, service, cleanliness, and value.

Innovative control procedures take place in front of the counter in the Moscow unit as well as behind the cash registers. To control for the timeliness of service, McDonald's tried to reduce the long waiting lines by hiring private security people to keep order and by using public-address systems to tell patrons how to place orders. In addition to verbal instructions, customers are given picture menus to simplify the ordering process. The Russian menu has also been streamlined to help speed up the service and the decision-making process. McDonald's has combated the growing black market problem by installing a one-door policy: This has eliminated large-scale pilferage, which usually occurs out the back door. A limit of ten Big Macs to each customer helps stop the black market sale to hungry customers anxiously waiting in line.

Top management at McDonald's anticipated difficulties with the setup and daily operations of this IJV and, indeed, had been working toward the opening day for 13 years. Through careful planning for the control of crucial operational factors, they solved the sourcing, distribution, and employment problems inherent in the former Soviet Union.

Over a decade later, in 2001, McDonald's Russia still imports chickens from France and cheese, fish, and apple segments from Poland, as well as potatoes—cut and frozen—from the Netherlands. Now a "chain" in Russia with 58 restaurants, McDonalds says it sources 75 percent of its supplies within the country, but that, for continued quality control, it opened its own "McComplex" farm to supply its outlets.

SOURCES: Updates by the author from: www.McDonalds.com, February 20, 2001; A. Jack, "Russians wake up to consumer capitalism," www.FT.com (*Financial Times*), January 30, 2001; earlier material adapted by the author from a term paper written by Gil George and Karsten Fetten, students at the State University of New York–Plattsburgh (December 1990). Copyright © 1993 by Helen Deresky.

Strategic plans are abstract sets of decisions that cannot affect a company's competitive position or bottom line until they are implemented. Having decided on the strategic direction for the company, international managers must then consider three of the key variables for implementing strategy—the organizational structure, the control and coordinating mechanisms, and the labor relations systems. The necessity of careful control systems to enable strategy implementation is illustrated in the opening profile "McDonald's in Moscow."

> There is no permanent organization chart for the world.... It is of supreme importance to be ready at all times to take advantage of new opportunities.
>
> ROBERTO C. GOIZUETA, (FORMER) CHAIRMAN AND CEO, COCA-COLA COMPANY.

ORGANIZATION STRUCTURE

Organizational structures must change to accommodate a firm's evolving internationalization in response to worldwide competition. Considerable research has shown that a firm's structure must be conducive to the implementation of its strategy.[1] In other words, the structure must "fit" the strategy, or it will not work. Managers are faced with how best to attain that fit in organizing the company's systems and tasks.

The design of an organization, as with any other management function, should be contingency based, taking into account the variables of that particular system at that specific point in time. Major variables include the firm's strategy, size, and appropriate technology as well as the environment in those parts of the world in which the firm operates. Given the increased complexity of the variables involved in the international context, it is no easy task to design the most suitable organizational structure and subsystems. In fact, research shows that most international managers find that it is easier to determine what to do to compete globally (strategy) than to decide how to develop the organizational capability (structure) to do it.[2] Additional variables affecting structural choices—geographic dispersion as well as differences in time, language, cultural attitudes, and business practices—introduce further layers of complication. We will show how organizational structures need to, and typically do, change to accommodate strategies of increasing internationalization.

EVOLUTION AND CHANGE IN MNC ORGANIZATIONAL STRUCTURES

Historically, a firm reorganizes as it internationalizes to accommodate new strategies. The structure typically continues to change over time with growth and with increasing levels of investment or diversity and as a result of the types of entry strategy chosen. Internationalization is the process by which a firm gradually changes in response to international competition, domestic market saturation, and the desire for expansion, new markets, and diversification. As discussed in Chapter 6, the firm's managers weigh alternatives and decide on appropriate entry strategies. Perhaps the firm starts by exporting or by acting as a licensor or licensee and then, over time, continues to internationalize by engaging in joint ventures or by establishing service, production, or assembly facilities, or alliances, abroad, moving into a global strategy. At each stage, the firm's managers redesign the organizational structure to optimize the strategy's chances to work, making changes in the firm's tasks and relationships and designating authority, responsibility, lines of communication, geographic dispersal of units, and so forth. This model of **structural evolution** has become known as the **stages model**, resulting from Stopford and Wells' research on 187 U.S. MNCs[2a]. Of course, many firms do not follow the stages model because they may start their internationalization at a higher level of involvement—perhaps a full-blown global joint venture without ever having exported, for example.

Even a mature MNC needs to make structural changes from time to time to facilitate changes in strategy—perhaps a change in strategy from globalization to regionalization (as discussed in Chapter 6) or an effort to improve efficiency or effectiveness. The reorganization of Aluminum Company of America (Alcoa), for example, split the company into smaller, more autonomous units. This reorganization gives more focus to growing businesses, such as automotive products, where the market for aluminum is strong. It also enables Alcoa to link businesses with similar functions that are divided geographically—that is, to improve previously insufficient communication between Alcoa's aluminum operations in Brazil and its Australian counterparts.[3]

The typical ways in which firms organize their international activities are shown in the following list. (Larger companies often use several of these structures in different regions or parts of their organization.) After discussing some of these structural forms, we will introduce new, transitional organizational arrangements.

- Domestic structure plus export department
- Domestic structure plus foreign subsidiary
- International division
- Global functional structure
- Global product structure

As discussed, many firms—especially the smaller ones—start their international involvement by exporting. For this they may simply use the services of an export management company, or they may reorganize into a simple **domestic structure plus export department**.

To facilitate access to and development of specific foreign markets, the firm can take a further step toward worldwide operations by reorganizing into a **domestic structure plus foreign subsidiary** in one or more countries (as illustrated in Exhibit 8-1). To be effective, subsidiary managers should have a great deal of autonomy and should be able to adapt and respond quickly to serve local markets. This structure works well for a company with one or a few subsidiaries located relatively close to headquarters.

With further market expansion, the firm may then decide to specialize by creating an **international division**, organized along functional, product, or geographic lines. With this structure, the various foreign subsidiaries are under the international division, and subsidiary managers report to its head, typically called

Exhibit 8-1
Domestic Structure
Plus Foreign
Subsidiary

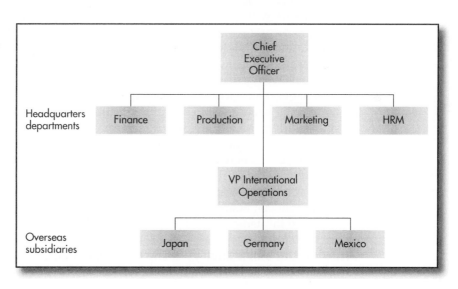

the vice president, international division, who in turn reports directly to the CEO of the corporation. The creation of an international division facilitates the beginning of a global strategy. It permits managers to allocate and coordinate resources for foreign activities under one roof and so enhances the firm's ability to respond, both reactively and proactively, to market opportunities. Some conflicts may arise among the divisions of the firm because more resources and management attention tend to get channeled toward the international division than toward the domestic divisions and because of the different orientations of various division managers.[4] Companies such as IBM, PepsiCo, and Gillette have international divisions, called, respectively, IBM World Trade, PepsiCola International, and Gillette International.

Integrated Global Structures

To respond to increased product diversification and to maximize benefits from both domestic and foreign operations, a firm may choose to replace its international division with an integrated global structure. This structure can be organized along functional, product, geographic, or matrix lines.[5]

The **global functional structure** is designed on the basis of the company's functions—production, marketing, finance, and so forth. Foreign operations are integrated into the activities and responsibilities of each department to gain functional specialization and economies of scale. This form of organization is used primarily by small firms with highly centralized systems. It is particularly appropriate for product lines using similar technology and for businesses with a narrow spectrum of customers. This structure results in plants that are highly integrated across products and that serve single or similar markets.[6]

Much of the advantage resulting from economies of scale and functional specialization may be lost if the managers and the work systems become too narrowly defined to have the necessary flexibility to respond to local environments. An alternative structure can be based on product lines.

For firms with diversified product lines (or services) that have different technological bases and that are aimed at dissimilar or dispersed markets, a **global product (divisional) structure** may be more strategically advantageous than a functional structure. In this structure, a single product (or product line) is represented by a separate division. Each division is headed by its own general manager, and each is responsible for its own production and sales functions. Usually, each division is a **strategic business unit** (SBU)—a self-contained business with its own functional departments and accounting systems. The advantages of this organizational form are market concentration, innovation, and responsiveness to new opportunities in a particular environment. It also facilitates diversification and rapid growth, sometimes at the expense of scale economies and functional specialization. H. J. Heinz Company CEO, William R. Johnson, came on board in April, 1998 and decided that the company should restructure to implement a global strategy. He changed the focus of the company from a multidomestic international strategy using the global geographic area structure, to a global strategy, using the global product divisional structure. His

Exhibit 8-2
Global Product
(Divisional)
Structure

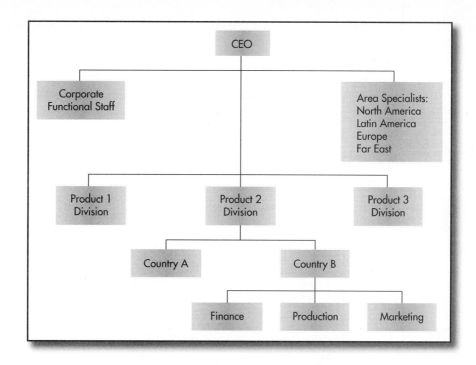

goal was further growth overseas by building international operations; this structure also readily incorporated their new specialty pet food division for marketing those products around the world.[7] Particularly appropriate in a dynamic and diverse environment, the global product structure is illustrated in Exhibit 8-2.

With the global product (divisional) grouping, however, ongoing difficulties in the coordination of widely dispersed operations may result. One answer to this, particularly for large MNCs, is to reorganize into a global geographic structure.

In the **global geographic (area) structure**—the most common form of organizing foreign operations—divisions are created to cover geographic regions (see Exhibit 8-3). Each regional manager is then responsible for the operations and performance of the countries within a given region. In this way, country and regional needs and relative market knowledge take precedence over product expertise. Local managers are familiar with the cultural environment, government regulations, and business transactions. In addition, their language skills and local contacts facilitate daily transactions and responsiveness to the market and the customer. While this is a good structure for consolidating regional expertise, problems of coordination across regions may arise. With the geographic structure, the focus is on marketing, since products can be adapted to local requirements. Therefore, marketing-oriented companies, such as Nestlé and Unilever, which produce a range of products that can be marketed through similar (or common) channels of distribution to similar customers, will usually opt for this structure.

Exhibit 8-3
Global Geographic Structure

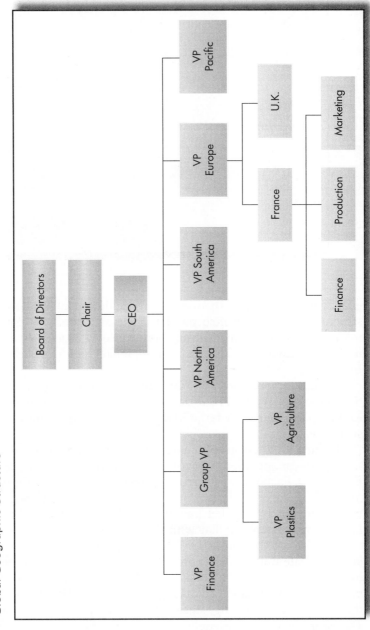

Nestlé SA, for example, uses this decentralized structure which is more typical of European companies, because:

> It is not Nestlé's policy to generate most of its sales in Switzerland, supplemented by a few satellite subsidiaries abroad. Nestlé strives to be an insider in every country in which it operates, not an outsider.
>
> www.Nestle.com, DECEMBER 7, 2000.

Grouping a number of countries under a region doesn't always work out, however, as experienced by Ford with its European Group; it soon discovered tensions among the units in Germany, Britain, and France resulting from differences in their national systems and culture and, in particular, management styles. Nevertheless, it has pursued its consolidation into five regionalized global centers for the design, manufacture, and marketing of 70 lines of cars around the world.[8] In 2001, under Ford's CEO Jacques Nasser—born in Lebanon and raised in Australia, Ford has a presence in over 200 countries, with 140 manufacturing plants.[9]

A **matrix structure**—a hybrid organization of overlapping responsibilities—is used by some firms, but has generally fallen into disfavor recently.

ORGANIZING FOR GLOBALIZATION

> If you misjudge the market [by globalizing], you are wrong in 15 countries rather than only in one.
>
> FORD EUROPEAN EXECUTIVE.[10]

No matter what the stage of internationalization, a firm's structural choices always involve two opposing forces: the need for **differentiation** (focusing on and specializing in specific markets) and the need for **integration** (coordinating those same markets). The way the firm is organized along the differentiation–integration continuum determines how well strategies—along a localization–globalization continuum—are implemented. This is why the structural imperatives of various strategies such as globalization must be understood to organize appropriate worldwide systems and connections.

As discussed earlier, global trends and competitive forces have put increasing pressure on multinational corporations to adopt a strategy of **globalization**—a specific strategy that treats the world as one market by using a standardized approach to products and markets. Recent examples of companies reorganizing to achieve globalization are the following:[11]

- **IBM**. Big Blue decided to move away from its traditional geographic structure to a global structure based on its 14 worldwide industry groups, such as banking, retail, and insurance, shifting power from country managers to centralized industry expert teams. IBM hopes the restructuring will help the company take advantage of global markets and break down internal barriers.
- **Bristol-Meyers Squibb**. The international drug company announced the formation of new worldwide units for consumer medicine businesses, such as Bufferin, and for its Clairol and hair-care products.

Organizing to facilitate a globalization strategy typically involves rationalization and the development of strategic alliances. To achieve rationalization, managers choose the manufacturing location for each product based on where the best combination of cost, quality, and technology can be attained. It often involves producing different products or component parts in different countries; typically, it also means that the product design and marketing programs are essentially the same for all end markets around the world—to achieve optimal economies of scale. The downside of this strategy is a lack of differentiation and specialization for local markets.

Organizing for global product standardization necessitates close coordination among the various countries involved. It also requires centralized global product responsibility (one manager at headquarters responsible for a specific product around the world), an especially difficult task for multiproduct companies. Henzler and Rall suggest that structural solutions to this problem can be found if companies rethink the roles of their headquarters and their national subsidiaries. Managers should center the overall control of the business at headquarters, while treating national subsidiaries as partners in managing the business—perhaps as holding companies responsible for the administration and coordination of cross-divisional activities.[12]

A problem many companies face in the future is that their structurally sophisticated global networks, built to secure cost advantages, leave them exposed to the risk of environmental volatility from all corners of the world. Such companies need to restructure their global operations to reduce the environmental risk that results from multicountry sourcing and supply networks.[13] In other words, the more links in the chain, the more chances for things to go wrong.

Comparative Management in Focus

The Overseas Chinese Global Network

The Chinese who left the mother country had to struggle, and that became a culture of its own. Because we have no social security, the Overseas Chinese habit is to save a lot and make a lot of friends.

LEE SHAU KEE, 65, REAL ESTATE DEVELOPER, HONG KONG (NET WORTH: $6 BILLION).[14]

Compared to the Japanese *keiretsu*, the emerging Chinese commonwealth is an interconnected, open system—a new market mechanism for conducting global business.[15] It is now becoming apparent to many business leaders who have finally figured out Japan's *keiretsu* that they "now need to understand a distinctively Chinese model, where tycoons cut megadeals in a flash and heads of state wheel and deal like CEOs."[16]

The "Chinese commonwealth" is a form of global network which has become the envy of Western multinationals. It is a network of entrepreneurial relationships spread across continents, though primarily in Asia. What is increasingly being referred to as the "big dragon of Greater China" includes mainland China's 1.3 billion citizens and over 55 million overseas Chinese—most of them from Taiwan, Indonesia, Hong Kong, and Thailand. It is estimated that the overseas Chinese control $2 trillion in liquid assets, and contribute about 80 percent of the capital for the PRC; if the overseas Chinese lived in one country, their GNP would exceed that of mainland China.[17] In addition, this "bamboo network," which transcends national boundaries, is estimated to contribute about 70 percent of the private sector in Malaysia, Thailand, Indonesia, and the Philippines."[18] Most observers believe that this China-based informal economy is the world leader in economic growth, industrial expansion, and exports. It comprises mostly midsize, family-run firms linked by transnational network channels. "These channels for the movement of information, finance, goods, and capital help to explain the relative flexibility and efficiency of the numerous ongoing informal agreements and transactions that bind together the various parts of the Chinese-based trading area.[19] The network alliances bind together and draw from the substantial pool of financial capital and resources available in the region—including those of entrepreneurial services in Hong Kong, technology and manufacturing capability in Taiwan, outstanding communications in Singapore, and vast endowments of land, resources, and labor in mainland China.[20]

The overseas Chinese, now models for entrepreneurship, financing and modernization for the world, and in particular for Beijing, are refugees from China's poverty, disorder, and communism. Business became the key to survival for those Chinese emigrants faced with uncertainties, hardships, and lack of acceptance in their new lands. The uncertainties, a survivor mentality, and the cultural basis in the Confucian tradition of patriarchical authority have led to a way of doing business which is largely confined to family and trusted friends. This business mentality and approach to life has led to many self-made billionaires among the overseas Chinese. Among them are Y. C. Wang, the Taiwanese plastics king, who had to leave school after the sixth grade, but taught himself what was necessary to develop a new industry. At 77, he still never takes a day off and views personal consumption as undue extravagance. His wife sneaks out his worn suits to the tailor to be copied and sneaks the new ones back into his closet.[21] The network of alliances of the ethnic Chinese is based on *guanxi*—personal connections—among families, business friends, and political associations, often rooted in the traditional clans. Massive amounts of cross-investment and trade are restricted primarily to families and long-standing connections, including those from the province of the PRC from which the overseas Chinese or their ancestors migrated. As examples, Chinese ties in Hong Kong have provided about 90 percent of the investment in the adjacent Guangong; and telephone calls from the special economic zone of Xiamen in the PRC to Taiwan now average 60 thousand a month, up from ten a month eight years ago.[22] The web of those connections has created an influential network that is the backbone of the East Asian economy.

The history, culture, and careful, personal approach to business of the overseas Chinese has led to some underlying values, which Kao calls "life-raft values," which have shaped a distinctive business culture. These values include thrift and a very high savings level, regardless of need, extremely hard work, trust in family before anyone else, adherence to patriarchal authority, investment based strictly on kinship and affiliations, a preference for investment in tangible goods, and an ever-wary outlook on life.[23] It is this shared web of culture and contacts that has spawned an intensely commercial and entrepreneurial network of capitalists and a dominant power in Asia. Two benefits of such a business culture are speed and patience. Because of their knowledge of and trust in their contacts, the overseas Chinese can smell profits quickly and make decisions even more quickly; a deal to buy a hotel in Asia can be completed in days, compared to months in the United States.[24] Patience to invest for the long term is an outcome of closely held ownership and management, often in a single family, so that outside shareholders are not demanding short-term profits. There is no doubt that sharing language and cultural bonds is a vital lubricant for business, especially with people in China, where there are few firm laws that businesspeople can rely on.[25]

Organizing to "Be Global, Act Local"

In their rush to get on the globalization bandwagon, too many firms have sacrificed the ability to respond to local market structures and consumer preferences. Managers are now realizing that—depending on the type of products, markets, and so forth—a compromise must be made along the globalization–regionalization continuum, and they are experimenting with various structural configurations to "be global and act local." Colgate-Palmolive's organization structure illustrates such a compromise. As described by Rosenzweig and illustrated in Exhibit 8-4, the primary operating structure is geographic, that is, localized. The presidents of four major regions—North America, Europe, Latin America, and Asia Pacific—report to the chief operating officer, while other developing regions such as Africa, Eastern Europe, the Middle East report to the chief of operations of international business development. Then that person reports to the CEO of Colgate-Palmolive, who oversees the centralized coordinating operations (that is, the "globalized" aspects), for technology, finance, marketing, human resources management, and so on.

Colgate-Palmolive's structure has evolved to this point to complement its evolving strategy. As described by Rosenzweig, at first, Colgate-Palmolive structured its international operations on a country-by-country basis, with the foreign subsidiaries each reporting directly to headquarters. With expansion into the 1950s, the structure was changed to a regional one, with regional presidents overseeing subsidiaries. But during the 1970s and 1980s there was increasing global competition in consumer goods, leading Colgate-Palmolive to strive more for global coordination than relying on geographic decentralization. Toward that end, the company reorganized in 1981, setting up a global business development unit to oversee and coordinate some worldwide operations and launch new products. And, as of 1994, the structure illustrated was a hybrid in order to seek the advantages of global coordination as well as local responsiveness.[26]

Levi Strauss is another example of a company attempting to maximize the advantages of different structural configurations. First, Levi has ensured its ability to respond to local needs in a different way, by allowing its managers to act independently. Levi's success turns on its ability to fashion a global strategy that doesn't snuff out local initiative. It's a delicate balancing act, one that often means giving foreign managers the freedom needed to adjust their tactics to meet the changing tastes of their home markets.[27] Second, Levi keeps centralized control of some aspects of its business but decentralizes control to its foreign operations, organized as subsidiaries. These subsidiaries are supplied by a global manufacturing network of Levi

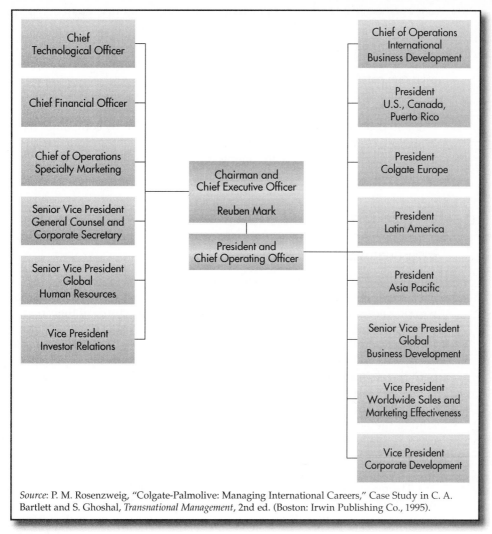

Source: P. M. Rosenzweig, "Colgate-Palmolive: Managing International Careers," Case Study in C. A. Bartlett and S. Ghoshal, *Transnational Management*, 2nd ed. (Boston: Irwin Publishing Co., 1995).

Exhibit 8-4
Colgate-Palmolive's "Glocal" Organizational Structure

plants and contract manufacturers. This approach allows local coordination and the flexibility to respond to ever-changing fashion trends and fads in denim shading.[28]

Another company's plan to go global by acting local does not involve changing the company's basic structure. Fujitsu, a Japanese high-technology conglomerate producing computers, telecommunications equipment, and semiconductors, has found a way to internationalize by proxy. Fujitsu has substantial stakes in two foreign companies that account for nearly half of Fujitsu's overseas revenues. They are Amdahl, a Silicon Valley maker of IBM-compatible mainframes, and International Computers Ltd. (ICL), Britain's biggest computer company. These firms are run by westerners, who are given free reign to manage and even compete against each other. The plan is doing so well that Fujitsu is looking for similar deals in Europe. As Fujitsu's president, Takuma Yamamoto, explains, "We are doing business in a borderless economy, but there is a rising tide of nationalism, and you have to find ways to avoid conflict. That is one reason we give our partners autonomy."[29]

While strategy may be the primary means to a company's competitive advantage, the burden of realizing that advantage rests on the organizational structure and design. Because of the difficulties experienced by companies trying to be a "glocal" company (global and local), researchers are suggesting new, more flexible organizational designs, involving interorganizational networks and transnational design.

EMERGENT STRUCTURAL FORMS

Interorganizational Networks

Whether the ever-expanding transnational linkages of an MNC consist of different companies, subsidiaries, suppliers, or individuals, they result in relational networks. These networks may adopt very different structures of their own because they operate in different local contexts within their own national environments.[30] By regarding the MNC's overall structure as a network of interconnected relations, we can more realistically consider its organizational design imperatives at both the global and the local levels. Exhibit 8-5 illustrates the network structure of N. V. Philips, a multinational with headquarters in the Netherlands and operating units in 60 countries. These units range from large subsidiaries, which might be among the largest companies in a country, to very small single-function operations, such as research and development or marketing divisions for one of Philips's businesses. Some have centralized control at Philips's headquarters; others are quite autonomous.

The network of exchange relationships shown in Exhibit 8-5, say Ghoshal and Bartlett, is as representative of any MNC as it is of Philips. The network framework makes clear that the company's operating units link vastly different environmental and operational contexts based on varied economic, social, and cultural milieus. This complex linkage highlights the intricate task of a giant MNC to rationalize and coordinate its activities globally to achieve an advantageous cost position while simultaneously tailoring itself to local market conditions (to achieve benefits from differentiation).[31] In fact, N. V. Philips has recently fallen far behind its Japanese competitors in productivity because of its lumbering bureaucratic organization, which it needs to simplify and decentralize.[32]

The Transnational Corporation Network Structure

To address the globalization–localization dilemma, firms that have evolved through the multinational form and the global company are now seeking the advantages of horizontal organization in the pursuit of transnational capability—that is, the ability to manage across national boundaries, retaining local flexibility

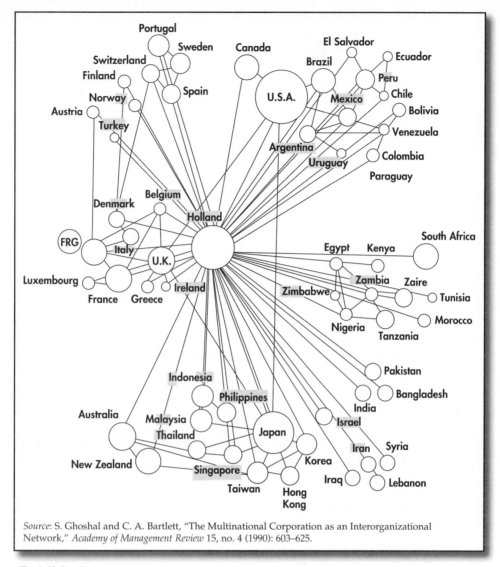

Exhibit 8-5
The Network Structure of N. V. Philips

Source: S. Ghoshal and C. A. Bartlett, "The Multinational Corporation as an Interorganizational Network," *Academy of Management Review* 15, no. 4 (1990): 603–625.

while achieving global integration.[33] This capability involves linking their foreign operations in a flexible way to each other and to headquarters, thereby leveraging local and central capabilities.[34] ABB (Asea Brown Boveri) is an example of such a decentralized horizontal organization. ABB operates in 140 countries with 1,000 companies with only one management level separating the business units from top management. ABB prides itself in being a truly global company, with 11 board members representing 7 nationalities. Thus, this structure is less a matter of boxes on an organizational chart and more a matter of a network of the company's units and their system of horizontal communication. This involves lateral communication across networks of units and alliances rather than in a hierarchy. The system requires the dispersal of responsibility and decision making to local subsidiaries and alliances. The effectiveness of that localized decision making depends a great deal on the ability and willingness to share current and new learning and technology across the network of units.

Whatever the names given to the organizational forms emerging to deal with global competition and logistics, the MNC organizational structure as we know it, with its hierarchical pyramid, subsidiaries, and world headquarters, is gradually evolving into a more fluid form to adapt to strategic and competitive imperatives. Facilitating this change, Kilmann points out, is the information technology explosion fueled by computers, fax machines, teleconferencing, the Internet, and so forth:

> Competitive companies in the future will be elaborate networks of people and information, each exerting an influence on the other. [These networks will comprise] a small hub of staff connected to each other by their physical proximity, which is electronically connected to global associates who help control assets and negotiate agreements to extend the company's business influence.[35]

In this new global web, the location of a firm's headquarters is unimportant. It may even be, says Reich, "a suite of rooms in an office park near an international airport—a communications center where many of the web's threads intersect."[36] The web is woven by decisions made by managers around the world, both decisions within the company and those between other companies. Various alliances tie together units and subunits in the web. Corning Glass, for instance, changed from its national pyramid-like organization to a global web, giving it the capability of making optical cable through its European partner, Siemens AG, and medical equipment with Ciba-Geigy.[37]

CHOICE OF ORGANIZATIONAL FORM

Two major variables in choosing the structure and design of an organization are the opportunities and need for (1) globalization and (2) localization. Exhibit 8-6 depicts alternative structural forms appropriate to each of these variables and to the strategic choices regarding the level and type of international involvement desired by the firm. This figure thereby updates the evolutionary stages model to reflect alternative organizational responses to more recent environments and to the anticipated competitive environments ahead. The updated model shows that, as the firm progresses from a domestic to an international company—and perhaps later to a multinational and then a global company—its managers adapt the organizational structure to accommodate their relative strategic focus on globalization versus localization, choosing a global product structure, a geographic area structure, or perhaps a matrix form. The model proposes that, as the company becomes larger, more complex, and

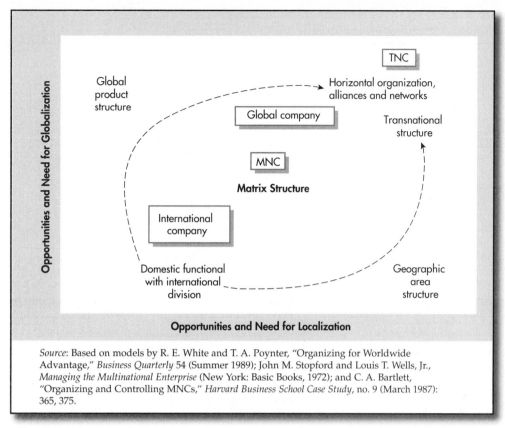

Exhibit 8-6
Organizational Alternatives and Development for Global Competition

more sophisticated in its approach to world markets (no matter which structural route it has taken), it may evolve into a **transnational corporation** (TNC). The TNC strategy is to maximize opportunities for both efficiency and local responsiveness by adopting a transnational structure that uses alliances, networks, and horizontal design formats. The relationships between choice of global strategy and the appropriate structural variations necessary to implement each strategic choice are further illustrated in Exhibit 8-7.

Organizational Change and Design Variables

When a company makes drastic changes in its goals, strategy, or scope of operations, it is usually quite clear that a change in organizational structure is called for as well. However, other, less obvious, indications of organizational inefficiency also signal a need for structural changes: conflicts among divisions and subsidiaries over territories or customers, conflicts between overseas units and headquarters staff, complaints regarding overseas customer service, and overlapping

Exhibit 8-7

Global Strategy–Structure Relationships

	MULTIDOMESTIC STRATEGY	INTERNATIONAL STRATEGY	GLOBALIZATION STRATEGY	TRANSNATIONAL STRATEGY
	Low ⟷ Need for Coordination ⟷ High			
	Low ⟷ Bureaucratic Costs ⟷ High			
Centralization of authority	Decentralized to national unit	Core competencies centralized; others decentralized to national units	Centralized at optimal global location	Simultaneously centralized and decentralized
Horizontal differentiation	Global area structure	International division structure	Global product group structure	Global matrix structure "Matrix in the Mind"
Need for complex integrating mechanisms	Low	Medium	High	Very high
Organizational culture	Not important	Quite important	Important	Very important

Source: C. W. L. Hill and E. R. Jones, *Strategic Management*, 5th ed. (Boston: Houghton Mifflin, 2001): 462.

responsibilities are some of these warning signals. Exhibit 8-8 lists some indications of the need for change in organizational design.

At persistent signs of ineffective work, a company should analyze its organizational design, systems, and work flow for the possible causes of those problems. The nature and extent of any design changes must reflect the magnitude of the problem. In choosing a new organizational design or modifying an existing structure, managers must establish a system of communication and control that will provide for effective decision making. At such times, managers need to localize decision making and integrate widely dispersed and disparate global operations.

Besides determining the behavior of the organization on a macro level (in terms of what divisions, subsidiaries, departments, and units are responsible for), the organizational design must determine behavior on a micro level. For example, the organizational design affects the level at which certain types of decisions will be made. Determining how many and what types of decisions can be made and by whom can have drastic consequences; both the locus and the scope of authority must be carefully considered. This centralization–decentralization variable actually represents a continuum. In the real world, companies are neither totally centralized nor totally decentralized: The level of centralization imposed is a matter of degree. Exhibit 8-9 illustrates this **centralization–decentralization continuum** and the different ways that decision making can be shared between headquarters and local units or subsidiaries. In general, centralized decision making is common for some functions (finance and research and development) that are organized for the entire corporation, whereas other functions (production, marketing, and sales) are more appropriately decentralized. Two key issues are the speed with which the decisions have to be made and whether they primarily affect only a certain subsidiary or other parts of the company as well.

Exhibit 8-8

When Is Change Needed?

- A change in the size of the corporation—due to growth, consolidation, or reduction
- A change in key individuals—which may alter management objectives, interests, and abilities
- A failure to meet goals, capitalize on opportunities, or be innovative
- An inability to get things done on time
- A consistently overworked top management that spends excessive hours on the job
- A belief that costs are extravagant or that budgets are not being met
- Morale problems
- Lengthy hierarchies that inhibit the exercise of strategic control
- Planning that has become increasingly staff-driven and is thus divorced from line management
- Innovation that is stifled by too much administration and monitoring of details
- Uniform solutions that are applied to nonuniform situations. The extreme opposite of this condition—when things that should or could function in a routine manner do not—should also be heeded as a warning. In other words, management by exception has replaced standard operating procedures

The following are a few specific indicators of *international* organizational malaise:

- A shift in the operational scope—perhaps from directing export activities to controlling overseas manufacturing and marketing units, a change in the size of operations on a country, regional, or worldwide basis, or failure of foreign operations to grow in accordance with plans and expectations
- Clashes among divisions, subsidiaries, or individuals over territories or customers in the field
- Divisive conflicts between overseas units and domestic division staff or corporate staff
- Instances wherein centralization leads to a flood of detailed data that is neither fully understood nor properly used by headquarters
- Duplication of administrative personnel and services
- Underutilization of overseas manufacturing or distribution facilities
- Duplication of sales offices and specialized sales account executives
- Proliferation of relatively small legal entities or operating units within a country or geographic area
- An increase in overseas customer service complaints
- Breakdowns in communications within and between organizations
- Unclear lines of reporting and dotted-line relationships, and ill-defined executive responsibilities

Source: Business International Corporation, *New Directions in Multinational Corporate Organization* (New York: Business International Corporation, 1981).

As noted, culture is another factor that complicates decisions on how much to decentralize and how to organize the work flow and the various relationships of authority and responsibility. In Part 4, we discuss more fully how cultural variables affect people's attitudes about working relationships and about who should have authority over whom. At this point, simply note that cultural variables must

Exhibit 8-9

Locus of Decision Making in an International Organization

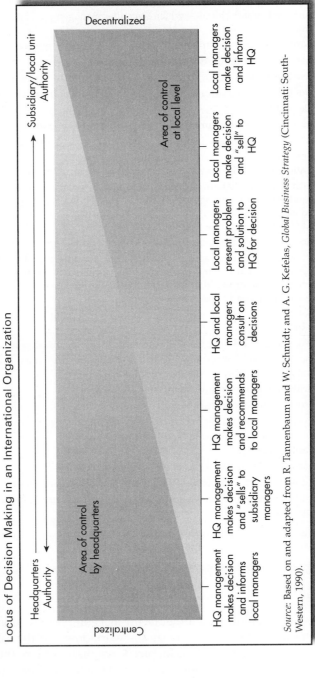

Source: Based on and adapted from R. Tannenbaum and W. Schmidt; and A. G. Kefelas, *Global Business Strategy* (Cincinnati: South-Western, 1990).

be taken into account when designing an organization. Delegating a high level of authority to employees in a country where the workers usually regard "the boss" as the rightful person to make all the decisions is not likely to work well. Clearly, managers must think through the interactions of organizational, staffing, and cultural issues before making final decisions.

In sum, there is no one best way to organize. Contingency theory applies to organizational design as much as to any other aspect of management. The best organizational structure is the one that facilitates the firm's goals and is appropriate to its industry, size, technology, and competitive environment. Structure should be fluid and dynamic and highly adaptable to the changing needs of the company. The structure should not be allowed to get bogged down in the **administrative heritage** of the organization (that is, "the way we do things around here," or "what we've always done") to the point that it undermines the very processes that will enable the firm to take advantage of new opportunities.

Most likely, however, the future for MNC structure lies in a global web of networked companies. Ideally, a company tries to organize in a way that will allow it to carry out its strategic goals; the staffing is then done to mesh with those strategic goals and the way the organizational structure has been set up. In reality, however, the existing structural factors often affect strategic decisions, so the end result may be a trade-off of desired strategy with existing constraints. So too with staffing: "ideal" staffing plans have to be adjusted to reflect the realities of assigning managers from various sources and the local regulations or cultural variables that make some organizing and staffing decisions more workable than others.

What may at first seem a linear management process of deciding on strategy, then on structure, then on staffing is actually an interdependent set of factors that must be taken into consideration and worked out as a set of decisions. In the next chapter, we will explore how staffing decisions are—or should be—intricately intertwined with other decisions regarding strategy, structure, and so forth. In fact, a unique set of management cadre and skills in a particular location can be a competitive advantage in itself, and so it may be a smart move to build strategic and organizational decisions around that resource, rather than risk losing that advantage. But first let's look at some other processes that are involved in implementing strategy which are interconnected with coordinating functions through organizational structure.

CONTROL SYSTEMS FOR GLOBAL OPERATIONS

> The establishment of a single currency makes it possible, for the first time, to establish shared, centralized accounting and administrative systems.
>
> FRANCESCO CAIO, CEO MERLONI ELETTRODOMESTICI, FABRIANO, ITALY.
> *HARVARD BUSINESS REVIEW*, JANUARY–FEBRUARY 1999.

To complement the organization structure, the international manager must design efficient coordinating and reporting systems to ensure that actual performance conforms to expected organizational standards and goals. The challenge is to coordinate far-flung operations in vastly different environments with various work processes and rules and economic, political, legal, and cultural norms. The feedback from the control process and the information systems should signal any necessary change in strategy, structure, or operations in a timely manner. Often, the strategy or the coordinating processes, or both, need to be changed to reflect conditions in other countries.

Monitoring Systems

The design and application of coordinating and reporting systems for foreign subsidiaries and activities can take any form that management wishes. MNCs usually employ a variety of direct and indirect coordinating and control mechanisms suitable for their organization structure. Some of the typical control methods used for the major organizational structures discussed here are shown in Exhibit 8-10. These are self-explanatory. For example, in the transnational network structure, decision-making control is decentralized to key network nodes, greatly reducing emphasis on bureaucratic control. Output control in this exhibit refers to the assessment of a subsidiary or unit based only on the results attained. Other specific mechanisms are summarized below.

Direct Coordinating Mechanisms

Direct mechanisms that provide the basis for the overall guidance and management of foreign operations include the design of appropriate structures (discussed earlier in this chapter) and the use of effective staffing practices (discussed in

Exhibit 8-10
Control Mechanisms in Multinational Organizational Structures

MULTINATIONAL STRUCTURES	OUTPUT CONTROL	BUREAUCRATIC CONTROL	DECISION-MAKING CONTROL	ORGANIZATION CONTROL
International division structure	Most likely profit control	Must follow company policies	Some centralization possible	Treated like other divisions
Global geographic structure	Profit center most common	Some policies and procedures necessary	Local units have autonomy	Local subsidiary culture often more important
Global product structure	Unit output for supply; sales volume for sales	Tight process controls for product quality and consistency	Centralized at product division headquarters	Possible for some companies but not always necessary
Transnational network structure	Used for supplier units and some independent profit centers	Less important	Few decisions centralized at headquarters; more decisions centralized in key network nodes	Organizational culture transcends national cultures; supports sharing and learning; the most important control mechanism

Source: Adapted from John B. Cullen, *Multinational Management* (Cincinnati: South-Western 2 ed., 2002): 288.

Chapter 9). Such decisions proactively set the stage for operations to meet goals, rather than troubleshooting deviations or problems after they have occurred. The opening profile describes how McDonald's Corp. successfully set up direct control systems in advance of its entry into Moscow.

Other direct mechanisms are visits by head-office personnel and regular meetings. Top executives from headquarters may use periodic visits to subsidiaries to check performance, troubleshoot, and help to anticipate future problems. International Telephone and Telegraph Corporation (ITT) holds monthly management meetings at its New York headquarters. Performance data are submitted by each ITT subsidiary general manager from around the world, and problems and solutions are shared.[38] The meetings allow each general manager to keep in touch with her or his associates, with the overall mission and strategy of the organization, and with comparative performance data and new problem-solving techniques. Increasingly, the tools of technology are being applied as direct mechanisms to ensure up front that operations will be carried out as planned, in particular in countries where processes such as efficient infrastructure and goods forwarding cannot be taken for granted. An example of this is the logistics monitoring system set up by Air Express International in Latin America to minimize its many problems there.[39] As an example of controlling (B2B) supply-chain processes and helping customers control their business, FedEx introduced a suite of e-business solutions for Asia (described in the accompanying *E-Biz Box*).

Indirect Coordinating Mechanisms

Indirect coordinating mechanisms typically include sales quotas, budgets, and other financial tools, and feedback reports, which give information about the sales and financial performance of the subsidiary for the last quarter or year.

Domestic companies invariably rely on budgets and financial statement analyses, but for foreign subsidiaries, financial statements and performance evaluations are complicated by **financial variables in MNC reports**, such as exchange rates, inflation levels, transfer prices, and accounting standards.

To reconcile accounting statements, MNCs usually require three different sets of financial statements from subsidiaries. One set must meet the national accounting standards and procedures prescribed by law in the host country—this set also aids management in comparing subsidiaries in the same country. A second set must be prepared according to the accounting principles and standards required by the home country. This set allows some comparison with other MNC subsidiaries. The third set of statements translates the second set of statements (with certain adjustments) into the currency of the home country for consolidation purposes, in accordance with Financial Accounting Standards Board (FASB) Ruling Number 52 of 1982. A foreign subsidiary's financial statements must be consolidated line-by-line with those of the parent company according to the International Accounting Standard Number 3, adopted in the United States.[40]

Researchers have noted comparative differences between the use of direct versus indirect controls among companies headquartered in different countries. One study by Egelhoff examined the practices of 50 U.S., U.K., and European MNCs over their foreign subsidiaries. It compared the use of two mechanisms—the assignment

Hong Kong, December 6, 1999—Federal Express Corporation ("FedEx"), the world's largest express transportation company, today unveiled a range of new e-commerce services. This new suite of services provides customers in Asia with tailored electronic-commerce solutions over the Internet that further streamline their supply chains and distribution systems.

"We believe that this new suite of customized solutions will enable FedEx customers in Asia to unlock the enormous potential for electronic commerce. These innovative new information technology solutions will be a tremendous boost to our e-commerce portfolio, facilitating business-to-business and business-to-consumer Internet commerce" said Rajesh Subramaniam, vice president, Electronic Commerce and Customer Services (ECCS), Marketing and Communications, FedEx Asia Pacific.

The FedEx suite of e-commerce services offers solutions for the differing needs of customers doing business on-line from virtual shopping and shipping to inventory management and procurement.

- Virtual Order Plus™: An electronic-commerce solution that enables a retailer to easily set up an electronic on-line storefront and provide its customers with a display of its goods, special deals and promotions. Customers can select goods and make payments in a variety of ways via a secure link and arrange shipping on-line.

- GIVSship™: An electronic-commerce solution that empowers merchants to use their order number to ship and track packages directly without leaving the merchant website.

- Global Inventory Visibility System™: An electronic inventory-management system that allows companies, using FedEx's warehouse logistics services, to efficiently access via the Internet updated information on inventory stock located virtually anywhere in the world. Companies can also place orders on-line to shi0 their stock from FedEx's warehouse to the customer.

- FullView™: An electronic-commerce solution that offers buyers and merchants an on-line business trading platform comprising integrated logistics, transportation and other value-added services and provides the flexibility of a one-stop shop for on-line supply chain management.

FedEx is a total-solutions provider offering an unparalleled worldwide transportation network interwoven with an extensive warehousing and information technology network. This suite of value-added services, enhanced by the Internet and new technology, serves to further strengthen FedEx's integrated capabilities.

"In today's increasingly competitive environment, companies are constantly looking for better and more efficient ways to do business. More and more, they are recognizing the importance of supply-chain management combined with e-commerce as a strategic weapon. The new FedEx electronic suite of services, with our unmatched reliability and unparalleled AsiaOne network, caters to the needs of both small and medium sized enterprises (SMEs) and large corporations, giving them powerful tools to win the competitive advantage" said Mr. Subramaniam.

Source: www.fedex.com, December 6, 1999. Copyright 1995–2001, Federal Express Corporation.

of parent-company managers to foreign subsidiaries and the use of performance reporting systems (that is, comparing behavior mechanisms with output reporting systems).[41] The results of this study show that considerable differences exist in practices across MNC nationalities. For example, says Egelhoff, U.S. MNCs monitor subsidiary outputs and rely more upon frequently reported performance data than do European MNCs. The latter tend to assign more parent company nationals to key positions in foreign subsidiaries and can count on a higher level of behavior control than their U.S. counterparts.[42]

These findings imply that the American system, which measures more quantifiable aspects of a foreign subsidiary, provides the means to compare performance among subsidiaries. The European system, on the other hand, measures more qualitative aspects of a subsidiary and its environment, which vary among subsidiaries, allowing a focus on the unique situation of the subsidiary but making it difficult to compare its performance to other subsidiaries.[43]

MANAGING EFFECTIVE MONITORING SYSTEMS

Management practices, local constraints, and expectations regarding authority, time, and communication are but a few of the variables likely to affect the **appropriateness of monitoring systems**. How transferable headquarters' practices and goals are probably depends on whether top managers are from the head office, the host country, or a third country. In addition, information systems and evaluation variables must all be considered when deciding on appropriate systems.

The Appropriateness of Monitoring and Reporting Systems

One example of differences in the expectations regarding monitoring practices, and therefore in the need for coordination systems, is indicated by a study of Japanese and American firms. Exhibit 8-11 shows the mean responses of the American and Japanese managers concerning budget control practices in their firms. Ueno and Sekaran say that their research shows that "the U.S. companies, compared to the Japanese companies, tend to use communication and coordination more extensively, build budget slack to a greater extent, and use long-term performance evaluations to a lesser extent."[44] Further, Ueno and Sekaran conclude that those differences in reporting systems are attributable to the cultural variable of individualism in American society, compared to collectivism in Japanese society. For example, American managers are more likely to use formal communication and coordination processes, whereas Japanese managers use informal and implicit processes. In addition, American managers, who are evaluated on individual performance, are more likely to build slack into budget calculations for a safety net than their Japanese counterparts, who are evaluated on group performance. The implications of this study are that managers around the world who understand the cultural bases for differences in control practices will be more flexible in working with those systems in other countries.

Exhibit 8-11

Mean Responses of American and Japanese Managers Regarding Their Budget Control Practices

VARIABLES	U.S. MEAN	JAPAN MEAN
Communication and coordination	4.03	3.70
Planning time horizons	3.51	3.52
Structuring of budgetary processes	2.95	2.90
Budget slack	3.08	2.89
Controllability of budgets	3.42	3.17
Budget performance evaluation time horizons	2.80	3.11

Response scale: 1–strongly disagree; 2–disagree; 3–neutral; 4–agree; 5–strongly agree

Source: Susumo Ueno and Uma Sekaran, "The Influence of Culture on Budget Control Practices in the U.S.A. and Japan: An Emprical Study," *Journal of International Business Studies* 23 (Winter 1992): 659–674.

The Role of Information Systems

Reporting systems such as those described in this chapter require sophisticated information systems to enable them to work properly—not only for competitive purposes, but also for purposes of performance evaluation. Top management must receive accurate and timely information regarding sales, production, and financial results to be able to compare actual performance with goals and to take corrective action where necessary. Most international reporting systems require information feedback at one level or another for financial, personnel, production, and marketing variables.

The specific types of functional reports, their frequency, and the amount of detail required from subsidiaries by headquarters will vary. Neghandi and Wedge surveyed the types of functional reports submitted by 117 MNCs in Germany, Japan, and the United States. They found that U.S. MNCs typically submit about double the number of reports than do German and Japanese MNCs, with the exception of performance reviews. German MNCs submit a few more reports than do Japanese MNCs. U.S. MNCs thus seem to monitor far more through specific functional reports than do German and Japanese MNCs. The Japanese MNCs put far less emphasis on personnel performance reviews than do the U.S. MNCs and the German MNCs—a finding consistent with their culture of group decision making, consensus, and responsibility.

Unfortunately, the accuracy and timeliness of information systems are often less than perfect. This is particularly so in less developed countries, where managers typically operate in conditions of extreme uncertainty. Government information, for example, is often filtered or fabricated; other sources of data for decision making are usually limited. Employees are not used to the kinds of sophisticated information generation, analysis, and reporting systems common in developed countries. Their work norms and sense of necessity and urgency may also confound the problem. In addition, the hardware technology and the ability to manipulate and transmit data are usually limited. The **adequacy of management information systems (MIS)** in foreign affiliates is a sticky problem for headquarters managers in their attempt to maintain efficient coordination of activities and consolidation of results. Another problem is the **noncomparability of performance data across countries**, which hinders the evaluation process.

The use of the Internet has, of course, made the availability and use of information attainable instantaneously. Many companies are starting to supply Internet MIS systems for supply-chain management. European partners Nestlé S.A. and Danone Group, world leaders in the food industry, set up Europe's first Internet marketplace for e-procurement in the consumer goods sector, called CPGmarket.com, saying:

> CPGmarket.com will enhance the efficiency of logistics while at the same time reducing procurement costs for businesses producing, distributing and selling consumer goods. CPG (based on mySAP.com e-business platform) allows companies not only to buy and sell, but also to access industry information. . . . Participants will benefit from a more efficient market, reducing costs through higher transaction efficiency and simplified processes.

www.Nestle.com, PRESS RELEASE, MARCH 21, 2000.

Evaluation Variables Across Countries

A major problem in the evaluation of the performance of foreign affiliates is the tendency by headquarters managers to judge subsidiary managers as if all of the evaluation data were comparable across countries. Unfortunately, many variables can make the evaluation information from one country look very different from that of another country due to circumstances beyond the control of a subsidiary manager. For example, one country may experience considerable inflation, significant fluctuations in the price of raw materials, political uprisings, or governmental actions. These factors are beyond the manager's control and are likely to have a downward effect on profitability. And yet, that manager may in fact have maximized the opportunity for long-term stability and profitability compared with a manager of another subsidiary who was not faced with such adverse conditions. Other variables influencing profitability patterns include transfer pricing, currency devaluation, exchange-rate fluctuations, taxes, and expectations of contributions to local economies.

Clearly, one way to ensure more meaningful performance measures is to adjust the financial statements to reflect the uncontrollable variables peculiar to each country where a subsidiary is located. This provides a basis for the true evaluation of the comparative return on investment (ROI), which is an overall control measure. Another way to provide meaningful, long-term performance standards is to take into account other nonfinancial measures. These measures include market share, productivity, sales, relations with the host-country government, public image, employee morale, union relations, and community involvement.[45]

> If you have to close a plant in Italy, in France, in Spain, or in Germany,
> you have to discuss the possibility with the state, the local communities,
> the trade unions; everybody feels entitled to intervene . . . even the
> Church.
>
> JACOB VITTORELLI, FORMER DEPUTY CHAIRMAN OF PIRELLI.

An important variable in organizing work, in control, and in strategic planning is that of the labor relations environment and system within which the managers of an MNE will operate in a foreign country. Differences in economic, political, and legal systems result in considerable variation in labor relations systems across countries. Pan-European firms, for example, are still dealing with disparate national labor and social systems as the EC directors wrestle with the goal of the harmonization of labor laws.[46] In addition, European businesses continue to be undermined by their poor labor relations and by inflexible regulations. As a result businesses are having to move jobs overseas to cut labor costs, resulting from a refusal of unions to grant any reduction in employment protection or benefits in order to keep the jobs at home.[47] As well, non-European firms wishing to operate in Europe have to carefully weigh the labor relations systems and their potential effect on strategic and operational decisions.

The term **labor relations** refers to the process through which managers and workers determine their workplace relationships.[48] This process may be through verbal agreement and job descriptions, or through a union-written labor contract which has been reached through negotiation in collective bargaining between workers and managers. The labor contract determines rights regarding workers' pay, benefits, job duties, firing procedures, retirement, layoffs, and so on.

The importance to the international manager of the prevailing labor relations system in a country is that it can constrain the strategic choices and operational activities of a firm operating there. The three main dimensions of the labor–management relationship which the manager will consider are: (1) the participation of labor in the affairs of the firm, especially as this affects performance and well-being; (2) the role and impact of unions in the relationship; and (3) specific human resource policies in terms of recruitment, training, and compensation.[49] Constraints take the form of (1) wage levels which are set by union contracts and leave the foreign firm little flexibility to be globally competitive; (2) limits on the ability of the foreign firm to vary employment levels when necessary; (3) limitations on the global integration of operations of the foreign firm because of incompatibility and the potential for industrial conflict.[50]

Organized Labor Around the World

Exhibit 8-12 shows the percentage of workforce in trade unions in industrialized countries. Notably, there is a trend of falling union membership. This trend is attributable to various factors, including an increase in the proportion of white-collar and service workers as proportionate to manufacturing workers, a rising

Exhibit 8-12

Trade Union Decline in
Industrialized Countries

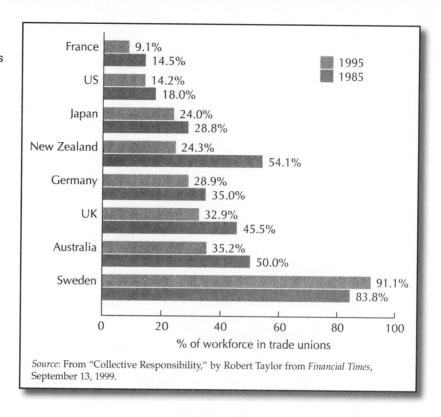

	1995	1985
France	9.1%	14.5%
US	14.2%	18.0%
Japan	24.0%	28.8%
New Zealand	24.3%	54.1%
Germany	28.9%	35.0%
UK	32.9%	45.5%
Australia	35.2%	50.0%
Sweden	91.1%	83.8%

% of workforce in trade unions

Source: From "Collective Responsibility," by Robert Taylor from *Financial Times*, September 13, 1999.

proportion of temporary and part-time workers, and a reduced belief in unions in the younger generations.[51] But the numbers do not show the nature of the system in each country. In most countries, a single dominant industrial relations system applies to almost all workers. But in both Canada and the United States there are two systems—one for the organized and one for the unorganized; each, according to Adams, has "different rights and duties of the parties, terms and conditions of employment, and structures and processes of decision making." Basically, in North America, an agent represents unionized employees whereas unorganized employees can only bargain individually, usually with little capability to affect major strategic decisions or policies or conditions of employment.[52]

The traditional trade union structures in Western industrialized societies have been in the following categories: industrial unions, representing all grades of employees in a specific industry and craft unions, based on certain occupational skills. More recently, the structure has been conglomerate unions, representing members in several industries, for example, the Metal Workers unions in Europe which cut across industries, and general unions, open to most employees within a country.[53] The system of union representation varies among countries. In the United States most unions are national and represent specific groups of workers—for example, truck drivers or airline pilots—so a company may have to deal with several different national unions. A single U.S. firm, rather than an association of firms representing a worker classification, engages in its own negotiations.[54] In

Japan, on the other hand, it is common for a union to represent all workers in a company. In recent years, company unions in Japan have increasingly coordinated their activities, leading to some lengthy strikes.

Industrial labor relations systems across countries can only be understood in the context of the variables in their environment and the sources of origins of unions; these include government regulation of unions, economic and unemployment factors, technological issues, and the influence of religious organizations.[55] Any of the basic processes or concepts of labor unions, therefore, may vary across countries, depending on where and how the parties have their power and achieve their objectives, such as through parliamentary action in Sweden. For example, collective bargaining in the United States and Canada refers to negotiations between a labor union local and management; but in Europe collective bargaining takes place between the employer's organization and a trade union at the industry level.[56] This difference means that the North American decentralized, plant-level, collective agreements are more detailed than the European industrywide agreements because of the complexity of negotiating a myriad details in multiemployer bargaining. In Germany and Austria, for example, such details are delegated to works councils by legal mandate.[57]

The resulting agreements from bargaining also vary around the world. A written, legally binding agreement for a specific period, common in Northern Europe and North America, is less prevalent in Southern Europe and Britain. In Britain, France, and Italy, bargaining is frequently informal and results in a verbal agreement valid only until one party wishes to renegotiate.[58]

Other variables of the collective bargaining process are the objectives of the bargaining and the enforceability of collective agreements. Because of these differences, managers in MNEs overseas realize that they must adapt their labor relations policies to local conditions and regulations. They also need to bear in mind that, while U.S. union membership has declined by about 50 percent in the last 20 years, in Europe overall membership is still quite high; it, too, has been falling, but from much higher levels.

Most Europeans are covered by collective agreements, whereas most Americans are not. Unions in Europe are part of a national cooperative culture between government, unions and management, and they hold more power than in the United States. In June, 1998, for example, thousands of employees at the state-owned Air France airline staged protests in Paris airports against proposed job and pay cuts, thereby causing the government to back down.[59]

Increasing privatization will make governments less vulnerable to this kind of pressure. It is also interesting to note that there are labor courts in Europe that deal with employment matters separately from unions and works councils. In Japan, labor militancy has long been dead, since labor and management agreed 40 years ago on a deal for industrial peace in exchange for job security. Unions in Japan have little official clout, especially in the midst of the Japanese recession.

In addition, there is not much to negotiate, since wage rates, working hours, job security, health benefits, overtime work, insurance, and so on are legislated. Local working conditions and employment issues are all that's left to negotiate. Also, the managers and labor union representatives are usually the same people, which serves to limit confrontation, as well as does the cultural norm of maintaining harmonious relationships. In the industrialized world, tumbling trade barriers are also reducing the power of trade unions, because competitive multinational companies have more freedom to choose alternative productive and sourcing locations. Most new union workers—about 75 percent—will be in emerging nations, like China and Mexico, where wages are low and unions are scarce.[60]

In China the government ordered all 47,000 foreign firms there to be unionized by mid-1996, and new foreign firms to establish unions in their first year of operation. This was in response to a sharp rise in labor tension and protests about poor working conditions and industrial accidents. The All-China Federation of Trade Unions claimed that "foreign employers often force workers to work overtime, pay no heed to labor-safety regulations and deliberately find fault with the workers as an excuse to cut their wages or fine them."[61] Much of the unrest has been caused by workers who are angry about losing their socialist safety net under the government's new economic reforms. Johnson & Johnson's three consumer-products manufacturing plants in China were already unionized and have a cooperative relationship with the unions.[62]

Convergence Versus Divergence in Labor Systems

In South Africa, the elimination of apartheid has given rise to a rapidly growing labor movement. The African National Congress is pro-union, and local unions receive assistance from the AFL-CIO branch in Johannesburg.[63]

Although no clear direction is evident at this point, political changes, external competitive forces, increased open trade, and frequent moves of MNCs around the world are forces working toward convergence in labor systems. **Convergence** occurs as the migration of management and workplace practices around the world results in the reduction of workplace disparities from one country to another. This occurs primarily as MNCs seek consistency and coordination among their foreign subsidiaries, and as they act as catalysts for change by "exporting" new forms of work organization and industrial relations practices.[64] It also occurs as harmonization is sought, such as for the EC countries, and as competitive pressures in free-trade zones, such as the NAFTA countries, eventually bring about demands for some equalization of benefits for workers.[65] It would appear that economic globalization is leading to labor transnationalism and will bring about changes in labor rights and democracy around the world.[66] In East European societies in transition to market economies, for example, newly structured industrial relations systems are being created.[67] Trends in industrial relations, such as the flattening of organizations and decline in the role of trade unions are viewed by many as global developments pointing to convergence in labor systems.[68]

Other pressures toward convergence of labor relations practices around the world come from the activities and monitoring of labor conditions worldwide by various organizations. One of these is the International Labor Organization (ILO)—comprising union, employer, and government representation—whose mission is to ensure that humane conditions of labor are maintained. Other associations of unions in different countries include various international trade secretariats representing workers in specific industries. These include the International

Confederation of Free Trade Unions (ICFTU) and the World Confederation of Labor (WCL). The activities and communication channels of these associations provide unions and firms with information about differences in labor conditions around the world.[69] One result of their efforts to provide awareness and changes in labor conditions was the pressure they brought to bear on MNCs operating in South Africa in the late 1980s. The result was the exodus of foreign companies and the eventual repeal of apartheid laws. Now there is a rapidly growing labor union movement there, thanks to the prounion African National Congress. In fact, the AFL-CIO opened an office in Johannesburg and assists the South African unions.[70]

Political and cultural shifts are also behind the new labor law in South Korea, as the country moves from a system founded on paternalism and authoritarianism to one based on more liberal values.[71]

Although there are forces for convergence in labor relations systems around the world, as discussed above, for the most part, MNCs still adapt their practices to a great extent to the traditions of national industrial relations systems, and there is considerable pressure to do so. Those companies, in fact, act more like local employers, subject to local and country regulations and practices. While the reasons for continued divergence in systems seem fewer, they are very strong; not the least of these are political ideology and the overall social structure and history of industrial practices. It is highly unlikely that China, for example, would accept Western practices which threaten their political ideology. And in the EU, where states are required to maintain parity in wage rates and benefits under the Social Charter of the Maastricht Treaty, there is still a powerful defense of cultural identity and social systems and considerable resistance by unions to comply with those requirements. Managers in those MNCs also recognize that a considerable gap often exists between the labor laws and the enforcement of those laws—in particular in less developed countries. Exhibit 8-13 shows the major forces for and against convergence in labor relations systems.

Exhibit 8-13

Trends in Global Labor Relations System

FORCES FOR GLOBAL CONVERGENCE ← CURRENT SYSTEM → FORCES TO MAINTAIN OR ESTABLISH DIVERGENT SYSTEMS	
Global competitiveness	National labor relations systems and traditions
MNC presence or consolidation initiatives	Social systems
Political change	Local regulations and practices
New market economies	Political ideology
Free-trade zones: harmonization (EU), competitive forces (NAFTA)	Cultural norms
Technological standardization, IT	
Declining role of unions	
Agencies monitoring world labor practices	

The NAFTA and Labor Relations in Mexico

About 40 percent of the total workforce in Mexico is unionized, with about 80 percent of workers in industrial organizations which employ over 25 workers, unionized. However, government control over union activities is very strong, and although there are some strikes, union control over members remains rather weak.[72] Multinational Corporations are required by government regulation to hire Mexican nationals for at least 90 percent of their workforce; preference must be given to Mexicans and to union personnel. However, in reality, the government permits hiring exceptions.

Currently, the only labor issues that are subject to a formal trinational review under the North American Foreign Trade Agreement (NAFTA) labor side pact are minimum wages, child labor, and safety issues. But foreign firms like Honeywell operating in Mexico are faced with pressures from various stakeholders in their dealings with unions. In fact, in early 1998 the AFL-CIO President John Sweeney flew to Mexico to try "to develop coordinated cross-border organizing and bargaining strategies."[73] Although no deals were made at that time, the seeds were sown in the direction of more open union activity and benefits for employees.

Many foreign firms set up production in Mexico at least in part for the lower wages and overall cost of operating there—utilizing the advantages of NAFTA—and the Mexican government wants to continue to attract that investment, as it has for many years before NAFTA. But Mexican workers claim that some of the large U.S. companies in Mexico violate the basic labor rights and cooperate with progovernment labor leaders in Mexico to break up independent unions. MNCs are believed by workers there to routinely use blacklists, physical intimidation, and economic pressure against union organization and independent labor groups that oppose Mexican government policies or the progovernment Confederation of Mexican Workers (CTM). GE, for example, has been accused of firing 11 employees in its Juarez plant who were involved in organizing a campaign for the Authentic Labor Front, Mexico's only independent labor group. The company was also accused of "blacklisting" union activists (a list of "undesirable employees" which is circulated around some employers). In February 1994, formal complaints were filed to the U.S. National Administration office of the Department of Labor by two U.S. unions—the Teamsters and the United Electrical, Radio, and Machine Workers Union. (U.S. unions have an interest in increasing wages and benefits in Mexico so as to offset some of the reasons that American companies take productive facilities there, along with U.S. jobs.) The Labor Department's National Administrative Office (NAO), which was set up by NAFTA to monitor labor policies in the United States, Mexico, and Canada, reviewed complaints that GE may have violated Mexican labor law. That office later ruled that those claims against GE were unsubstantiated; further they ruled that neither that office (the NAO) nor the Mexican counterpart could punish other nations for failing to address union-organization rights, although they could issue formal complaints.[74]

This incident illustrates the complexities of labor relations when a firm operates in other countries—particularly when there are linkages and interdependence among those countries, such as through NAFTA or the EC. Of interest are the differences in labor law in the private sector among NAFTA nations; for example, while the minimum wage in Mexico is far less than that in Canada or the United

States, there are a number of costly required benefits for Mexican workers, such as 15 days pay for a Christmas bonus and 90 days severance pay.

Comparative Management in Focus

Labor Relations in Germany

Codetermination has proved to be efficient, and several northern European countries adopted similar systems, while others, such as the UK, did not. The combined influences made dialogue between management and the workers a natural component of decision making.

ANDRE LEYSEN, CHAIRMAN, SUPERVISORY BOARD, AGLA GEBERT.[75]

Germany's **codetermination** law (*mitbestimmung*), which refers to the participation of labor in the management of a firm, mandates representation for unions and salaried employees on the supervisory boards of all large companies, and "works councils" of employees at every work site. Unions are well integrated into managerial decision making and can make a positive contribution to corporate competitiveness and restructuring; this seems different from the traditional adversarial relationship of unions and management in the United States.[76] However, the fact is that firms, in the form of affiliated organizations of companies, have to contend with negotiating with powerful industrywide unions. Employment conditions that would be negotiated privately in the United States, for example, are subject to federal mandates in Germany—a model unique in Europe.

Union membership in Germany is voluntary, usually with one union for each major industry, and union power is quite strong. Negotiated contracts with firms by the employers' federation stand to be accepted by firms who are members of the federation, or used as a guide for other firms; these contracts therefore result in setting the pay scale for about 90 percent of the country's workers.[77]

The union works councils play an active role in hiring, firing, training, and reassignment during times of reorganization and change.[78] Because of the depth of works council penetration into personnel and work organization matters, as required by law, their role has been termed by some as "comanager of the internal labor market."[79] This situation has considerable implications for how managers of MNCs plan to operate in Germany. IG Metall, for example, which is Germany's largest metalworking union, with 2.6 million workers, negotiates guidelines regarding pay, hours, and working conditions on a regional basis. Then works councils use those guidelines to make local agreements. IG Metall's proactive role on change illustrates the evolving role of unions by leading management thinking instead of reacting to it. In addition, management and workers tend to work together because of the structure of the unions. Indeed, Adams suggests that such institutional accord is a powerful factor in changing deeply ingrained cultural traits.

Codetermination has clearly helped to modify German managerial style from authoritarian to something more akin to humanitarian, without, it should be noted, altering its capacity for efficiency and effectiveness.[80] This system compares to the lack of integration and active roles for unions in the U.S. auto industry, for example, conditions that limit opportunities for change.

DaimlerChrysler, the German-American company headquartered in Germany, includes a works council in its decision making, as mandated by German law. This means that the company's labor representatives pay close attention to U.S. attitudes which may lead to changes in the tone of the collective bargaining processes. The two-tiered system of a supervisory and a management board will remain. It is likely that the company will exert pressure to bring down the high labor costs and taxes in Germany, under the threat of moving its plants elsewhere in order to remain globally competitive. With the DaimlerChrysler company accounting for about 13 percent of the DAX index of 30 German blue-chip stocks, U.S. shareholders and managers in the company will no doubt hold some power to bring about change and reduce operating costs in the company—and perhaps eventually in the country. Pay for German production workers is among the highest in the world, about 150 percent of that in the United States, and about ten times that in Mexico. German workers also have the highest number of paid vacation days in the world, and they prefer short work days. The stores are open very little in the evenings or weekends. Termination costs are also very high (including severance pay, retraining costs, time to find another job, etc.) and that is assuming that you are successful in terminating the employee in the first place, which is very difficult in Europe. This was brought home to Colgate-Palmolive when it tried to close its factory in Hamburg in 1996. The company offered the 500 employees an average of $40,000 each, but the union would not accept and eventually Colgate had to pay a much higher (undisclosed) amount.

The German model, according to Rudiger Soltwedel of the Institute for the World Economy at Kiel, holds that competition should be based on factors other than cost.[81] Thus the higher wage level in Germany should be offset by higher-value goods like luxury cars and machine tools which have been the hallmark of Germany's products. To the extent that the West German unions have established the high-wage, high-skill, and high-value-added production pattern, then, they have also become dependent on the continued presence of that pattern.[82] In recognition of that dependency, German auto firms are in the process of remaking themselves after the Japanese model—reducing supplies and cutting costs in order to compete on a global scale. However, this social contract which has underpinned Germany's manufacturing success is fraying at the edges as Germany's economy weakens under the $100 billion cost of absorbing East Germany, and under competitive EC pressures.[83]

Conclusion

The structure, control and coordination *processes* are the same whether they take place in a domestic company, a multinational company with a network of foreign affiliates, or a specific IJV. It is the extent, the focus, and the mechanisms used to organize those activities that differ. More coordination is needed in global companies because of uncertain working environments and information systems and because of the variable loci of decision making. Additional complexities attributable to varying labor relations systems compound the challenge of organization and control. These dynamic conditions confound the task of integrating and controlling a worldwide network of subsidiaries, joint ventures, and contractual relationships. Headquarters managers must design appropriate systems to take into account those variables and to evaluate performance.

SUMMARY OF KEY POINTS

1. An organization must be designed to facilitate the implementation of strategic goals. Other variables to consider when designing an organization's structure include environmental conditions, the size of the organization, and the appropriate technology. The geographic disperson of operations as well as differences in time, language, and culture affect structure in the international context.

2. The design of a firm's structure reflects its international entry strategy and tends to change over time with growth and increasing levels of investment, diversity, or both.

3. Global trends are exerting increasing pressure on MNCs to achieve economies of scale through globalization. This involves rationalization and the coordination of strategic alliances.

4. MNCs can be regarded as interorganizational networks of their own dispersed operations and other strategic alliances. Such relational networks may adopt unique structures for their particular environment, while also requiring centralized coordination.

5. The transnational structure allows a company to "be global and act local" by using networks of decentralized units with horizontal communication; this allows local flexibility while achieving global integration.

6. Indications of the need for structural changes include inefficiency, conflicts among units, poor communication, and overlapping responsibilities.

7. Coordinating and monitoring systems are necessary to regulate organizational activities so that actual performance conforms to expected organizational standards and goals. MNCs use a variety of direct and indirect controls.

8. Financial monitoring and evaluation of foreign affiliates is complicated by variables such as exchange rates, levels of inflation, transfer prices, and accounting standards.

9. The design of appropriate monitoring systems must take into account local constraints, management practices and expectations, uncertain information systems, and variables in the evaluation process.

10. Two major problems in reporting for subsidiaries must be considered: (1) inadequate management information systems and (2) the noncomparability across countries of the performance data needed for evaluation purposes.

11. Labor relations refers to the process through which managers and workers determine their workplace relationships. The labor relations environment, system, and processes vary around the world and affect how the international manager must plan strategy and organize work and control systems.

INTERNET RESOURCES

Visit the Deresky companion Web site at http://prenhall.com/Deresky for this chapter's Internet resources.

Chapter 9

Developing a Global Management Cadre

Opening Profile: Oleg and Mark —
Equal Work but Unequal Pay

Oleg and Mark are project managers at the Moscow sub-sidiary of a multibillion dollar international company. Oleg is a Russian local and Mark an American expatriate. Although raised in vastly different countries, they have a lot in common. Both 30 years old, they graduated from top universities in their home countries with degrees in economics, worked for prestigious organizations, went back to graduate school, and now work side by side in the challenging environment of Russia's emerging market economy. They work long hours, have unpredictable schedules, manage difficult relations with vendors and government agencies, and endure the ups and downs in corporate attitudes toward the Russian market. They often work together, attend the same meetings, face similar problems, and send countless faxes and e-mail messages to corporate headquarters in North America. They have an excellent relationship and often help each other. They like what they do and their boss sees a bright future for both of them.

But when the working day is over, the similarity abruptly ends. Mark drives his Volvo 760 to a lavish four-room apartment in the prestigious Southeast district of Moscow, while Oleg has to take the subway to the dark apartment in a run-down building downtown that he shares with four roommates. On the weekends Mark likes to dine out at the fashionable Savoy restaurant, where dinner costs as much as $200, while Oleg has a few beers at a friend's apartment. Three times a year Mark goes on vacation to Western Europe, the Caribbean, or the United States; once a year Oleg goes to see his parents in Siberia. Neither his car, apartment, or vacation costs Mark anything. They are part of the "hardship package" he receives as compensation for living in Moscow on top of his regular salary of U.S. $6,000 per month. Oleg does not get any "hardship benefits" since he is a local resident and his salary is $200 per month.

Says Oleg: "I like my job and I like the people I work with. I think we have a great organization here in Moscow. Most of our expatriates are very open and knowledgeable. I think we learn a lot from each other and the company benefits from having this multinational team.

"My compensation? Well, it's a bit frustrating to know that your buddies, who do the same work you do and who you often help, since many of them don't speak Russian, make 30 times more than you do. This summer we had an intern from an American business school, who worked under me. He used to take me out for lunch to hard-currency restaurants and pay as much as my monthly salary for it! He was a nice guy, but I don't think our relations were quite normal, because I could not even buy a bottle of wine for that lunch, and he knew it.

"But at work I don't think about it. I'm too busy to think like that. Sometimes, late at night, some crazy thoughts come to my mind: "Gee, something must be wrong—they treat you like a second-class citizen, cheap labor, they exploit you." ... But the next morning, I am up for work and those thoughts are gone. How long will my patience last? I don't know."

According to the company's managing director for Russia: "Some of our Russian managers, such as Oleg, are equally, if not better qualified than expatriates. They perfectly understand our business and they are truly bilingual, while most of our expatriates can barely speak Russian. We are very fortunate to have these Russian employees—their contribution is hard to overestimate. Compensation? We pay them what the market tells us here in Moscow. Yes, it is extremely low pay according to Western standards, but why should I pay a manager $5,000 if I can hire him for $200? Are they bothered by the inequity? I don't think so. I haven't heard any complaints so far, and I think we have very good relations among Russians and expatriates."

Mark comments, "Oleg is a great guy. We get along well, he helps me a lot, especially with my Russian. Do I feel sorry for him? No, I think he has a bright future. One day he will manage this subsidiary. As far as money goes, we live in a market economy. I was hired in the United States and what I get is what the job market pays there. It's different in Russia, so Oleg is being compensated differently. And I think he makes more than Russians working for Russian organizations. Plus, one of the reasons why our company is here is the cheap, skilled labor, and we've got to take advantage of this."

SOURCE: Sheila M. Puffer and Stanislav V. Shekshnia, "Compensating Nationals in Post Communist Russia; The Fit Between Culture and Compensation Systems" (Paper presented at the Annual Academy of International Business Conference, Boston, November 1994). Used with permission.

[In the new millennium], the caliber of the people will be the only source of competitive advantage.

ALLAN HALCROW, EDITOR, *PERSONNEL JOURNAL*, FEBRUARY, 1996.

Of the 100 top UK firms surveyed by Cendant International Assignment Services, 63 reported failed foreign assignments.

www.expat.FT.com, MARCH 5, 2001.

This chapter's Opening Profile describes a contemporary problem of salary differentials between expatriates and their counterpart host-country managers. There are many challenges to the human resource management function of any organization, domestic or international. However, given the greater complexity of managing international operations, the need to ensure high-quality management is even more critical than in domestic operations.

A vital component of implementing global strategy is **international human resource management** (IHRM). IHRM is increasingly being recognized as a major determinant of success or failure in international business. In fact, in a highly competitive global economy, where the other factors of production—capital, technology, raw materials and information—are increasingly able to be duplicated, "the caliber of the people in an organization will be the only source of sustainable competitive advantage available to U.S. companies.[1] Corporations operating overseas need to pay careful attention to this most critical resource, which also provides control over other resources. Most U.S. multinationals underestimate the importance of the human resource planning function in the selection, training, acculturation, and evaluation of managers assigned abroad. And yet the increasing significance of this resource is evidenced by the numbers. Over 37,000 MNCs are currently in business worldwide. They control over 200,000 foreign affiliates and have over 73 million employees. In the United States, foreign MNCs employ three million Americans—over 10 percent of the U.S. manufacturing workforce.[2] In addition, about 80 percent of mid- and large-size U.S. companies send managers abroad and most plan to increase that number.[3] The National Foreign Trade Council (NFTC) estimates that 300,000 U.S. expatriates are on assignment at any given time. Of those companies responding to Arthur Andersen's Global Best in Class Study . . .

> Those companies generate 43 percent of their revenues outside their headquarters country; consequently, they need expatriates who can support their expansion through both technical expertise and cultural understanding.[4]

However, recent advances in technology are enabling firms to effectively and efficiently manage the IHRM function and maximize the firm's global management cadre, as illustrated in the accompanying *E-Biz Box.*

At the first level of planning, decisions are required on the staffing policy suitable for a particular kind of business, its global strategy, and its geographic locations. Key issues involve the difficulty of control in geographically dispersed operations, the need for local decision making independent of the home office, and the suitability of managers from alternate sources.

The interdependence of strategy, structure, and staffing is particularly worth noting. Ideally, the desired strategy of the firm should dictate the organizational structure and staffing modes considered most effective for implementing that strategy. In reality, however, there is usually considerable interdependence among those functions. Existing structural constraints often affect strategic decisions; similarly, staffing constraints or unique sets of competences in management come into play in organizational and sometimes strategic decisions. It is thus important to achieve a system of fits among those variables that facilitates strategic implementation.

Companies operating in several countries need to globalize the human resource management systems (HRMS). Compelling reasons for doing so include the need to get an accurate count of the international workforce, to monitor expatriates, to track and analyze employee benefits, to evaluate compensation models, and to streamline payroll. MNCs also need to access data on knowledge and abilities, make up-to-date information easily accessible to line managers, and study career planning and succession planning models. Creating a global HRMS, however, is not an easy task. The different laws, cultures, business practices and technological limitations of various countries have to be taken into consideration.

Michael P. Corey, head of human resource (HR) systems for British Airways, knows how challenging it is to coordinate HRMS when your company has a presence in 83 countries. Without efficient hardware, software, and HR strategies to back it all up, the corporate data highway can easily resemble a one-lane, unpaved roadway in a developing nation: chaotic, crowded and swarming with obstacles. But Corey is adamant about implementing a system that provides HR with the tools to truly excel. "In an era of intense competition and pressure, at a time when HR must provide value, it's essential to automate and streamline as much as possible," he explains. With more than 50,000 employees working worldwide, and many of them in a different location every day of the week, it's no simple task.

When HR needs to notify employees of a change in benefits or policy, for example, many of the workers are 40,000 feet above the earth. When it needs to track headcount or update employee records, it has to deal with 24 time zones and dozens of languages and cultures. In addition, systems and technologies that work in one place can come to a grinding halt elsewhere. Yet British Airways' automated system handles recruiting, benefits, headcount, basic record keeping and an array of other functions—cutting across technology platforms and breaking language barriers. Moreover, the system, dubbed ACHORD (Airline Corporate Human and Organisation Resources Database), links to 35 other systems that require staff data within British Airways. Plans are now under way to link to 40 additional business systems.

When a manager in Kuala Lumpur needs information on terminations or company share schemes, it's accessible within seconds. When an HR specialist in New York requires data on pensions or concessional travel arrangements, it's visible in a flash. With a network of IBM mainframe computers linked to PCs and dumb terminals, data flows seamlessly between offices and across national boundaries. What's more, the worldwide network has almost eliminated duplicate data input, paperwork, disks, and delays in processing work. "It fits into the concept of reengineering and making HR accountable and involved in corporate matters," says Corey. "It provides us with a powerful tool."

SOURCE: Adapted from: S. Greengard, "When HRMS Goes Global: Managing the Data Highway," *Personnel Journal* 74, no. 6 (June 1995): 90–91.

> We found the most successful formula is to hire people in-country and then bring them to our U.S. headquarters to get acquainted and have them interact with our organization.
>
> STUART MATHISON, VICE PRESIDENT STRATEGIC PLANNING,
> SPRINT INTERNATIONAL, 1995.

Alternate philosophies of managerial staffing abroad are known as the ethnocentric, polycentric, regiocentric, and global approaches. Firms using an **ethnocentric staffing approach** fill key managerial positions with people from headquarters—that is, **parent-country nationals (PCNs)**. Among the advantages of this approach, PCNs are familiar with company goals, products, technology, policies, and procedures, and they know how to get things accomplished through headquarters. This policy is likely to be used where a company notes the inadequacy of local managerial skills and determines a high need to maintain close communication and coordination with headquarters. It is also the preferred choice when the organization has been structured around a centralized approach to globalization and is primarily at the internationalization stage of strategic expansion.

Frequently, companies use PCNs for the top management positions in the foreign subsidiary—in particular, the chief executive officer (CEO) and the chief financial officer (CFO)—to maintain close control. PCNs are usually preferable where a high level of technical capability is required. They are also chosen for new international ventures requiring managerial experience in the parent company and where there is a concern for loyalty to the company rather than to the host country: in cases, for example, where proprietary technology is used extensively.

Disadvantages of the ethnocentric approach include (1) the lack of opportunities or development for local managers, thereby decreasing their morale and their loyalty to the subsidiary, and (2) the poor adaptation and lack of effectiveness of expatriates in foreign countries. Procter & Gamble, for example, routinely appointed managers from its headquarters for foreign assignments for many years. After several unfortunate experiences in Japan, the firm realized that such a practice was insensitive to local cultures and also underutilized its pool of high-potential non-American managers.[5] Further, an ethnocentric recruiting approach does not enable the company to take advantage of its worldwide pool of management skill. This approach also serves to perpetuate particular personnel selections and other decision-making processes because the same types of people are making the same types of decisions.

With a **polycentric staffing approach**, local managers—**host-country managers (HCNs)**—are hired to fill key positions in their own country. This approach is more likely to be effective when implementing a multinational strategy. If a company wants to "act local," there are obvious advantages to staffing with HCNs. These managers are naturally familiar with the local culture, language, and ways of doing business, and they already have many contacts in place. HCNs are more likely to be accepted by people both inside and outside the subsidiary, and they provide role models for other upwardly mobile personnel.

As far as cost, it is usually less expensive for a company to hire a local manager than to transfer one from headquarters, frequently with a family and often at a higher rate of pay. Transferring from headquarters is a particularly expensive policy when it turns out that the manager and her or his family do not adjust and have to be transferred home prematurely. In fact, rather than building their own facilities, some companies acquire foreign firms as a means of obtaining qualified local personnel. Local managers also tend to be instrumental in staving off or more effectively dealing with problems in sensitive political situations. Some countries, in fact, have legal requirements that a specific proportion of the firm's top managers must be citizens of that country.

One disadvantage of a polycentric staffing policy is the difficulty of coordinating activities and goals between the subsidiary and the parent company, including the potentially conflicting loyalties of the local manager. Poor coordination among subsidiaries of a multinational firm could constrain strategic options. An additional drawback of this policy is that the headquarters managers of multinational firms will not gain the overseas experience necessary for any higher positions in the firm that require the understanding and coordination of subsidiary operations.

In the **global staffing approach**, the best managers are recruited from within or outside of the company, regardless of nationality—a practice used for some time by many European multinationals. Recently, as more major U.S. companies adopt a global strategic approach, they are also considering foreign executives for their top positions. General Motors hired J. Ignacio Lopez de Arriortua as vice president for worldwide purchasing, Xerox hired Vittorio Cassoni as executive vice president, and Esprit de Corp hired Fritz Ammann as president.[6]

There are several important advantages of a global staffing approach. First, this policy provides a greater pool of qualified and willing applicants from whom to choose, which, in time, results in further development of a global executive cadre. A further advantage is that the skills and experiences that those managers use and transfer throughout the company result in a pool of shared learning, which is necessary for the company to compete globally. Second, where third-country nationals (TCNs) are used to manage subsidiaries, they usually bring more cultural flexibility and adaptability—as well as bilingual or multilingual skills—to a situation than parent-country nationals, especially if they are from a similar cultural background as the host-country coworkers and are accustomed to moving around. In addition, when TCNs are placed in key positions, they are perceived by employees as an acceptable compromise between headquarters and local managers, which works to reduce resentment. Third, it can be more cost-effective to transfer and pay managers from some countries than from others because their pay scale and benefits packages are lower. Indeed, those firms with a truly global staffing orientation are phasing out the entire ethnocentric concept of a home or host country; and as part of that focus, the term **transpatriates** is increasingly replacing that of expatriates.[7] Firms such as Philips, Heinz, Unilever, IBM, and ABB, have a global staffing approach, which makes them highly visible and seems to indicate a trend.[8]

Generally, it seems that "the more distant geographically and culturally the subsidiary, the more expatriates are used in key positions, especially in less developed countries."[9] Clearly, this situation arises out of concern about uncertainty and the ability to control implementation of the corporation's goals. However, given the generally accepted consensus that staffing, along with structure and systems must "fit" the desired strategy,[10] firms desiring a truly global posture should adopt a global staffing approach. That is easier said than done. As shown in Exhibit 9-1, such an approach requires the firm to overcome barriers such as the availability and willingness of high-quality managers to transfer frequently around the world, dual career constraints, time and cost constraints, conflicting requirements of host governments, and ineffective human resource management policies.

In a **regiocentric staffing approach**, recruiting is done on a regional basis— say within Latin America for a position in Chile. This staffing approach can produce a specific mix of PCNs, HCNs, and TCNs, according to the needs of the company or the product strategy.[11]

What factors influence the choice of staffing policy? Among them are the strategy and organizational structure of the firm as well as the factors related to the particular subsidiary (such as the duration of the particular foreign operation, the types of technology used, and the production and marketing techniques necessary). Factors related to the host country also play a part (such as the level of economic and technological development, political stability, regulations regarding ownership and staffing, and the sociocultural setting).[12] As a practical matter, however, the choice often depends on the availability of qualified managers in the

Exhibit 9-1

Maintaining a Globalization Momentum Through a Global Staffing Policy

Source: Adapted from D. Welch, "HRM Implications of Globalization," *Journal of General Management* 19, no. 4 (Summer 1994): 52–69.

host country. Most MNCs use a greater proportion of PCNs (also called **expatriates**) in top management positions, staffing middle- and lower-management positions with increasing proportions of HCNs ("inpatriates") as one moves down the organizational hierarchy. The choice of staffing policy has a considerable influence on organizational variables in the subsidiary, such as the locus of decision-making authority, the methods of communication, and the perpetuation of human resource management practices. These variables are illustrated in Exhibit 9-2.

Exhibit 9-2
Relationships Among Strategic Mode, Organizational Variables, and Staffing Orientation

ASPECTS OF THE ENTERPRISE	ORIENTATION			
	ETHNOCENTRIC	POLYCENTRIC	REGIOCENTRIC	GLOBAL
Primary Strategic Orientation/Stage	International	Multidomestic	Regional	Transnational
Perpetuation (recruiting, staffing, development)	People of home country developed for key positions everywhere in the world	People of local nationality developed for key positions in their own country	Regional people developed for key positions anywhere in the region	Best people everywhere in the world developed for key positions everywhere in the world
Complexity of organization	Complex in home country, simple in subsidiaries	Varied and independent	Highly interdependent on a regional basis	"Global Web": complex, independent, worldwide alliances/network
Authority; decision making	High in headquarters	Relatively low in headquarters	High regional headquarters and/or high collaboration among subsidiaries	Collaboration of headquarters and subsidiaries around the world
Evaluation and control	Home standards applied to people and performance	Determined locally	Determined regionally	Globally integrated
Rewards	High in headquarters; low in subsidiaries	Wide variation; can be high or low rewards for subsidiary performance	Rewards for contribution to regional objectives	Rewards to international and local executives for reaching local and worldwide objectives based on global company goals
Communication; information flow	High volume of orders, commands, advice to subsidiaries	Little to and from headquarters; little among subsidiaries	Little to and from corporate headquarters, but may be high to and from regional headquarters and among countries	Horizontal; network relations
Geographic identification	Nationality of owner	Nationality of host country	Regional company	Truly global company, but identifying with national interests ("glocal")

Source: Updated and adapted by H. Deresky in 1998, from original work by D. A. Heenan and H. V. Perlmutter, *Multinational Organization Development* (Reading, MA: Addison Wesley, 1979): 18–19.

The conclusions drawn by the researchers some time ago are still valid today. The ethnocentric staffing approach, for example, usually results in a higher level of authority and decision making in headquarters compared to the polycentric approach.[13]

A study by Rochelle Kopp found that ethnocentric staffing and policies are associated with a higher incidence of international human resource management problems. Exhibit 9-3A shows the breakdown of staffing among PCNs, HCNs and TCNs of the 81 Japanese, European, and American companies studied. In addition, Kopp found that Japanese firms scored considerably lower than European and American firms in their practice of implementing policies such as preparing local nationals for advancement and keeping inventory of their managers around the world for development purposes. As a result of these ethnocentric practices, Japanese firms seem to experience various IHRM problems, such as high turnover of local employees, more than European and American firms, as shown in Exhibit 9-3B.

Without exception, all phases of human resources management should support the desired strategy of the firm.[14] In the staffing phase, having the right people in the right places at the right times is a key ingredient to success in international operations. An effective managerial cadre can be a distinct competitive advantage for a firm. How the "right" selections are made is the focus of the next section.

GLOBAL SELECTION

The initial phase of setting up criteria for global selection, then, is to consider which overall staffing approach or approaches would most likely support the company's strategy, as discussed above, such as HCNs for localization (multilocal) strategic approach and transpatriates for globalization. These are typically just starting points using idealized criteria, however; in reality other factors creep into the process, such as host-country regulations, stage of internationalization, and—most often—who is both suitable and available for the position. It is also vital to integrate long-term strategic goals into the selection process and development process, especially when rapid global expansion is intended. Insufficient projection of staffing needs for global assignments will likely result in constrained strategic opportunities because of a shortage of experienced managers suitable to place in those positions.

The selection of personnel for overseas assignments is a complex process. The criteria for selection are based on the same success factors as in the domestic setting, but additional criteria must be considered, related to the specific circumstances of each international position. Unfortunately, many personnel directors have a long-standing, ingrained practice of selecting potential expatriates simply on the basis of their domestic track record and their technical expertise.[15] Too often overlooked is the need to ascertain whether potential expatriates have the necessary cross-cultural awareness and interpersonal skills for the position. It is also important to assess whether the candidate's personal and family situation is such that everyone is likely to adapt to the local culture. There are five categories

Exhibit 9-3A
Nationality of Top Managers in Overseas Operations

HEADQUARTERS COUNTRY		% HOME-COUNTRY NATIONALS	% LOCAL NATIONALS	% THIRD-COUNTRY NATIONALS
Japan	(n = 26)	74%	26%	0.2%
Europe	(n = 21)	48%	44%	8%
U.S.	(n = 20)	31%	49%	18%

Source: R. Kopp, "International Human Resource Policies and Practices in Japanese, European, and United States Multinationals," *Human Resource Management* 33, no. 4 (Winter 1994): 581–599.

Exhibit 9-3B
Incidence of International Personnel Problems

	% OF JAPANESE FIRMS REPORTING PROBLEM (N = 34)	% OF EUROPEAN FIRMS REPORTING PROBLEM (N = 23)	% OF U.S. FIRMS REPORTING PROBLEM (n = 24)
Expatriate-related			
Lack of home-country personnel who have sufficient international management skills	68%	39%	29%
Lack of home-country personnel who want to work abroad	26%	26%	13%
Expatriates experience reentry difficulties (e.g., career disruption) when returning to the home country	24%	39%	42%
Average of expatriate-related problems	39%	35%	28%
Local national staff related			
Difficulty in attracting high-caliber local nationals to work for the firm	44%	26%	21%
High turnover of local employees	32%	9%	4%
Friction and poor communication between home-country expatriates and local employees	32%	9%	13%
Complaints by local employees that they are not able to advance in the company	21%	4%	8%
Local legal challenges to the company's personnel policies	0 (0)	0	8%
Average of local national staff related problems	26%	10%	11%

Source: R. Kopp, "International Human Resource Policies and Practices in Japanese, European, and United States Multinationals," *Human Resource Management* 33, no. 4 (Winter 1994): 581–599.

of success for expatriate managers: job factors, relational dimensions such as cultural empathy and flexibility, motivational state, family situation, and language skills. The relative importance of each factor is highly situational and difficult to establish.[16]

These **expatriate success factors** are based on studies of American expatriates. One could argue that the requisite skills are the same for managers from any country—and particularly so for third-country nationals.

A more flexible approach to maximizing managerial talent, regardless of the source, would certainly consider more closely whether the position could be suitably filled by a host-country national, as put forth by Tung, based on her research.[17] This contingency model of selection and training depends on the variables of the particular assignment, such as the length of stay, the similarity with the candidate's own culture, and the level of interaction with local managers in that job. Tung concludes that the more rigorous the selection and training process, the lower the failure rate.

The selection process is set up as a decision tree in which the progression to the next stage of selection or the type of orientation training depends on the assessment of critical factors regarding the job or the candidate at each decision point. The simplest selection process involves choosing a local national, because minimal training is necessary, regarding the culture or ways of doing business locally. However, local managers often require additional training regarding the MNC's companywide processes, technology and corporate culture to be successful. If the position cannot be filled by a local national, but yet the job requires a high level of interaction with the local community, there needs to be a very careful screening of candidates from other countries and a vigorous training program.

Most MNCs tend to start out their operations in a particular region by selecting primarily from their own pool of managers. Over time, and with increasing internationalization, they tend to move to a predominantly polycentric or regiocentric policy because of (1) increasing pressure (explicit or implicit) from local governments to hire locals (or sometimes legal restraints on the use of expatriates), and (2) the greater costs of expatriate staffing, particularly when the company has to pay taxes for the parent-company employee in both countries.[18] In addition, in recent years, MNCs have noted an improvement in the level of managerial and technical competence in many countries, negating the chief reason for using a primarily ethnocentric policy in the past. One researcher's comment represents a growing attitude: "All things being equal, a local national who speaks the language, understands the culture and the political system, and is often a member of the local elite, should be more effective than an expatriate alien."[19] However, concerns about the need to maintain strategic control over subsidiaries and to develop managers with a global perspective remain a source of debate about staffing policies among human resource management professionals.[20] A globally oriented company such as ABB (Asea Brown Boveri), for example, has 500 roving transpatriates who are moved every two to three years, thus developing a considerable management cadre with global experience.

For MNCs based in Europe and Asia, human resource policies at all levels of the organization are greatly influenced by the home-country culture and policies. For Japanese subsidiaries in Singapore, Malaysia, and India, for example, promotion from within and expectations of long-term loyalty to and by the firm are culture-based practices transferable to subsidiaries.[21] At Matsushita, however, selection criteria for staffing seem to be similar to those of Western companies. Its candidates are selected on the basis of a set of characteristics the firm calls SMILE: specialty (required skill, knowledge), management ability (particularly motivational ability), international flexibility (adaptability), language facility, and endeavor (perseverance in the face of difficulty).[22]

Problems with Expatriation

> While 89 percent of companies formally assess a candidate's job skills prior to a foreign posting, less than half go through the same process for cultural suitability. Even fewer gauge whether the family will cope.
>
> www.expat.FT.com, MARCH 5, 2001.

Deciding on a staffing policy and selecting suitable managers are logical first steps but do not alone ensure success. When staffing overseas assignments with expatriates, for example, many other reasons, besides poor selection, contribute to **expatriate failure** among U.S. multinationals. A large percentage of these failures can be attributed to poor preparation and planning for the entry and reentry transitions of the manager and his or her family. One important variable, for example, often given insufficient attention in the selection, preparation, and support phases, is the suitability and adjustment of the spouse. The inability of the spouse to adjust to the new environment has been found to be a major—in fact, the most frequently cited—reason for expatriate failure in U.S. and European companies.[23] Yet only about half of those companies studied had included the spouse in the interviewing process. In addition, although research shows that human relational skills are critical for overseas work (a fact acknowledged by the companies in a study by Tung), most of the U.S. firms surveyed failed to include this factor in their assessment of candidates.[24,25] The following is a synthesis of the factors frequently mentioned by researchers and firms as the major causes of expatriate failure:

- Selection based on headquarters criteria rather than assignment needs
- Inadequate preparation, training, and orientation prior to assignment
- Alienation or lack of support from headquarters
- Inability to adapt to local culture and working environment
- Problems with spouse and children—poor adaptation, family unhappiness
- Insufficient compensation and financial support
- Poor programs for career support and repatriation

After careful selection based on the specific assignment and the long-term plans both of the organization and the candidates, plans must be made for the preparation, training, and development of expatriate managers.

> Some 81% of companies [around the world] said in 1998 that they expect to send an increasing number of people overseas through 2000. That means more folks confounded by foreign cultures and customs. What's key? Preparation.
>
> www.businessweek.com, MARCH 5, 2001.

It is clear that preparation and training for cross-cultural interactions is critical. In earlier discussions of the need for cultural sensitivity by expatriate managers, we noted that reports indicate that up to 40 percent of expatriate managers end their foreign assignments early because of poor performance or an inability to adjust to the local environment.[26] Moreover, about half of those who do remain function at a low level of effectiveness. The direct cost alone of a failed expatriate assignment is estimated to be from $50,000 to $150,000. The indirect costs may be far greater, depending on the position held by the expatriate. Relations with the host-country government and customers may be damaged, resulting in a loss of market share and a poor reception for future PCNs.

Both cross-cultural adjustment problems and practical differences in everyday living present challenges for expatriates and their families. Examples are evident from a 1998 survey of expatriates when they ranked the countries which presented the most challenging assignments to them, along with some pet peeves from their experiences:

China A continuing problem for expatriates; one complained that at his welcome banquet he was served duck tongue and pigeon head.

Brazil Expatriates stress that cell phones are essential because home phones don't work.

India Returning executives complain that the pervasiveness of poverty and street children is overwhelming.

Indonesia Here you need to plan ahead financially because landlords typically demand rent two to three years in advance.

Japan Expatriates and their families remain concerned that although there is excellent medical care, the Japanese doctors reveal little to their patients.

After these five countries, expatriates rank Russia, Mexico, Saudi Arabia, South Korea, and France also challenging.[27]

Even though cross-cultural training has proved to be effective, less than a third of expatriates are given such training. In a 1997 study by Harvey of 332 U.S. expatriates (dual-career couples) the respondents stated that their MNCs had not provided them with sufficient training or social support during the international assignment.[28] Much of the rationale for this lack of training is an assumption that managerial skills and processes are universal. In a simplistic way, a manager's domestic track record is used as the major selection criterion for an overseas assignment.

In most countries, however, the success of the expatriate is not left so much to chance. Foreign companies provide considerably more training and preparation for expatriates than American companies. Therefore, it is not hard to understand why Japanese expatriates experience significantly fewer incidences of failure than their American counterparts, although this may be partially attributable to the lower incidence of families accompanying Japanese assignees. Japanese multinationals typically have recall rates of below 5 percent, signifying that they send abroad managers who are far better prepared and more adept at working and flourishing in a foreign environment.[29] While this success is largely attributable to training programs, it is also a result of intelligent planning by the human resource management staff in most Japanese organizations, as reported in a study by Tung.[30] This planning begins with a careful selection process for overseas assignments, based on the long-term knowledge of executives and their families. An effective selection process, of course, will eliminate many potential "failures" from the start. Another factor is the longer duration of overseas assignments, averaging almost five years, which allows the Japanese expatriate more time to adjust initially and then to function at full capacity. In addition, Japanese expatriates receive considerable support from headquarters and sometimes even from local divisions set up for that purpose. At NEC Corporation, for example, part of the Japanese giant's globalization strategy is its permanent boot camp, with its elaborate training exercises to prepare NEC managers and their families for overseas battle.[31]

The demands on expatriate managers have always been as much a result of the multiple relationships that they have to maintain as they are of the differences in the host-country environment. Those relations include family relations, internal relations with people in the corporation, both locally and globally, especially with headquarters, external relations (suppliers, distributors, allies, customers, local community, etc.), and relations with the host government. It is important to pinpoint any potential problems that an expatriate may experience with those relationships so that these problems may be addressed during predeparture training. Problem recognition is the first stage in a comprehensive plan for developing expatriates shown in Exhibit 9-4. The three areas critical to preparation are cultural training, language instruction, and familiarity with everyday matters.[32] In the model shown in Exhibit 9-4, various development methods are used to address these areas during predeparture training, postarrival training, and reentry training. These methods continue to be valid and used by many organizations. Two-way feedback between the executive and the trainers at each stage helps to tailor the level and kinds of training to the individual manager. The desired goal is the increased effectiveness of the expatriate as a result of familiarity with local conditions, cultural awareness, and an appreciation of his or her family's needs in the host country.

Cross-Cultural Training

While training in language and practical affairs is quite straightforward, cross-cultural training is not; it is complex and deals with deep-rooted behaviors. The actual process of cross-cultural training should result in the expatriate learning both content and skills that will improve interactions with host-country individuals by reducing misunderstandings and inappropriate behaviors. Black and Mendenhall suggest that trainers should apply social learning theory to this process by using

Exhibit 9-4
A Model for Developing Key Expatriate Executives

Source: A. Rahim, "A Model for Developing Key Expatriate Executives," *Personnel Journal* (April 1983): 312–337.

the behavioral science techniques of incentives and rehearsal until the trainee internalizes the desired behaviors and reproduces them.[33] The result is a state of adjustment, representing the ability to effectively interact with host nationals.

Culture Shock

The goal of this training is to ease the adjustment to the new environment by reducing **culture shock**—a state of disorientation and anxiety about not knowing how to behave in an unfamiliar culture. The cause of culture shock is the trauma people experience in new and different cultures, where they lose the familiar signs and cues that they had used to interact in daily life and where they must learn to cope with a vast array of new cultural cues and expectations.[34] The symptoms of culture shock range from mild irritation to a deep-seated psychological panic or crisis. The inability to work effectively, stress within the family, and hostility toward host nationals are the common dysfunctional results of culture shock—often leading to the manager giving up and going home.

It is helpful to recognize the stages of culture shock to understand what is happening. Culture shock usually progresses through four stages, as described by Oberg: (1) *honeymoon*, when positive attitudes and expectations, excitement, and a tourist feeling prevail (which may last up to several weeks); (2) *irritation and hostility*, the crisis stage when cultural differences result in problems at work, at home, and in daily living. Expatriates and family members feel homesick and disoriented, lashing out at everyone (many never get past this stage); (3) *gradual adjustment*, a period of recovery in which the "patient" gradually becomes able to understand and predict patterns of behavior, use the language, and deal with daily activities, and the family starts to accept their new life; and (4) *biculturalism*, the stage in which the manager and family members grow to accept and appreciate local people and practices and are able to function effectively in two cultures.[35] Many never get to the fourth stage—operating acceptably at the third stage—but those who do report that their assignment is positive and growth-oriented.

Subculture Shock

Similar to culture shock, although usually less extreme, is the experience of subculture shock. This occurs when a manager is transferred to another part of the country where there are cultural differences—essentially from what she or he perceives to be a "majority" culture to a "minority" one. The shock comes from feeling like an "immigrant" in one's own country and being unprepared for such differences. For instance, someone going from New York to Texas will experience considerable differences in attitudes and lifestyle between those two states. These differences will exist even within Texas, with cultures that range from roaming ranches and high technology to Bible-belt attitudes and laws and to areas with a very Mexican heritage.[36]

Training Techniques

Many training techniques are available to assist overseas assignees in the adjustment process. These techniques are classified by Tung as (1) area studies, that is, documentary programs about the country's geography, economics, socio-political history, and so forth; (2) culture assimilators, which expose trainees to the kinds of situations they are likely to encounter that are critical to successful interactions; (3) language training; (4) sensitivity training; and (5) field experiences—exposure to people from other cultures within the trainee's own country.[37] Tung recommends using these training methods in a complementary fashion, giving the trainee increasing levels of personal involvement as she or he progresses through each method. Documentary and interpersonal approaches have been found comparable, with the most effective intercultural training occurring when trainees become aware of the differences between their own culture and the one they are planning to enter.[38]

Similarly categorizing training methods, Ronen suggests specific techniques, such as workshops and sensitivity training, including a field experience called the host-family surrogate, where the MNC pays for and places an expatriate family with a host family as part of an immersion and familiarization program.[39]

Most training programs take place in the expatriate's own country prior to leaving. While this is certainly a convenience, the impact of host-country (or in-country) programs can be far greater than those conducted at home because crucial skills, such as overcoming cultural differences in intercultural relationships, can actually be experienced during in-country training rather than simply discussed.[40] In fact, some MNCs are beginning to recognize that there is no substitute for on-the-job training (OJT) in the early stages of the careers of those managers whom they hope to develop into senior-level global managers. Colgate-Palmolive—whose overseas sales represent two-thirds of its $6 billion in yearly revenue—is one company whose management development programs adhere to this philosophy. After training at headquarters, Colgate employees become associate product managers in the United States or abroad—and, according to John R. Garrison, manager of recruitment and development at Colgate, they must earn their stripes by being prepared to country-hop every few years. In fact, says Garrison, "That's the definition of a global manager: one who has seen several environments firsthand."[41] Exhibit 9-5 shows some other global management development programs for junior employees.

Integrating Training with Global Orientation

In continuing our discussion on "strategic fit," it is important to remember that training programs, like staffing approaches, be designed with the company's strategy in mind. While it is probably impractical to break those programs down into a lot of variations, it is feasible to at least consider the relative level or stage of globalization that the firm has reached, because obvious major differences would be appropriate, for example from the initial export stage to the full global stage. Exhibit 9-6 suggests levels of rigor and types of training content appropriate for the firm's managers, as well as those for host country nationals, for four globalization stages—export, multidomestic, multinational, and global. It is noteworthy, for example, that the training for host-country nationals for a global firm has a considerably higher level of scope and rigor than for the other stages, and borders on the standards for the firm's expatriates.

Exhibit 9-5

Corporate Programs to Develop Global Managers

- ABB (Asea Brown Boveri) rotates about 500 managers around the world to different countries every two to three years in order to develop a management cadre of transpatriates to support their global strategy.
- PepsiCo Inc. has an orientation program for its foreign managers by bringing them to the United States for one-year assignments in bottling division plants.
- British Telecom uses informal mentoring techniques to induct employees into the ways of the country they are about to go to; existing expatriate workers talk to prospective assignees about the cultural factors to expect. (www.expat.FT.com)
- Honda of America Manufacturing Inc. gives its U.S. supervisors and managers extensive preparation in Japanese language, culture, and lifestyle and then sends them to Tokyo for up to three years to the parent company.[42]
- General Electric likes its engineers and managers to have a global perspective whether or not they are slated to go abroad. The company gives regular language and cross-cultural training for them so that they are equipped to conduct business with people around the world. (www.GE.com)

Exhibit 9-6

Stage of Globalization and Training Design Issues

EXPORT STAGE	MNC STAGE
Degree of Rigor: Low to moderate	*Degree of Rigor*: High moderate to high
Content: Emphasis should be on interpersonal skills, local culture, customer values, and business behavior.	*Content*: Emphasis should be on interpersonal skills, two-way technology transfer, corporate value transfer, international strategy, stress management, local culture, and business practices.
Host-Country Nationals: Low to moderate training of host nationals to understand parent country products and policies.	*Host-Country Nationals*: Moderate to high training of host nationals in technical areas, product and service systems, and corporate culture.
MDC STAGE	**GLOBAL STAGE**
Degree of Rigor: Moderate to high	*Degree of Rigor*: High
Content: Emphasis should be on interpersonal skills, local culture, technology transfer, stress management, and business practices and laws.	*Content*: Emphasis should be on global corporate operations and systems, corporate culture transfer, customers, global competitors, and international strategy.
Host-Country Nationals: Low to moderate training of host nationals; primarily focusing on production and service procedures.	*Host-Country Nationals*: High training of host nationals in global organization production and efficiency systems, corporate culture, business systems, and global conduct policies.

Source: J. S. Black, Mark E. Mendenhall, Hal B. Gregersen, and Linda K. Stroh, *Globalizing People Through International Assignments* (Reading, MA: Addison Wesley Longman, 1999).

Training Host-Country Nationals

The continuous training and development of HCNs and TCNs for management positions is also important to the long-term success of multinational corporations. As part of a long-term staffing policy for a subsidiary, the ongoing development of HCNs will facilitate the transition to an indigenization policy. Furthermore, multinational companies like to have well-trained managers with broad international experience available to take charge in many intercultural settings, whether at home or abroad. Such managerial skills are increasingly needed in U.S.–Japanese joint ventures—a good example being G.M.-Toyota in Freemont, California. There, managers as well as employees from both America and Japan learn to work side by side and adjust to a unique blend of country and corporate culture. For the Americans in this organization, helping to acculturate the Japanese employees not only demonstrates friendly goodwill but is a necessary part of securing their own future in the company.

Many HCNs are, of course, receiving excellent training in global business and Internet technology within their home corporations. Kim In Kyung, 24, for example, has a job involving world travel and high-technology with Samsung Electronics company, of Seoul, South Korea. It's part of Samsung's strategy to promote its new Internet focus, and this strategy has landed the farmer's daughter a $100,000 job. Her situation reflects Seoul's sizzling tech boom, where IT comprised 11 percent of its $400 billion economy in 2001, and is expected to reach 20 percent by 2010.[43]

In another common scenario also requiring the management of a mixture of executives and employees, American and European MNCs presently employ Asians as well as Arab locals in their plants and offices in Saudi Arabia, bringing together three cultures: well-educated Asian managers living in a Middle Eastern, highly traditional society who are employed by a firm reflecting Western technology and culture. This kind of situation involves the integration of multiple sets of culturally based values, expectations, and work habits.

COMPENSATING EXPATRIATES

The significance of an appropriate compensation and benefit package to attract, retain, and motivate international employees cannot be overemphasized. Compensation is a crucial link between strategy and its successful implementation; there must be a fit between compensation and the goals for which the firm wants managers to aim.[44] So that they will not feel exploited, MNC employees need to perceive equity and goodwill in their compensation and benefits, whether they are PCNs, HCNs, or TCNs. The premature return of expatriates or the unwillingness of managers to take overseas assignments can often be traced to their knowledge that the assignment is detrimental to them financially and usually to their career progression.

From the firm's perspective, the high cost of maintaining appropriate compensation packages for expatriates has led many companies—Colgate-Palmolive, Chase Manhattan Bank, Digital Equipment, General Motors, and General Electric among them—to cut back on PCN assignments as much as possible. "Transfer a $100,000-a-year American executive to London—and suddenly he [or she] costs the employer $300,000," explains the *Wall Street Journal*. "Move him to Stockholm or Tokyo, and he [or she] easily becomes a million-dollar [manager]."[45]

Designing and maintaining an appropriate compensation package is more complex than it would seem because of the need to consider and reconcile parent and host-country financial, legal, and customary practices. The problem is that although around the world there may be little variation in typical executive salaries at the level of base compensation, there is often a wide variation in net spendable income. American executives may receive more in cash and stock, but they have to spend more for things that foreign companies provide, such as cars, vacations, and entertainment allowances. In addition, the manager's purchasing power with that net income is affected by the relative cost of living. The cost of living is considerably higher in most of Europe than in the United States. In designing compensation and benefit packages for PCNs, then, the challenge to IHRM professionals is to maintain a standard of living for expatriates equivalent to their colleagues at home plus compensating them for any additional costs incurred. This policy is referred to as "keeping the expatriate whole."[46]

To ensure that expatriates do not lose out through their overseas assignment, the **balance sheet approach** is often used to equalize the standard of living between the host country and the home country and to add some compensation for inconvenience or qualitative loss. This approach is illustrated in Exhibit 9-7. However, there is a recent trend with some companies to base their compensation

Exhibit 9-7
The Balance Sheet Approach to International Compensation

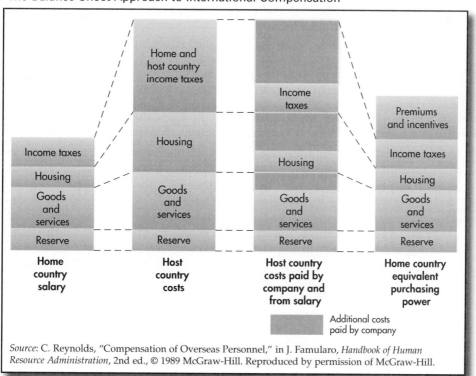

Source: C. Reynolds, "Compensation of Overseas Personnel," in J. Famularo, *Handbook of Human Resource Administration*, 2nd ed., © 1989 McGraw-Hill. Reproduced by permission of McGraw-Hill.

package on a goal of achieving a standard of living comparable to host-country managers, which does help resolve some of the problems of pay differential illustrated in the opening profile.

In fairness, the MNC is obliged to make up additional costs the expatriate would incur for taxes, housing, and goods and services. The tax differential is complex and expensive for the company, and generally MNCs use a policy of tax equalization: the company pays any taxes due on any type of additional compensation that the expatriate receives for the assignment; the expatriate pays in taxes only what she or he would be paying at home. The burden of foreign taxes can be lessened, however, by efficient tax planning—a fact often overlooked by small firms. The timing and methods of paying people determine what foreign taxes are incurred; for example, a company can save on taxes by renting an apartment for the employee instead of providing a cash housing allowance. All in all, MNCs have to weigh the many aspects of a complete compensation package, especially at high management levels, to effect a tax equalization policy.

Managing PCN compensation is a complex challenge for companies with overseas operations. Exhibit 9-8 shows the categories that must be considered. All components of the compensation package must be considered in light of both home- and host-country legalities and practices. Most important, to be strategically competitive, the compensation package must be comparatively attractive to the kinds of managers the company wishes to hire or relocate. Some of those managers will, of course, be local managers in the host country. This too is a complex situation requiring competitive compensation policies in order to attract, motivate, and retain the best local managerial talent. In many countries, however, it is a considerable challenge to develop compensation packages appropriate to the local situation and culture, while also recognizing the differences between local salaries and those expected by expatriates or transpatriates (that difference itself often being a source of competitive advantage).

COMPENSATING HOST-COUNTRY NATIONALS

How do firms deal with the kinds of situations posed by Mark and Oleg in the Opening Profile? Of course, there is no one set of solutions that can be applicable in any country. The variables are many—including local market factors and pay scales, government involvement in benefits, the role of unions, the cost of living, and so on.

In Eastern Europe, for example, people in Hungary, Poland, and the Czech Republic spend 35 to 40 percent of the disposable income on food and utilities, and that may run as high as 75 percent in the CIS.[47] Therefore, East European managers need to have cash for about 65 to 80 percent of their base pay, compared to about 40 percent for U.S. managers (the rest being long-term incentives, benefits, and perks). In addition, they still expect the many social benefits provided by the "old government." To be competitive, MNCs can focus on providing goods and services that are either not available at all or extremely expensive in Eastern Europe; such upscale perks can be used to attract high-skilled workers.

Exhibit 9-8

Components of an
Expatriate Compensation
Package

Salary
- Home rate/home currency
- Local rate/local currency
- Salary adjustments or promotions—home or local standard
- Bonus—home or local currency, home or local standard
- Stock options
- Inducement payment/hardship premium—percentage of salary or
  lump sum payment, home/local currency
- Currency protection—discretion or split basis
- Global salary and performance structures

Taxation
- Tax protection
- Tax equalization
- Other services

Benefits
- Home-country program
- Local program
- Social Security program

Allowances
- Cost-of-living allowances   • Perquisites
- Housing standard   • Home leave
- Education   • Shipping and storage
- Relocation

Source: P. J. Dowling and R. S. Schuler, *International Dimensions of Human Resource Management* (Boston: PWS-Kent, 1990).

Nestlé Bulgaria offers a company car and a cellular phone to new recruits. . . . Fuel prices are about $2 per gallon and cell phones cost $1,200 a year—equivalent to half a year's salary.[48]

In Japan, companies are revamping their HRM policies to compete in a global world, in response to a decade-long economic slump. The traditional lifetime employment and a guaranteed tidy pension is giving way to the more Western practices of competing for jobs, of basing pay on performance, rather than seniority, and of making people responsible for their own retirement fund decisions.[49]

In China, too, change is under way. University graduates may now seek their own jobs, rather than being assigned to state-owned companies, though nepotism is still common. In a study of HRM practices in China, Bjorkman and Lu found that a key concern of Western managers in China was the compensation of the HCNs. In Beijing and Shanghai, top Chinese managers have seen their salaries increase by 30 to 50 percent in the last few years. They also received considerable fringe benefits such as housing, company cars, pensions, and overseas training.

The difficulty, too, was that in Western–Chinese joint ventures, the Chinese partner opposed pay increases.[50] Yet when trying to introduce performance-based pay, the Western companies ran into considerable opposition and usually gave up, using salary increases instead. Setting up some kind of housing scheme, such as investing in apartments, seemed to be one way that foreign-owned firms were able to compete for good managers. Those managers were, understandably, maximizing their job opportunities now that they do not have to get permission to leave the Chinese state-owned companies.[51]

DEVELOPING A GLOBAL MANAGEMENT CADRE

A crucial factor in global competitiveness is the ability of the firm to maximize its long-term global human resources. To do this, attention must be paid to several important areas:

1. To maximize long-term retention and use of international cadre through career management so that the company can develop a top management team with global experience
2. To develop effective global management teams
3. To understand, value, and promote the role of women and minorities in international management in order to maximize those underutilized resources

Preparation, Adaptation, and Repatriation

We began to realize that the entire effectiveness of the assignment could be compromised by ignoring the spouse.

STEVE FORD, CORPORATION RELOCATIONS, HEWLETT-PACKARD.[52]

Effective human resource management of a company's global cadre does not end with the overseas assignment. It ends with the successful repatriation of the executive into company headquarters. In fact, long-term, proactive management of critical resources should begin with the end of the current assignment in mind—that is, it should begin with plans for the repatriation of the executive as part of his or her career path. The management of the reentry phase of the career cycle is as vital as the management of the cross-cultural entry and training; otherwise, the long-term benefits of that executive's international experience may be negated.[53] Shortsightedly, many companies do little to minimize the potential effects of **reverse culture shock** (return shock). In fact, a survey of companies belonging to the American Society of Personnel Administration International (ASPAI) revealed that only 31 percent had formal repatriation programs for executives and only 35 percent of those included spouses. In addition, only 22 percent of those had conducted the programs prior to the executive's departure for the assignment.[54] Those American companies without programs had various explanations: a lack of expertise in repatriation training, the cost of the programs, or a lack of a perceived need for such training.

The long-term implications of ineffective repatriation practices are clear—few good managers will be willing to take international assignments because they will see what happened to their colleagues. If a certain manager lost out on promotion opportunities while overseas and is now in fact worse off than before he or she left, the only people willing to take on foreign assignments in the future will be those who have not been able to succeed on the home front or those who think that a stint abroad will be like a vacation. In fact, research has shown that overseas assignments are commonly seen by employees as negative career moves in many U.S. multinational companies.[55] However, such moves are seen as positive in most European, Japanese, and Australian companies because they consider international experience necessary for advancement to top management.

In a recent study of dual-career couples, "the perceived impact of the international assignment upon returning to the United States," was one of the most important issues stated by managers regarding their willingness to relocate overseas.[56]

Reverse culture shock occurs primarily because of the difficulty of reintegration into the organization but also because, generally speaking, the longer a person is away, the more difficult it is to get back into the swing of things. Not only might the manager have been overlooked and lost in the shuffle of a reorganization, but her or his whole family might have lost social contacts or jobs and feel out of step with their contemporaries. These feelings of alienation from what has always been perceived as "home"—because of the loss of contact with family, friends, and daily life—delay the resocialization process. Such a reaction is particularly serious if the family's overall financial situation has been hurt by the assignment and if the spouse's career has also been kept "on hold" while he or she was abroad.

For companies to maximize the long-term use of their international cadre, they need to make sure that the foreign assignment and the reintegration process are positive experiences. This means careful career planning, support while overseas, and the use of the increased experience and skills of returned managers to benefit the home office. Research into the practices of successful U.S., European, Japanese, and Australian MNCs indicates the use of one or more of the following support systems, as recommended by Tung, for a successful repatriation program:

- A mentor program to monitor the expatriate's career path while abroad and upon repatriation
- As an alternative to the mentor program, the establishment of a special organizational unit for the purposes of career planning and continuing guidance for the expatriate
- A system of supplying information and maintaining contacts with the expatriate so that he or she may continue to feel a part of the home organization.[57]

The Role of the Expatriate Spouse

Many companies are beginning to recognize the importance of providing support for spouses and children—in particular because both spouses are often corporate fast-trackers and demand that both sets of needs be included on the bargaining table. Firms often use informal means, such as intercompany networking, to help find the trailing spouse a position in the same location. They know that, with the increasing number of dual-career couples (65 percent in the United States), if the spouse does not find a position the manager will very likely turn down the assignment. They decline because they can't afford to lose the income or they worry that it may derail the spouse's career entirely if he or she is out of the workforce for a few years. Indeed, as women continue to move up the corporate ladder, the accompanying ("trailing") spouse is often male—estimated at 25 percent in the year 2000.[58] Companies such as Hewlett-Packard, Shell, Medtronic, and Monsanto offer a variety of options to address the dual-career dilemma.

At Procter & Gamble, employees and spouses destined for China are sent to Beijing for two months of language training and cultural familiarization. Nissho Iwai, a Japanese trading company, gets together managers and spouses who are leaving Japan with foreign managers and spouses who are on their way there. In addition, the firm provides a year of language training and information and services for Japanese children to attend schools abroad. Recent research on 321 American expatriate spouses around the world shows that effective cross-cultural adjustment by spouses is more likely (1) when firms seek the spouse's opinion about the international assignment and the expected standard of living, and (2) when the spouse initiates his or her own predeparture training (thereby supplementing the minimal training given by most firms).[59]

Expatriate Career Management

Support services provide timely help for the manager and therefore are part of the effective management of an overseas assignment. The overall transition process experienced by the company's international management cadre over time is shown in Exhibit 9-9. It comprises three phases of transition and adjustment that must be managed for successful socialization to a new culture and resocialization back to the old culture. These phases are (1) the exit transition from the home country, the success of which will be determined largely by the quality of preparation the expatriate has received; (2) the entry transition to the host country, in which successful acculturation (or early exit) will depend largely on monitoring and support; and (3) the entry transition back to the home country or to a new host country, in which the level of reverse culture shock and the ease of reacculturation will depend on previous stages of preparation and support.[60] Although we discussed these broad issues earlier, this model offers an interesting overview of the interdependency and the timing of the three transitions.

The Role of Repatriation in Developing a Global Management Cadre

> Managers returning from expatriate assignments are two to three times more likely to leave the company within a year because attention has not been paid to their careers and the way they fit back into the corporate structure back home.
>
> www.expat.FT.com, MARCH 5, 2001.

One purpose of the international assignment is that both the manager and the company benefit from the enhanced skills and the experience gained by the expa-

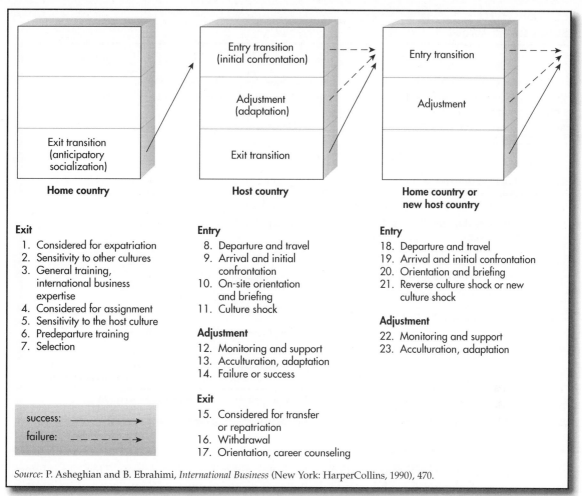

Exit
1. Considered for expatriation
2. Sensitivity to other cultures
3. General training, international business expertise
4. Considered for assignment
5. Sensitivity to the host culture
6. Predeparture training
7. Selection

Entry
8. Departure and travel
9. Arrival and initial confrontation
10. On-site orientation and briefing
11. Culture shock

Adjustment
12. Monitoring and support
13. Acculturation, adaptation
14. Failure or success

Exit
15. Considered for transfer or repatriation
16. Withdrawal
17. Orientation, career counseling

Entry
18. Departure and travel
19. Arrival and initial confrontation
20. Orientation and briefing
21. Reverse culture shock or new culture shock

Adjustment
22. Monitoring and support
23. Acculturation, adaptation

success: ─────────→
failure: ─ ─ ─ ─ ─→

Source: P. Asheghian and B. Ebrahimi, *International Business* (New York: HarperCollins, 1990), 470.

Exhibit 9-9
The Expatriate Transition Process

triate. Many returning executives report an improvement in their managerial skills and self-confidence. Some of these acquired skills, as reported by Adler, are shown in Exhibit 9-10.

In addition to the managerial and cross-cultural skills acquired by expatriates, the company benefits from the knowledge and experience those managers gain about how to do business overseas and what new technology, local marketing, and competitive information they acquire. The company should position itself to benefit from that enhanced management knowledge if it wants to develop a globally oriented and experienced management cadre—an essential ingredient for global competitiveness—in particular where there is a high degree of shared learning among the organization's global managers. If the company cannot retain good returning managers, then the potential shared knowledge is not only lost but

Exhibit 9-10
Skills Learned Abroad

Managerial Skills, Not Technical Skills

Working abroad makes you more knowledgeable about the questions to ask, not the answers.

I learned how to work in two cultures . . . to compromise, not to be a dictator. It's very similar to two domestic cultures . . . like marketing and engineering.

I'm more open-minded . . . more able to deal with a wider range of people . . . because I ran into many other points of view.

Tolerance for Ambiguity

Because I only understood a fraction of what was really going on overseas, maybe 50 percent, I had to make decisions on a fraction of the necessary information. Now I can tolerate nonclosure and ambiguity better.

Things you never thought you'd put up with, you learn to put up with . . . I always thought I was right, until I went overseas.

Multiple Perspective

I learned what it feels like to be a foreigner . . . I could see things from their perspective.

I learned to anticipate . . . it's the role of a diplomat.

Ability to Work with and Manage Others

I increased my tolerance for other people. For the first time, I was the underdog, the minority.

I became a soft-headed screamer. I'm definitely better with others now.

I used to be more ruthless than I am now . . . I was the all-American manager. Now, I stop and realize the human impact more. I use others as resources. I do more communicating with others in the organization.

Source: N. J. Adler, *International Dimensions of Organizational Behavior*, 4th ed. (Cincinnati: South-Western, 2002).

also conveyed to another organization who hires that person. This can be very detrimental to the competitive stance of the company. Some companies are becoming quite savvy about how to use technology to utilize shared knowledge to develop their global management cadre, to better service their customers, and—as a side benefit—to store the knowledge and expertise of their managers around the world in case they leave the company; that knowledge, it can be argued, is an asset in which the company has invested large amounts of resources. One such savvy company is Booz-Allen & Hamilton, which instituted a Knowledge On-Line Intranet.

Research by Black and Gregersen of 750 U.S., European, and Japanese companies concluded that those companies which reported a high degree of job satisfaction and strong performance and which experienced limited turnover used the following practices when making international assignments:

- They focus on knowledge creation and global leadership development.
- They assign overseas posts to people whose technical skills are matched or exceeded by their cross-cultural abilities.
- They end expatriate assignments with a deliberate repatriation process.[61]

A successful repatriation program, then, starts before the assignment. The company top management must set up a culture which conveys that the organization regards international assignments as an integral part of continuing career development and advancement, and that it values the skills of the returnees. The company's objectives should be reflected in its long-range plans, commitment, and compensation on behalf of the expatriate. GE sets a model for effective expatriate career management. With its 500 expatriates worldwide, it takes care to select only the best managers for overseas jobs and then commits to placing them in specific positions upon reentry.[62] In fact, a study of the IHRM policies of British multinationals indicates that careful planning for foreign assignments pays off. Farsighted policies, along with selection criteria based more on the adaptability of the manager and her or his family to the culture than on technical skills, apparently account for the low expatriate failure rate—estimated at less than 5 percent.[63]

Global Management Teams

The term **global management teams** describes collections of managers from several countries who must rely on group collaboration if each member is to experience the optimum of success and goal achievement.[64] Whirlpool International, for example, is a U.S.–Dutch joint venture, with administrative headquarters in Comerio, Italy, where it is managed by a Swede and a six-person management team from Sweden, Italy, Holland, the United States, Belgium, and Germany.[65] To achieve the individual and collective goals of the team members, international teams must "provide the means to communicate corporate culture, develop a global perspective, coordinate and integrate the global enterprise, and be responsive to local market needs."[66] The role and importance of international teams increases as the firm progresses in its scope of international activity.

Similarly, the manner in which multicultural interaction affects the firm's operations depends on its level of international involvement, its environment, and its strategy. In domestic firms, the effects of cross-cultural teams are limited to internal operations and some external contacts. In international firms that export products and produce some products overseas, multicultural teams and cultural diversity play important roles in the relationships between buyers, sellers, and other intermediaries at the boundary of the organization. For multinational firms, the role of multicultural teams again becomes internal to the company; the teams consist of culturally diverse managers and technical people located around the world and also working together within subsidiaries. The team's ability to work together effectively is crucial to the success of the company. In addition, technology facilitates effective and efficient teamwork around the world. This was found by the Timberland U.K. sales conference planning team. In the past their large sales conferences were cumbersome to organize with their offices in France, Germany, Spain, Italy, and the U.K. Then the team started using the British Telecom Conference Call system for the arrangements, which saved them much travel and expense; the company subsequently adopted the BT Conference Calls for the executive teams' country meetings.

> There really was no point in travelling for two hour meetings. So we would lock diaries for a couple of hours over BT Conference Call.
>
> www.BritishTelecom.com/cases, FEBRUARY 18, 2001.

For global organizations and alliances, we find the same cross-cultural interactions as in MNCs and, in addition, considerably more interaction with the external environment at all levels of the organization. Therefore, global teamwork is vital, as are the pockets of cross-cultural teamwork and interactions that take place at many boundaries.[67] For the global company, worldwide competition and markets necessitate global teams for strategy development, both for the organization as a whole and for the local units to respond to their markets.

As shown in Exhibit 9-11, when a firm responds to its global environment with a global strategy and then organizes with a networked "glocal" structure (discussed in Chapter 8), various types of cross-border teams are necessary for global integration and local differentiation. These include headquarters–subsidiary teams and those coordinating alliances outside the organization. In joint ventures, in particular, multicultural teams work at all levels of strategic planning and implementation and on the production and assembly floor.

Increasingly advances in communication now facilitate **virtual global teams**, with people around the world conducting meetings and exchanging information via the Internet, enabling the organization to capitalize on 24-hour productivity. In this way, too, knowledge is shared across business units and across cultures.[68] Virtual global teams are not without their challenges—including cultural misunderstandings, and the logistics of differences in time and space; group members must

Exhibit 9-11
International Teams in the Modern Global Enterprise

Source: T. Gross, E. Turner, and L. Cederholm, "Building Teams for Global Operations," *Management Review* (June 1987): 34.

build their teams bearing in mind the group diversity and the need for careful communication.[69]

Building Global Teams

The ability to develop effective transnational teams is essential in light of the increasing proliferation of foreign subsidiaries, joint ventures, and other transnational alliances. As noted by David Dotlich of Honeywell Bull Inc. (HBI), an international computer firm, effective international teamwork is essential because cross-cultural "double-talk, double agendas, double priorities, and double interests can present crippling business risks when your storefront stretches for 6000 miles."[70] HBI represents a joint venture of NEC (Japan), Campagnie de Machines Bull (France, and Honeywell (U.S.). To coordinate this joint venture, HBI considered it important to have transnational teams for front-end involvement in strategic planning, engineering, design, production, and marketing. Dotlich notes that HBI's primary corporate question is how to integrate a diverse pool of cultural values, traditions, and norms in order to be competitive.[71]

The effectiveness of global teams and their ability to integrate with organizational goals depends on the synergy it can attain despite the problems and setbacks that result from the workings of an intercultural group.[72] The advantages of synergy are confirmed by Moran in a survey of managers from two multinational organizations. He found that the respondents could more quickly generate the advantages of cultural diversity in their organizations than the disadvantages. The advantages they listed included a greater opportunity for global competition (by being able to share experiences, technology, and a pool of international managers) and a greater opportunity for cross-cultural understanding and exposure to different viewpoints. The disadvantages they listed included problems resulting from differences in language, communication, and varying managerial styles; complex decision-making processes; fewer promotional opportunities; personality conflicts, often resulting from stereotyping and prejudice; and greater complexity in the workplace.[73]

How can management find out how well its international teams are performing and what areas need to be improved? The following criteria for evaluating the success of such teams is proposed by Indrei Ratiu of the Intercultural Management Association in Paris:

- Do members work together with a common purpose? Is this purpose something that is spelled out and felt by all to be worth fighting for?
- Has the team developed a common language or procedure? Does it have a common way of doing things, a process for holding meetings?
- Does the team build on what works, learning to identify the positive actions before being overwhelmed by the negatives?
- Does the team attempt to spell out things within the limits of the cultural differences involved, delimiting the mystery level by directness and openness regardless of the cultural origins of participants?
- Do the members recognize the impact of their own cultural programming on individual and group behavior? Do they deal with, not avoid, their differences in order to create synergy?

- Does the team have fun? (Within successful multicultural groups, the cultural differences become a source of continuing surprise, discovery, and amusement rather than irritation or frustration.)[74]

The Role of Women in International Management

> Around the world, women are remaking companies, society, and themselves. But in each country, women have achieved different things, fought different battles—and made different sacrifices.[75]

Opportunities for female indigenous employees to move up the managerial ladder in a given culture depend on the values and the expectations regarding the role of women in that society. In Japan, for example, the workplace has traditionally been male domain as far as managerial careers are concerned (although rapid changes are now taking place). To the older generation, a working married woman represented a loss of face to the husband because it implied that he was not able to support her. Women were usually only allowed clerical positions, under the assumption that they would leave to raise a family and perhaps later return to part-time work. Employers thus made little effort to train them for upper-level positions.[76] As a result, very few women workers have been in supervisory or managerial posts—thus limiting the short-term upward mobility of women through the managerial ranks.[77]

The younger generation and increased global competitiveness have brought some changes to traditional values regarding women's roles in Japan. Over 60 percent of Japanese women are now employed, including half of Japanese mothers.[78] But how and when these cultural changes will affect the number of Japanese women in managerial positions remains to be seen.

Where one finds limitations on managerial opportunities for women in their own country, there are obviously even more limitations on their opportunities as expatriates. Overall, more managerial opportunities are available for American women than for women in most other countries. But, even for American women, who now fill over 25 percent of the managerial positions at home, commensurate opportunities are not available to them abroad: about 6 percent of North American expatriate managers are women.[79] The reasons for this anomaly can often be traced to the cultural expectations of the host countries—the same cultural values that keep women in these countries from the managerial ranks.

An explanation for the lack of expatriates who are female or represent other minority groups does not include their lack of desire to take overseas assignments; studies indicate their strong willingness to work abroad. Nor can the situation be explained by their lack of success: for example, a major study by Adler of North American women working as expatriate managers in countries around the world showed that they are, for the most part, successful.[80]

The most difficult job seems to be getting the assignment in the first place. One of the major reasons is that North American executives are reluctant to send minorities abroad because they assume they will be subject to the same culturally based biases as at home, or they assume a lack of understanding and acceptance, particularly in certain countries. Research on 52 female expatriate managers, for example, shows this assumption to be highly questionable. Adler showed, first and foremost, that foreigners are seen as foreigners; further, a woman who is a foreigner (called a *gaijin* in Japan) is not expected to act like a local woman. In fact, Adler and Izraeli say, "Asians see female expatriates as foreigners who happen to be women, not as women who happen to be foreigners." The other women in the study echoed this view. One woman based in Hong Kong noted, "'It doesn't make any difference if you are blue, green, purple, or a frog. If you have the best product at the best price, they'll buy.'"[81]

Women and minorities represent a significant resource for overseas assignments—whether as expatriates or as host-country nationals, that is underutilized by American companies. Adler studied this phenonomen regarding women and recommends that businesses (1) avoid assuming that a female executive will fail because of the way she will be received or because of problems experienced by female spouses; (2) avoid assuming that a woman will not want to go overseas; and (3) give female managers every chance to succeed by giving them the titles, status, and recognition appropriate to the position—as well as sufficient time to be effective.[82]

Conclusion

The effectiveness of managers at foreign locations is crucial to the success of the firm's operations, particularly because of the lack of proximity to, and control by, headquarters executives. The ability of expatriates to initiate and maintain cooperative relationships with local people and agencies will determine the long-term success, even viability, of the operation. In a real sense, a company's global cadre represents its most valuable resource. Proactive management of that resource by headquarters will result in having the right people in the right place at the right time, appropriately trained, prepared, and supported. MNCs using these IHRM practices can anticipate the effective management of the foreign operation, the fostering of expatriates' careers, and ultimately, the enhanced success of the corporation.

INTERNET RESOURCES

Visit the Deresky companion Web site at http://prenhall.com/Deresky for this chapter's Internet resources.

1. Global Human Resource management is a vital component of implementing global strategy and is increasingly being recognized as a major determinant of success or failure in international business.

2. The main staffing alternatives for global operations are the ethnocentric, polycentric, regiocentric, and global approaches. Each approach has its appropriate uses, according to its advantages and disadvantages.

3. The causes of expatriate failure include the following: poor selection based on inappropriate criteria, inadequate preparation before assignment, alienation from headquarters, inability of manager or family to adapt to local environment, inadequate compensation package, and poor programs for career support and repatriation.

4. Appropriate and attractive compensation packages must be designed by IHRM staffs to sustain a competitive global management cadre. Compensation packages for host-country managers must be designed to fit the local culture and situation as well as the firm's objectives.

5. Support programs for expatriates should include information from and contact with the home organization, as well as career guidance and support after the overseas assignment.

6. Global management teams offer greater opportunities for competition—by sharing experiences, technology, and international managers—and greater opportunities for cross-cultural understanding and exposure to different viewpoints. Disadvantages can result for communication and cross-cultural conflicts and greater complexity in the workplace.

7. Women and minorities represent an underutilized resource in international management; a major reason for this situation is the assumption that culturally based biases may limit the opportunities and success of females and minorities.

Chapter 10

Motivating and Leading

Opening Profile: Starbucks' Java Style Helps to Recruit, Motivate, and Retain Leaders in Beijing

Starbucks Coffee International, already operating in London, Japan, Singapore, Taiwan, the Philippines, and Thailand, is continuing its aggressive global expansion. It plans to have 500 coffee shops in Europe by end 2003, and had 35 shops in Beijing and Shanghai in 2002. No stranger to training leaders from around the world in the Starbucks' style, the company nevertheless has had a challenge in recruiting, motivating and retaining managers for its Beijing outlets—to say nothing of getting a nation of tea-drinkers to switch to java.

Starbucks' first challenge has been to recruit good managers in a country where the demand for local managers by foreign companies expanding there is far greater than the supply of managers with any experience in capitalist-style companies. Chinese recruits have stressed that they are looking for opportunity to get training and to advance in global companies, more than money; they know that managers with experience in Western organizations can always get a job. The brand's pop-culture reputation is also an attraction to young Beijingers.

In order to expose the recruits to java-style culture as well as to train them for management, Starbucks brings them to Tacoma, Washington, for three months to give them a taste of West-Coast lifestyle and the company's informal culture, such as Western-style backyard barbecues. Then they are exposed to the art of cappuccino-making at a real store before dawn and how to concoct dozens of fancy coffees. They get the same intensive training as anyone else anywhere in the world. One recruit, Mr. Wang, who worked in a large Beijing hotel before finding out how to make a triple grand latte, said that he enjoys the casual atmosphere and respect. The training and culture is very different from the expectations at a traditional state-owned company in China, where the work is strictly defined and has no challenge for employees.

Starbucks has found that motivating their managers in Beijing is multifaceted. They know that people won't switch jobs for money alone. They want to work for a company that gives them an opportunity to learn. They want to have a good working environment and a company with a strong reputation. The recruits have expressed their need for trust and participation, in an environment where local nationals are traditionally not expected to exercise initiative or authority; in all, what seems to motivate them more than anything else is dignity.

SOURCES: www.Starbucks.com, "Starbucks' Expansion in China Is Slated," *Wall Street Journal*, October 5, 1998; *The Economist*, October 6, 2001.

MOTIVATING

> In Mexico, everything is a personal matter; but a lot of managers don't get it.
>
> ROBERT HOSKINS, MANAGER, LEVITON MANUFACTURING, JUAREZ.

After managers set up a firm's operations by planning strategy, organizing the work and responsibilities, and staffing those operations, they turn their attention to everyday activities. This ongoing behavior of individual people carrying out various daily tasks enables the firm to accomplish its objectives. Getting those people to perform their jobs efficiently and effectively is at the heart of the manager's challenge.

As this chapter's Opening Profile illustrates, motivation—and therefore appropriate leadership style—is affected by many powerful variables (societal, cultural, and political). In China, there is a long history behind workers' assumptions about "the way we do things around here," and a strong culture which determines attitudes toward work. But in the big cities like Beijing, employees are eager to learn Western ways in order to make themselves more marketable. Foreign companies are challenged to find the right mix of old and new in order to motivate and retain good employees.

Our objective in this chapter is to consider motivation and leadership in the context of diverse cultural milieus. We need to know what, if any, differences there are in the societal factors that elicit and maintain behaviors that lead to high employee productivity and job satisfaction. Are effective motivational and leadership techniques universal or culture based?

CROSS-CULTURAL RESEARCH ON MOTIVATION

Motivation is very much a function of the context of a person's work and personal life. That context is greatly influenced by cultural variables, which affect the attitudes and behaviors of individuals (and groups) on the job. The framework of this context was described in Chapter 3 and illustrated in Exhibit 3-1. In applying Hofstede's research on cultural dimensions of individualism, uncertainty avoidance, masculinity, and power distance, for example, we can make some generalized assumptions about motivation, such as:

- High uncertainty avoidance suggests the need for job security, whereas people with low uncertainty avoidance would probably be motivated by more risky opportunities for variety and fast-track advancement.
- High power distance suggests motivators in the relationship between subordinates and their boss, whereas low power distance implies that people would be more motivated by teamwork and relations with their peers.
- High individualism suggests people would be motivated by opportunities for individual advancement and autonomy; collectivism (low individualism) suggests that motivation will more likely work through appeals to group goals and support.

- High masculinity suggests that most people would be more comfortable with the traditional division of work and roles; in a more feminine culture, the boundaries could be looser, motivating people through more flexible roles and work networks.

Misjudging the importance of these cultural variables in the workplace may result not only in a failure to motivate, but also in demotivation. An example given by Rieger and Wong-Rieger:

> In Thailand, the introduction of an individual merit bonus plan, which runs counter to the societal norm of group cooperation, may result in a decline rather than an increase in productivity from employees who refuse to openly compete with each other.[1]

In considering what motivates people, we have to understand their needs, goals, value systems, and expectations. No matter what their nationality or cultural background, people are driven to fulfill needs and to achieve goals. But what are those needs, what goals do they want to achieve, and what can motivate that drive to satisfy their goals?

The Meaning of Work

Because our focus here is on the needs that affect the working environment, it is important to understand first what work means to people from different backgrounds. For most people, the basic meaning of work is tied to economic necessity (money for food, housing, and so forth) for the individual and for society. However, the additional connotations of work are more subjective, especially about what work provides other than money—achievement, honor, social contacts, or whatever.

Another way to view work, though, is through its relationship to the rest of a person's life. The Thais call work *ngan*, which is the same as their word for "play," and they tend to introduce periods of play in their workdays. On the other hand, most people in China, Germany, and the United States have a positive attitude toward work. Especially in work-oriented China, seven-day workweeks with long hours and few days off are common.[2] A study of average work hours in various countries conducted by Steers found that Koreans worked longer hours and took fewer vacation days than workers in Thailand, Hong Kong, Taiwan, Singapore, India, Japan, and Indonesia.[3] The study concluded that the Koreans' hard work was attributable to loyalty to the company, group-oriented achievement and emphasis on group harmony and business relationships.

Studies on the meaning of work in eight countries were carried out by George England and a group of researchers who are called the Meaning of Work (MOW) International Research Team.[4] Their research sought to determine a person's idea of the relative importance of work compared to that of leisure, community, religion, and family. They called this concept **work centrality**, defined as "the degree of general importance that working has in the life of an individual at any given point in time." The mean score on the work centrality index for the eight countries studied is shown in Exhibit 10-1.

The obvious general implication from these findings is that the higher the mean work centrality score, the more motivated and committed the workers would be. Of even more importance to managers (as an aid to understanding culture-based differences in motivation) are the specific reasons for valuing work. What kinds of needs does the working environment satisfy and how does this differ among populations?

Some excellent insights into this question were provided by the MOW research team when they asked people in the eight countries to what extent they regarded work as satisfying six different functions. The six functions were as follows: work (1) provides a needed income, (2) is interesting and satisfying, (3) provides contacts with others, (4) facilitates a way to serve society, (5) keeps one occupied, and (6) gives

Exhibit 10-1

The Relative Meaning of Work in Eight Countries

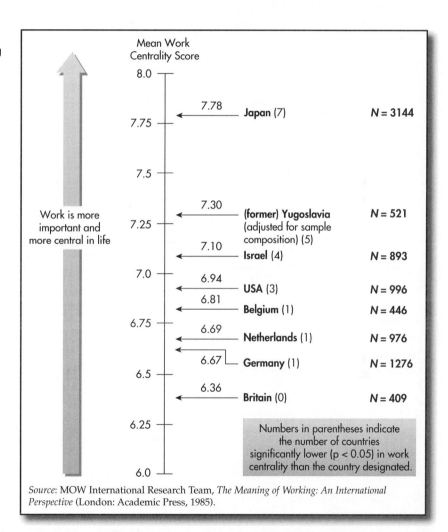

Source: MOW International Research Team, *The Meaning of Working: An International Perspective* (London: Academic Press, 1985).

status and prestige. The results are shown in Exhibit 10-2. Note the similarities of some of these functions with Maslow's need categories and Herzberg's categories of motivators and maintenance factors. Clearly, these studies can help international managers to anticipate what attitudes people have toward their work, what aspects of work in their life context are meaningful to them, and therefore what approach the manager should take in setting up motivation and incentive plans.

In addition to the differences among countries within each category—such as the higher level of interest and satisfaction derived from work by the Israelis as compared with the Germans—it is interesting to note the within-country differences. While income was clearly the most important factor for all countries, it apparently has a far greater importance than any other factor in Japan. In other countries, like the Netherlands, the relative importance of different factors was more evenly distributed.

The broader implications of such comparisons about what work means to people are derived from considering the total cultural context: the low rating given by the Japanese to the status and prestige found in work, for instance, suggests that those needs are more fully satisfied elsewhere in their lives, such as within the family and community. In the Middle East, religion plays a major role in all aspects of life, including work. The Islamic work ethic is a commitment toward fulfillment and so business motives are held in the highest regard.[5] The ori-

Exhibit 10-2
The Perceived Utility of the Functions of Work (Mean Number of Points)

COUNTRY	N	WORKING PROVIDES YOU WITH AN INCOME THAT IS NEEDED	WORKING IS BASICALLY INTERESTING AND SATISFYING TO YOU	WORKING PERMITS YOU TO HAVE INTERESTING CONTACTS WITH OTHER PEOPLE	WORKING IS A USEFUL WAY FOR YOU TO SERVE SOCIETY	WORKING KEEPS YOU OCCUPIED	WORKING GIVES YOU STATUS AND PRESTIGE
Japan	3180	45.4	13.4	14.7	9.3	11.5*	5.6‡
Germany	1264	40.5	16.7	13.1	7.4	11.8	10.1
Belgium	447	35.5	21.3	17.3	10.2	8.7	6.9
Britain	471	34.4	17.9	15.3	10.5	11.0	10.9
Yugoslavia	522	34.1	19.8	9.8	15.1	11.7	9.3
United States	989	33.1	16.8	15.3	11.5	11.3	11.9
Israel	940	31.1	26.2	11.1	13.6	9.4	8.5
Netherlands	979	26.2	23.5	17.9	16.7	10.6	4.9
All countries combined	8792	35.0†	19.5	14.3	11.8	10.8	8.5

Working keeps you occupied was translated in Japan in such a manner that there is real question about how similar its meaning was to that intended.
†The combined totals weight each country equally regardless of sample size.
‡The mean points assigned by a country to the six functions add to approximately 100 points.

Source: Meaning of Work International Research Team, *The Meaning of Working: An International Perspective* (London: Academic Press, 1985).

gin of the Islamic work ethic is in the Muslim holy book, the Qur'an, and the words of the Prophet Mohammed:

> On the day of judgment, the honest Muslim merchant will stand side by side with the martyrs.

MOHAMMED

Muslims feel that work is a virtue and an obligation to establish equilibrium in one's individual and social life. The Arab worker is defined by his or her level of commitment to family, and work is perceived as the determining factor to the ability to enjoy social and family life.[6] A study of 117 managers in Saudi Arabia by Ali found that Arab managers are highly committed to the Islamic work ethic and that there is a moderate tendency toward individualism.[7]

Exhibit 10-3 shows the results of the study and gives more insight into the Islamic work ethic. Another study by Kuroda and Suzuki found that Arabs are

Exhibit 10-3
The Islamic Work Ethic Responses by Saudi Arabian Managers

ITEM	MEAN*
Islamic Work Ethic	
1. Laziness is a vice.	4.66
2. Dedication to work is a virtue.	4.62
3. Good work benefits both one's self and others.	4.57
4. Justice and generosity in the workplace are necessary conditions for society's welfare.	4.59
5. Producing more than enough to meet one's personal needs contributes to the prosperity of society as a whole.	3.71
6. One should carry work out to the best of one's ability.	4.70
7. Work is not an end in itself but a means to foster personal growth and social relations.	3.97
8. Life has no meaning without work.	4.47
9. More leisure time is good for society.	3.08
10. Human relations in organizations should be emphasized and encouraged.	3.89
11. Work enables man to control nature.	4.06
12. Creative work is a source of happiness and accomplishment.	4.60
13. Any man who works is more likely to get ahead in life.	3.92
14. Work gives one the chance to be independent.	4.35
15. A successful man is the one who meets deadlines at work.	4.17
16. One should constantly work hard to meet responsibilities.	4.25
17. The value of work is derived from the accompanying intention rather than its results.	3.16

*On scale of 1–5 (5 highest)

Source: Adapted from Abbas J. Ali, "The Islamic Work Ethic in Arabia," *Journal of Psychology* 126, no. 5 (1992): 507–519 (513).

serious about their work and that favoritism, give-and-take, and paternalism have no place in the Arab workplace; they compared this attitude to that of the Japanese and Americans who consider friendship to be an integral part of the workplace.[8]

Other variables affect the perceived meaning of work and how it satisfies various needs, such as the relative wealth of a country.[9] When people have a high standard of living, work can take on a different meaning other than simply to provide the basic economic necessities of life. In fact, economic differences among countries was found to explain variation in attitudes toward work in a study by Furnham et. al., of over 12,000 young people from 41 countries on all five continents. Specifically, they found that young people in Far and Middle Eastern countries reported highest competitiveness and acquisitiveness for money, while those from North and South America scored highest on worth ethic and "mastery" (i.e., to continue to struggle to master something).[10] Such studies show the complexity of the underlying reasons for differences in attitudes toward work—cultural, economic, and so on—which must be taken into account when considering what needs and motivations people bring to the workplace. All in all, research shows a considerable cultural variability affecting how work meets employees' needs.

The Need Hierarchy in the International Context

How can a manager know what motivates people in a specific country? Certainly, by drawing on the experiences of others who have worked there; also, by inferring the likely type of motivational structure present by studying what is known about the culture in that region. In addition, some research and comparative studies about needs in specific countries are available and can provide another piece of the puzzle.

Some researchers have used Maslow's hierarchy of needs to study motivation in other countries. A classic study by Haire, Ghiselli, and Porter surveyed 3641 managers in 14 countries. They concluded that Maslow's needs, in particular the upper-level ones, are important at the managerial level, although the managers reported that the degree to which their needs were fulfilled did not live up to their expectations.[11]

In a similar study, Ronen investigated whether work-related values and needs are similar across nationalities and whether the motivation categories of Maslow and Herzberg apply universally. Studying trained, nonmanagerial male employees (in Germany, Canada, France, Japan, and the United Kingdom), he found that such similarities do exist and that there are common clusters of needs and goals across nationalities. These clusters include (1) job goals, such as working area, work time, physical working conditions, fringe benefits, and job security; (2) relationships with coworkers and supervisors; and (3) work challenges and opportunities for using skills.[12] Ronen concludes that **need clusters** are constant across nationalities and that Maslow's need hierarchy is confirmed by those clusters. In addition, he claims that Herzberg's categories are confirmed by the **cross-national need clusters** in his study.

One clear conclusion is that managers around the world have similar needs but show differing levels of satisfaction of those needs derived from their jobs. Variables other than culture may be at play, however. One of these may be the country's stage of economic development. In the transitioning economy in Russia, for example, it was found in a study by Elenkov that Russian managers stress security and belongingness needs as opposed to higher-order needs.[13] Whatever the reason, many companies that have started operations in other countries have experienced differences in the apparent needs of the local employees and how they expect work to be recognized. Mazda, of Japan, experienced this problem in its Michigan plant. Japanese firms tend to confer recognition in the form of plaques, attention, and applause. Hence Japanese workers are likely to be insulted by material incentives because such rewards imply that they would work harder to achieve them than they otherwise would. Instead, Japanese firms focus on group-wide or companywide goals, compared with the American emphasis on individual goals, achievement, and reward.

When considering the cross-cultural applicability of Maslow's theory, then, it is not the needs that are in question as much as the ordering of those needs in the hierarchy. The hierarchy reflects the Western culture where Maslow conducted his study, and different hierarchies might better reflect other cultures. For example, Eastern cultures focus on the needs of society rather than on those of individuals. Nevis proposes that a hierarchy more accurately reflecting the needs of the Chinese would comprise four levels: (1) belonging, (2) physiological needs, (3) safety, and (4) self-actualization in the service of society.[14] It is difficult to observe or measure the individual needs of a Chinese person because, from childhood, these are intermeshed with the needs of society. Clearly, however, along with culture, the political beliefs at work in China dominate many facets of motivation. As the backbone of the industrial system, cadres (managers and technicians) and workers are given exact and detailed prescriptions of what is expected of them as members of a factory, workshop, or work unit; this results in conformity at the expense of creativity. Workers are accountable to their group, which is a powerful motivator. Because being "unemployed" is not an option in China, it is important for employees to maintain themselves as cooperating members of the work group.[15] Money is also a motivator, stemming from the historical political insecurity and economic disasters which have perpetuated the need for a high level of savings.[16] A Gallup opinion poll cited in the 1998 World Competitiveness Yearbook, found that a priority among Chinese is to "work hard and get rich," compared to Europeans and Americans who value self-achievement over wealth.[17]

The Intrinsic–Extrinsic Dichotomy in the International Context

The intrinsic–extrinsic dichotomy is another useful model (researched by a number of authors) for considering motivation in the workplace. Herzberg's research, for example, found two sets of needs: (1) motivational factors (intrinsic) and (2) maintenance factors (extrinsic).

Results from others' research using Herzberg's model provide some insight into motivation in different countries and also help us to determine whether the intrinsic–extrinsic dichotomy is generalizable across cultures. Research on managers in Greece and on workers in general in an Israeli kibbutz indicate that all these people are motivated more by the nature of the work itself; dissatisfactions resulted from the conditions surrounding the work.[18,19] Another study in Zambia found, in general, the same dichotomy. Work motivation was found to result from the intrinsic factors of the opportunity for growth and the nature of the work and, to some extent, physical provisions; factors that produced dissatisfaction and were not motivators were extrinsic—relations with others, fairness in organizational practices, and personal problems.[20]

In addition to research on single countries, Herzberg's theory has been used to compare different countries on the basis of job factors and job satisfaction. A study of MBA candidates from the United States, Australia, Canada, and Singapore, for example, indicated that Herzberg's motivational factors were more important to these prospective managers than hygiene factors.[21] In a broader study of managers from Canada, the United Kingdom, France, and Japan to determine the relative importance of job factors to them and how satisfied they were with those factors, Kanungo and Wright drew a number of interesting conclusions. Interpreting their results, we can draw some overall conclusions: the managers indicated that internally mediated factors (intrinsic, job content factors) were more important than organizationally controlled factors (extrinsic, job context factors). However, they found differences across countries, in particular between the United Kingdom and France, in how much importance the managers placed on job outcomes and also in their relative levels of satisfaction with those outcomes.[22] As a practical application of their research results, Kanungo and Wright suggest the following implications for motivation in the workplace:

> Efforts to improve managerial performance in the UK should focus on job content rather than on job context. . . . Job enrichment programs are more likely to improve performance in an intrinsically oriented society such as Britain, where satisfaction tends to be derived from the job itself, than in France, where job context factors, such as security and fringe benefits, are more highly valued.[23]

To answer common questions about whether Japanese-style management practices—work groups, quality circles, and long-term employment—make a difference to commitment and job satisfaction, Lincoln studied 8302 workers in 106 factories in the United States and Japan (though not specifically using Herzberg's factors). He concluded that those practices had similar positive or negative effects on work attitudes in both countries. But, while the level of commitment to the company was essentially the same in both samples, the Japanese indicated a lower level of job satisfaction.[24]

The lower level of satisfaction is contrary to popular expectations because of the well-known Japanese environment of teamwork, productivity, long-term employment, and dedication to the company. However, previous research has also found a lower level of job satisfaction in Japan.[25] Lower work satisfaction indicates a higher level of motivation to fulfill personal and company goals (that is, to do better), compared to a lower level of motivation indicated by complacency. As Lincoln points out, however, these research findings could be the result of another cultural variable introducing a measurement bias: the Japanese tendency to "color their evaluations of nearly everything with a large dose of pessimism, humility and understatement" in their persistent quest to do better.[26] This underscores the need to consider carefully all the cultural variables involved in observing or managing motivation.

Clearly, there is a need for more cross-cultural research on motivation, but one can draw the tentative conclusion that managers around the world are motivated more by intrinsic than by extrinsic factors. Considerable doubt remains, however, about the universality of Herzberg's or Maslow's theories because of the inability to take into account all of the relevant cultural variables when researching motivation. Different factors have different meaning within the entire cultural context and must be taken into account on a situation-by-situation basis. The need to consider the entire national and cultural context is shown in the following Comparative Management in Foucs, which highlights motivational issues for Mexican workers and indicates the importance to them of what Herzberg calls maintenance factors. As you read, consider whether this situation supports or refutes Herzberg's theory.

Comparative Management in Focus

Motivation in Mexico

To get anything done here, the manager has to be more of an instructor, teacher, or father figure than a boss.

ROBERT HOSKINS, MANAGER, LEVITON MANUFACTURING, JUAREZ.

It is particularly important for an aspiring international manager to become familiar with Mexican factory workers because of the increasing volume of manufacturing that is being outsourced there.[27]

To understand the cultural milieu in Mexico, we can draw on research that concludes that Latin American societies, including Mexico, rank high on power distance (the acknowledgment of hierarchical authority) and on uncertainty avoidance (a preference for security and formality over risk). In addition, they rank low on individualism, preferring collectivism, which values the good of the group, family, or country over individual achievement.[28] In Mexico, the family is of central importance; loyalty and commitment to the family frequently determines employment, promotion, or special treatment for contracts. Unfortunately, it is this admirable cultural norm that often results in motivation and productivity problems on the job by contributing to very high absenteeism and a turnover rate especially in the *maquiladoras*. This high turnover and absenteeism are costly to employers, thereby offsetting the advantage of relatively low labor cost per hour. "Family reasons" (taking care of sick relatives or elderly parents) are the most common reasons given for absenteeism and for failing to return to work.[29] Workers often simply do not come back to work after vacations or holidays. In fact, for many Mexican males, the value of work is primarily that it enables them to fulfill their culturally imposed responsibilities as head of household and breadwinner rather than to seek individual achievement.[30] Machismo (sharp role differentiation based on gender) and prestige are important characteristics of the Mexican culture.

As a people, speaking very generally, Mexicans are very proud and patriotic; *respeto* (respect) is important to them, and slights against personal dignity are regarded as a grave provocation.[31] Mexican workers expect to be treated in the same respectful manner that they use toward one another. As noted by one U.S. expatriate, foreign managers must adapt to Mexico's "softer culture"; Mexican workers "need more communication, more relationship-building, and more reassurance than employees in the U.S."[32] The Mexican people are very warm and have a leisurely attitude toward time; face-to-face interaction is best for any kind of business, with time allowed for socializing and appreciating their cultural artifacts, buildings, and so forth. Taking time to celebrate a worker's birthday, for instance, will show that you are a *simpatico* boss and will increase workers' loyalty and effort. The workers' expectations of small considerations which seem inconsequential to U.S. managers, should not be discounted. In one maquiladora, when the company stopped providing the annual Halloween candy, the employees filed a grievance to the state arbitration board—Junta de Conciliacion y Arbitraje.

Most managers in Mexico find that the management style that works best there is authoritative and paternal. In fact, paternalism is expected; the manager is regarded as the *"el patron" (pahtrone)*, or father figure, whose role it is to take care of the workers as an extended family.[33] Employees expect managers to be the authority; they are the "elite"—power rests with the owner or manager and other prominent community leaders. For the most part, if not told to do it, the workers won't do it; nor will they question the boss or make any decisions for the boss.[34] Nevertheless, employees perceive the manager as a person, not as a concept or a function, and success often depends on the ability of a foreign manager to adopt a personalized management style, such as by greeting all the workers as they come in for their shift.

Generally speaking, many Mexican factory workers doubt their ability to personally influence the outcome of their lives; they are apt to attribute events to the will of God, luck, timing, or relationships with higher authority figures. For many, decisions are made on the basis of ideals, emotions, and intuition, rather than objective information. However, there is increasing evidence of individualism and materialism, particularly among the upwardly mobile high-tech and professional Mexican employees.

Corrective discipline and motivation must occur through training examples, cooperation, and, if necessary, subtle shaming. As a disciplinary measure, it is a mistake to insult a Mexican directly; an outright insult implies an insult to the whole family. As a motivation, one must appeal to the pride of the Mexican employees and avoid causing them to feel humiliated. Given that "getting ahead" is often associated more with outside forces than with one's own actions, the motivation and reward system becomes difficult to structure in the usual ways. Past experiences have indicated that, for the most part, motivation through participative decision making is not as effective as that through the more traditional and expected autocratic methods. However, with careful implementation, the mutual respect and caring the Mexican people have for one another can lead to positive team spirit needed for the team structure to be used successfully by companies such as GM in its highest-quality plant in the world in Ramos Arizpe, near Saltillo, Mexico.[35] Although a study by Nicholls, Lane, and Brechu concluded that there are considerable cultural constraints on using self-managing teams in Mexico, the Mexican executives surveyed suggested that the relative success depends on the implementation.[36] The conflicts are between the norms of behavior in self-managed teams (typical of U.S. and Canadian culture), and typical values in Mexican business culture, as shown in Exhibit 10-4.

While self-managed teams require individual risk-taking of leaders to spearhead team initiatives, those behaviors, according to the survey of Mexican executives, "are in sharp contrast to the behavioral norms of the paternalistic and hierarchical tradition of managers and workers in the Mexican work place." The workers expect the mangers to give instructions and make decisions.[37] The business culture in Mexico is also attributable to prevailing conditions in Mexico's economy of low levels of education, training, and technical skills. The Mexican executives surveyed gave some suggestions for

Exhibit 10-4

Contrasting Cultures: Self-Managed Teams and the Mexican Business Culture

SELF-MANAGED TEAMS	MEXICAN BUSINESS CULTURE
NORMS	VALUE EXPECTATIONS
Individualism	*Collectivism*
Personal accountability	Shared responsibility
Individual responsibility	Moral obligation
Confidence in ability	Paternalistic management
Confrontation and debate	Harmony
Low uncertainty avoidance	*High uncertainty avoidance*
Take self-initiative	Resist change
Low power distance	*High power distance*
Self-leadership	Respect status roles
Bottom-up decision making	Top-down hierarchical structure
REQUIRED BEHAVIORS	EXPECTED BEHAVIORS
Team members solve problems, resolve conflicts, set goals, assess performance, initiate change, and communicate upward. Managers delegate, provide information, and encourage open communication.	Workers follow instructions, respect managers, receive feedback, avoid conflict and criticism, and save face. Managers make decisions, direct, control, and discipline.

Source: C. E. Nicholls, H. W. Lane, M. B. Brechu, "Taking Self-Managed Teams to Mexico," *Academy of Management Executive* 13, no. 3 (1999).

implementing work teams, given below, and cautioned that the process of implementation will take a long time.

- Foster a culture of individual responsibility among team members.
- Anticipate the impact of changes in power distribution.
- Provide leadership from the top throughout the implementation process.
- Provide adequate training to prepare workers for team work.
- Develop motivation and harmony through clear expectations.
- Encourage an environment of shared responsibility.[38]

For the most part, Mexican workers expect that authority will not be abused, but rather that it follow the family model where everyone works together in a dignified manner according to their designated roles.[39] Any event which may break this harmony, or seem to confront authority, will likely be covered up. This may result in a supervisor hiding defective work, for example, or, as in the case of a steel conveyor plant in Puebla, a total worker walkout rather than use of the grievance process.[40] Contributing to these kinds of problems is the need to save face for oneself and to respect others' place and honor. Public criticism is regarded as humiliating. Employees like an atmosphere of formality and respect. They typically use flattery and call people by their titles rather than their names, to maintain an atmosphere of regard for status and respect.

A context of continuing economic problems and a relatively low standard of living for most workers helps explain why Maslow's higher order needs (self-actualization, achievement, status) are generally not very high on most Mexican workers' list of needs. In discussing compensation, Mariah de Forest, who consults for American firms in Mexico, suggests that:

> Rather than an impersonal wage scale, Mexican workers tend to think in terms of payment now for services rendered now. A daily incentive system with automatic payouts for production exceeding quotas, as well as daily/monthly attendance bonuses, works well.[41]

Because of economic reforms and the peso devaluation, money is now a pressing motivational factor for most employees. Since the enjoyment of life is highly valued by workers, many companies in Mexico provide recreation facilities—a picnic area, a soccer field, and so forth. Bonuses are expected regardless of productivity; in fact, it is the law to give Christmas bonuses of 15 days' pay to each worker. Fringe benefits are also important to Mexicans; because most Mexican workers are poor, the company provides the only source of such benefits for them. In particular, benefits that help to manage family-related issues are positive motivators for employees to at least turn up for work. To this end, companies often provide on-site health care facilities for workers and their families, nurseries, free meals, and even small loans in crisis situations.[42] In addition, those companies which understand the local infrastructure problems often provide a company bus to minimize the pervasive problems of absenteeism and tardiness.

The foregoing statements are broad generalizations about Mexican factory workers. There are increasing numbers of American managers in Mexico because NAFTA has encouraged more U.S. businesses to move operations there. For firms on American soil, managers may employ many Mexican-Americans in an intercultural setting. As the second-largest and fastest-growing ethnic group, Mexican-Americans represent an important subculture requiring management attention as they take an increasing proportion of the jobs in the United States. Yet, they remain the least assimilated ethnic group in the majority mainstream, partially from economic or occupational causes, and partially from choice.[43]

From the research, it appears that little conclusive information is available to answer a manager's direct question of exactly how to motivate in any particular culture, because we cannot assume the universal applicability of the motivational theories, or even concepts, that have been used to research differences among cultures. Further, the entire motivational context must be taken into account. For example, Western firms entering markets in Eastern Europe invariably run into difficulties in motivating their local staff. Those workers have been used to working under entirely different circumstances and usually do not trust foreign managers. Typically, then, the work systems and responsibilities must be highly structured because workers in Eastern Europe are not likely to use their own judgment in making decisions and managerial skills are not developed.[44]

In sum, motivation is situational, and savvy managers use all they know about the relevant culture or subculture—consulting frequently with local people—to infer the best means of motivating in that context. Further, tactful managers consciously avoid an ethnocentric attitude, in which they make assumptions about a person's goals, motivation, or work habits based on their own frame of reference, and they do not make negative value judgments about a person's level of motivation because it differs from their own.

There are many cultural variables that affect people's sense of what is attainable, and thus affect motivation. One, for example is how much control people believe they have over their environment and their destiny—whether they believe that they can control certain events, not just be at the mercy of external forces. While Americans typically feel a strong internal locus of control, others attribute results to, for example, the will of God (in the case of Muslims) or to the good fortune of being born in the right social class or family (in the case of many Latin Americans). Whereas Americans feel that hard work will get the job done, many Hong Kong Chinese believe that outcomes are determined by *joss*, or luck. Clearly, then, managers must use persuasive strategies to motivate employees when they do not readily connect their personal work behaviors with outcomes or productivity.

The role of culture in the motivational process is shown in Exhibit 10-5. An employee's needs are largely determined by the cultural context of values and attitudes—along with the national variables—in which he or she lives and works; those needs then determine the meaning of work for that employee. The manager's understanding of what work means in that employee's life can then lead to the design of a culturally appropriate job context and reward

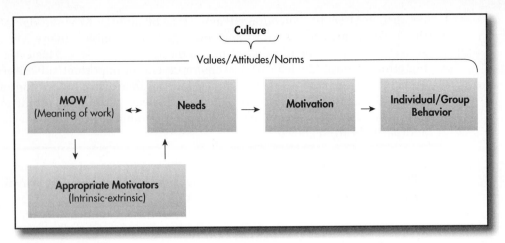

Exhibit 10-5
The Role of Culture in Job Motivation

system to guide individual and group employee job behavior to meet mutual goals.

Reward Systems

Incentives and rewards are an integral part of motivation in a corporation. Recognizing and understanding different motivational patterns across cultures leads to the design of appropriate reward systems. In the United States, there are common patterns of rewards, varying among levels of the company and types of occupations and based on experience and research with Americans. Rewards usually fall into five categories: financial, social status, job content, career, and professional.[45] The relative emphasis on one or more of these five categories varies from country to country. In Japan, for example, reward systems are based primarily on seniority, and much emphasis is put on the bonus system. In addition, distinction is made there between the regular workforce and the temporary workforce, which usually comprises women expected to leave when they start a family. As is usually the case, the regular workforce receives considerably more rewards than the temporary workforce, both in pay and benefits and in the allocation of interesting jobs.[46] For the regular workforce, the emphasis is on the long-term effectiveness of the employee in terms of behavior, personality, and group output. Rewarding the individual is frowned on in Japan because it encourages competition rather than the desired group cooperation. Therefore, specific cash incentives are usually limited. In Taiwan, recognition and affection are important; company departments compete for praise from top management at their annual celebration.

In contrast, the entire reward system in China is very different from that of most countries. The low wage rates are compensated for by free housing, schools, and medical care. While egalitarianism still seems to prevail, the recent free-enterprise reform movements have encouraged *duo lao, duo de* (more work, more pay). One important incentive is training, which gives workers more power. One approach used in the past—and one that seems quite negative to Americans—is best illustrated by the example of a plaque award labeled "Ms. Wong—Employee of the Month." While Westerners would assume that Ms. Wong had excelled as an employee, actually this award given in a Chinese retail store was for the worst employee; the plaque was designed to shame and embarrass her.[47] Younger Chinese in areas changing to a more market-based economy have seen a shift toward equity-based rewards, no doubt resulting from a gradual shift in work values.[48]

There is no doubt that culture plays a significant role in determining the appropriate incentive and reward systems around the world. Employees in collectivist cultures such as Japan, Korea, and Taiwan would not respond well to the typical American merit-based reward system to motivate employees because that would go against the traditional value system and disrupt the harmony and corporate culture.[49]

LEADING

> The manager's quintessential responsibility is to help his people realize their own highest potential.
>
> JACQUES MAISONROUGE, IBM WORLD TRADE CORPORATION.

As you read this section on leadership, consider the following questions: To what extent, and how, do leadership styles and practices around the world vary? What are the forces perpetuating that divergence? Where and why, will that divergence continue to be the strongest? Is there any evidence for convergence of leadership styles and practices around the world? What are the forces leading to that convergence, and how and where do you think this convergence will occur in the future? What are the implications of these questions for cross-cultural leaders?

The task of helping employees realize their highest potential in the workplace is the essence of leadership. The goal of every leader is to achieve the organization's objectives while achieving those of each employee. Today's global managers realize that increased competition requires them to be open to change and to rethink their old culturally conditioned modes of leadership.

The Global Leader's Role and Environment

The greatest competitive advantage global companies in the twenty-first century can have is effective global leaders. Yet this competitive challenge is not easy to meet. People tend to rise to leadership positions by proving themselves able to lead in their home-country corporate culture and meeting the generally accepted behaviors of that national culture. However, global leaders must broaden their horizons, both strategically and cross-culturally, and develop a more flexible model of leadership that can be applied anywhere—one that is adaptable to locational situations around the world.[50] From their recent research involving 125 global leaders in 50 companies, Morrison, Gregersen, and Black concluded that effective leaders must have global business and organizational savvy. They explain global business savvy as the ability to recognize global market opportunities for their company and having a vision of doing business worldwide. Global organizational savvy requires an intimate knowledge of the company's resources and capabilities in order to capture global markets; to understand each subsidiary's product lines and how the people and business operates on the local level. Morrison, Gregersen, and Black outline four personal development strategies through which companies and managers can meet these requirements of effective global leadership: travel, teamwork, training, and transfers (the four *ts*).[51]

Travel, of course, exposes managers to various cultures, economies, political systems and markets. Working on global teams teaches managers to operate on an interpersonal level while dealing with business decision-making processes which are embraced by differences in cultural norms and business models. While formal training seminars also play an important role, most of the global leaders interviewed said that the most influential developmental experience in their lives was the international assignment. In fact, increasingly global companies are requiring that their managers have overseas assignment experience in order to progress to top management positions.[52] Of course, the benefits accruing to the organization depend on how effectively the assignment and repatriation is handled, as discussed in Chapter 9.

Effective global leadership involves the ability to inspire and influence the thinking, attitudes, and behavior of people anywhere in the world.[53,54] The importance of the leadership role cannot be overemphasized because the leader's interactions strongly influence the motivation and behavior of employees, and ultimately, the entire climate of the organization. The cumulative effects of one or more weak managers can have a significant negative impact on the ability of the organization to meet its objectives.

Managers on international assignments try to maximize leadership effectiveness by juggling several important, and sometimes conflicting, roles as (1) a representative of the parent firm, (2) the manager of the local firm, (3) a resident of the local community, (4) a citizen of either the host country or of another country, (5) a member of a profession, and (6) a member of a family.[55]

The leader's role comprises the interaction of two sets of variables—the content and the context of leadership. The **content of leadership** comprises the attributes of the leader and the decisions to be made; the **context of leadership** comprises all those variables related to the particular situation.[56] The increased number of variables (political, economic, and cultural) in the context of the managerial job abroad requires astute leadership. Some of the variables in the content and context of the leader's role in foreign settings are shown in Exhibit 10-6. The multicultural leader's role thus blends leadership, communication, motivational, and other managerial skills within unique and ever-changing environments. We will examine the contingent nature of such leadership throughout this section.

Exhibit 10-6
Factors Affecting Leadership Abroad

<table>
<tr><td colspan="2" align="center">CONTENT</td></tr>
<tr><td>ATTRIBUTES OF THE PERSON</td><td>CHARACTERISTICS OF DECISIONS SITUATION</td></tr>
<tr>
<td>
Job position knowledge, experience, expectations

Longevity in company, country, functional area

Intelligence and cultural learning or change ability

Personality as demonstrated in values, beliefs, attitudes toward foreign situations

Multiple memberships in work and professional groups

Decision and personal work style
</td>
<td>
Degree of complexity, uncertainty, and risk

In-country information needs and availability

Articulation of assumptions and expectations

Scope and potential impact on performance

Nature of business partners

Authority and autonomy required

Required level of participation and acceptance by employees, partners, and government

Linkage to other decisions

Past management legacy

Openness to public scrutiny and responsibility
</td>
</tr>
<tr><td colspan="2" align="center">CONTEXT</td></tr>
<tr><td>ATTRIBUTES OF THE JOB OR POSITION</td><td>CHARACTERISTICS OF THE
FIRM AND BUSINESS ENVIRONMENT</td></tr>
<tr>
<td>
Longevity and past success of former role occupants in the position

Technical requirements of the job

Relative authority or power

Physical location (e.g., home office, field office)

Need for coordination, cooperation, and integration with other units

Resource availability

Foreign peer group relations
</td>
<td>
Firm structure: size, location, technology, tasks, reporting, and communication patterns

Firm process; decision making, staffing, control system, reward system, information system, means of coordination, integration, and conflict resolution

Firm outputs: products, services, public image, corporate culture, local history, and community relations

Business environment: social-cultural, political-economic, and technological aspects of a country or market
</td>
</tr>
</table>

Source: R. H. Mason and R. S. Spich, *Management—An International Perspective* (Homewood, IL: Irwin, 1987), 186.

An additional factor—that of technology—is becoming increasingly pervasive in its ability to influence the global leader's role and environment, and perhaps will contribute to a lessening of the differences in motivation and leadership around the world. More and more often, companies like Italtel spa, featured in the accompanying *E-Biz Box*, are using technology in global leadership techniques to set up systems for their geographically dispersed employees to enable them to expand and coordinate their global operations. In the case of Italtel, this required wide delegation and empowerment of their employees so that they could decentralize.

EXECUTIVE SUMMARY

Company: Italtel spa

Industry: Telecommunications

Business Challenge: To "flatten" the organization and expand globally.

Solution: An intranet based on Netscape products that enables Italtel to share knowledge and product information throughout the company.

Plant operations, antenna functioning, and network traffic are monitored online.

Solution Features: Employees can access Italtel's technical product documentation online.

Employees can book training courses via the intranet.

Reduced costs for information, documentation, and software distribution.

Business Benefits: Network and service monitoring online contributes to improved customer service.

Centralized employee database and single network login for every user dramatically reduces system administration time and costs.

Italtel spa is an international supplier of telecommunications networks that specializes in the design, development, and installation of integrated telecommunications systems. The company employs 16,000 people, 21 percent of whom are involved in research and development. Italtel invests 12 percent of its annual revenues in R&D, addressing a wide range of applications.

BUSINESS CHALLENGE

With the globalization of the telecommunications market, Italtel had to expand internationally in order to compete successfully. To do so, Italtel management felt that it should "flatten" the organization, moving from a hierarchical structure to one in which employees are empowered with all the tools and information they need to do their jobs better, thereby improving customers service and time to market.

In addition to the business challenges associated with international expansion, the company faces several technical challenges. Sweeping changes spurred by the convergence of communication and information technologies force Italtel to innovate faster than ever before. As a result, Italtel needs to share knowledge and information and improve communication throughout the company—all within a distributed, extremely heterogeneous computing environment. This environment includes a wide range of client systems, such as Unix workstations and PCs running Windows 3.1, 95, and NT, and servers that include Digital, Hewlett-Packard, IBM, Sun, and Windows NT-based systems. The company needed a new information technology solution that would provide global information access, flexibility, and ease of use. Among the goals for the new system were to create a centralized, easily accessible source for all company information resources, to monitor the company's telecommunications services and network online for better performance, to organize training courses, and to set up working groups in different departments.

SOLVING THE CHALLENGE

Italtel selected key components of the Netscape SuitSpot server software family to deploy an enterprisewide intranet and messaging solution. Netscape Enterprise Server distributes Web-based intranet and Internet services.

SOURCE: www.Netscape.com case studies, May 1, 2000.

CROSS-CULTURAL RESEARCH ON LEADERSHIP

Numerous leadership theories variously focus on individual traits, leader behavior, interaction patterns, role relationships, follower perceptions, influence over followers, influence on task goals, and influence on organizational culture.[57] Our task in this chapter is to understand how the variable of societal culture fits into these theories and what implications can be drawn for international managers as they seek to provide leadership around the world. While the *functions* of leadership are similar across cultures, anthropological studies, such as those by Mead, indicate that leadership is a universal phenomenon and that effective leadership varies across cultures.[58]

In addition to research studies that indicate variations in leadership profiles, the generally accepted image that people in different countries have about what they expect and admire in their leaders tends to become a norm over time, forming an idealized role for these leaders. Industry leaders in France and Italy, for example, are highly regarded for their social prominence and political power. In Latin American countries, leaders are respected as the total person and leaders in society, with appreciation for the arts being important. In Germany, polish, decisiveness, and a wide general knowledge are respected, with their leaders granted a lot of formality by everyone. Foreigners are often surprised at the informal off-the-job lifestyles of executives in the United States and would be surprised to see them pushing a lawn mower for example.[59]

Most research on American leadership styles describes managerial behaviors on, essentially, the same dimension, variously termed autocratic versus democratic, participative versus directive, relations-oriented versus task-oriented, or initiating structure versus consideration continuum.[60–62] These studies were developed in the West, and conclusions regarding employee responses largely reflect the opinions of American workers. The democratic, or participative, leadership style has been recommended as the one more likely to have positive results with most American employees.

CONTINGENCY LEADERSHIP—THE CULTURE VARIABLE

Modern leadership theory recognizes that no single leadership style works well in all situations.[63] A considerable amount of research, directly or indirectly, supports the notion of cultural contingency in leadership. Much of this research also provides insight on the relative level of preference for autocratic versus participative leadership styles. For example, Hofstede's four cultural dimensions (discussed in Chapter 3) provide a good starting point to study leader–subordinate expectations and relationships. We can assume, for example, that employees in countries that rank high on power distance (India, Mexico, the Philippines) are more likely to prefer an autocratic leadership style and some paternalism because they are more comfortable with a clear distinction between managers and subordinates rather than with a blurring of decision-making responsibility.

Employees in countries that rank low on power distance (Sweden and Israel) are more likely to prefer a consultative, participative leadership style, and they expect superiors to adhere to that style. Hofstede, in fact, concludes that the participative management approaches recommended by many American researchers can be counterproductive in certain cultures.[64]

The GLOBE Leadership Project

Recent research on culturally-contingent leadership behaviors was conducted in 62 countries with 18,000 managers by 170 researchers who made up the GLOBE leadership research project, led by Robert House. Following is a small sample of their findings.[65] Those leadership styles and behaviors that were found to be culturally contingent are: charismatic, team-oriented, self-protective, participative, humane, and autonomous. The charismatic leader as in this research is someone who is, for example, a visionary, an inspiration to subordinates, and performance-oriented. Although charisma was ranked as important to leaders everywhere, those countries where it seemed to be most important were Israel, the Philippines, Canada, Australia, and the United States, for example. The managers in those countries where team orientation was regarded as very important for leaders were in Greece, Brazil, Turkey, and Argentina, although the ratings were all quite high and close together. The self-protective dimension describes a leader who is self-centered, conflictual and status conscious. Not surprisingly, the ratings were generally lower than the previous two dimensions mentioned although managers in some countries—for example, Albania, Egypt, Indonesia, and Taiwan—thought those attributes of leaders were fairly important to facilitate leadership (scores more than 4.0 on a 1–7 point scale). The lowest scores were found in the Nordic countries. The participative leader was deemed to be most important (out of the 62 countries researched) in Austria, Brazil, and Canada, while those countries in which those behaviors were deemed the least important compared with the others were Russia, Mexico, and Taiwan. An autonomous leader is, as expected, an individualist, so countries that ranked participation as important tended to rank autonomy in leadership as relatively unimportant. Humane leaders are compassionate to their employees. Most ratings on that dimension were fairly high, with the highest being South Africa (white sample), India, the Philippines, and Malaysia. The lower scores were from Finland, western Germany, Italy, Russia, and Morocco.[66]

Clearly, this path-breaking research can be very helpful to managers going abroad to enable them to develop a culturally-appropriate profile of requisite leadership skills and to exercise them accordingly.

Expectations about managerial authority versus participation were also among the managerial behaviors and philosophies studied by Laurent, a French researcher. In a study conducted in nine Western European countries, the United States, Indonesia, and Japan, he concluded that national origin significantly affects the perception of what is effective management.[67] For example, Americans and Germans subscribe more to participation than do Italians and Japanese; Indonesians are more comfortable with a strict autocratic structure. Managers in Sweden, the Netherlands, the United States, Denmark, and Great Britain believe that employees should participate in problem solving rather than simply be "fed" all the answers by managers, compared with managers in those countries on the higher end of this scale, such as Italy, Indonesia, and Japan. Laurent's findings about Japan, however, seem to contradict common knowledge about Japan's very participative decision-making culture. In fact, research by Hampden-Turner and Trompenaars places Japan as second highest, after Sweden, in the extent to which leaders delegate authority.[68] Findings regarding the other countries are similar, as shown in Exhibit 10-7. However, participative leadership should not mean a lack of initiative or responsibility.

Other classic studies indicate cross-cultural differences in the expectations of leadership behavior. Haire, Ghiselli, and Porter surveyed over three thousand managers in 14 countries. They found that, although managers around the world consistently favored delegation and participation, those managers also had a low appreciation of the capacity and willingness of subordinates to take an active role in the management process.[69]

Exhibit 10-7
Comparative Leadership Dimensions: Participation and Initiative

MANAGERIAL INITIATIVE, MANAGERS' SENSE OF DRIVE AND RESPONSIBILITY (0 = LOW; 100 = HIGH)		EXTENT TO WHICH LEADERS DELEGATE AUTHORITY (0 = LOW; 100 = HIGH)	
USA	73.67	Sweden	75.51
Sweden	72.29	Japan	69.27
Japan	72.20	Norway	68.50
Finland	69.58	USA	66.23
Korea	67.86	Singapore	65.37
Netherlands	67.11	Denmark	64.65
Singapore	66.34	Canada	64.38
Switzerland	65.71	Finland	62.92
Belgium/Lux	65.47	Switzerland	62.20
Ireland	64.76	Netherlands	61.33
France	64.64	Australia	61.22
Austria	62.56	Germany	60.85
Denmark	62.79	New Zealand	60.54
Italy	62.40	Ireland	59.53
Australia	62.04	UK	58.95
Canada	61.56	Belgium/Lux	54.55
Spain	61.55	Austria	54.29
New Zealand	59.46	France	53.62
Greece	58.50	Italy	46.80
UK	58.25	Spain	44.31
Norway	54.50	Portugal	42.56
Portugal	49.74	Greece	37.95

Source: C. Hampden-Turner and A. Trompenaars, *The Seven Cultures of Capitalism* (New York: Doubleday, 1993).

In addition, several studies of individual countries or areas conclude that a participative leadership style is frequently inappropriate. Managers in Malaysia, Indonesia, Thailand, and the Philippines were found to prefer autocratic leadership, whereas those in Singapore and Hong Kong are less autocratic.[70] Similarly, the Turks have been found to prefer authoritarian leadership, as do the Thais.[71,72]

In the Middle East, in particular, there is little delegation. A successful company must have strong managers who make all the decisions and who go unquestioned; much emphasis is placed on the use of power through social contacts and family influence, and the chain of command must be rigidly followed.[73] A comparison of these and other management dimensions between Middle Eastern and Western managers is shown in Exhibit 10-8.

These stereotypical extremes of Middle Eastern and Western leadership styles were exemplified at the highest level by President George Bush and President

Exhibit 10-8
Comparison of Middle Eastern and Western Management Practices

MANAGERIAL FUNCTION	MIDDLE EASTERN STEREOTYPE	WESTERN STEREOTYPE
Organizational design	Highly bureaucratic, overcentralized with power and authority at the top. Vague relationships. Ambiguous and unpredictable organization environments.	Less bureaucratic, more delegation of authority. Relatively decentralized structure.
Patterns of decision making	Ad hoc planning, decisions made at the highest level of management. Unwillingness to take high risk inherent in decision making.	Sophisticated planning techniques, modern tools of decision making, elaborate management information systems.
Performance evaluation and control	Informal control mechanisms, routine checks on performance. Lack of vigorous performance evaluation systems.	Fairly advanced control systems focusing on cost reduction and organizational effectiveness.
Manpower policies	Heavy reliance on personal contacts and getting individuals from the "right social origin" to fill major positions.	Sound personnel management policies. Candidates' qualifications are usually the basis for selection decisions.
Leadership	Highly authoritarian tone, rigid instructions. Too many management directives.	Less emphasis on leader's personality, considerable weight on leader's style and performance.
Communication	The tone depends on the communicants. Social position, power, and family influence are ever-present factors. Chain of command must be followed rigidly. People relate to each other tightly and specifically. Friendships are intense and binding.	Stress usually on equality and a minimization of differences. People relate to each other loosely and generally. Friendships not intense and binding.
Management methods	Generally old and outdated.	Generally modern and more scientific.

Source: Copyright © 1980 by The Regents of the University of California. Reprinted from the *California Management Review* 22, no 3. By permission of The Regents.

Saddam Hussein during the 1991 Gulf War. Underlying these styles—and the misunderstandings that persist between Arabs and the West—are many cultural and national factors (including differences in religion, logic, and ideas about truth, freedom, honor, trust, family, and friends). Most of these factors are based on elements of Arab history that Westerners find difficult to comprehend. Arabs tend to use the past as their basis of reference, whereas Americans look to the future.

From various accounts, Hussein thinks that his strong leadership means the fulfillment of destiny: Iraq was meant to be the dominant power in the region. Others, however, attest to his use of internal power for personal aggrandizement. His leadership style is, obviously, dictatorial, and to most people in the world he seems a ruthless tyrant and a master of manipulation. However, he is seen as a hero by most Iraqis and by many other Arabs in the region. Participation and delegation in decision making are clearly not among his leadership behaviors, nor is he likely to seek consensus even on radical plans. In contrast, most Western leaders quietly go about team building—consulting widely and building consensus around whatever action they feel should be taken. After Iraq invaded Kuwait in August 1990, President Bush took time to build strong support behind the scenes, forging a powerful alliance among Arabs, Israelis, Europeans, Japanese, Chinese, and Soviets. Based on continued support, President Clinton ordered further attacks on Iraq in 1998–99 after Iraq's lack of compliance with agreements made in 1990, and President George W. Bush followed suit in 2001, keeping up to pressure for compliance.[74]

The effects of participative leadership can vary even in one location when the employees are from different cultural backgrounds—from which we can conclude that a subordinate's culture is usually a more powerful variable than other factors in the environment. Research that supports this conclusion includes a study conducted in Saudi Arabia that found participative leadership to be more effective with American workers than with Asian and African employees, and a study in a U.S. plant that found that participative leadership resulted in greater satisfaction and communication in American employees than in Mexican employees.[75,76]

In Exhibit 10-9 we depict our integrative model of the leadership process by pulling together the variables described in this book and in the research on culture, leadership, and motivation. It shows the powerful contingency of culture as it affects the leadership role. Reading from left to right, it covers the broad environmental factors through to the outcomes affected by the entire leadership situation. As shown in the exhibit, the broad context in which the manager operates necessitates adjustments in leadership style to all those variables relating to the work and task environment and the people involved. Cultural variables (values, work norms, the locus of control, and so forth), as they affect everyone involved— leader, subordinates, and work groups—then shape the content of the immediate leadership situation.

The leader–follower interaction is then further shaped by the leader's choice of behaviors (autocratic, participative, and so on) and the employees' attitudes toward the leader and the incentives. Motivation effects—various levels of effort, performance, and satisfaction—result from these interactions, on an individual and a group level. These effects determine the outcomes for the company (productivity, quality) and for the employees (satisfaction, positive climate). The

Exhibit 10-9

The Culture Contingency in the Leadership Process: An Integrative Model

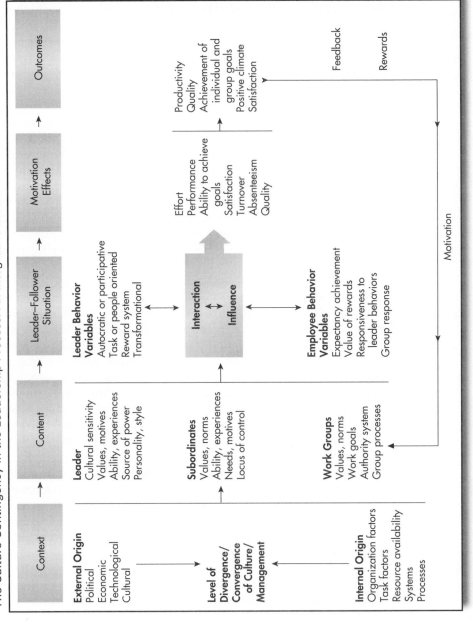

results and rewards from those outcomes then act as feedback (positive or negative) into the cycle of the motivation and leadership process.

Clearly, then, international managers should take seriously the **culture contingency** in their application of the contingency theory of leadership: They must adjust their leadership behaviors according to the context, norms, attitudes, and other variables in that society. One example of the complexity of the leadership situation involving obvious contextual as well as cultural factors can be seen from the results of a study of how Russian employees responded to participative management practices of North American managers. It was found that the performance of the Russian workers decreased, which the researchers attributed to a history of employee ideas being ignored by Russian managers, as well as cultural value differences.[77] To gain more insight into comparative leadership situations, the following Comparative Management in Focus highlights the leadership context in India, along with the implications for appropriate leadership by expatriates.

Comparative Management in Focus

Leadership in India

The most effective leadership style in India would thus combine integrity, being organized, an action orientation, being a self starter, charisma, and a collective orientation; with being a problem solver, a visionary, entrepreneurial, and inspirational, in that order.

JAGDEEP S. CHHOKER, THE GLOBE LEADERSHIP RESEARCH PROJECT,
WWW.UCALGARY.CA NOVEMBER 5, 2001.

Many subtle effects of the caste system still remain and affect life in organizations in the form of a strict adherence to hierarchy. Indians are disposed to structure all relationships hierarchically; for this reason they usually work better individually than in groups.[78] Management in India is often autocratic, based on formal authority and charisma. Family norms emphasizing loyalty to the family authority figure underlie the limited decision-making experience and unfamiliarity with responsibility found in some employees. Consequently, decision making is centralized, with much emphasis on rules and a low propensity for risk.[79] In addition, intricate family ties and strong authority figures perpetuate a managerial style of paternalism.

Under the pervasive influences of religion, caste, and family on the life of the Hindu, the Indian culture stresses moral orientation and loyalty, as in the pursuit of *dharma*, one's obligation to society, rather than personal goals. Work tends to be viewed primarily in the context of family or intercaste relationships, rather than being valued for itself.[80] Nepotism is common both at the lowest and highest levels. Unsurprisingly, power based on expertise frequently takes a back seat to power based on position.[81] Generally, American managers in India need to make connections with the right families, make contact at the highest levels, and provide incentives for middle managers and assistants to help nudge proposals upward.[82]

On the micro level of leadership—manager to employees—American managers in India are wise to tread slowly while trying to understand the culture and find what works. Various proposals have been put forward to help managers move toward more effective leadership. Tripathi suggests that "indigenous values, such as familism, need to be synthesized with the values of industrial democracy."[83] Similarly, Sinha proposes that, while a leader in India has to be a "nurturant," taking a personal interest in the well-being of each subordinate; he or she can use that nurturance to encourage increasing levels of participation. The manager may accomplish this by guiding and directing subordinates to work hard and maintain a high level of productivity, reinforcing each stage with increased nurturance.[84] According to Sinha and Sinha, a prerequisite to effective cross-cultural leadership in India is to establish work as the "master value." Once this is done, "other social values will reorganize themselves to help realize the master value."[85]

Multiple problems abound on the macro level of leadership of a global enterprise in India, as discovered by companies such as Gillette, Rank Xerox, Texas Instruments, and Hewlett-Packard. Investment opportunities are very attractive, with a potential for great sales and a pool of cheap, highly educated, and skilled labor. But, even after getting through the entrenched bureaucracy to set up business, managers may face many operating problems because of the undeveloped infrastructure and difficult climate. Gaining control and integrating leadership styles with local managers are additional hurdles. American managers, used to being boss in their own companies, may have difficulty taking orders from Indian partners and prefer to operate at a faster pace.[86] Gill, of Gillette, suggests, "You've got to find the right partner and convince him to give you complete management control."[87] Failure to include an Indian partner or to build local support was behind the cancellation of Enron's $2.8 billion power project in Dhabol, as part of a resurgence of economic nationalism in India in 1995 pending national elections. The project was reinstated in 1999; but as of 2001, problems between Enron and the Indian government continued and Enron decided not to build more plants in India.[88,89] In other areas, such as telecommunications, liberalization is progressing well, to the benefit of companies such as AT&T, Motorola, and Texas Instruments (TI). It is noteworthy that these companies have Indian joint-venture partners and Indian CEOs. TI India's managing director, Srini Rajam, noted that the Bagalore plant was responsible for one-third of TI's design automation for semiconductor products worldwide.[90]

India is expected to be an economic giant someday. Meanwhile, American managers must realize that setting up and running a successful business in India requires astute leadership skills, including integrating and collaborating at all levels of the community for the long term.

As we have said, leadership refers not just to the manager-subordinate relationship, but to the important task of running the whole company, division, or unit for which the manager is responsible. In Japan, for example, in spite of recent economic distress, many companies there continue to provide a model for quality control techniques. One executive, who has worked ten years for Japanese companies, says that a key to Japanese-style success is "to take many small steps, consistently, every day."[91] One of the areas in which Japanese managers use this process of **continuous improvement**—or *kaizen*—is quality control, which has been the hallmark of success for many Japanese industries.

Although anecdotal evidence in late 2000 indicated that Japan's long economic decline and the increased global competitiveness was eroding the system of lifetime employment and causing Japanese employees to be more independent, it is still common for employees to have a great sense of loyalty and duty to the firm.[92] In fact, hard work and loyalty have resulted in widespread workaholism among Japanese because of "the intense pressures on them to conform and to identify with their corporate 'family.'"[93] Conformity and dedication are instilled since childhood; for example, it is typical for a group of employees to participate in a company song and creed recitation before work.

For some time, American companies have studied successful Japanese companies for the purpose of emulating management styles to improve productivity, in particular the practice of employee involvement. Recently, increased global competitiveness and further exposure to Western culture and managerial practices, have led Japanese firms to adopt more American practices. This partial blending of management practices indicates a trend toward convergence of leadership styles. Nevertheless, management processes, while ostensibly similar, will usually manifest themselves differently as a function of the entire cultural context in which they are enacted.

Conclusion

Because leadership and motivation entail constant interactions with others (employees, peers, superiors, outside contacts), cultural influences on these critical management functions are very strong. Certainly, other powerful variables are intricately involved in the international management context, particularly those of economics and politics. Effective leaders carefully examine the entire context and develop a sensitivity to others' values and expectations regarding personal and group interactions, performance, and outcomes—and then act accordingly.

INTERNET RESOURCES

Visit the Deresky companion Web site at http://prenhall.com/Deresky for this chapter's Internet resources.

1. Motivation and leadership are factors in the successful implementation of desired strategy. But while many of the basic principles are universal, much of the actual content and process is culture-contingent—a function of an individual's needs, value systems, and environmental context.

2. One problem in using content theories, such as those created by Maslow and Herzberg, for cross-cultural research is the assumption of their universal application. Because they were developed in the United States, even the concepts, such as achievement or esteem, may have different meanings in other societies, resulting in a noncomparable basis of research.

3. Implicit in motivating an employee is an understanding of which of the employee's needs are satisfied by work. Studies on the "meaning of work" indicate considerable cross-cultural differences.

4. Other studies on cross-cultural motivation support Herzberg's two-factor theory. They also indicate, as do studies using Maslow's theory, support for the greater importance of intrinsic factors to motivation, at least on the managerial level. One problem with Herzberg's theory is that it does not account for all relevant cultural variables.

5. A reexamination of motivation relative to Hofstede's dimensions of power distance, uncertainty avoidance, individualism, and masculinity provides another perspective on the cultural contexts that can influence motivational structures.

6. Incentives and reward systems must be designed to reflect the motivational structure and relative cultural emphasis on five categories of rewards: financial, social status, job content, career, and professional.

7. Effective leadership is crucial to the ability of a company to achieve its goals. The challenge is to decide what is effective leadership in different international or mixed-culture situations.

8. The perception of what makes a good leader—both traits and behaviors—varies a great deal from one society to another.

9. Contingency theory is applicable to cross-cultural leadership situations because of the vast number of cultural and national variables that can affect the dynamics of the leadership context. These include leader–subordinate and group relations, which are affected by cultural expectations, values, needs, attitudes, perceptions of risk, and loci of control.

10. Joint ventures with other countries present a common but complex situation in which leaders must work together to anticipate and address cross-cultural problems.

Case 1 Colgate-Palmolive in Postapartheid South Africa

After a month of intense contemplation, Carol Lewis decided to accept the position of head of Colgate-Palmolive Foundation (South Africa). Carol learned in her job interview that the American subsidiary, based in South Africa, was committed to extending its leadership role in generating social responsibility (SR) activities in a postapartheid South Africa (see appendix).

"Ever since 1967, when four dental educators first went into the surrounding black townships to educate residents about teeth that can be strong and healthy through receiving daily care and nourishment, investing in communities where the firm earns its living had been—and would continue to be—integral to its South African mission," Vice President David Moore told her.

Indeed, Carol had studied the American firm and learned that Colgate-Palmolive had achieved an outstanding Category 1 rating on the Sullivan Code for South Africa (see Exhibit C1-1). She discovered that compliance to the code requires a firm to direct 12 percent of its salary budget to social responsibility efforts. And she knew the company meant business about their SR activities. The firm had recently launched the $3 million Colgate-Palmolive Foundation. Many South African firms believed this level of achievement was beyond even their financial reach.

So Carol was glad to have been selected to lead Colgate-Palmolive's SR initiatives. With more than $100 million annual sales and a workforce of 600 employees, she believed that the American firm could continue to build on its stellar track record (see Exhibit C1-2 for Mission Statement).

After a month spent doing MBWA (management by wandering around) on the job, Carol had listened to the opinions of individual and group stakeholders in the firm. She had learned about the kinds of SR initiatives they thought the firm should consider in a postapartheid South Africa.

Exhibit C1-1
Signatory Code for South Africa

These were devised in 1977 by the Reverend Leon Sullivan of Philadelphia as a code of conduct for American multinationals in South Africa.

Principle 1
Nonsegregation of the races in all eating, comfort, locker room and work facilities.

Principle 2
Equal and fair employment practices for all employees.

Principle 3
Equal pay for all employees doing equal or comparable work for the same period of time.

Principle 4
Initiation and development of training programs that will prepare blacks, coloured, and Asians in substantial numbers for supervisory, administrative, clerical and technical jobs.

Principle 5
Increasing the number of blacks, coloured, and Asians in management and supervisory positions.

Principle 6
Improving the equality of employees' lives outside the work environment in such areas as housing, transportation, schooling, recreations and health facilities.

Principle 7
Working to eliminate laws and customs that impede social and political justice.

First, she discovered that Colgate-Palmolive employees were the highest-paid workers in the industry. In fact, she learned that the firm pays employees in excess of stipulations listed in the Sullivan principles.

Exhibit C1-2
Mission Statement

Colgate-Palmolive is committed, through its social investment program, to support social and socio-economic projects; in particular, those that promote the principles and structures of a nonracial society, equality of opportunity, advancement based on merit and freedom of association and speech.

We are dedicated to the upliftment of the quality of life for all South Africans through education, health and youthful sporting activities, which will encourage self-development and confidence-building to create an improved social climate in the South African community.

Second, she learned of the overwhelming support of all employees to the SR initiatives of Colgate-Palmolive. Indeed, she'd been frequently stopped in hallways and on factory floors by employees who thanked her and the company profusely for, among other things, helping their kids with school bursaries, receiving funds for school fees for employees (on the condition they pass their subjects), and nutritional classes. She learned from her briefing by senior management that the primary mission of the firm's SR efforts was to "accelerate economic empowerment through education by developing formal and informal educational skills and motivating communities to become self-sufficient" (see a list and description of specific SR activities of Colgate-Palmolive at conclusion of case). In fact, the firm had "adopted" seven schools that could approach an employee committee with requests for anything from photocopying ink to teacher and pupil upgrading programs.

Third, she learned that Colgate-Palmolive sponsors professional nurses to help daycare centers, schools, and community groups with primary health care education.

Fourth, she learned of the strategic initiative of top management to institute a formal "affirmative action" plan for black employees that would be implemented as a strategy to accelerate economic empowerment and remove any barriers to advancement into senior corporate positions.

Fifth, Carol listened to the appreciative comments from union leaders and community activists about the "social justice" role the firm had performed for its surrounding communities. She learned the firm had become politically active to assist neighboring communities in two ways. First, she discovered that Colgate-Palmolive had provided legal assistance to members of a neighboring squatter camp who had been intimidated by the local town council while steps were being taken to solve the squatter problem. Second, she discovered that although the American firm explicitly advocated nonalignment with any political party, initiatives were in place, at the request of community leaders, to provide "democracy training" as a social justice program. Indeed, materials she studied indicated that the firm sponsored lectures for the community by academics and other experts on specific subjects, such as voting procedures of issues connected with a bill of rights (these courses were offered for both white and black groups and communities).

Finally, Carol found out that the SR projects that "worked" and achieved Colgate-Palmolive's mission were ones in which people who were beneficiaries of the project were actively involved in formulating and implementing each activity. Colgate-Palmolive followed the process of consultation with all stakeholders throughout their SR initiatives.

Carol paused, however, to reflect on a number of disturbing issues that had surfaced in personal interviews with some trade union leaders and community activists. In one of her meetings with trade union shop stewards, they argued that union leaders, not management, should direct and manage Colgate-Palmolive's SR budget since they believed their constituency was the primary stakeholder group who were recipients of the firm's SR activities.

Carol countered that the SR budget should remain with the Foundation since Colgate-Palmolive's unionized workforce comprised only 50 percent of employees and the firm had to ensure fair representation for all employees. Besides, Carol indicated to the shop stewards that the firm's SR activities were for "underprivileged" communities represented by all employee stakeholder race and ethnic groups.

Carol speculated on another issue that had surfaced with trade union leaders that made her uncomfortable. She wondered about the extent to which union leaders were genuinely interested in the needs of their community. She considered whether, based on her interviews with union leaders, they were more inclined to support issues to gain "political" favor with their followers inside the firm than the company's stakeholders and surrounding communities outside the firm. For example, she remembered a discussion she'd had with union leaders about the best method to provide bursaries to the children of employees. Union leaders pressed hard to have ten bursaries that paid all fees. What's more, the union wanted to announce this decision to employees as a concession they'd obtained from management. On the other hand, she argued for shared responsibility of bursaries where parents paid a nominal amount and Colgate-Palmolive contributed the remainder so that the budget would allow for an additional 20 bursaries and thus provide funding assistance to more in need. She believed this alternative was consistent with the notion that "shared help" is more effective than a "hand-out" in the firm's commitment to economic empowerment for underprivileged communities.

Finally, Carol reflected on an issue that several union representatives had raised during her interviews. Some leaders saw a dilemma for the firm. They pointed out that the firm was self-serving in promoting SR initiatives because a number of products were "sold" under the umbrella of social responsibility activities. For example, one leader described how the firm had supported primary healthcare education activities for a local community. He conceded that parents and children who received healthcare and nutritional hand-outs, posters, and other reading materials featuring a cartoon and logo depicting the "Colgate Smile" were helped by the program. On the other hand, they also received information promoting the "purchase" of oral care products sold by Colgate-Palmolive. He queried her, "Is it right to help underprivileged communities while at the same time also promoting your products to these communities?"

Carol frowned as she considered these issues; then the phone rang and she had to dash out, reminding herself to gain closure on the issues facing her.

CASE QUESTIONS

1. What method did Carol use to probe stakeholder opinion about Colgate-Palmolive's social responsibility initiatives in South Africa? Assume you have arrived from the United States to manage your firm's operations in a foreign country, what are the advantages and disadvantages of using this method to discover what employees think?

2. Colgate-Palmolive is politically active in a postapartheid South Africa as part of its social responsibility initiatives. Should American firms continue their political activism in a postapartheid South African society? What implications does your answer have for U.S. firms conducting similar activities in other countries, or foreign firms conducting similar activities in the United States?

3. If you believe trade union criticisms that Colgate-Palmolive is selling several products in South Africa under the umbrella of social responsibility activities, what ethical issues need to be considered?

4. From your reading of this case, what specific knowledge and skills do you believe American managers need to learn?

APPENDIX
Social Responsibility Activities Through Education

Primary school. Colgate-Palmolive was at the forefront of the adopted school initiative in South Africa. In 1977, Kutloanong Primary School in Vosloorus was the first school to receive assistance under this scheme, and Colgate-Palmolive now has five adopted primary schools in Vosloorus and Daveyton, all receiving assistance for teacher upgrade, media equipment, books, sports equipment, and even basics such as electricity and burglar-proofing.

High school. The St. Andrews Outreach and Bridging Program takes disadvantaged children from Daveyton to St. Andrews for additional and remedial tuition. Recreational days and fun events are also organized.

University. Preprimary- to tertiary-level bursaries are offered to employees' dependents. The bursaries, which cover fees and textbooks, are also offered to dependents of retired and deceased employees.

Colgate-Palmolive's assistance to the Academic Support Program at the University of the Witwatersrand is structured to supplement students' lectures, particularly at first-year level.

Colgate-Palmolive recognizes the lack of adequate career guidance material and funds a high school career guidance program at the Medical University of South Africa.

An annual bursary donation is made to Medunsa and awarded by the university to dental students. A number of students also benefit each year from bursary funding to the University of Cape Town.

Forty schools on the East Rand participated in the Deved Trust's Career Guidance Teachers' Program. Regular workshops and visits to industries give the teachers a better perception of the education necessary to enter identified careers.

The foundation supports teacher upgrade programs at the East Rand College of Education, Vista, and Promat. It also funds research surveys undertaken by Amcham's Policy Research Unit into open, nonracial education in East Rand schools. This includes high school teacher training in cultural issues, and symposia for principals from TED and DET schools in the Boksburg area.

As part of their college diploma course, Technikon students are required to undertake six months' practical experience in industry. Colgate-Palmolive has assisted many students to obtain their diplomas in analytical chemistry, chemical engineering, and production management through these six-month practical training periods.

Social Responsibility Activities Through Community Projects

The Colgate-Palmolive Youth for South Africa program, started in January 1993, highlights the positive side of today's young people. It is aimed at encouraging youth groups to become more responsible to their communities, and rewards their efforts in diverse ways, as follows:

- Support is given to the Institute of Natural Resources project in KwaZulu, which includes water purification and basic sanitation work.
- Funding is provided for the St. Anthony's Aged Center in Johannesburg.

- Colgate-Palmolive organizes and manages the nonracial Colgate 15-km Road Race, which attracts more than 4,500 runners each year. A percentage of the entrance money, matched by Colgate-Palmolive, is given to the Retinitis Pigmentosa Organization.
- Assistance is provided to the House of Mercy drug and alcohol rehabilitation center run by St. Anthony's.
- Colgate-Palmolive sponsors the running costs of the St. Francis House for the terminally ill.
- AIDs Education Programs include sponsorship of an AIDs awareness page in school exercise books piloted by the Johannesburg City Council Health Department, as well as in-house programs for Colgate-Palmolive employees.
- The Medunsa/Colgate Mobile Dental Unit provides treatment to underprivileged communities in the northeastern Transvaal.
- Mobile Dental Units provide treatment to underprivileged communities in South Africa. Colgate-Palmolive sponsorship has enabled the Departments of Community Dentistry at the Universities of Witwatersrand, Pretoria, and Medunsa to operate the three units currently providing this much needed service in both rural and urban areas.
- The Business Development Training–East Rand Townships Project offers basic business skills training courses. This program gives opportunities to informal businesses to develop and create additional job opportunities in these areas of high unemployment.
- Colgate-Palmolive supports the nonracial Eagle Tumbling Club, which offers gymnastics and tumbling training to children; it also covers transport and equipment costs.
- The Durban Lifesaver project sponsors the training and equipment needs of black lifesavers.
- Assistance and funding is provided to the Daveyton Physically Handicapped Training Center, where a workshop offers sheltered employment.
- A Mobile Health Clinic has been built, using a bus, and is utilized in the expanding township of Vosloorus.
- Health education programs are provided by medical and dental students at rural clinics as part of the Medunsa–Children's Clinic and

Case 2　　　*Footwear International*

John Carlson frowned as he studied the translation of the front-page story from the afternoon's edition of the *Meillat*, a fundamentalist newspaper with close ties to an opposition political party. The story, titled "Footwear's Unpardonable Audacity," suggested that the company had knowingly insulted Islam by including the name of Allah in a design used on the insoles of sandals it was manufacturing. To compound the problem, the paper had run a photograph of one of the offending sandals on the front page. As a result, student groups were calling for public demonstrations against Footwear the next day. As managing director of Footwear Bangladesh, Carlson knew he would have to act quickly to defuse a potentially explosive situation.

FOOTWEAR INTERNATIONAL

Footwear International is a multinational manufacturer and marketer of footwear. Operations span the globe and include more than 83 companies in 70 countries. These include shoe factories, tanneries, engineering plants producing shoe machinery and moulds, product development studios, hosiery factories, quality control laboratories, and approximately 6,300 retail stores and 50,000 independent retailers.

Footwear employs more than 67,000 people and produces and sells in excess of 270 million pairs of shoes every year. The head office acts as a service center and is staffed with specialists drawn from all over the world. These specialists, in areas such as marketing, retailing, product development, communications, store design, electronic data processing, and business administration, travel for much of the year to share their expertise with the various companies. Training and technical education, offered through company-run colleges and the training facility at headquarters, provide the latest skills to employees from around the world.

Although Footwear requires standardization in technology and the design of facilities, it also encourages a high degree of decentralization and autonomy in its operations. The companies are virtually self-governing, which means their allegiance belongs to the countries in which they operate. Each is answerable to a board of directors that includes representatives from the local business community. The concept of "partnership" at the local level has made the company welcome internationally and has allowed it to operate successfully in countries where other multinationals have been unable to survive.

BANGLADESH

With a population approaching 110 million in an area of 143,998 square kilometers (see Exhibit C2-1), Bangladesh is the most densely populated country in the world. It is also among the most impoverished, with a 1987 per capita gross national product of $160 and a high reliance on foreign aid. More than 40 percent of the gross domestic product is generated by agriculture, and more than 60 percent of its economically active population works in the agriculture sector. Although the land in Bangladesh is fertile, the country has a tropical monsoon climate and suffers from the ravages of periodic cyclones. In 1988, the country experienced the worst floods in recorded history.

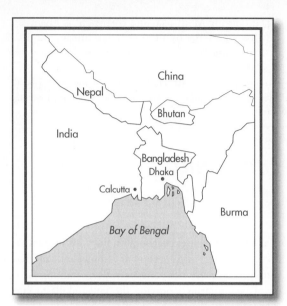

Exhibit C2-1
Bangladesh

The population of Bangladesh is 85 percent Muslim, and Islam was made the official state religion in 1988. Approximately 95 percent of the population speaks Bengali, with most of the remainder speaking tribal dialects.

Bangladesh has had a turbulent history in the 20th century. Most of the country was part of the British-ruled East Bengal until 1947. In that year, it joined with Assam to become East Pakistan, a province of the newly created country of Pakistan. East Pakistan was separated from the four provinces of West Pakistan by 1,600 kilometers of Indian territory, and although the East was more populous, the national capital was established in West Pakistan. Over the following years, widespread discontent built in the East whose people felt that they received a disproportionately small amount of development funding and were under-represented in government.

Following a period of unrest starting in 1969, the Awami League, the leading political party in East Pakistan, won an overwhelming victory in local elections held in 1970. The victory promised to give the league, which was pro-independence, control in the National Assembly. To prevent that happening, the national government suspended the convening of the Assembly indefinitely. On March 26, 1971, the Awami League proclaimed the independence of the People's Republic of Bangladesh, and civil war quickly followed. In the ensuing conflict, hundreds of thousands of refugees fled to safety across the border in India. In December, India, which supported the independence of Bangladesh, declared war, and 12 days later Pakistan surrendered. Bangladesh had won its independence, and the capital of the new country was established at Dhaka. In the years immediately following independence, industrial output declined in major industries as a result of the departure of many of the largely non-Bengali financier and managerial class.

Throughout the subsequent years, political stability proved elusive for Bangladesh. Although elections were held, stability was threatened by the terrorist tactics resorted to by opposition groups from both political extremes. Coups and countercoups, assassinations, and suspension of civil liberties became regular occurrences.

Since 1983, Bangladesh had been ruled by the self-proclaimed President General H. M. Ershad. Despite demonstrations in 1987 that led to a state of emergency being declared, Ershad managed to retain power in elections held the following year. The country remains politically volatile, however. Dozens of political parties continually maneuver for position, and alliances and coalitions are the order of the day. The principal opposition party is the Awami League, an alliance of eight political parties. Many of the parties are closely linked with so-called opposition newspapers, which promote their political positions. Strikes and demonstrations are frequent and often result from cooperation among opposition political parties, student groups, and unions.

FOOTWEAR BANGLADESH

Footwear became active in what was then East Bengal in the 1930s. In 1962, the first major investment took place with the construction of a footwear manufacturing facility at Tongi, an industrial town located 30 kilometers north of Dhaka. During the following years, the company expanded its presence in both conventional and unconventional ways. In 1971, the then managing director became a freedom fighter, while continuing to oversee operations. He subsequently became the only foreigner to be decorated by the government with the "Bir Protik" in recognition of both his and the company's contribution to the independence of Bangladesh.

In 1985, Footwear Bangladesh went public and two years later spearheaded the largest private-sector foreign investment in the country, a tannery and footwear factory at Dhamrai. The new tannery produced leather for local Footwear needs and the export market, and the factory produced a variety of footwear for the local market.

By 1988, Footwear Bangladesh employed 1,800 employees and sold through 81 stores and 54 agencies. The company introduced approximately 300 new products a year to the market using their in-house design and development capability. Footwear managers were particularly proud of the capability of the personnel in these departments, all of whom were Bangladeshi.

Annual sales in excess of 10 million pairs of footwear gave the company 15 percent of the national market in 1988. Revenues exceeded $30 million and after-tax profit was approximately $1 million. Financially, the company was considered a medium contributor within the Footwear organization. With a population approaching 110 million, and per capita consumption of one pair of shoes every two years, Bangladesh was perceived as offering Footwear enormous potential for growth both through consumer education and competitive pressure.

The managing director of Footwear Bangladesh was John Carlson, one of only four foreigners working for the company. The others were the managers of production, marketing, and sales. All had extensive and varied experience within the Footwear organization.

THE INCIDENT

On Thursday, June 22, 1989, John Carlson was shown a copy of that day's *Meillat*, a well-known opposition newspaper with pro-Libyan leanings. Under the headline "Footwear's Unpardonable Audacity," the writer suggested that the design on the insole of one model of sandal produced by the company included the Arabic spelling of the word *Allah* (see Exhibit C2-2). The story

Exhibit C2-2
Translation of the Meillat Story*

UNPARDONABLE AUDACITY OF FOOTWEAR

In Bangladesh a Sandal with Allah as Footwear trade mark in Arabic designed in calligraphy has been marketed although last year Islam was made the State Religion in Bangladesh. The Sandal in black and white contains Allah in black. Prima facie it appears it has been designed and the Alif "the first letter in Arabic" has been jointly written. Excluding Alif it reads LILLAH. In Bangladesh after the Satan Rushdie's[†] Satanic Verses which has brought unprecedented demonstration and innumerable strikes (Hartels). This International shoe manufacturing organization under Jewish ownership with the design of Allah has made religious offense. Where for sanctity of Islam one million people of Afghanistan have sacrificed their lives and wherein occupied Palestine many people have been gunned down by Jews for sanctity of Islam in this country the word Allah under this guise has been put under feet.

Last night a group of students from Dhaka University came to Meillat office with a couple of pairs of Sandal. The management staff of Footwear was not available over telephone. This sandal has got two straps made of foam.

*The translation is identical to that which Carlson was given at work.
[†]Salman Rushdie was the author of the controversial book The Satanic Verses. The author had been sentenced to death, in absentia, by Ayatollah Khomeini, the late leader of Iran, for crimes against Islam.

went on to suggest that Footwear was under Jewish ownership and to link the alleged offense with the gunning down of many people in Palestine by Jews. The story highlighted the fact that the design was on the insole of the sandal and therefore, next to the bottom of the foot, a sign of great disrespect to Muslims.

Carlson immediately contacted the supervisor of the design department and asked for any information he could provide on the design on the sandals. He already knew that they were from a medium-priced line of women's footwear that had the design on the insole changed often as a marketing feature. Following his investigation, the supervisor reported

*The company's name and logo appeared prominently on the insole of the sandal. Both of the images in the exhibit were redrawn from copies of facsimiles sent to headquarters by John Carlson.

Exhibit C2-3
The Temple Bells and the Design Used on the Sandal

that the design had been based on a set of Chinese temple bells that the designer had purchased in the local market. Pleased by the appearance of the bells, she had used them as the basis for a stylized design, which she submitted to her supervisor for consideration and approval (see Exhibit C2-3).

All the employees in the development and marketing department were Muslims. The supervisor reported that the woman who had produced the offending design was a devout Bengali Muslim who spoke and read no Arabic. The same was true of almost all the employees in the department. The su-

pervisor confirmed to Carlson that numerous people in the department had seen the new design prior to its approval, and no one had seen any problem or raised any objection to it. Following the conversation, Carlson compared the design to the word *Allah*, which he had arranged to have written in Arabic (see Exhibit C2-4).

Carlson was perplexed by the article and its timing. The sandals in question were not new to the market and had not been subject to prior complaints. As he reread the translation of the *Meillat* article, he wondered why the Jewish reference had been made

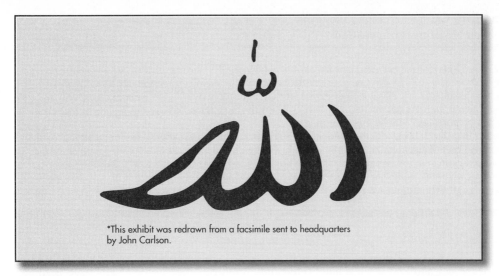

*This exhibit was redrawn from a facsimile sent to headquarters by John Carlson.

Exhibit C2-4
The Arabic Spelling of Allah*

when the family that owned Footwear International was Christian. He also wondered if the fact that students from the university had taken the sandals to the paper was significant.

As the day progressed, the situation got worse. Carlson was shown a translation of a proclamation that had been circulated by two youth groups calling for demonstrations against Footwear to be held the next day (see Exhibit C2-5). The proclamation linked Footwear, Salman Rushdie, and the Jewish community, and ominously stated that "even at the cost of our lives we have to protest against this conspiracy."

Exhibit C2-5
Translation of the Student Group's Proclamation*

The audacity through the use of the name "Allah" in a sandal.

Let Rushdie's Jewish Footwear Company be prohibited in Bangladesh.

Dear people who believe in one God it is announced in the holy Quran Allahs name is above everything but shoe manufacturing Jewish Footwear Shoe Company has used the name Allah and shown disrespect of unprecedented nature and also unpardonable audacity. After the failure of Rushdie's efforts to destroy the beliefs of Muslims in the Quran, Islam and the prophet (SM) who is the writer of Satanic verses the Jewish People have started offending the Muslims. This time it is a fight against Allah. In fact Daud Haider, Salman Rushdie Viking Penguin and Footwear Shoe Company all are supported and financed by Jewish community. Therefore no compromise with them. Even at the cost of our lives we have to protest against this conspiracy.

For this procession and demonstration will be held on 23rd. June Friday after Jumma prayer from Baitul Mukarram Mosque south gate. Please join this procession and announce we will not pardon Footwear Shoe Company's audacity. Footwear Shoe Company has to be prohibited, don't buy Jewish products and Footwear shoes. Be aware Rushdie's partner.

Issued by Bangladesh Islamic Jubashibir (Youth Student Forum) and Bangladesh Islamic Satrashbir (Student Forum).

Source: *The translation is identical to that which Carlson was given at work.

Exhibit C2-6
Section 295 of the Criminal Code

295-A. *Deliberate and malicious acts intended to outrage religious feelings of any class by insulting its religion or religious believers.* Whoever, with deliberate and malicious intention of outraging the religious feelings of any class of [the citizens of Bangladesh], by words, either spoken or written, or by visible representations, insults, or attempts to insult the religion or religious beliefs of that class, shall be punished with imprisonment . . .

. . . In order to bring a matter under S. 295-A it is not the mere matter of discourse or the written expression but also the manner of it which has to be looked to. In other words the expressions should be such as are bound to be regarded by any reasonable man as grossly offensive and provocative and maliciously and deliberately intended to outrage the feelings of any class of citizens. . . . If the injurious act was done voluntarily without a lawful excuse, malice may be presumed.

More bad news followed. Calls had been made for charges to be laid against Carlson and four others under a section of the criminal code that forbade "deliberate and malicious acts intended to outrage feelings of any class by insulting its religion or religious believers" (see Exhibit C2-6). A short time later, Carlson received a copy of a statement that had been filed by a local lawyer although no warrants were immediately forthcoming (see Exhibit C2-7).

Exhibit C2-7
The Statement of the Plaintiff

The plaintiff most respectfully states that:

1) The plaintiff is a lawyer, and a Bangladeshi Citizen and his religion is Islam. He is basically a devout Muslim. According to Islamic tradition he regularly performs his daily work.

2) The first accused of this . . . is the Managing Director of Footwear Shoe Company, the second accused is the Production Manager of the said company, the third accused is the Marketing Manager, the fourth accused is the Calligrapher of the said company and last accused is the Sales Manager of the said company. The said company is an international organization having shoe business in different countries.

3) The accused persons deliberately wanted to outrage the religion of Muslims by engraving the calligraphy of "Allah" in Arabic on a sandal thereby to offend the Religion of majority this Muslim Country. By marketing this sandal with the calligraphy of "Allah" they have offended the religious feelings of millions of Muslims. It is the solemn religious duty and responsibility of every devout Muslim to protect the sanctity of "Allah." The plaintiff first saw the sandal with this calligraphy on 22nd June 1989 at Elephant road shop.

The accused persons collectively and deliberately wanted this calligraphy under the feet thereby to offend the religion of mine and many other Muslims and have committed a crime under provisions of section 295-A of the Penal Code. At the time of hearing the evidence will be provided.

Therefore under the provisions of section 295A of the Penal Code the accused persons be issued with warrant of arrest and be brought to court for justice.

The names of the Witnesses
1)
2)
3)

While he was reviewing the situation, Carlson was interrupted by his secretary. In an excited voice, she informed him that the prime minister was being quoted as calling the sandal incident an "unforgivable crime." The seriousness of the incident seemed to be escalating rapidly, and Carlson wondered what he should do to try to minimize the damage.

CASE QUESTIONS

You are in John Carlson's position. Analyze the situation facing Footwear, and prepare a detailed plan of action to deal with your immediate responsibilities as well as the entire situation and a long-term plan.

The following suggestions may help you develop your plan:

- Use a stakeholder analysis to assess the role and objectives of various interest groups and evaluate what is going on and why, and to look beyond the immediate situation.
- Consider what role or roles local politics play in the Footwear case, and who are the principal actors in this real-life business drama.
- What issues are of greatest concern to Footwear Bangladesh? To Footwear International?

Note: These events actually happened. Ask your professor for the information on the follow-up events. Do you think this situation could happen again?

SOURCE: Reproduced by permission of the author. (Copyright © R. William Blake, Faculty of Business Administration, Memorial University of Newfoundland, St. Johns, Canada.)

Case 3   Moto: Coming to America

Moto arrived in Chicago in the middle of winter, unprepared for the raw wind that swept off the lake. The first day he bought a new coat and fur-lined boots. He was cheered by a helpful salesgirl who smiled as she packed his lined raincoat into a box. Americans were nice, Moto decided. He was not worried about his assignment in America. The land had been purchased, and Moto's responsibility was to hire a contracting company and check on the pricing details. The job seemed straightforward.

Moto's firm, KKD, an auto parts supplier, had spent 1½ years researching American building contractors. Allmack had the best record in terms of timely delivery and liaisons with good architects and the best suppliers of raw materials. That night Moto called Mr. Crowell of Allmack, who confirmed the appointment for the next morning. His tone was amiable.

Moto arrived at the Allmack office at nine sharp. He had brought a set of *kokeshi* dolls for Crowell. The dolls, which his wife had spent a good part of a day picking out, were made from a special maple in the mountains near his family home in Niigata. He would explain that to Crowell later, when they knew each other. Crowell also came from a hilly, snowy place, which was called Vermont.

When the secretary ushered him in, Crowell stood immediately and rounded the desk with an outstretched hand. Squeezing Moto's hand, he roared, "How are you? Long trip from Tokyo. Please sit down, please."

Moto smiled. He reached in his jacket for his card. By the time he presented it, Crowell was back on the other side of the desk. "My card," Moto said seriously.

"Yes, yes," Crowell answered. He put Moto's card in his pocket without a glance.

Moto stared at the floor. This couldn't be happening, he thought. Everything was on that card: KKD, Moto, Michio, Project Director KKD meant University of Tokyo and years of hard work to earn a high recommendation from Dr. Iwasa's laboratory. Crowell had simply put it away.

"Here." Crowell handed his card.

"Oh, John Crowell, Allmack, President," Moto read aloud, slowly trying to recover his equilibrium. "Allmack is famous in Japan."

"You know me," Crowell replied and grinned. "All those faxes. Pleased to meet you, Moto. I have a good feeling about this deal."

Moto smiled ant lay Crowell's card on the table in front of him.

"KKD is pleased to do business with Allmack," Moto spoke slowly. He as proud of his English. Not only had he been a top English student in high school and university, but he had also studied English in a *juku* (an afterschool class) for five years. As soon as he received this assignment, he took an intensive six-week course taught by Ms. Black, an American, who also instructed him in American history and customs.

Crowell looked impatient. Moto tried to think of Ms. Black's etiquette lessons as he continued talking about KKD and Allmack's history. "We are the best in the business," Crowell interrupted. "Ask anyone. We build the biggest and best shopping malls in the country."

Moto hesitated. He knew Allmack's record—that's why he was in the room. Surely Crowell knew that. The box of *kokeshi* dolls pressed against his knees. Maybe he should give the gift now. No, he thought, Crowell was still talking about Allmack's achievements. Now Crowell had switched to his own achievements. Moto felt desperate.

"You'll have to come to my house," Crowell continued. "I live in a fantastic house. I had an architect from California build it. He builds for all the stars, and for me." Crowell chuckled. "Built it for my wife. She's the best wife, the very best. I call her my little sweetheart. Gave the wife the house on her birthday. Took her right up to the front door and carried her inside."

Moto shifted his weight. Perhaps if he were quiet, Crowell would change the subject. Then they could pretend the conversation never happened. "Moto-san, what's your first name? Here, we like to be on a first-name basis."

"Michio," Moto whispered.

"Michio-san, you won't get a better price than from me. You can go down the block to Zimmer or Casey, but you got the best deal right here."

"I brought you a present," Moto said, handing him the box of *kokeshi* dolls.

"Thanks," Crowell answered. He looked genuinely pleased as he tore open the paper. Moto looked away while Crowell picked up a *kokeshi* doll in each hand. "They look like Russian dolls. Hey, thanks a lot, my daughter will love them."

Moto pretended that he hadn't heard. I'll help by ignoring him, Moto thought, deeply embarrassed.

Crowell pushed the *kokeshi* dolls aside and pressed a buzzer. "Send George in," he said.

The door opened and a tall, heavyset man with a dark crew cut stepped inside the room.

"George Kubushevsky, this is Moto-san. Michio . . ."

"How do you do?" Kubushevsky's handshake was firm.

Moto took out his card.

"Thanks," Kubushevsky said. "Never carry those." He laughed and hooked his thumbs in his belt buckle. Moto nodded. He was curious. Kubushevsky must be a Jewish name—or was it Polish, or maybe even German? In Japan he'd read books about all three groups. He looked at Kubushevsky's bone structure. It was impossible to tell. He was too fat.

"George, make sure you show Michio everything. We want him to see all the suppliers, meet the right people, you understand?"

"Sure." George grinned and left the room.

Moto turned to Crowel. "Is he a real American?" Moto asked.

"A real American? What's that?"

Moto flushed. "Is he first generation?" Moto finished lamely. He remembered reading that Jews, Lebanese, and Armenians were often first generation.

"How do I know? He's just Kubushevsky."

During the next few weeks Moto saw a great deal of Kubushevsky. Each morning he was picked up at nine and taken to a round of suppliers. Kubushevsky gave him a rundown on each supplier before they met. He was amiable and polite, but never really intimate. Moto's response was also to be polite. Once he suggested that they go drinking after work, but Kubushevsky flatly refused, saying that he had to work early the next morning. Moto sighed, remembering briefly his favorite bar and his favorite hostess in Tokyo. Yuko-san must be nearly fifty now, he thought affectionately. She could make him laugh. He wished he were barhopping with his colleagues from his *ringi* group at KKD. Moto regretted that he had not brought more *kokeshi* dolls, since Kubushevsky had not seemed delighted with the present of the KKD pen.

One morning they were driving to a cement outlet.

"George."

"Yes, Michio-san."

Moto paused. He still found it difficult to call Kubushevsky by his first name. "Do you think I could have some papers?"

"What kind of papers?" Kubushevsky's voice was friendly. Unlike Crowell, he kept an even tone. Moto liked that.

"I need papers on the past sales of these people."

"We're the best."

"I need records for the past five years on the cement place we are going to visit."

"I told you, Michio-san, I'm taking you to the best! What do you want?"

"I need some records."

"Trust me, I know what I'm doing."

Moto was silent. He didn't know what to say. What did trust have to do with anything? His *ringi* group in Tokyo needed documentation so they could discuss the issues and be involved in the decision. If the decision to go with one supplier or the other was correct, that should be reflected in the figures.

"Just look at what's going on now," George said. "Charts for the last five years, that's history."

Moto remained silent. George pressed his foot to the gas. The car passed one truck, and then another. Moto looked nervously at the climbing speedometer. Suddenly Kubushevsky whistled and released his foot. "All right, Michio-san, I'll get you the damned figures."

"Thanks," Moto said softly.

"After we see the cement people, let's go for a drink."

• • •

Moto looked uneasily at the soft red light bulb that lit the bar. He sipped his beer and ate a few peanuts. Kubushevsky was staring at a tall blonde at the other end of the bar. She seemed to notice him also. Her fingers moved across the rim of the glass.

"George," Moto said gently. "Where are you from, George."

"Here and there," Kubushevsky said idly, still eyeing the blonde.

Moto laughed. "Here and there."

Kubushevsky nodded. "Here and there," he repeated.

"You Americans," Moto said. "You must have a home."

"No home, Michio-san."

The blonde slid her drink down the bar and slipped into the next seat. Kubushevsky turned more toward her.

Moto felt desperate. Last week Crowell had also acted rudely. When Imai, KKD's vice president, was visiting from Japan, Crowell had dropped them both off at a golf course. What was the point?

He drained his beer. Immediately the familiar warmth of the alcohol made him buoyant. "George," he said intimately. "You need a wife. You need a wife like Crowell has."

Kubushevsky turned slowly on his seat. He stared hard at Moto. "You need a muzzle," he said quietly.

"You need a wife," Moto repeated. He had Kubushevsky's full attention now. He poured Kubushevsky another beer. "Drink," he commanded.

Kubushevsky drank. In fact they both drank. Then suddenly Kubushevsky's voice changed. He put his arm around Moto and purred in his ear. "Let me tell you a secret, Moto-san. Crowell's wife is a dog. Crowell is a dog. I'm going to leave Allmack, just as soon as possible. Want to join me, Michio-san?"

Moto's insides froze. Leave Crowell. What was Kubushevsky talking about? He was just getting to know him. They were a team. All those hours in the car together, all those hours staring at cornfields and concrete. What was Kubushevsky talking about? Did Crowell know? What was Kubushevsky insinuating about joining him? "You're drunk, George."

"I know."

"You're very drunk."

"I know."

Moto smiled. The blonde got restless and left the bar. Kubushevsky didn't seem to notice. For the rest of the night he talked about his first wife and his two children, whom he barely saw. He spoke of his job at Allmack and his hopes for a better job in California. They sat at a low table. Moto spoke of his children and distant wife. It felt good to talk. Almost as good as having Yuko next to him.

As they left the bar, Kubushevsky leaned heavily on him. They peed against a stone wall before getting in the car. All the way home Kubushevsky sang a song about a folk hero named Davy Crockett, who "killed himself a bear when he was only three." Moto sang a song from Niigata about the beauty of the snow on the rooftops in winter. Kubushevsky hummed along.

They worked as a team for the next four months. Kubushevsky provided whatever detailed documentation Moto asked for. They went drinking a lot. Sometimes they both felt a little sad, sometimes happy, but Moto mostly felt entirely comfortable. Kubushevsky introduced him to Porter, a large, good-natured man in the steel business who liked to hunt and cook gourmet food; to Andrews, a tiny man who danced the polka as if it were a waltz; and to many others.

Just before the closing, Kubushevsky took him to a bar and told him of a job offer in California. He had tears in his eyes and hugged Moto good-bye. Moto had long since accepted the fact that Kubushevsky would leave.

Two weeks later Moto looked around the conference room at Allmack. Ishii, KKD's president, and Imai had flown in from Tokyo for the signing of the contract for the shopping mall, the culmination of three years of research and months of negotiation. John Crowell stood by his lawyer, Sue Smith. Sue had been on her feet for five hours. Mike Apple, Moto's lawyer, slammed his fist on the table and pointed at the item in question. The lawyers argued a timing detail that Moto was sure had been worked out weeks before. Moto glanced nervously at Ishii and Imai. Ishii's eyes were closed. Imai stared at the table.

Moto shifted uneasily in his seat. Sue was smarter than Mike, he thought. Perhaps a female lawyer wouldn't have been so terrible. While it was not unusual to see females in professional positions in Japan, this was America. Tokyo might have understood. After all, this was America, he repeated to himself. Internationalization required some adjustment. A year ago he would have had total loss of face if confronted with this prolonged, argumentative closing. Today he did not care. He could not explain to Tokyo all he'd learned in that time, all the friends he'd made. When he tried to communicate about business in America, the home office sent him terse notes by fax.

Now the lawyers stood back. President Ishii opened his eyes. Crowell handed a pen to Ishii. They signed the document together. The lawyers smiled. Sue Smith looked satisfied. She should be pleased, Moto thought. Her extensive preparation for the case made him realize again that the Japanese stereotype of the "lazy" American was false. Sue's knowledge of the case was perfect in all details. I'll have to use her next time, Moto thought. She's the smart one. Yes, he thought, his friend Kubushevsky had taught him many things. Suddenly he felt Kubushevsky's large presence. Moto lowered his head in gratitude.

CASE QUESTIONS

1. What was Moto's purpose and agenda for the first meeting with Crowell? How does he try to implement his agenda?
2. What happened to introduce "noise" in the communication from Moto to Crowell, and then from Crowell to Moto?
3. What was the significance of the doll? What went wrong?
4. Why did Crowell's remarks about Allmack threaten a loss of *face* from Moto's perspective?
5. How did Moto feel about Kubushevsky's behavior early on? How did their relationship change?

SOURCE: Patricia Gercik, *On Track with the Japanese*, 1992. (New York: Kodansha International, 114 Fifth Ave., NY, NY 10011) (OR Kudanske America).

Case 4   *Reorganization at AB Telecom (1998)*[1]

In early 1998, the top managers at AB Telecom were debating how to change its worldwide organization. AB Telecom is a Canadian telecommunications hardware firm that manufactures fixed wireless systems. This $200 million company earned more than 95 percent of its revenues from outside Canada, with 40 percent coming from Asia in 1997. In 1998, AB Telecom conducted all of its manufacturing and R&D within Canada; much of its market development and project engineering is maintained in its Canadian headquarters.

AB Telecom was founded in 1981 and is publicly traded on several Canadian stock exchanges. It had been profitable since 1990, with an average 7 percent net profitability between 1990 and 1997. Given its strong presence outside Canada, ABT has been awarded the prestigious Canadian Export Award several times by the Canadian government.

AB Telecom's traditional customer is a national telephone company that wants to improve telecommunications to its rural locations. Sixty percent of ABT's sales in 1997 were turnkey projects for national telephone companies. Its structure had been a regional sales and marketing structure with three regions: Asia/Pacific, Latin America, and Europe/Middle East/Africa. Each region had a headquarters and several sales subsidiaries in different countries. These regional offices had autonomy in booking small deals, but headquarters became involved with deals worth over $2 million. The regional offices are also reliant on some project engineering support provided by the headquarters.

Several significant changes had created a need for top management to review its current structure:

- early signs of economic difficulty in Malaysia and other southeast Asian countries could po-

tentially stall or stop agreed-to projects in this region
- opportunities to use their existing fixed wireless systems for industrial application were growing
- Europe, Middle East, and Africa provided many opportunities for sales to traditional national telephone companies for rural applications
- potential is unknown for its new wireless product for urban data transmissions to telephone companies and new competitors

In March 1998, the CEO, his top management team, and some board members met to discuss how to restructure the company.

PRODUCT APPLICATIONS

Rural telephony. AB Telecom researchers, designs, and manufactures fixed wireless systems mostly for installation in rural and remote areas, to aid in rural telecommunications. ABT manufactures all components required for rural installation. It subcontracts with local contractors to install the systems.

The main application of the AB Telecom product is to connect remote villages and towns to the national telephone system grid. Fixed wireless is a cost-effective solution for many national telephone companies to connect to rural locations; the cost of installing a fixed wireless system is far less than that of laying miles of fiber or copper cable to the same locale. ABT's traditional customers have been national telephone companies.

For this business, ABT considers Alcatel, NEC Japan, and Lucent to be its direct competitors, but the fixed wireless systems are a very small portion of these large multinational firms' sales, whereas ABT specializes in the fixed wireless systems and technology.

Industrial applications. New applications of ABT's wireless systems have been recently recognized. Companies in industries such as oil, gas, and electricity

---

[1]This is a real company, but the company name, location and a few aspects of the firm are disguised because of a pledge of confidentiality by the researcher.

Exhibit C4-1
AB Telecom at Time of Case

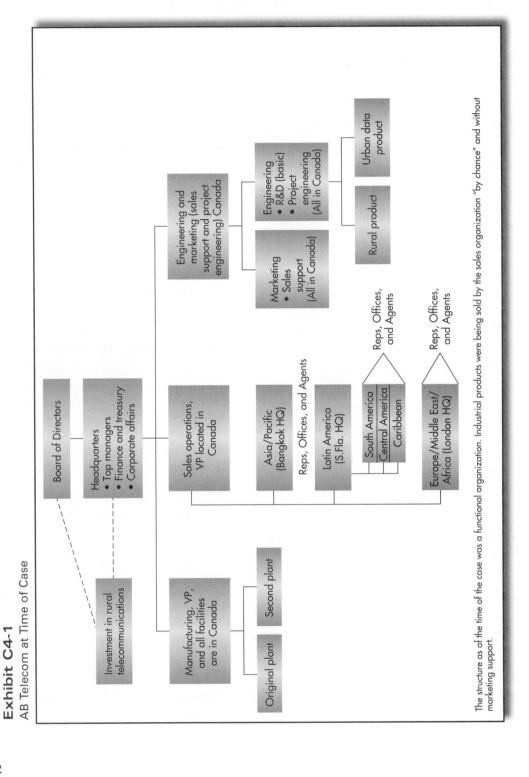

The structure as of the time of the case was a functional organization. Industrial products were being sold by the sales organization "by chance" and without marketing support.

generation require remote sensing of dispersed operations. In early 1998, this type of business had grown to comprise 25 percent of ABT's revenues. Much of this business was developed "by chance," as explained by one top manager:

> We realized that the industrial portion of sales could be more significant. The industrial market was not properly marketed to, nor were their needs involved in, our R&D efforts. We realized that this area could become significant if we added more products that customers wanted because we are one of the largest companies selling to this fragmented and diverse market.

This manager went on to explain how industrial customers were developed in one Asian country:

> Our industrial customers developed just by chance [in this country]. Now, we have 100 industrial customers. We had no idea what the customer wanted. Because selling to this national telephone company was slow and government controlled, we stumbled upon the electric companies who were interested. It started off with a change of attention of one salesperson already located in this market, but it developed in a mostly word of mouth way . . . this counts for a lot in [this country]. We gained a reputation for being a reliable supplier, but growing this business was not part of a plan . . . it just happened.

The estimated potential revenue from this market is around $100 million per year, but it is spread among hundreds of industrial customers. One ABT manager explained, "Tremendous sales and marketing efforts are required to obtain a $5 million order, but once a customer orders and is satisfied, they are more likely to repeat the purchase. . . . We need more information to develop the business. . . . It is difficult to find out where the big industrial users are worldwide. . . . mostly trial and error," stated one top ABT manager.

Urban wireless. ABT also had developed and was testing fixed wireless systems in urban settings. The potential customers for this product were telephone companies, both the incumbent telephone company as well as start-up carriers, especially in Europe. A start-up company would offer data services in competition with the original telephone company. The ABT system would be used to transmit data reliably within dense urban settings. This application has required some modification to the original ABT product lines. "With data applications, we are really starting from zero, but we should be able to double or triple them in the future." In 1998, this system was being tested in the U.K. Only a few technical and marketing people were involved and only in a haphazard way.

INVESTMENT IN RURAL LICENSE

In 1996, ABT deviated from its sales and delivery of operation systems to invest in the telecommunications infrastructure of a Latin American country. This investment in rural infrastructure in Latin America was a major departure from ABT's short-term, project-oriented, turnkey operations. For several years, top executives had discussed the possibility of pursuing investment as opposed to sales-only deals. This investment was initiated, managed, and controlled by top managers in Montreal, but local managers were hired to help with the installation and operations of this investment.

Top executives outlined several reasons for ABT to pursue an investment in rural telecommunications operations. According to one manager close to this deal, "Many people confuse rural with poverty, but they miss out on a very good investment and tremendous pent-up demand." Most of the large hardware equipment manufacturers have moved from selling equipment and services to investing and buying up licenses in international markets. As one top manager stated, "It was a difficult decision to invest in rural telecom, but our board of directors was convinced it was a good idea . . . we realized that we could supply our equipment at no markup and then sell a 51 percent stake in our investment, perhaps using this to fund future investments in rural telecommunications."

Concerning the challenges inherent in starting this new venture, one manager explained, "We are not experts at running a telephone company; we don't know how to bill or do maintenance." In 1998, ABT hired a local manager away from the national telephone company to run the firm. Consultants with experience with Bell Canada were also helping with the venture. By 1998, ABT had set up 1,000 telephone lines and had 100 employees; the push was to install pay phones, a legal requirement of the license. ABT managers estimated that it would take about 8,000 to 10,000 installed lines to break even, probably in 1999. Once this rural venture establishes a proven track record, ABT managers plan to sell off a portion to a local partner. If this venture is successful, ABT managers are considering future investments in rural telecommunications. One top manager stated, "We are being approached by people in many markets around the world about potential investments."

CURRENT REGIONAL SALES AND MARKETING STRUCTURE

From 1981 until 1988, ABT's Canadian headquarters controlled all of the details of the business. Then, as one top manager explained, "We felt that we had to get closer to the customer, and we went first to Asia because that was where the action was." So, in the late 1980s, ABT placed several sales people in the field in three regions: Asia/Pacific, Latin America, and Europe/Africa/Middle East. In 1997, Asia/Pacific markets were 50 percent of all revenues, Latin America 36 percent, and Europe/Africa/Middle East 19 percent of sales. The United States was not a market for ABT's equipment given the significant rural infrastructure already in place in the United States.

Asia/Pacific. The first subsidiary was in Hong Kong as "an easy way into China," according to a top ABT manager. There were no customers, and it was expensive to maintain an office there. "Because we weren't even paying the light bills, we decided to move the Asia/Pacific headquarters to Manila to save on taxes and expenses, and in order to have access to a skilled labor force." Soon after this move, a sales subsidiary was set up in China, followed by another office in Bangkok after a large project was won there.

By the early 1990s, ABT had more than 60 people on the ground in these three operations. These offices were staffed with technical sales people with an engineering background. They were rewarded on meeting a quota, and they operated autonomously from the headquarters. Their sales efforts centered on selling ABT's equipment and solutions to national telephone companies. These technical sales people placed orders with headquarters and provided service to the firm once the system was installed and in place. Many times, they relied on project engineering for technical details related to a bid or final customer proposal.

In the early 1990s, the Asian headquarters was moved again to Bangkok. As one manager stated, "With these regional offices, we cultivated relationships." If a project or bid was around $1 million, headquarters would rarely get involved. If the order was more strategic (from $5 million to $10 million in size), headquarters would interact closely with sales, working together on pricing, delivery, and technical specifications.

Latin America. The Latin America office was located in south Florida. At first, this region was staffed with sales engineers. Then, managers for different areas within Latin America were brought in to strengthen the region's marketing abilities. In 1998, there were three area managers: one each for South America (included Brazil, Argentina, Colombia, and Peru), Caribbean U.S., and Central America. The total number of engineers and managers in this office was 12 in 1998. Sales support and project engineers were still located in Montreal to support Latin America project bids technical assistance, or operations. Most of the activity within this area was repeat customers, the national telephone companies. This Latin American sales and marketing area had nothing to do with the 1997 investment in rural telecommunications by ABT. In fact, most of the managers knew very few details about this investment transaction.

With the privatization of many Latin American telephone companies, managers from AB Telecom's Latin American office had developed a close working relationship with Telefonica (Spain's national telephone company) and STET (Italy's national telephone company) because these two companies have purchased significant stakes in many national telephone companies in Latin America. This area had been growing consistently for AB Telecom in the 1990s.

One manager explained how deals are developed in this region: "We follow regulatory changes in countries that are considering privatization. We know that a piece will be rural, and money will be made available for rural according to the bids for this privatization. Our local representatives keep us advised." Another manager explained, "We have not pushed much into the industrial business in Latin America except for one excellent industrial client—an oil company in Venezuela— and this relationship was gained through a technical representative on the ground with this oil company." When asked about how they interact with R&D in Canada, one manager stated, "We don't worry about technology. . . . we worry about satisfying a need . . . we have the best product technically, reflected in our high quality and high price. . . . this combined with being close to the customer lands us deals . . . many of our deals in Latin America are renewals."

One area manager in the Latin American division stated, "The greatest impediment to our international growth is resources—human resources. We are looking for people with language, engineering, project skills, and good interpersonal skills."

Europe/Middle East/Africa. In 1998, the Europe/Middle East/Africa region was the most difficult, according to several managers. This was attributed to too many different regulations and frequencies across this region. Sales subsidiaries have been developed where a strong relationship with a national telephone company existed. Sales subsidiaries had been set up in Nairobi, Saudi Arabia, South Africa, Sweden, and the U.K. The head of this regional structure had recently resigned.

DILEMMA

In reviewing the evolution of their structure, top managers recognized that they had moved from a domestic functional structure to a geographic regional sales and marketing structure. They realized that each existing sales subsidiary was organized to develop and maintain a close relationship with the national telephone company of countries within its region, focusing mostly on its rural telephony needs.

Sales persons were not rewarded to develop new markets (such as industrial business or urban data transmission) because they were paid on the basis of meeting quarterly sales quotas. According to one top manager, "They could not focus on such a diverse market as industrial because it is going to take two or three years of working closely with an industrial customer or a new telephone competitor to land a deal, and this just doesn't fit within our reward system of sales persons."

In 1998, traditional Asian markets and telephone companies were beginning to suffer, and top managers anticipated that revenues from these markets would be flat or, worse, fall by the end of the year. There were opportunities to expand their presence in non-Asian markets with their traditional customers or to push for entry into other applications such as industrial and urban data.

Therefore, the top managers were focused on developing a structure to manage the tension within its wireless technology division (traditionally housed in the R&D area in Canada), its current regional structure (responsive to customers needs, cultural differences mostly in its current rural applications), and emerging new customer groups (such as the industrial and urban wireless data products).

CASE QUESTION

How should ABT top managers reorganize to resolve the tensions among the regional organization selling to national telephone customers, new applications for industrial and urban data, and investments in rural telephony?

SOURCE: Case written by Professor Anne Smith, University of New Mexico, based on her research of the firm discussed. © 1998 by Professor Anne Smith. Used with permission.

Case 5   *Softbank Corp.*

Internet and Web-Related Acquisitions, Market Expansion, and Global Strategies in 2001/02

Syed Tariq Anwar

INTRODUCTION

Softbank Corp. is a Japanese business group that controls more than 600 Internet and technology-related companies and other businesses worldwide (see Exhibits C5-1–C5-4). The company is headquartered in Tokyo and was started by Masayoshi Son in 1981. Even after the 1999/2000's dot.com downturn, the company ranks as one of the largest distributors of software and technology-related products as well as a provider of Internet-based information in the world. In 2001, Softbank Group is divided into the following segments: IT-related distribution and e-commerce, financial services, publishing and marketing, Internet infrastructure, technology service, and broadcast media (see Exhibit C5-4). Because of its massive acquisitions, Softbank is often called the Internet *Keiretsu* (Lynskey and Yonekura, 2001; Webber 1992). The company is the largest investor in the Internet, e-commerce, and technology-related areas in the world. Since 1992, Softbank has grown into one of the most influential and dynamic players in the Internet and e-commerce industry. Because of Son's unique entrepreneurial style and flamboyant personality, the Western media often called him "The Bill Gates of Japan," "Cyber-Mogul," "Master *of* the Internet," "Japan's Mr. Internet," etc. Son's entrepreneurial style has become a powerful force in the Internet world. Son started Softbank after receiving his degree in economics from the University of California at Berkeley in 1980. Since 1994, Softbank's shares have been traded on the Tokyo over-the-counter market. In 1998, Softbank's consolidated revenues reached $4.38 billion with a pre-tax profit of $339 million. In 1999, Softbank's market capitalization surpassed $11.5 billion and the company employed 7,000 workers worldwide (refer to Exhibit C5-1; *Business*

Week, 1999a&b; *Financial Times,* 1997a-c; *The Wall Street Journal,* 1996,1999a-c).

In the last ten years, Softbank has sought aggressive global diversification by acquiring high-profile Internet companies and investing millions of dollars in long-term Internet technologies. In September 1999, Softbank's selected acquisitions and majority share holdings included: Yahoo, Yahoo Japan, E-Trade-Japan, E-Trade Group, Buy.com, Concentric, E-Loan, USWeb, ZDNet, Ziff Davis, ZD Comdex, Kingston Technology, SB Networks, and Japan Digital Broadcasting Services (see Exhibit C5-5). Softbank's venture capital subsidiary (Softbank Technology Ventures) has actively pursued and sought equity-related investments in companies from the areas of digital information technology, Internet communications, network services, and e-commerce.

Softbank's shift in its core-competence and long-term strategies results from a massive growth in the Internet and technology-related markets in the U.S., Japan, and Western Europe. According to industry analysts, Softbank plans to become one of the largest Internet and technology communication companies in the world. Softbank is truly the first-mover company in its product markets. Analysts believe that in the next five years, Softbank will become a major force in the Internet and technology-related and software distribution areas because of increasing demand and growth. On the other hand, Softbank will be impacted by heightened global competition and will be challenged by newcomers in the industry. The case is intended to have students look at Softbank's future market growth and its global strategies within the concept of internationalization and competitive advantage issues.

Exhibit C5-1

Softbank Corp.: Selected Financial and Corporate Data (1999 vs. 2001)*

A: *Financial Data*	1999	2001
Consolidated Revenues:	$4.3 billion	$4.6 billion
Pre-Tax Profit:	$339 million	$286 million
Net Profit:	$311 million	$75 million
Market Capitalization:	$11.3 billion	$12.81 billion
Global Rank:	—	447

B: *Corporate Data*		
Head Office:	24–1, Nihonbashi-Hakozakicho, Chuco-ku, Tokyo, Japan	
Employees Worldwide (2001):	7,000	7,219
Incorporated:	September 3, 1981	
Stock Information:	Stock traded on *Tokyo Stock Exchange* (first section)	
	Symbol: *9984*	

Company Structure:	Softbank Corp.
	Softbank Global Ventures
	Softbank International Ventures
	Softbank Venture Capital
	Softbank Capital Partners
	Softbank Europe Ventures
	Softbank Latin American Ventures
	Softbank China Venture Capital
	Softbank Ventures Korea

Board of Directors (as of June 21, 2001)

President & CEO: Masayoshi Son

Directors: Yoshitaka Kitao, Ken Miyauchi, Kazuhiko Kasai, Masahiro Inoue, Ronald Fisher, Jun Murai, Toshifumi Suzuki, Tadashi Yanai, Mark Schwartz.

Source: (1). Softbank Corp., Tokyo, Japan: September 1999, <www.softbank.com/corporate_data.htm>; *Forbes*. "Master of the Internet," July 5, 1999, pp. 146–151; *Financial Times*, May 11, 2001, pp. 1–55.

Who Is Masayoshi Son?

Son was born in 1957 on Kyushu Island and grew up in a small town, Tosu City, Saga Prefecture. Son belongs to an ethnic Korean family. His grandparents migrated to Japan from Korea. In 1973, at the age of 16, Son attended high school in California and later moved to Holy Names College in Oakland, California. In 1980, Son graduated from the University of California at Berkeley with a B.A. degree in Economics. While an undergraduate student, Son invented a multilingual pocket translator and sold his patent to Sharp Corp., which later brought him a $1 million windfall (Lynskey and Yonekura, 2001). Son also founded Unison Computer Company, which is now owned by Kyocera Corp. (Webber, 1992; <www.softbnk.com/bios.htm>.

In 1981, Son returned to Japan and founded Softbank Corp. The company initially started with two part-time workers and later grew to 570 employees in 1991. Softbank supplied computer software, books and magazines, and other technology-related products to 200 dealer outlets. In 1991, the company expanded at a very fast pace and grew to 15,000 dealer outlets because of the changing market conditions

Exhibit C5-2

Softbank Corp.: Major Entities and Product Lines (1999)

A: Media & Marketing:

Ziff-Davis, Inc. (NYSE: **ZD**):
  —Integrated media & marketing company
  —PC Magazine
  —PC Week
  —Computer Shopper
  —50 licensed publication (combined circulation: 8 million readers)
  —COMDEX (the largest U.S. show)

ZDNet (NYSE: **ZDZ**)
  —Web site (news, information, entertainment)

ZDTV
  —Cable TV Channel – Digital Information Topics

Ziff-Davis – Market Research Division
  —Computer intelligence unit; market research firm

B: Internet & Technology-Related Companies:

  —*Softbank Technology Ventures*
  —*Asymetrix Learning Systems* (NASDAQ: **ASYM**): Online trading programs
  —*BackWeb*: Markets software; deliver personalized information
  —*Buy.com*: Operates retail web site
  —*Concentric* (NASDAQ: **CNCX**): Provides Virtual Private Networks & extranets; operates the *Quicken Financial Network* for Intuit
  —*E-Loan*: Online mortgage
  —*E*Trade* (NASDAQ: **EGRP**): Online Investment brokerage and stock trading services
  —*InterTrust*: Develops and sells a software system in the areas of medical records, movies, audio, stock transactions, etc.
  —*MessageMedia* (NASDAQ: **MESG**): Develops, markets, and installs messaging systems on the Internet; two-way communications
  —*Reciprocal*: Provides service in the areas of selling software, music, magazines and other types of digital property
  —*USWeb/CKS* (NASDAQ: **USWB**): Helps design Web sites for Fortune 1000 companies; deals with strategic consulting
  —*Yahoo* (NASDAQ: **YHOO**): Premier global Internet media company; Softbank is the largest shareholder of Yahoo, which recently acquired *GeoCities*

Source: Softbank Corp., Tokyo, Japan: September 1999, <www.softbank.com/corporate_data.htm>.

and strong consumer demand for software and computer products. In 1991, Son netted $350 million in sales and its retailers' network expanded to 25,000. During this period, Softbank was distributing products from companies such as Microsoft, Novell, Sun Microsystems, and Oracle (Lynskey and Yonekura, 2001). After 1991, Son started to expand into the Internet area and made numerous acquisitions. In 1994, Softbank's stock started trading on the Tokyo over-the-counter market. After four years, Softbank's shares were listed on the Tokyo Stock Exchange. Since 1994 the stock has split four times. Son's recent initiatives, acquisitions, and major alliances include Nihon Cisco Systems, Ziff-Davis trade show,

Exhibit C5-3
Softbank Corp.: Company Structure and Portfolio Companies (December 2001)

A: Company Structure
—Softbank in Japan
—Softbank Corp.
—Softbank e-Commerce Corp
—Softbank Finance Corp.
—Softbank Media & Marketing Corp.
—Softbank Technology Corp.
—Softbank Networks Inc.
—Softbank Broadmedia Corp.
—Softbank Venture Capital (Mountain View, Calif.)
—Softbank Capital Partners
—Softbank Europe Ventures
—Softbank Latin America Ventures
—Softbank China Holdings
—Softbank Ventures Korea
—Softbank Emerging Markets

B: Portfolios Companies
United States:

—BUY.COM, Inc.,
—CompuBank-National Associates
—E*Trade
—E-LOAN, Inc.
—Key3media
—Kinesoft Development Corp.

—SayIt,
—Sonnet Financial, Inc.
—UTStarcom
—Viacore, Inc.
—Yahoo! Inc.
—ZDNet

SOFTBANK Venture Capital
United States:

—Neomeo
—ProSavvy
—ADIR Technologies
—AppGenesys
—Aqueduct
—Art Technology Group, Inc.
—Asia Online
—Asymetrix
—Atreus Systems
—B2SB Technologies
—beMANY!
—Blue-Silicon
—BlueLight.com Corporation
—BlueTiger Networks
—Broad Daylight, Inc.

—BUY.COM, Inc.
—CBCA, Inc.
—ChannelWave Software, Inc.
—Comergent Technologies, Inc.
—Concentric Network Corporation
—Connected Corporation
—Critical Path, Inc.
—Cybercash
—Danger Research
—dbDoctor
—deuxo
—Differential Inc.
—Digimarc Corporation
—E-Loan, Inc.
—Electron Economy

SOFTBANK Venture Capital (*cont.*)

—etrieve, Inc.
—Evant
—Everest Broadband Networks, Inc.
—Exactis.com.
—EYT
—FastParts, Inc.
—FileFish
—Finali Corporation
—FinaPlex
—Game Change
—GenericMedia
—Gold Systems, Inc
—Group Sense PDA Holdings Limited
—Guggenheim
—HeyAnita
—Hubstorm
—HVC Technologies
—iBoost Technology, Inc.
—iGeneration
—Ignition Corporation
—Intend Change Group, Inc.
—Interliant, Inc.
—InterTrust Technologies
—Corporation invesmart
—Invisible Worlds, Inc.s
—iPrint.com
—Kefta
—Latis
—Law.com
—Legal Knowledge Company
—LIMITrader.com
—Maaya
—MessageMedia, Inc.
—Mondo Media
—Net2Phone, Inc.
—Netgov.com
—NETSEC
—New Moon
—Novare
—Oediv
—PayTrust.com

—PeoplePC, Inc.
—Perfect Commerce
—Photopoint
—PocketThis
—Preview Systems, Inc.
—Proxinet, Inc.
—Pulse Entertainment
—Purple Yogi, Inc.
—Quova
—Raindance Communications
—ReachCast Corporation
—REBAR
—Reciprocal, Inc.
—Reelplay.com
—Rentals.com
—Rivio
—SecurityFocus
—ServiceMagic.com
—ServiceMagic.com
—ShareWave, Inc.
—SportBrain
—StartSampling
—Support.com
—TelEvoke, Inc.
—Terabeam Networks
—The Feld Group
—TheStreet.Com, Inc.
—Tonos
—Toysrus.com
—Transilica
—Trapezo
—United Devices, Inc.
—UTStarcom
—Veripost
—Verisign, Inc.
—Viathan
—Voice Works
—Vytek Wireless
—Wideforce Systems
—WiredCapital
—Xythos

Exhibit C5-3
(*cont.*)

SOFTBANK Capital Partners
United States:
—1–800-FLOWERS.Com, Inc.
—AllAdvantage.com
—BlueLight.com Corporation
—BUY.COM, Inc.
—ClearCross
—DoveBid, Inc.
—Electron Economy
—Global Sports, Inc.
—Ignition Corporation
—Law.com
—Webhire

—Legal Research Network, Inc.
—Mysmart.com, Inc.
—Naviant, Inc.
—Odimo.com
—Optimark Technologies, Inc.
—PeoplePC, Inc.
—Rivals.com
—SmartAge.com Corp.
—Toysrus.com
—Web MD

SOFTBANK Europe Ventures
Finland
—LPG Innovations
France
—CONSUL
—Cril Telecom Software (CTS)
Israel
—iSeg
Netherlands
—StiVentures
Sweden
—Picofun
—Startupfactory
Switzerland
—uB-mobile
United Kingdom
—Picsel
—RIOT-E
—theworkx.net

—Enition
—NeTarget

—Venation
—Volantis

SOFTBANK Latin America Ventures
Argentina
—Dineronet
Brasil
—ConnectMed.com
—Springwireless
United States
—BitTime
—From2.com (Merged with Arzoon)

—LearningSoft Corporation
—Tiaxa

Exhibit C5-3
(cont.)

SOFTBANK China Venture Capital
China
- —51Marry.com
- —Airoam Technology
- —Alibaba
- —Asiawise.com
- —ChinaQuest
- —eBao
- —ExhibitionOne
- —EZnova
- —Good Doctor
- —Goodbaby
- —Guardian Auction
- —Jia2000
- —NewLido
- —Precom
- —Prosys
- —Universiti

SOFTBANK Ventures Korea
Korea
- —Alibaba Korea
- —Anysteel.com
- —B2B Cons
- —CrossCert
- —Cyberdigm
- —HeyAnita Korea
- —I-Cube
- —I-Textile Korea
- —I-World
- —JoyinBox
- —MediOn (n-Health)
- —MediService (n-Health)
- —SecureSoft
- —SOFTBANK Media
- —SOFTBANK Web Institute
- —SOFTBANKnPlatform
- —Yahoo! Korea

Source: Softbank <www.softbank.com>.

Comdex, Windows World, Yahoo, Yahoo Japan, and Softbank Technology Ventures (refer to Exhibits C5-1–C5-3). In 1994, when the Internet market in North America started to take off, Softbank was the only Japanese company making high-profile acquisitions. This shows Son's visionary personality and aggressive entrepreneurial style (*Business Week*, 1996; *Business Week E-Biz*, 1999; *U.S. News & World Report*, 1999; Weinberg, 1999). Abrahams & Nakamoto (1999, p. 16) commented:

> Softbank is a unique Japanese company. Led by Masayoshi Son, its flamboyant president, it has been touted as Japan's answer to Microsoft. Son's multimedia empire has expanded at breathtaking speed to become a global enterprise, but in the past year the group's shares have tumbled, raising concerns about Softbank's future.

Forbes (1999, p. 148) commented on Softbank's massive acquisitions:

> Masayoshi Son's golden touch in Web investing has made him fabulously rich. His 42% stake in Softbank gives him a personal worth of $6.4 billion. The $6.4 billion question: Is he really that much smarter than everyone else—or is he just lucky?

Far Eastern Economic Review (1999, p. 11) commented on Son's bold moves and his entrepreneurial style:

> Son's vision is to build Softbank into a global Internet consortium or zaibatsu[1], with the same

---

[1]*Zaibatsu* group of companies' structure was based on the concept of holding companies. These companies were very strong before World War II. After the war, the U.S. dissolved these groups, which later took the form of *Keiretsu* companies based on the Main-Bank structure and network connections.

Exhibit C5-4

Softbank Group as of December 2001

A. IT-Related Distribution Service & E-Commerce:

Softbank EC Holdings Corp., Softbank Commerce Corp., Softbank Frameworks Corp., Onsale Japan K.K., e-Shopping! Information Corp., e-Shopping! Books Corp., e-Shopping! Toys Corp., e-Shopping! Cargoods Corp., e-Shopping! Wine Corp., e-Career Corp., CarPoint K.K., e-Best Corp., Vector Inc., VerticalNet Japan Corp., eEntry Corp., SmartFirm Corp., Tavigator Inc., e-Express Co., Ltd., Style Index Corp., Diamon.com Corp., Softbank Mobile Corp., GWP Japan Corp., eselect Corp., BridalConcierge Corp., Eupholink, Inc., AIP Bridge Corp., CreativeBank Corp., Nihon Ariba K.K., Cmnet Corp., BluePlanet Corp., Ability Design, Ltd.

B. Financial Service:

Softbank Finance Corp., E*Advisor Co., Ltd., E*Trade Japan K.K., E8Trade Securities Co., Ltd., Ascot Co., Ltd., E-Loan Japan K.K., Insweb Japan K.K., Softbank Investment Corp., Cognotec Japan K.K., Cybercash K.K., Morningstar Japan K.K., Web Lease Co., Ltd., Softbank Frontier Securities Co., Ltd., SophiaBank Ltd., Office Work Corp., HousePortal Co., Ltd., Goodloan Co., Ltd., e-Commodity Co., Ltd., Online IR Co., Ltd., E-Real Estate Co., Ltd., SF Realty Co., Ltd., Web Portal Co., Ltd., Softbank Asset Management Co., Ltd., SBI Capital Co., Ltd., SBI Promo Corp., Benefit Systems, Inc., Utopian Life Co., Ltd., Finance All Corp., Arsnova Capital Research, Inc., SBF Auction, Inc., Dream Support, Inc., TechTank Corp., SF Aggregation Service Co., Ltd.

C. Publishing & Marketing:

Softbank Media & Marketing Corp., Softbank Publishing Inc., Key3Media Events Japan, Inc., Com-Path, Inc., Cyber Communications, Inc., Softbank ZDNet, Inc., WebMD Japan K.K., Barks K.K., Click2learn Japan K.K., Rivals Japan Corp., JaJa Entertainment Inc., Aplix Net Inc., Englishtown Ltd., DirektPlanet Co., Ltd, iWeb Technologies Japan K.K., EC Research Corp.

D. Internet Infrastructure:

Softbank Networks Inc., IP Revolution Inc., Internet Facilities Inc., GlobalCenter Japan Corp.,

E. Technology Service:

Softbank Technology Holdings Corp., Softbank Technology Corp., E-cosmos, Inc., Broadbank Technology Corp., EC Architects Corp., Softbank Mobile Technology Corp., e-Commerce, Technology Corp.

F. Broadcast & Media:

Softbank Broadmedia Corp., Digital Club Corp., Computer Channel Corp., Xdrive Japan K.K., YesNoJapan Corp., Akamai Technologies Japan K.K., Digital Media Factory Inc., Sky Perfect Communications, Inc., J Sky Sports Corp., Nihon Eiga Satellite Broadcasting Corp., Aliss-Net Co., Ltd..

G. Other:

Yahoo Japan Corp., AtWork Corp., Softbank Digital Rights Corp., Nasdaq Japan, Inc., Aozora Bank, Ltd., SpeedNet Inc., BB Technologies Corp..

Source: Softbank < www.softbank.com >.

Exhibit C5-5

Softbank's Internet and Technology-Related Revenues (as of June 1999)

A: Software & Network Products

Sales (1998): $1.58 billion (9.7 % up)

Operating Profit: $30.1 million (38.4% down)

Major Companies: SB Networks, UTStarcom, Trend Micro

B: Media & Broadcasting

Sales (1998): $0.96 billion (17.3 % up)

Operating Profit: $114.2 million (10.8% up)

Major Companies: Ziff-Davis, Japan Digital Broadcasting Corp. (TV, radio & data transmission)

C: Technology Events & Trade Shows:

Sales (1998): $0.3 billion (30.4% up)

Operating Profit: $78.8 million (8.0% up)

Selected Companies: ZD Comdex & Forums, Inc.,

D: Technology Services

Sales (1998): $1.35 billion (185.4 % up)

Operating Profit: $48.5 million (22.7% up)

Selected Companies: Kingston Technology (memory modules), Pasona Softbank (computer temp. agency)

E: Internet Sector

Sales (1998): NA

Operating Profit: NA

Selected Companies: Yahoo Japan (ownership: 51%), E*Trade Japan (58%), GeoCities Japan (60%), ZDNet (online news & magazines)

Source: *The Wall Street Journal*. "Japan's Softbank Unveils New Internet Deals," June 25, 1999, p. A17.

---

landscape-shifting impact as the zaibatsu of the Meiji era who created Japan's first modern industries. He is doing this by identifying businesses where substantial efficiencies can be gained by going on-line. In particular, Son has zoomed in on Japan's stuffy world of brokerage, insurance, and banking. . . . Should Son succeed, he will be known not just as the man who dominates the Internet, but as a major financial-services player.

ACQUISITIONS, DIVERSIFICATION, AND GLOBAL STRATEGIES IN 1999

According to *Forbes* (1999), Softbank has invested $2.4 billion in 100 Internet, technology, communications, and computer publishing companies. As of July 1999, the total market value of these companies surpassed $14 billion. In many companies, Softbank became one of the major investors (see Exhibit C5-6). Softbank's venture capital subsidiary (Softbank Technology Ventures) has provided $906 million to many internet firms in the United States and Japan. Analysts believe that Softbank has plans to invest $1.2 billion in the coming months to seek additional acquisitions and new Internet start-ups. As of September 1999, Softbank held 7% to 8% ownership in the Internet and e-commerce industry worldwide. Softbank's Internet and technology acquisitions fall into two categories. First, in the area of media and marketing, Softbank owns 70 percent of Ziff-Davis, Inc., which is the largest computer trade show company in the world. Ziff-Davis publishes computer maga-

Exhibit C5-6

Softbank's Selected Internet & Technology-Related Acquisitions & Market Value in 1999 & 2001

A: As of July 1999:

ACQUISITION	DATE ACQUIRED	PRICE PAID ($ MILLION)	CURRENT HOLDING (%)	MARKET VALUE ($ MILLION)
E-Trade Group (*Online Investing*)	July 98	$409	27%	$2,364
Message Media (*Message Technology*)	May-Sept. 98	8	24	124
Pasona Softbank (*Temp. Agency*)	Feb. 95	NA	20	62
Trend Micro (*Anti-Virus Software*)	Dec. 96	64	27	768
USWeb (*Web Consulting*)	Feb. 96	14	7	131
Yahoo (*Internet Portal*)	Nov. 95-Aug. 98	410	27	8,424
Yahoo Japan (*Internet Portal*)	April 96	10	51	2,287
Ziff-Davis (*Media & Marketing*)	Oct. 94-Feb. 96	1,500	70	833
Total:		$2,415	$14,993	

B. As of January 2001:

INTERNET/WEB SECTOR	INVESTMENT MADE	RETURN	TOTAL COMPANIES
Web Infrastructure:	$771 million	$2.8 billion	142
Wireless:	143 million	238 million	41
Portals & Content:	484 million	15 billion	155
Consumer E-Commerce:	924 million	1.4 billion	108
Business-to-Business E-Commerce:	484 million	612 million	140

Source: Financial Times. "Softbank Widens Its Net," July 9, 1999, p. 12; *Forbes.* "Master of the Internet," July 5, 1999, pp. 146–151; *Business Week.* "The Last True Believer," January 22, 2001, pp. EB23–28.

zines such as *PC Magazine*, *PC Week*, and *Computer Shopper*. Second, in the Internet, communications, and technology sectors, Softbank has invested in some of the top Internet brands; i.e., Yahoo, Yahoo Japan, E-Trade Group, E-Loan, Concentric, USWeb, Message Media, and Asymetrix Learning Systems. These acquisitions have placed Softbank among the top Internet and technology players in the world.

A quick look at Softbank's global strategy reveals two areas. First, Softbank is the main Internet and communications company in the world. This was achieved by acquiring some of the strategic Internet brands in the world markets. Second, Softbank plans to get out of the computer publishing business and will start refocusing on the Internet and e-commerce areas. This could be attributed to high growth in the Internet and e-commerce industry. Although risky in nature, this long-term strategic move by Softbank carries an excellent market share and will place it

among the top Internet companies in Japan and other markets. Very few Japanese companies have pursued this kind of risky growth strategy in the Internet and e-commerce areas.

GLOBAL OPPORTUNITIES AND PROBLEMS AREAS IN 1999
Company Plans and Global Opportunities

Unlike Microsoft, Dell, AOL, Amazon.com, Intel, and other high-tech and e-commerce companies, Softbank has not been able to become a household name in the Western world. Most of its markets and customers are located in Japan and Asian countries. On the other hand, Softbank ranks as a global player in the Internet and e-commerce. In 1999, Softbank's initial investment of $358 million in the Internet and technology-related industry has grown to a value of $10 billion (*Far Eastern Economic*

Review, 1999). Most of Softbank's visibility lies in Japan where it has changed the traditional Japanese corporate culture. Unlike the American business environment, the Japanese market is limited in venture capital firms. Analysts believe that Japan lags about 4–6 years behind in the Internet and e-commerce areas. For this reason, Softbank represents one of the few Japanese companies having significant entrepreneurial potential and future growth prospects. Very few Japanese companies are well positioned to capitalize on the changing Internet and e-commerce industry.

Unlike other Japanese Internet and service companies, Softbank has acquired companies that are complementary in nature and may carry good growth potential in the future. Since its inception in 1981, Softbank has become a small conglomerate having its influence in many high-tech and Internet sectors. Although the Internet and its related industries are still in their infancy in Japan and other developed markets of Asia, Softbank has fully exploited these markets. This is the main reason why Softbank captured a significant market share and changed the mainstream Japanese corporate culture. Son's entrepreneurial style made many inroads in the Japanese corporate environment. Son, the main pace setter in the Internet industry, has forced other competitors to follow him. The change process pursued and managed by Softbank represents a classic textbook case study. As Brown & Eisenhardt (1998, pp. 4–5) states on managing the change process:

> At one level, managing change means reacting to it. . . . But managing change also means anticipating it. . . . Finally, at the highest level, managing change is about leading change. By this we mean creating the change to which others must react. It means launching a new market, raising the industry standard of service, redefining customer expectations, or increasing the pace of industry product cycles. It means being ahead of change or even changing the rules of the game. At the extreme, the best performing firms consistently lead change in their industries.

Softbank fits perfectly in the change process stated by Brown & Eisenhardt (1998) by not only becoming the industry leader but also forcing others to make changes.[2]

Many analysts believe that in the coming years, Softbank's markets will grow significantly. In the areas of product development and worldwide brand visibility, Softbank holds a good position to capitalize on its learning curve and knowledge-related areas. Some of Softbank's investments in the Internet companies doubled in the last three years and have brought massive fortune to Son (refer to Exhibit C5-6). Selected companies include Yahoo, Yahoo Japan, E-Trade, Ziff-Davis, ZDNet, and Geo Cities. In June 1999, Softbank announced a joint venture with NASDAQ to initiate the process of setting up the NASDAQ-type stock market in Japan (*The Wall Street Journal*, 1999b). In September 1999, Softbank announced another strategic alliance with Microsoft and Global Crossing to provide telecommunications services in the Asian markets. Global crossing will take 93% equity in the venture whereas Softbank and Microsoft each will invest 3.5 % in the venture. Softbank and Microsoft may increase their stakes to 19% <http://www.quicken.com>. These recent alliances and ventures show that Softbank plans to go beyond its traditional Japanese market.

Problem Areas and Weaknesses

In the coming years, Softbank may face problems because of the changing Internet and e-commerce industry (see Exhibit C5-7). Some of the problems include:

1. Unlike Microsoft, Dell, AOL, Amazon.com, and other high-tech companies, Softbank is not a household name in the U.S. and the Western world. The company is very well known in Japan but carries limited influence in other markets.
2. Softbank mostly stayed in Japan and sought its growth through acquisitions. These acquisitions have accumulated debt, which may limit future growth if some of its entities go sour.
3. Ziff-Davis, Inc., which publishes *PC Magazine* and *Computer Shopper* faces problems because of its declining ad revenues, heightened competition, and debt problems. Analysts believe that Ziff-Davis may take some time to recover since the world PC industry now faces lower profits and an invasion of cheaper machines

---

[2]For further discussion, see Kim & Mauborgne (1999a–c).

(*Advertising Age*, 1998; *Business Week*, 1999a; <cbs.marketwatch.com/news/current>).

4. Softbank is not listed on the New York Stock Exchange or NASDAQ. This weakens Softbank's ability to attract mutual fund managers and institutional investors from the U.S. In addition, this may hamper Softbank's future growth in Japan, the U.S., and Western Europe.

5. The East Asian crisis has affected Softbank's expansion in the Asian markets. Although economic conditions are improving, Softbank may be affected because of currency depreciations in the weaker economies; i.e., Indonesia, Thailand, Malaysia, and others.

6. Historically, Softbank has targeted the distribution of software, computer publications, and selected consumer e-commerce areas. It is still a small player in the e-commerce industry because of entry barriers and heightened competition.

7. Softbank plans to enter into Japan's online financial and insurance industry, which is somewhat untapped. Some analysts believe that Softbank may face tough competition because of its unfamiliarity with these sectors. Softbank's strong know-how in the Internet areas may not be replicated in the finance and insurance sectors.

8. The Internet and e-commerce industry at the global level is a complex industry because of regulations and country-specific standards. Softbank may face these hurdles beyond the Japanese market.

9. Since 1996, Softbank's stock has plunged many times because of its massive acquisitions and debt problems. Some analysts are concerned about Softbank's handling of its debt and negative cash flows because Son owns 43 percent of the company (*Fortune*, 1997).

10. In the U.S. market, Softbank has devised a new strategy to cope with its new competitors. Some of the smaller companies in the e-commerce industry are perceived to be more successful and profitable.

GLOBAL STRATEGIES AND PROBLEMS AREAS IN 2001/02

Between 1996 and 1999, Softbank was in a strong position to capitalize on its Internet and technology-related acquisitions worldwide. Since the dot.com downturn, the company has encountered difficulties regarding its consumer markets and new technologies. Like other dot.com and Internet companies, Softbank has lost its market value significantly and the company was ranked 447 by *Financial Times* (2001) among 1000 companies worldwide. In the coming years, Softbank may face the following problems (refer to Exhibit C5–7):

1. As stated earlier, Softbank is not a household name in the U.S. and Western Europe. The company is well positioned in Japan but carries limited clout in other markets.

2. As of 2001, Softbank has lost its market value by $188 billion and its share price has declined by 94 percent. On the other hand, the company continues to be the first-mover in the Internet areas. In 2000/2001, Softbank incurred some of its heaviest losses in ventures such as Webvan, Buy.com, and other consumer-related Net companies. In 2001, Softbank is concentrating on niche/unique segments in the area of wireless and other Internet technologies (*Business Week*, 2001; *The Wall Street Journal*, 2001a-c).

3. Compared with other Internet companies, Softbank's financial position remains to be strong for future growth. As of 2001, the company has a $2 billion venture fund and has accumulated $10 billion in unrealized gains because of its early investments in the Internet area. In addition, Softbank maintains $ 1.6 billion in corporate cash and marketable securities (*Business Week*, 2001).

4. Softbank's strategy of seeking expansion in the Web infrastructure, portals/content, consumer e-commerce, and B2B commerce may backfire if markets do not recover. As of 2001, the company has a portfolio of more than 600 Internet companies worldwide (refer to Exhibit C5-3). Softbank's corporate structure resembles a *Keiretsu* network, which may not bring lucrative opportunities if markets go down. On the other hand, as a first-mover company, Softbank's diversification strategy has been successful. As of 2001, Softbank continues to amass massive fortune by having partial and full ownerships in technology companies worldwide.

5. Like its earlier initiatives, Softbank's future growth strategies are expected to revolve around three information asymmetries: (a) value-chain asymmetry, which may help

Exhibit C5-7
Softbank Corp.: Strengths and Weaknesses

Strengths	Weaknesses
• Softbank is one of the largest and innovative Internet and communications companies in the world • Has built/acquired 100 plus Internet companies; aims to be the leader in the Internet and e-commerce industry • Excellent potential in the areas of software distribution, web publishing, and computer trade shows • Excellent growth through acquisitions • Recent joint venture with NASDAQ looks very promising • First-Mover in the Internet and technology related-industry • Excellent learning curve; knows the Japanese market • Knows how to expedite the product development process and target new markets • Plans to bring significant changes in Japan's Internet market • Masayoshi Son (President/CEO) is U.S. educated; knows the Western corporate system and culture; also has a good vision • Good market share in the niche-oriented Internet and communications industry	• Softbank is not a household name in the U.S. and Western Europe • Some acquisitions have gone sour; some of the future startups may also go sour if Softbank expands into unrelated areas • Softbank may encounter more competition in the Internet market • Softbank's shifting focus on its core strategy may create problems in the coming years • Softbank's may not be able to manage its hundreds of alliances and joint ventures because of changing technologies and competition in the e-commerce areas • The stock is not listed in the U.S. (NYSE or NASDAQ) • East Asian markets are somewhat stagnant; may take some years to recover • Softbank is a small player in the e-commerce and retailing industry • Ineffective handling of debt and cash flows have created problems

coordinate the information industry (between suppliers and buyers); (b) financial asymmetry, which may leverage procurement cost differences; and (c) technology asymmetry, which may leverage technological gaps (Lynskey and Yonekura, 2001, pp. 10–12).

6. According to Son, in the coming years, Softbank's core competence will solely rely on the Internet sector and will continue to acquire companies from the areas of infrastructure, hardware, content, commerce, and distribution (Lynskey and Yonekura, 2001, p. 12).

WHAT LIES AHEAD?

Many analysts see Softbank as a unique Japanese company. Under the leadership of Son, the company stands to reap huge rewards if markets do not tumble in 2001/02. In the short-term, Softbank can acquire all the benefits by being the market leader. More acquisitions are expected in the Internet and mobile commerce.

Some analysts believe that Softbank plans on consolidating its position in the Internet market. It is also expected that Softbank will gradually reduce its holdings in the area of media, publications, and software distribution and will concentrate on the consumer and B2B commerce. There is a huge growth potential expected in B2B commerce in the Western world. Of course, it may also carry risks because of competition and changing business markets. At the global level, the Internet and its technology-related markets are highly fragmented (*The Economist*, 1999; U.S. Department of Commerce, 1999). Companies have to be vigilant to capitalize on the changing technologies, growth, and customers. Softbank is well positioned to be part of the growing market. As *Forbes* (1999, p. 151) commented on Son's future plans:

Son wants to be number one in "eyeball traffic, finance, e-commerce and content'. . . not by controlling a single behemoth like Amazon.com, but by taking sizable stakes in top players in myriad niches.

Softbank's venture capital subsidiary, Softbank Technology Ventures, has established a 40,000 square-foot site in Mountain View, California (*Fortune*, 1999), but the dot.com downturn has impacted its growth. This facility is used as a "startup incubator" for promising Internet and technology firms (refer to Exhibit C5-3).

After having a portfolio of 600 Internet companies, Softbank plans to become a major player in every aspect of technology and e-commerce areas. This includes telecommunications, finance and banking, insurance, publishing, distribution, retailing, and other Web-based service products (refer to Exhibit C5-3).

In Japan, Softbank has formed a joint venture with NASDAQ. There is a huge potential in the NASDAQ-style market in Japan (see Exhibit C5-8).

Exhibit C5-8
Softbank Corp.: Potential Growth Areas and Global Internet Markets

A: Future NASDAQ Market in Japan & Breakdown of Consumer Assets (as of Dec. 1997)

Time Deposits:	40.5%
Insurance:	24.4%
Demand Deposits:	8.6%
Securities:	7.3%
Trusts:	5.9%
Stocks:	4.8%
Cash Currency:	3.7%
Bonds:	2.5%
Investment Trusts:	2.3%
Total Assets:	*$10.3 trillion (1,230 Yen)*

B: Global Internet Access by Regions (as of May 1999)

Canada & U.S.:	97.0 million consumers (56.6%)
Europe:	40.1 (23.4)
Asia/Pacific:	27.0 (15.8)
Latin America:	5.3 (3.1)
Africa:	1.1 (0.6)
Middle East:	0.9 (0.5)
Total:	*171 million*

C: Selected Countries with Internet Access: Home and Work (as of 1998)

U.S.:	37%
Canada:	36
Nordics:	33
Australia:	31
U.K.:	15
Germany:	10
Japan:	10
France	8

Source:(1). *Financial Times*. "Electronic Trading to Open Up the World to Japan's Investors," (June 16), 1999, p. 20; (2). U.S. Department of Commerce. *The Emerging Digital Economy-II*, Washington, DC.: U.S. Dept. of Commerce, (June), 1999, p. 3.

According to one estimate, consumer savings and assets are used inefficiently because of the unavailability of U.S.-style individual investors. Softbank's initiative in this segment with NASDAQ is expected to bring big structural changes in the stock markets in Japan if economy improves in 2001/02 (*Financial Times*, 1999a-c; *The Wall Street Journal*, 1999b). In addition, Softbank plans to consolidate its position in Japan's online industry in virtually every sector; i.e., education, e-commerce (business and retailing), retailing, banking, finance, insurance and bond markets, distribution, and the broadcasting industry. Within the present circumstances, Softbank is one of the main Internet companies in the world. It will be interesting to see if Softbank can hold its position as the world Internet company or just be run over by another Softbank-type company. As *Business Week* (2001, p. EB23 & 24) calls Son "the last true believer in the Internet revolution" and states:

> Undaunted by the tech slump, Softbank's Masayoshi Son is thinking bigger than ever; his master plan: to create a cyberconglomerate that will transform the Net into a truly global phenomenon.

CASE QUESTIONS

1. What are your views of Softbank's recent Internet-related diversification and its technology-based acquisitions?
2. Analyze and evaluate Softbank's market niche in the Internet and e-commerce industry.
3. What kind of specific global strategies does Softbank need to undertake to be the key player in the Internet and technology-related markets in Japan, North America, and other global markets?
4. What did you learn from Softbank's global diversification initiatives and expansion strategy?
5. Compare and contrast Softbank with other multinationals from Japan and the Western world regarding internationalization, diversification, and global competition issues.
6. Evaluate Softbank's market expansion and global strategies in 2001/02.

REFERENCES

Abrahams, Paul & Michiyo Nakamoto. 1999. "Heat Turns Up on the Rising Star," *Financial Times* (November 13): 16.

Advertising Age. 1998. "Softbank Woes Rattle Clients of Web Ad Firms" (March 23): 1& 48.

Brown, Shona L. & Kathleen Eisenhardt. 1998. *Competing on the Edge: Strategy as a Structured Chaos*, Boston, MA: Harvard Business School Press.

Business Week. 1996. "Cyber-Mogul: to Conquer the Net, Masayoshi Son Takes to the High Wire" (August 12): 56–62.

Business Week. 1999a. "Ziff-Davis Is Printing in Red Ink" (January 25): 107.

Business Week. 1999b. "Time for This Behemoth to Evolve?" (September 20): 48.

Business Week e.Biz. 1999. "The E-Biz 25: Masters of the Web Universe" (September 27): 20–56.

Business Week e.Biz. 2001. "The Last True Believer" (January 22): EB23–28.

Butler, Steve. 1999. "Empire of the Son," *U.S. News & World Report* (July 5): 48–50.

The Economist. 1999. "The Real Internet Revolution" (August 21): 53–54.

Far Eastern Economic Review. 1998. "Prodigal Son" (January 22): 42–44.

Far Eastern Economic Review. 1999. "Japan's Mr. Internet" (July 29): 11–12.

Far Eastern Economic Review. 2000. "Internet Warrior on the Defensive" (November 16): 54–60.

Financial Times. 1997a. "Softbank Spree Has Investors in a Jitter" (April 23): 21.

Financial Times. 1997b. "Softbank Shares Take Further Dive" (October 4/5): 23.

Financial Times. 1997c. "Softbank Falls into the Perception Gap" (December 3): 19.

Financial Times. 1999a. "Softbank Set for Online Investors" (April 21): 24.

Financial Times. 1999b. "Electronic Trading to Open up the World to Japan's Investors" (June 16): 20.

Financial Times. 1999c. "Softbank Widens Its Net" (July 9): 12.

Financial Times. 2001. "Lehman, Softbank Close Web Venture" (April 10): 17.

Financial Times. 2001. "Softbank and Yahoo Japan in Broadband Plan" (July 20): 20.

Forbes. 1999. "The World's Working Rich" (July 5): 222.

Fortune. 1997. "Japan's Top Technology Investor Takes a Hit" (September 8): 150–151.

Fortune. 1999. "How Son Captured Japan's Internet Economy" (August 16): 156–160.

<http://www.quicken.com>. "Global Crossing, Microsoft, Softbank Announces Asian Network Venture" (September 8, 1999).

Kim, W. Chan & Renee Mauborgne. 1999a. "How to Discover the Unknown Market," *Financial Times* (May 6): 12.

Kim, W. Chan & Renee Mauborgne. 1999b. "How Southwest Airlines Found a Route to Success," *Financial Times* (May 13): 20.

Kim, W. Chan & Renee Mauborgne. 1999c. "From Trend to Quantum Leap," *Financial Times* (June 10): 24.

Lynskey, Michael and Seiichiro Yonekura. 2001. "Softbank: An Internet Keiretsu and Its Leveraging of Information Asymmetries," *European Management Journal*, 19(1): 1–15.

Softbank, Tokyo, Japan, September 1999, </www.softbank.com>

Softbank, Tokyo, Japan, September 2001, </www.softbank.com>

U.S. Department of Commerce. 1999. *The Emerging Digital Economy-II* (June): Washington, DC.: U.S. Dept. of Commerce.

The Wall Street Journal. 1996. "Softbank's Buying Spree May Be Hard Act to Follow " (August 19): B4.

The Wall Street Journal. 1999a. "Softbank Cleans Up on the Internet" (February 3): B4.

The Wall Street Journal. 1999b. "NASDAQ Plans to Set Up a New Stock Market in Japan" (June 16): A19&21.

The Wall Street Journal. 1999c. "Japan's Softbank Unveils New Internet Deals" (June 25): A15&17.

The Wall Street Journal, 2001a. "Softbank-Cisco Deal Nourishes Alliance" (January 25): A3.

The Wall Street Journal, 2001b. "Masayoshi Son's Role as Internet Kingpin in Japan Is Shrinking" (March 29): A1&A8.

The Wall Street Journal, 2001c. "Softbank's Corp.'s Net Profit Quadruples, but Web-Stock Plunge Still Poses Problem" (May 29): A19.

Webber, Alan M. 1992. "Japanese Style Entrepreneurship: An Interview with Softbank's CEO, Masayoshi Son," *Harvard Business Review*, 70(1): 93–103.

Weinberg, Neil. 1999. Master of the Internet, *Forbes* (July 5): 146–151.

Yip, George S. 1992. *Total Global Strategy: Managing for Worldwide Competitive Advantage*, Upper Saddle River, NJ: Prentice Hall.

Ziff-Davis Rebuts News Corp. Story, (Sept.13, 1999), <cbs.marketwatch.com/news/current>.

SOURCE: This case was prepared by Syed Tariq Anwar of T. Boone Pickens College of Business. Copyright 2001 by Syed Tariq Anwar. Reprinted by permission. The discussion in this case is intended to be used as a basis for discussion rather than to illustrate either effective or ineffective handling of a managerial situation or corporate strategies.

Case 6   A First-Time Expatriate's Experience in a Joint Venture in China

John Stanbury

THE LONG TRIP HOME

James Randolf was traveling back to his home state of Illinois from his assignment in China for the last time. He and his wife were about three hours into the long flight when she fell asleep, her head propped up by the airline pillow against the cabin wall. James was exhausted, but for the first time in many days he had the luxury of reflecting on what had just happened in their lives.

He was neither angry nor bitter, but the disruption of the last few weeks was certainly unanticipated and in many ways unfortunate. He had fully expected to complete his three-year assignment as the highest ranking U.S. manager of his company's joint venture (JV) near Shanghai. Now, after only 13 months, the assignment was over and a manager from the regional office in Singapore held the post. Sure, the JV will survive, he thought, but how far had the relationship that he had been nurturing between the two partnered companies been set back? His Chinese partners were perplexed by his company's actions and visibly affected by the departure of their friend and colleague.

Was this an error in judgment resulting from Controls relative inexperience as a multinational company and a partner in international joint ventures, James wondered? Or, had something else caused the shift in policy that resulted in the earlier-than-planned recall of several of the corporation's expatriates from their assignments? There had always been plans to reduce the number of expatriates at any particular location over time, but recently the carefully planned timetables seemed to have been abandoned.

Next week, James had to turn in his report covering the entire work assignment. How frank should he be? What detail should he include in his report? To whom should he send copies? There had been rumors that many senior managers were being asked to take early retirement. James did not really want to retire but could hardly contain his dissatisfaction as to how things had turned out. Maybe it would be better to take the offer, if it was forthcoming, and try to find some consulting that would make the best use of his wide spectrum of technical and managerial experience, which now included an expatriate assignment in what was considered to be one of the most difficult locations in the world.

James reflected with satisfaction on his accomplishment of the initial primary objectives, which were to establish a manufacturing and marketing presence. In fact, he was quite pleased with his success at putting in place many things that would allow the operation to prosper. The various departments within the joint venture were now cooperating and coordinating, and the relationships he had established were truly the evidence of this achievement. He would like to have seen the operations become more efficient, however.

The worklife that awaited him upon his return was a matter of considerable concern. Reports from the expatriates who preceded him in the last few months indicated that there were no established plans to utilize their talents, and often early retirement was strongly encouraged by management. Beyond the obligatory physical examinations and debriefings, he had been told there was little for them to do. Many of the recalled expatriates found themselves occupying desks in Personnel waiting for responses about potential job opportunities.

He gazed at his wife, Lily, now settled into comfortable slumber. At least she had had a pretty good experience. She was born in Shanghai, but left China in 1949. The country was then in the middle of a revolution but, aside from her memory of her parents appearing extremely anxious to leave, she remembered little else about the issues surrounding their emigration to the United States. Most of her perceptions about "what it was like" in China came from U.S. television coverage, some fact, some fiction.

As the plane droned on into the night, James thought back to how this experience began.

THE COMPANY

The world headquarters of Controls, Inc. were in Chicago, Illinois. It had operations in several countries in Europe, Asia, and South America but, with the exception of several *maquiladoras*, all of its expansion had occurred very recently. Its first involvement in joint ventures began only three years ago. As an in-house supplier to Filtration Inc., a huge Chicago-based international manufacturing conglomerate specializing in the design and production of temperature control and filtration systems, it had been shielded from significant competition, and most of its product lines of various electronic control mechanisms had been produced in North America. Ten years ago, however when Controls became a subsidiary of Filtration Inc. and it was given a charter to pursue business beyond that transacted with its parent. At the same time, the rules for acquiring in-house business changed as well. Controls now bid for Filtration Inc.'s business against many of the world's best producers of this equipment. The need to use cheaper labor and to be located closer to key prospective customers drove the company to expand internationally at a rate that only a few years earlier would have been completely outside its corporate comfort zone.

A JV in China would provide Controls with an opportunity to gain a foothold in this untapped market for temperature control systems. This could pave the way for a greater thrust into the expanding Chinese economy. If the JV were successful, it could also lead to the establishment of plants to manufacture various products for the entire Asia/Pacific market.

The corporation's involvement in the joint venture seemed less planned than its other expansion efforts. The Freezer and Cooler Controls Business Unit (one of Controls' key business units), headquartered in Lakeland, Minnesota, sent a team of four, consisting of two engineers and two representatives from the Finance and Business Planning Departments to investigate the possibility of partnering with a yet-to-be-identified Chinese electronics assembly operation. The team was not given an adequate budget and was limited to a visit of one month. Not being experienced international negotiators, they were only able to identify one potential partner, a Chinese state-owned firm. They quickly realized that they did not have time to conclude negotiations and returned to HQ without having met their objective. After debriefing them upon their return to the United States, the corporation's planners decided that the Chinese JV presented a good opportunity and sent another team to continue these negotiations. Eventually an agreement was reached with the Chinese state-owned firm. Exhibit C6-1 shows the organizational relationships between Filtration Inc. and its subsidiaries.

HOW IT ALL BEGAN

James had always been intrigued by the idea of securing an international assignment. His interest heightened on the day that Controls Inc. announced its intentions to expand the business through establishing a more international presence worldwide. By age 51, James had worked in managerial positions in Engineering, Quality, Customer Support, and Program Management for the last 15 of his 23 years with the company, but always in positions geographically based in Pauley, Illinois. He frequently mentioned the idea of working on an international assignment to his superiors during performance reviews and in a variety of other settings. He did not mentally target any specific country, but preferred an assignment in the Pacific Rim, due to his life-long desire to gain an even deeper understanding of his wife's cultural heritage.

Finally, two years ago, he was able to discuss his interests with the corporation's International Human Resources Manager. During this interview, he was told of the hardships of functioning as an expatriate. There could be a language problem as well as difficulties caused by the remoteness from home office. He remained interested.

A year later, James was first considered for a position that required venture development in Tokyo. At one point he was even told he had been chosen for that position. With little explanation, the company instead announced the selection of a younger, more "politically" connected "fast tracker."

When, a few months later, a discussion about the position in China was first broached by personnel, it was almost in the context of it being a consolation prize. The position, however, appeared to be one for which James was even better suited and one that

Exhibit C6-1
Organization Chart: Filtration Inc.

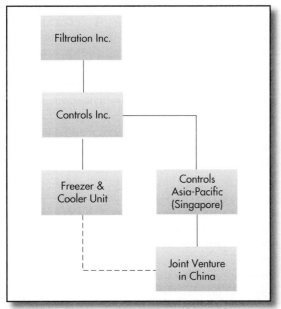

would be challenging enough to "test the mettle" of any manager in the company. The assignment was to "manage a joint venture manufacturing facility" located on Chongming Dao Island, about 25 miles north of Shanghai. The strategic objective of the JV was market entry into China.

Soon thereafter, in mid August of 1992, James was asked to go immediately to Lakeland to meet one on one with Joe Whistler, the Director of the Freezer and Cooler Controls Business Unit, to discuss the JV. The negotiating team was still in China in the process of "finalizing" the JV agreement with the Chongming Electro-Assembly Company, a state-owned electronic device assembly operation. The corporation felt that there was a dire need to put someone on site. Joe asked if he could leave next week! James indicated that he was interested in accepting the position and that he was willing to do whatever the corporation required of him to make it happen as soon as possible. It was understood that a formal offer for the position would be processed through Personnel and communicated through James's management. When this trip didn't materialize, James wondered if this was going to be a repeat of the Tokyo assignment. Finally, in late September, James's supervisor approached him and said "If you still want it, you've got the prize."

ORIENTATION

Filtration Inc. has a defined set of procedures to deal with expatriate work assignment orientation. When it was determined that James was a strong candidate to go overseas, it was arranged for James and his wife to go to Chicago for orientation training. The training began with a day-long session conducted by Filtration Inc.'s International Personnel function. James thought the training was exceptionally well done. Filtration Inc. brought in experts to discuss pay, benefits, moving arrangements, and a multitude of other issues dealing with working for the corporation in an international assignment. Part of the orientation process was a "look-see trip," the normal length of which was seven days. The trip was quickly arranged to begin two weeks later. The Randolfs were extremely excited. This would be Lily's first trip back to China. They even extended the duration of the trip to 10 days to do some investigation on their own time.

There was a considerable mix-up in the planning of the "look-see" trip. Although the Personnel Department in Pauley wanted to arrange the entire trip, Controls' Asia-Pacific regional office in Singapore insisted it was better for them to handle it locally. The Randolfs were supposed to have a rental car available upon arrival, but discovered that no arrangements had been made and they were forced to secure their own car. Their itinerary indicated that they had reservations at the Shanghai Inn, but they soon discovered that no reservations had been made there, either.

In Shanghai they went sightseeing on their own for three days. Afterwards, they were scheduled for seven days of official activities. They spent the following two days with an on-site consultant, who was on retainer from the JV and who showed the potential expatriates around the city. Her tour consisted of what she perceived a typical American might most like to see.

The wife of an expatriate herself, the consultant didn't speak Shanghainese or any other Chinese dialects. Travel with her was somewhat of a nightmare. As opposed to discussing the planned locations with the Chinese driver at the beginning of a day, she directed the trip one step at a time. She would show the driver a card on which was written the address of the next location and say "go here now." This approach caused considerable delays due to the inefficiencies of transversing the city numerous times and touring in a disorderly sequence. They were shown American-style shopping, American-style restaurants, and potential living accommodations. The Randolfs were told that leasing a good apartment commonly required a "kickback."

After visiting the JV's factory near Shanghai, they traveled to the regional headquarters, Controls Asia-Pacific, in Singapore to participate in an extensive orientation workshop. Again the topics included compensation policies and other matters of interest to potential expatriates, this time from the perspective of Controls Inc. James and Lily both noted a significant contrast in dealings with the regional Controls Inc. personnel staff as opposed to the "first rate" Filtration Inc. International Human Resources people. The former was by far a less polished and informed operation. Even as they departed Singapore for the United States, they were still unsure that the move was right for them. They spent the next several days reflecting on the trip and discussing their decision. They were discouraged by the lack of maintenance apparent in the factory, which was clearly inferior to U.S. standards. Things were dirty, and little effort was expended on environmental controls. The days seemed awfully gray. However, they had quickly become enamored with the Shanghai people, and this became a key factor in their ultimate decision to accept the position. As the result of their interactions with the Chinese partners and Shanghai area residents, James and Lily truly felt the promise of exciting, new, deep, long-lasting relationships.

Once they were firmly committed to the assignment, they attended a two-day orientation on living and working in China. This was provided by Prudential Relocation Services Inc. in Boulder, Colorado, and was tailored to the needs and desires of the participants. Optional curriculum tracks included the history, culture, political climate, business climate, and the people of the region. James focused his training on a business-related curriculum, which was taught by professors from a local university. Additionally, whenever an expatriate returned from China to the home office on home leave, James was given an opportunity to interface with him.

Between November (1992) and January (1993), James worked an exhausting schedule, alternating two-week periods in Pauley and at the JV in China, where lodging and meals were provided in a hotel. During this time, his wife, Lily, remained in Lakewood preparing for their permanent relocation to China. Also, Filtration Inc. held scheduled, intensive Mandarin language courses in Chicago, which James planned to attend, but due to his work schedule he was unable to take advantage of the opportunity. Finally, in January, James attended the language school for a week. Fortunately, he and Lily already spoke some Cantonese, another Chinese dialect. After James was finally on-site full time in February, he hired a language tutor to supplement this training. The orientation procedure concluded with a checklist of things that James and Controls were to accomplish after the commencement of his on-site assignment. Although all of these checklist items were eventually accomplished, priorities on the job didn't allow them to be completed in a very timely manner.

WORKPLACE ORIENTATIONS

Mandarin, China's official language, was spoken at the factory. In regions where Mandarin was not the primary language of the people, it was the language most commonly used in industry and trade and in dealing with the government. Most residents were proficient in Mandarin, although the oldest members of the population had learned it only after they had completed their formal education, if at all. Mandarin became China's official language when the alphabet was standardized in 1955. Away from the workplace, people preferred to speak Shanghainese or Chongming Dao's own similar dialect.

Chongming Dao, the actual site of the factory, was situated in the Chuang Yangtze river. At approximately 50 miles long and 18 miles wide, it is China's third largest island. Its population is approximately one million people. The residents were perceived by the Shanghainese to be poor, backward farmers.

James found that he was able to maintain residencies in Shanghai and in Chongming Dao, although all the Chinese workers, including managers, lived close to their place of work. The trip from downtown Shanghai to the plant took more than two hours. First there was an hour and a half trip to the site of the ferry departure, then came a 20-minute ferry ride, followed by another 20 minutes of travel by car. Work days at the factory were scheduled from Tuesdays through Saturdays. As is common in China, the schedules were centrally planned to alternate with those of other factories in a manner that conserved power consumption.

The Chinese partner had warehouses and a business center on the island, which, in addition to the factory, became part of the JV. The people worked under conditions that would be totally unacceptable to most American workers. There were no temperature or humidity controls. In the winter, the plant was so cold that workers wore up to six layers of clothing. In contrast, summers were very hot and humid. None of the machinery had safety guards. Tools were generally either nonexistent or inadequate. Lighting was also very poor.

The Chinese factory's workforce was primarily young women. This was in contrast to the Chinese partner's factories that James had visited, where most of the workers were men who appeared to be over the age of 40. The plant's organization and operation fostered considerable inefficiencies. There were no process controls to prevent errors and scrap. The only visible methods of quality control were extensive amounts of 100% testing and inspection performed after the product was completely assembled. The layout of the plant was awkward. There were numerous little rooms and no large expansive production areas. Operations were not laid out sequentially or even in a line. The typical mode of operation was to have numerous workers working elbow to elbow around the perimeter of a large table.

Material movement was most commonly performed by dragging large tubs of materials across the floor. Storage was disorderly and bins were generally not stacked, due to a lack of shelving. Consequently, containers of parts, partially assembled products, scrap materials, and finished assemblies could be found anywhere and everywhere. Instead of scheduling plant output, the system scheduled only the number of man-hours to be expended. This lack of direction caused a considerable amount of confusion and inefficiency. It was really more of a way of accounting for the use of the excessive labor force that existed in the factory and in the area. James often commented that he could produce as much or more output with only the number of Quality Control (QC) operators that were in the plant. By his estimates, the JV employed three times as many people as were needed. James did not think that he could change this immediately, but he felt that he could convince the Chinese management that this practice need to be changed eventually.

ADAPTING TO LIFE IN CHINA

Beyond some terrific people in the Personnel Department in Pauley, who could help with specific employment-related issues, James quickly came to realize that there would be little operational support from the home office. His links back to his corporation came more from Filtration Inc. than from Controls. Filtration Inc. at least sent a monthly package of news clippings, executive briefs, and memos that had been specifically prepared for expatriates. The package allowed James to keep up somewhat on what was happening in the larger corporate setting.

Filtration Inc. had a couple dozen employees in Shanghai. It was their role to establish and implement a joint venture that the parent had negotiated with a different Chinese manufacturer than the one with which Controls had partnered. As part of this team, there were also a few representatives from Controls Inc. They were all co-located in a small office building in downtown Shanghai. It was in this corporate office environment that James found a great deal of support, a lot of helpful advice, and his unofficial mentor, a Filtration Inc. manager who had spent four years in China. At the time James wondered why he hadn't visited this office during his orientation trip.

The help that James received from Controls Inc.'s subsidiary, Controls Asia-Pacific, was often ineffective and inconsistent. Nagging policies and obligatory paperwork were typical characteristics of their assistance. There were ongoing problems finding and retaining a qualified translator for James. In the agreement, the JV was responsible for providing each expatriate with a translator. Controls-Asia/Pacific was responsible for the wage structure at the JV. The Personnel Department in Singapore established a maximum wage rate for the translator position at 2000 yuan. This rate was fair for the area, but there were few high-quality translators available. When an area translator was identified, he or she would often be lost to another multinational company in the area who offered a salary of 3000 yuan. To attract translators from Shanghai would require a wage comparable to the wages one would receive in Shanghai, and 2000 yuan was significantly lower than that paid in the city.

Another aspect of employment in China that merited consideration was the movement of one's "personnel file" from a former employer to the present one. This is the rough equivalent of changing one's residency to another state in the United States. The reputation and perception of Chongming Dao was that of a rural community. This would have a negative impact on transferring a translator's file back to Shanghai in the future. Singapore didn't understand the economics and implications of this situation and refused to increase the wage rate to a level that would entice qualified translators to accept the position. James, as a result, was without a qualified translator for significant periods during his time in China. The impact on his ability to function in that setting was therefore also significant, resulting in less being accomplished than if Singapore had been more flexible.

The residence in Shanghai was available because the JV had committed to a two-year lease of an executive apartment on the twenty-second floor of the Shanghai Inn. These accommodations were quite nice and offered most of the comforts of home. The hotel complex included a supermarket, exercise facilities, a theater, and several restaurants, including Shanghai's Hard Rock Cafe. The three-bedroom apartment, which James measured to be around 1,500 square feet, was converted into a two-bedroom apartment to his specifications. Amenities included cable TV with five English-language channels. Accommodations on the island were significantly rougher. The original plan was for James to temporarily stay at the government's guest house on the factory grounds until a 12-unit housing compound was constructed in the immediate vicinity. The small rooms, intense heat, and fierce mosquitoes at the guest house proved to be unbearable, and by June, James decided to make other arrangements. These entailed staying in a hotel 17 miles away with the two other expatriates from Controls Inc. to manage the JV. Although the building was new, the quality of the construction was quite poor, which seemed to be common in China. The costs associated with constructing their compound were, by this time, estimated to be much larger than expected. Eventually a solution was reached to fix up certain aspects of the guest house and retain it as the long-term island living arrangements for them. After this, Lily always traveled with him to and from the factory.

ADAPTING TO THE WORK

In addition to James, there were three other Controls Inc. expatriates assigned to the JV. The Director of Engineering and the Director of Manufacturing were on assignment from the United States. The Director of Finance was from Singapore. Each of these individuals had dual roles, that of heading up their respective departments and the assignment to bring to the JV new technology associated with their departments. The Finance Director had the particularly challenging assignment of introducing a new accounting system to the JV, one that was compatible with the Controls Inc. system. The existing system, installed by the Chinese partner, was not designed to report profits and losses, irrelevant concepts in the formerly state-owned company.

The other expatriates occasionally complained of not getting good cooperation from the Chinese workers. James never encountered this problem, as he always communicated his requests directly to the workers.

One of the first problematic situations that evolved related to differences between expatriate conditions of employment for Filtration Inc. and Controls Inc. employees. Most Filtration employees enjoyed a per diem of US$95, but Controls employees were limited to US$50 per day. Additionally, the Filtration Inc.'s visitation policies were more liberal in terms of allowing college-age children to visit their expatriate parents.

ONGOING NEGOTIATIONS

In China, a JV contract is "nice framework" from which to begin the real negotiation process. The Controls JV negotiating team viewed the contract as a conclusion to negotiations and returned to the United States in late December of 1992. James soon discovered that the process of negotiations would be ongoing. On almost a daily basis, some element of the agreement was adjusted or augmented with new understanding.

A misconception held by the Controls negotiating team related to the ease of obtaining appropriate governmental approvals. There were various annexes and subcontracts that were yet to be finalized and approved when they departed. Some of these approvals were required from government officials with whom they had had very little interface. The impact of this miscalculation was that production in the JV didn't commence on January 1, 1993, as anticipated. Instead it took until August 1, 1993, to get the operation going.

One of the most serious issues affecting the operation of the JV that directly impacted James's

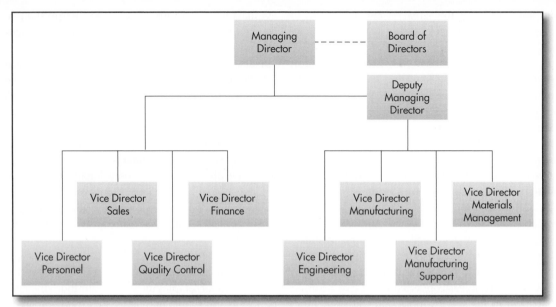

Exhibit C6-2
Organization Chart: Controls-Shanghai

effectiveness was the JV's organization structure, which was negotiated by the Controls' team. The organization chart for the JV is shown in Exhibit C6-2. Controls perceived the position of Chairman of the Board (COB) of Directors to be of greater importance in operating the company than that of Managing Director, thinking that they could "run the company" from that position. Consequently, when the organization chart was drawn up, Controls conceded the position of Managing Director to the Chinese partner in exchange for the right to appoint the COB for the first three of the five years. James noted that in Chinese JVs negotiated by Filtration Inc., the U.S. partner always secured the position of Managing Director.

OBSERVATIONS OF CHINESE MANAGEMENT METHODS

James observed that when Chinese managers were dealing with subordinates, decision making was very top-down. This resulted in virtually all decisions of any consequence being made by the Managing Director. James was extremely fortunate that the Managing Director appointed by the Chinese partner was willing to share his power. He and the Managing Director developed an excellent relationship, which James consciously worked on in the firm belief that this was the key to business success in China. Toward the end of his time at the JV, James was frequently being left in charge of running the factory while the Managing Director was visiting outside friends of influence, customers, and potential customers. The only other manager that shared this distinction was the Director of Personnel.

The Personnel Department in this JV, as in the state-owned Chinese companies, was unusually powerful when compared to most U.S. companies with which James was familiar. It maintained the all-important employment files and was very connected to the Communist Party.

OBSERVATIONS OF CHINESE MANAGEMENT TEAM

Chinese managers at the JV were considerably more educated than the workers. They had matriculated at various universities and graduated with degrees in Engineering, Management, and the like. In one case, the manager's experience and education came from his time as a career-soldier in the Army.

INTERACTIONS WITH THE CHINESE GOVERNMENT

Prior to the formation of the JV, the Secretary for the Communist Party and the Managing Director were co-equals when it came to "running the Chongming Electro Assembly company." About 325 of the 1819 employees at the JV were Communists. After James's arrival, there was always a question as to what would happen to the Party office, which was located adjacent to the Managing Director's office. In many ways, the Party served a function similar to that of labor unions in the United States. It represented the workers and entered into discussions related to labor relations issues. The Communist Party could be viewed as a different channel to deal with issues, and James quickly recognized them as an ally.

James's only personal experience with a government bureau was while getting his residency papers established. The rules he encountered were extremely inflexible, everything had to be just right, and no copies were allowed because the Bureau required originals. The Bureau office, which was the size of a walk-in closet in the United States, was extremely crowded, and the process required forcing one's way up through the lines to get to the table where female police officers would process the paperwork. After it was all over, he noticed that they had spelled his name wrong. He did not return to correct the mistake.

INTERACTIONS WITH THE UNION

The JV also had a labor union, but by comparison to the United States, the organization was extremely weak and superficial. James's only dealings with the union related to a request for donations for a retirees' party the union wanted to hold. Since the JV had no retirees and this was new ground for him, he referred them to the Managing Director.

GETTING IT TOGETHER

James loved to walk the floor and see what was happening in the factory. His position gave him the authority to direct actions to be taken, but often he did not have to use this authority in that way. The Chinese workers seemed to be influenced by his every action. If he would make a point to pick up trash in the parking lot, the next day he would observe that the trash had all been cleaned up. Another example was when he straightened some papers in the pigeon holes of a filing system. The next day every stack of papers was perfectly arranged. He felt that there had never been a time when he had walked the floor and it hadn't paid off in some way. He found Chinese workers to be very attentive to detail.

He was often tested by the Chinese managers and workers alike, as is not uncommon in other parts of the world. He perceived that they would test his commitment, leadership, and decision-making ability. They would determine how far this manager could be pushed. These tests provided him with the opportunity to do the right thing. A case in point was when a drunken salesperson accosted a woman in a nightclub. James took him to a private place and severely chastised him.

During his assignment, he remained cognizant of the fact that one of his jobs was to make the Managing Director look good. This required him to fire a translator on the spot when the translator remarked that anyone who wanted to stay in China was stupid.

He had great admiration for the Chinese workers at the JV. They proved to be very cooperative people. They had a great deal of pride and were very loyal to their company and the industry in which they worked. James often commented that, with informed leadership, Chinese workers would be as good as workers anywhere in the world.

What James liked best, however, was his interactions with the Chinese people. Every day brought him a new experience.

OBSERVATIONS ABOUT THE CHINESE PEOPLE

Most of the Chinese people were not Communists. They would rather ignore the political situations going on around them and get on with their lives. They were eager to learn anything they could about what Westerners could teach them. Almost without exception, they looked up to Americans and would begin to imitate them after a while. James found it very gratifying. He was also delighted with their treatment of his wife Lily, which bordered on reverence. James wondered about the reasons for this.

Perhaps it had something to do with the fact that she, through her parents, had previously escaped Communist oppression and found a better life, which symbolized to the Chinese that there was hope for all.

James never saw a Chinese man leering at a woman, as is common in the United States. In China, sexuality was a private matter. They tended to live a simpler life than do most Westerners. Their children were treated with reverence, even doted over. Their chaotic traffic jams seemed always to be dealt with very calmly. James never observed swearing or anger, as is common in the United States. James also found that the Chinese have an attitude that they know more than Westerners do, but that this never manifested itself a boastful way. The attitude was more that at some point in time, Westerners would come around to their way of thinking. It was almost as though they played the role of a wiser urban patriarch guiding his young country cousin during the latter's first visit to the city. See Exhibit C6-3 for more information on Chinese culture and management.

ACTIVITIES AWAY FROM THE JOB

James and Lily had a different social life than that enjoyed in the United States. They spent hours walking and talking. Occasionally, when they were in Shanghai, they had the opportunity to see shows. They saw the acrobats, went to symphony concerts and ballet, and even joined the crowds when Foster Beer brought Australian bands to perform in a Shanghai park.

The concerns Lily had expressed prior to expatriating disappeared as she made friends and became integrated into the social fabric of the area. Because her appearance was indistinguishable from the indigenous Shanghai-area people, she was more readily accepted and learned more about local happenings than most Westerners. At one point, two months after their arrival, Lily was hospitalized with a lung infection. Even this was resolved satisfactorily. She particularly noted that the skill level of the medical practitioners seemed to be very good, from the diagnosis to the way they painlessly took blood samples. Overall she found it easy to occupy her time. She was a traditional wife, who had not worked full-time

since her children were born and never had difficulty occupying the time in her life because she was a woman who was compelled to learn about everything and everybody. She spent much of her time traveling with James to and from the site and when he was working, she sought out the people and assisted at a mission nearby because she had some experience in nursing, having earned her RN before marrying James.

The Randolfs preferred to eat food with fresh ingredients, and were happy away from the "supermarket" society, so Lily also spent a lot of time shopping. They felt that they were able to eat quite well in China.

James and Lily learned as much of the local Shanghai dialect as they could. In spite of never becoming fully proficient, the fact that they attempted to speak it greatly pleased the local residents. They spent much of their spare time interacting with the people of the area.

Sometimes Filtration Inc. would put on a social affair for the expatriates in Shanghai. James and Lily were always invited. While on the island, however, they always ate at the restaurant in the factory. Contrary to what they were told at their orientation training, they found the Chinese to be gregarious and fun loving during meals. Meals were used as an opportunity to build relationships and share experiences.

JAMES'S RECALL AND DEPARTURE

Then one day, early in February 1994, James received the call from Singapore, which proved to be the most disappointing news he had heard during his entire China experience. Controls had chosen to recall him back to home office. He was directed to train his replacement and return home within the month.

Things had been going very well for several months now, and he was accomplishing a great many things. There was still so much he planned to do, including to convince the Chinese JV partner that they needed to reduce the number of workers significantly.

Although he and Lily handled the news and the return arrangements with a great deal of dignity,

Culture

One of the strong cultural beliefs among the Chinese is that their culture is the oldest and the best. It is the center of the universe, the Zhong guo—center country. They believe themselves to be totally self-sufficient. In Chinese, the character of the word "China" means "middle kingdom," thus implying that everyone other than themselves is beneath them.

Concept of Face and Time

The concept of face is of paramount importance in China. It is a person's most precious possession. Without it, one cannot function in China. It is earned by fulfilling one's duties and other obligations. Face often requires little effort, but merely an attention to courtesy in relationships with others. Face involves a high degree of self-control, social consciousness, and concern for others. In Chinese society, a display of temper, sulking, loss of self-control, or frustration creates further loss of face rather than drawing respect.

Despite having invented the clock, the Chinese never define or segment time in the way that it is approached in the West. Even today, for Chinese, time simply flows from one day to another. If a job is not completed today, they will carry it forward to the next day or the day after next. This is a manifestation of the concept of polychronic (nonlinear) time. In Western cultures, people see time as monochronic (linear).

An important cultural difference between the West and China is the Chinese custom of giving precedence to form and process in completing a task, over the task itself, an approach that is typically more time consuming.

Behavior

Chinese behavior is influenced by their brutal history. This has created a careful people. They give consideration to the repercussions of every move or decision that they make.

An important aspect of behavior involves the way the Chinese think. They think about thinking and relationships, whereas the Westerner thinks in linear patterns of cause and effects.

Another aspect that confuses the Westerner is the Chinese willingness to discuss endless possibilities even when things look hopeless.

A Chinese philosophy that relates to interacting with Westerners can be stated: Whereas a Westerner will try to tell you everything he knows in a conversation, a Chinese will listen to learn everything the Westerner knows, so that, at the end of the day, he would know both what he knew and what the Westerner knew.

Gift Giving

Chinese are conditioned to express appreciation in tangible ways, such as by giving gifts and other favors. They regard the Westerner's frequent use of "thank you" as a glib and insincere way of passing off obligations to return favors. When they do someone a favor, they expect appreciation to be expressed in some very concrete way. If all you choose to do is say "Thanks," it should be very specific and sincere, and then stop. The Chinese do not like gushy thanks. Gift giving in China is a highly developed art. Although it has greatly diminished today (there is a law forbidding government officials from accepting gifts of any kind or value), the practice remains a vital aspect of creating and nurturing relationships with people.

Living as a Foreign Guest in the People's Republic of China

Foreigners who have gone to the People's Republic of China in the last decade to help the Chinese have been given preferential treatment. Their quarters are often far more modern than those of a typical native Chinese. The expatriate is given perquisites in excess of those available to all but the top officials, fed with highest quality food, and paid salaries that are many times higher than their Chinese counterpart of the same status. They are sheltered from the harsh realities of the Chinese life and are recipients of enormous courtesy and care.

There are three main reasons for this preferential treatment. First, as a poverty stricken nation, the Chinese need to attract and retain foreigners to help them achieve a higher standard of living, by increasing their economic and technical level. Second, the Chinese believe that people from the developed nations are so used to modern comforts that they would not be able to function competently without them. Finally, there is simple pride. They want their country to be thought of favorably.

Social

Generally the sociocultural behavior of the Chinese differs greatly from that of Western societies. Family is very important to them, and obligation to them takes precedence when it conflicts with work responsibilities. Those outside the family are treated with indifference and sometimes with contempt. Decision making evolves from the opinion and support of the family. The highest respect is given to elders and ancestors. The reverence for authority and order explains why the Chinese are so careful about getting consensus from everyone. An important ideal that is fostered by the family is harmony.

The Chinese do not believe in the concept of privacy. This absence of individuality and freedom is a way of life in China.

Laws Made to Be Broken

Due to their history of being encumbered by rules and taboos, the Chinese have developed a perverse and seemingly contradictory attitude toward laws and regulations. They tend to ignore them and break them to suit their purpose, as long as they think they can get away with it. A significant proportion of public Chinese behavior is based on political expediency and not on their true feelings. Since their public, official behavior is more of a survival technique than anything else, they do not feel guilty about ignoring or subverting the system. It is something they do naturally as a way of getting by.

Importance of Human Resources Management in Organizations in China

The labor environment in China is influenced by six major factors. They are National Economic Plans, the Four Modernization Programs, Political Leadership, Chinese Cultural Values, Labor Unions, and the Special Economic Zones (SEZs). The SEZs were created specially for the conduct of the joint ventures with overseas countries. The main characteristics of the SEZs that are found in a joint venture are their dominating influence on matters pertaining to the employment wage system, organizational structure, management roles, and decision making.

One of the most interesting aspects of Chinese human resource management is the unmistakable influence of some of the traditional cultural values such as guanxi (relationship), renqing (favor), mianzi (face), and bao (reciprocation) in recruitment and selection, training and development, and placement and promotion.

A definite political element is involved in the behavior of Chinese Personnel managers; those who are more party oriented base their decisions on party policies rather than on what is for the good of the company.

Maintaining Personnel Files and Their Implications

Chinese-style personnel management generally does not forgive or forget any real or imagined past transgressions by employees under their jurisdiction. Any past mistakes or offenses committed by the employee are duly recorded in the employee's file and are often used against that person.

To hire someone from another company, the other company must release the prospective employee's file. This contains the employee's work record and entitles him or her to benefits accorded to workers in the state sector. If the employer is not willing to release the file and the employee leaves, he or she loses the benefits, a risk few Chinese are willing to take. Many foreign companies have been able to complete transfers only after compensating the other company. The average payoff has been c1000 yuan (in 1992), a very modest amount in $US but one-half of one month's salary for a translator.

The Chinese can be said to be ethnocentric when it comes to their perception of people from other provinces. This can carry over into the review and acceptance of an employee's file from another province. The employee's previous place of employment can impact his future job prospects. In this case, the Shanghainese would look with disfavor on an employee file (and therefore the individual) from the poorer, less sophisticated Chongming Dao area.

A related cultural difference is that a foreign manager would examine an employee's file from the perspective of performance, whereas a Chinese manager would review the file to learn of an individual's seniority and to see if there is a history of causing dissention.

Rank

There are no official class distinctions in China, but rank among businesspeople and government bureaucrats is very important. It is very important that you know the rank of the individual you are likely to deal with and your response should be consistent with the rank. Connections and rank gain one access to the *te-quan*, or special privileges. If the top official is accompanied by the second in rank, all the discussion should be directed toward the top official and the second in rank might as well not be present.

Manufacturing and Quality Control in China

In general, the Chinese have only a rudimentary understanding of quality concepts. They almost always carry out 100% inspections to "control" quality. Because the Chinese have become accustomed to inferior quality goods, workers often do not perceive producing goods of high quality to be important. Items that do not pass quality control are offered to the employees free of charge.

The quality of technology used in China varies greatly. For the most part, the technological level resembles that of the United States in the 1950s. Computerization is scant. Materials handling is done manually. Machinery is bulky and frequently needs repair.

Scheduling of work is almost nonexistent, though work itself is assigned to groups. A typical manufacturing operation is very labor intensive, and in most cases, the workforce is excessively large. Production planning is usually based on the number of hours to be worked rather than on the number of units to be manufactured.

Infrastructure

China's economy suffers from a weak infrastructure. Electricity is unavailable at times (especially if the firm has exceeded its quota). Roads need repairs, train shipments are more often than not late, factory allocations of raw materials are (occasionally) routed to other units, and the communication systems can be considered a nightmare.

Additional Note

Neither Geert Hofstede's original study (Hofstede 1980), nor his later work (Hofstede and Bond 1988) included China as a country of analysis. However, Hong Kong and Taiwan were included in both instances. The results were similar for Power Distance (Large), Individualism (Low), Uncertainty Avoidance (Low), and Confucianism (High), differing only in Masculinity (Hong Kong, high, and Taiwan low). We would therefore expect top down decision making, centralized authority, little participative management, tolerance of uncertainty, and authority vested only in the most senior employees. This confirms the events described in the case.

---

there was a great sense of disbelief and sadness associated with the recall. Jimmy Chao, his replacement, arrived two weeks later. Jimmy was a Singaporean engineer whose experience was limited to supervising production at one of Controls' factories in that country. James spent as much time getting him up to speed as was possible. Jimmy was 18 years younger than James, quite cocky, very opinionated, and aggressive. Although James provided all the coaching that he could, Jimmy was bound to do things his way.

The scene at the ferry when they departed the island for the last time was incredible. Many of the workers and all of the managers supplied by the Chinese partner were there to see them off. Many tokens of appreciation and affection were exchanged.

The plane droned inexorably on. James had, by this point in the trip, "rerun the tapes" of his whole experience over and over in his mind, and again he thought about how blessed he felt to have had the experience at all. What recommendations should I make in my report and during my debriefings? If I really think they are heading for the "ditch," it is my responsibility to steer them away from it. Oh well, these questions will have to wait until another day. It is time to get some sleep. I wonder what the temperature is in Pauley?

References

Steven R. Hendryx, "The China Trade: Making the Deal Work," *Harvard Business Review* (July–August, 1986), pp. 75–84.

———, and Michael H. Bond, "The Confucius Connection: From Cultural Roots to Economic Growth," *Organizational Dynamics* (Spring 1988), pp. 5–21.

Geert Hofstede, *Cultures' Consequences: International Differences in Work Related Values*, Sage Publications, Beverly Hills, CA, 1980.

Wenzhong Hu, and Cornelius Grove, *Encountering the Chinese: A Guide for the Americans*, Intercultural Press Inc. Yarmouth, ME, 1993.

Saha Sudhir Kumar, "Managing Human Resources in China," *Canadian Journal of Administrative Science* (Summer 1991), pp. 167–177.

Roderick Macleod, *How to Do Business with the Chinese*, Bantam Books, New York, 1988.

James J. Wall, Jr., "Managers in the People's Republic of China," *Academy of Management Executives*, (1990), pp. 19–32.

Irene Y. M. Yeung, and Rosalie L. Tung, "Achieving Business Success in Confucian Societies: The Importance of Gunaxi," *Organizational Dynamics* (Autumn 1996), pp. 54–65.

BOOK NOTES

CHAPTER 1: ASSESSING THE ENVIRONMENT—POLITICAL, ECONOMIC, LEGAL, TECHNOLOGICAL

1. "Nokia's China Strategy: Exchanging Technology for Market Access," www.businessweek.com, January 22, 2001.
2. D. Pearl and A. Freedman, "Behind Cipla's Offer of Cheap AIDS Drugs," *Wall Street Journal*, March 12, 2001.
3. K. Ohmae, "Putting Global Logic First," *Harvard Business Review* (January–February 1995): 119–125.
4. *Business Week*, August 31, 1998.
5. www.WTO, November 10, 1998.
6. Jeremy Kahn, "The Fortune Global 500," *Fortune*, August 3, 1998.
7. K. Ohmae, *The Borderless World* (New York: Harper Business, 1990).
8. Ibid.
9. "EU Members play the numbers game," *Financial Times*, November 17, 2000.
10. *Wall Street Journal*, February 28, 1995.
11. "South Korean Chaebol Enter Series of Mergers," *Wall Street Journal*, September 4, 1998.
12. "How Japan's Toshiba Got Its Focus Back," *Wall Street Journal*, December 28, 2000.
13. "A Kinder, Gentler Way to Open Up Japan," *Wall Street Journal*, January 12, 2001.
14. G. Becker, "It's Time for NAFTA to Look Further South," *Business Week*, January 8, 2001.
15. *Fortune Investors' Guide*, December 18, 2000.
16. W. E. Halal and A. I. Nikitin, "One World: The Coming Synthesis of New Capitalism and a New Socialism," *Futurist* (November–December 1990): 8–14.
17. J. A. Quelch, E. Joachimsthaler, and J. L. Nueno, "After the Wall: Marketing Guidelines for Eastern Europe," *Sloan Management Review* (Winter 1991): 82–93.
18. "Piling into Central Europe," *Business Week*, July 1, 1996.
19. M. Forney, P. Yatski, "No More Free Lunch," *Far Eastern Economic Review*, October 16, 1997, 62–63.
20. "China's Effort to Join WTO Gaining Urgency," *Wall Street Journal*, January 12, 2001.
21. UPI Newswire, November 7, 1995.
22. K. Ohmae.
23. W. B. Johnston, "Global Work Force 2000: The New World Labor Market," *Harvard Business Review* (March–April 1991): 115–127.
24. Ibid.
25. N. J. Adler, "Cross-Cultural Management: Issues to Be Faced," *International Studies of Management and Organization* 13 (Spring–Summer 1983): 7–45.
26. B. Weiner, "What Executives Should Know About Political Risks," *Management Review* (January 1991): 19–22.
27. Ibid.
28. S. H. Robock and K. Simmonds, *International Business and Multinational Enterprises*, 4th ed. (Homewood, IL: Irwin, 1989): 378.
29. Ibid.
30. D. F. Simon, "After Tiananmen: What Is the Future for Foreign Business in China?" *California Management Review* (Winter 1990): 106–108.
31. A. Jack, Moscow: "Europe reinvented: Russians wake up to consumer capitalism," www.FT.com, January 30, 2001.
32. A. Clark, "Japan Goes to Europe," *World Monitor* (April 1990): 36–40.

33. E. F. Micklous, "Tracking the Growth and Prevalence of International Terrorism," in *Managing Terrorism: Strategies for the Corporate Executive*, ed. P. J. Montana and G. S. Roukis (Westport, CT: Quorum Books, 1983): 3.

34. Robock and Simmonds.

35. G. M. Taoka and D. R. Beeman, *International Business* (New York: HarperCollins, 1991).

36. Rahul Jacob, "Asian Infrastructure: The Biggest Bet on Earth," *Fortune*, October 31, 1994, 139–146.

37. D. R. Beeman, "An Empirical Analysis of the Beliefs Held by the International Executives of United States Firms Regarding Political Risks and Risk Reduction Methods in Developing Nations" (unpublished doctoral diss., Indiana University Graduate School of Business, 1978), reprinted in G. M. Taoka and D. R. Beeman, *International Business* (New York: HarperCollins, 1991): 36–41.

38. T. W. Shreeve, "Be Prepared for Political Changes Abroad," *Harvard Business Review* (July–August 1984): 111–118.

39. M. C. Schnitzer, M. L. Liebrenz, and K. W. Kubin, *International Business* (Cincinnati, OH: South-Western, 1985).

40. C. Erol, "An Exploratory Model of Political Risk Assessment and the Decision Process of Foreign Direct Investment," *International Studies of Management and Organization* (Summer 1985): 75–90.

41. T. Morrison, W. Conaway, J. Bouress, *Dun & Bradstreet's Guide to Doing Business Around the World* (Englewood Cliffs, NJ: Prentice-Hall, 1997).

42. M. C. Schnitzer, M. L. Liebrenz, and K. W. Kubin, *International Business* (Cincinnati, OH: South-Western, 1985).

43. P. Smith Ring, S. A. Lenway, and M. Govekar, "Management of the Political Imperative in International Business," *Strategic Management Journal* 11 (1990): 141–151.

44. Ibid.

45. L. D. Howell and B. Chaddick, "Models of Political Risk for Foreign Investment and Trade," *Columbia Journal of World Business*, Fall 1994.

46. Taoka and Beeman.

47. Ibid.

48. Overseas Private Investment Corporation, *Investment Insurance Handbook*, 4.

49. Schnitzer, Liebrenz, and Kubin.

50. B. O'Reilly, "Business Copes with Terrorism," *Fortune*, January 6, 1986, 48.

51. *Wall Street Journal*, December 29, 2000.

52. J. Dahl, "Firms Warn Workers Traveling Abroad," *Wall Street Journal*, April 10, 1989, B1.

53. A. Paul, "Indonesia," *Fortune*, April 13, 1998.

54. F. John Mathis, "International Risk Analysis," in *Global Business Management in the 1990s*, ed. R. T. Moran (Washington, D.C.: Beacham, 1990): 33–44.

55. Mathis, 40.

56. Ibid.

57. Much of this section is drawn from A. Paul, "Indonesia," *Fortune*, April 13, 1998.

58. Ibid.

59. "Why Sweet Deals are Going Sour in China," *Business Week*, December 19, 1994, 50–51.

60. Loeb.

61. P. Hui-Ho Cheng, "A Business Risk in China: Jail," *Asian Wall Street Journal*, April 22, 1994.

62. M. Litka, *International Dimensions of the Legal Environment of Business* (Boston: PWS-Kent, 1988): 5.

63. Ibid.

64. Jacob.

65. Litka.

66. Jacob.

67. Ibid.

68. R. J. Radway, "Foreign Contract Agreements," in *Global Business Management in the 1990s*, ed. R. T. Moran (Washington, D.C.: Beacham, 1990): 93–103.

69. S. P. Robbins and R. Stuart-Kotze, *Management* (Scarborough, Ontario: Prentice-Hall, Canada, 1990): 4–11.

70. Ibid.

71. "Lacking Roads, Village Building Information Highway," *Wall Street Journal*, December 29, 2001.

72. Sylvia Ostry, "Technological Productivity and the Multinational Enterprise," *Journal of International Business Studies* 29,1 (1st quarter, 1998) 85–99.

73. Ibid.

74. "Where Technology Is the Appropriate Word," *Economist*, April 18, 1987, 83.

75. "How to Sell Soap in India," *Economist*, September 1988, 82.

76. Hans Dieter Zimmerman, "E-Business" www.businessmedia.org.

77. "What Is E-Business," PriceWaterhouseCoopers, www.pwglobal.com, July 21, 2000.

78. J. Rajesh, "Five E-Business Trends," Net.Columns, www.indialine.com, February 18, 1999.

79. Ibid.

80. "E-Management," *The Economist*, November 11, 2000.

81. "E-Commerce Report, *The New York Times*, March 26, 2001.

82. PricewaterhouseCoopers, www.pwcglobal.com

83. This section draws from a term paper by Ms. Laura Harrison, student at the State University of New York, December 2000.

84. "What Is E-Business," PricewaterhouseCoopers, www.pwcglobal.com, July 21, 2000.

85. B. James, "Reducing the Risks of Globalization," *Long-Range Planning* 23, no. 1 (1990): 80–88.

CHAPTER 2: MANAGING INTERDEPENDENCE: SOCIAL RESPONSIBILITY AND ETHICS

1. "Killer in a Bottle," *Economist* 279, no. 7184, May 9, 1981, 50.

2. A. M. Freedman and S. Stecklow, "As Unicef Battles Baby-Formula Makers, African Infants Sicken," *Wall Street Journal*, December 5, 2000.

3. Ibid.

4. J. C. Laya, "Economic Development Issues," in *Multinational Managers and Host Government Interactions*, ed. Lee A. Tavis (South Bend, IN: University of Notre Dame Press, 1988).

5. John A. Quelch and James E. Austin, "Should Multinationals Invest in Africa?" *Sloan Management Review* (Spring 1993): 107–119.

6. Milton Friedman, *Capitalism and Freedom* (Chicago: University of Chicago Press, 1962).

7. S. Prakash Sethi, "A Conceptual Framework for Environmental Analysis of Social Issues and Evaluation of Business Response Patterns, " *Academy of Management Review* (January 1979): 63–74.

8. A. B. Carroll, "A Three Dimensional Conceptual Model of Corporate Peformance," *Academy of Management Review* 4 (1979): 497–505.

9. John Dobson, "The Role of Ethics in Global Corporate Culture," *Journal of Business Ethics* 9 (1990): 481–488.

10. Ibid.

11. N. Bowie, "The Moral Obligations of Multinational Corporations, " in *Problems of International Justice*, ed. Luper-Fay (New York: Westview Press: 1987): 97–113.

12. A. C. Wicks, "Norman Bowie and Richard Rorty on Multinationals: Does Business Ethics Need 'Metaphysical Comfort'?" *Journal of Business Ethics* 9 (1990): 191–200.

13. Joanna Ramey, "Clinton Urges Industry to enlist in the War Against Sweatshops, " www.labordepartment.com, April 15, 1997.

14. Shu Shin Luh, "Report Claims Abuses by Nike Contractors," *Wall Street Journal*, February 22, 2001.

15. *Asian Wall Street Journal*, April 8, 1994.

16. "Staunching the Flow of China's Gulag Exports," *Business Week*, April 13, 1992.

17. J. Carlton, "Ties With China Will Be Severed by Levi Strauss," *Wall Street Journal*, May 5, 1993, A3.

18. G. P. Zachary, "Levi Tries to Make Sure Contract Plants in Asia Treat Workers Well," *Wall Street Journal*, July 28, 1994.

19. "Sweatshop Police," *Business Week*, October 20, 1997.

20. Kathleen A. Getz, "International Codes of Conduct: An Analysis of Ethical Reasoning," *Journal of Business Ethics* 9 (1990): 567–577.

21. Swee Hoon Ang, "The Power of Money: A Cross-Cultural Analysis of Business-Related Beliefs, " *Journal of World Business*, 35, no. il (Spring 2000): 43.

22. D. Vogel, "Is U.S. Business Obsessed with Ethics?" *Across the Board* (November/December, 1993): 31–33; A. Singer, "Ethics—Are Standards Lower Overseas?" *Across the Board* (September 1991): 31–34.

23. Parviv Asheghian and Bahman Ebrahimi, *International Business* (New York: Harper and Row, 1990).

24. Ibid.

25. Vogel.

26. Singer.

27. Ibid.

28. J. G. Kaikati and W. A. Label, "American Bribery Legislation: An Obstacle to International Marketing, " *Journal of Marketing* (Fall 1980): 38–43.

29. G. R. Laczniak and J. Naor, "Global Ethics: Wrestling with the Corporate Conscience," *Business* (July–August–September, 1985): 3–10.

30. Singer.

31. G. A. Steiner and J. F. Steiner, *Business, Government and Society*, 6th ed. (New York: McGraw-Hill, 1991).

32. Larry Luxner, "IBM Feeling Blue in Argentina," *Mutlinational Monitor*, October, 1996, vol. 17, no. 10: 14 (4).

33. T. L. Carson, "Bribery and Implicit Agreements: A Reply to Philips," *Journal of Business Ethics* 6 (1987): 123–125.

34. M. Philips, "Bribery," *Ethics* 94 (July 1984).

35. Ibid.

36. Singer.

37. L. H. Newton and M. M. Ford, *Taking Sides* (Guilford, CT: Dushkin, 1990).

38. Ibid.

39. K. Gillespie, "Middles East Response to the U.S. Foreign Corrupt Practices Act, " *California Management Review* (Summer 1987): 9.

40. K. M. Bartol and D. C. Martin, *Management* (New York: McGraw-Hill, 1991).

41. Vogel.

42. A. Cadbury, *Harvard Business Review* (September–October 1987): 63–73.

43. M. E. Shannon, "Coping with Extortion and Bribery," in *Multinational Managers and Host Government Interactions*, ed. Lee A. Tavis (South Bend, IN: University of Notre Dame Press, 1988).

44. Laczniak and Naor.

45. "A World of Greased Palms," *Business Week*, November 6, 1995.

46. D. E. Sanger, "Nippon Telegraph Executive Demoted for Role in Scandal," *New York Times*, December 10, 1988.

47. Susan Chira, "Another Top Official in Japan Loses Post in Wake of Scandal," *New York Times*, January 25, 1989, 1, 5; and "Remember the Recruit Scandal? Well . . ." *Business Week*, January 8, 1990, 52.

48. Sadehei Kusomoto, "We're Not in Honshu Anymore," *Across the Board* (June 1989): 49–50.

49. Ibid.

50. P. W. Beamish et al., *International Management* (Homewood, IL: Irwin, 1991).

51. J. N. Behrman, *National Interests and the Multinational Enterprise* (Englewood Cliffs, N.J.: Prentice-Hall, 1970): 31.

52. Adapted from P. Asheghian and B. Ebrahimi, *International Business* (New York: Harper and Row, 1990): 640–641.

53. R. Grosse and D. Kujawa, *International Business* (Homewood, IL: Irwin, 1988): 705.

54. R. H. Mason and R. S. Spich, *Management, An International Perspective* (Homewood, IL: Irwin, 1987).

55. Yves L. Doz and C. K. Prahalad, "How MNCs Cope with Host Government Intervention," *Harvard Business Review* (March–April 1980).

56. Mason and Spich.

57. Simcha Ronen, *Comparative and Multinational Management* (New York: John Wiley and Sons, 1986): 502–503.

58. R. T. De George, *Competing with Integrity in International Business* (NY: Oxford University Press, 1993) 3-4.

59. *Fortune*-Investors' Guide, December 18, 2000.

60. "Two Years Later, the Promises Used to Sell NAFTA Haven't Come True, but Its Foes Were Wrong, Too," *Wall Street Journal*, October 26, 1995.

61. *Wall Street Journal*, October 28, 1994.

62. Ibid.

63. *Fortune*, 2000.

64. *Wall Street Journal*, 1994.

65. "The Border," *Business Week*, May, 1997.

66. Ibid.

67. *Wall Street Journal*, June 29, 1994.

68. B. Ward and R. Dubois, *Only One Earth* (New York: Ballantine Books, 1972).

69. Ronen.

70. S. Tifft, "Who Gets the Garbage," *Time*, July 4, 1988, 42–43.

71. Jang B. Singh and V. C. Lakhan, "Business Ethics and the International Trade in Hazardous Wastes," *Journal of Business Ethics* 8 (1989): 889–899.

72. R. A. Peterson and M. H. Sauber, "International Marketing Ethics: Is There a Need for a Code?" (paper presented at the International Studies Association Southwest, Houston, TX, March 16–19, 1984).

73. M. Reza Vaghefi, S. K. Paulson, and W. H. Tomlinson, *International Business Theory and Practice* (New York: Taylor and Francis, 1991): 249–250.

74. T. E. Graedel and B. R. Allenby, *Industrial Ecology* (Englewood Cliffs, NJ: Prentice Hall, 1995).

75. M. Sharfman, Book Review of Graedel and Allenby, *Academy of Management Review* 20, no. 4 (1995): 1090–1107.

76. Ronen.

77. Asheghian and Ebrahimi.
78. H. Becker and D. J. Fritzsche, "A Comparison of the Ethical Behavior of American, French and German Managers, " *Columbia Journal of World Business* (Winter 1987): 87–95.

CHAPTER 3: UNDERSTANDING THE ROLE OF CULTURE

1. David A. Ricks, *Big Business Blunders: Mistakes in Multinational Marketing* (Homewood, IL: Dow Jones-Irwin, 1983).
2. Carla Joinson, "Why HR Managers Need to think Globally," *HR Magazine*, April, 1998, 2–7.
3. Ibid.
4. J. Stewart Black and Mark Mendenhall, "Cross-Cultural Training Effectiveness: A Review and a Theoretical Framework for Future Research," *Academy of Management Review* 15, no. 1 (1990): 113–136.
5. Adapted from Bernard Wysocki, Jr., "Global Reach: Cross-Border Alliances Become Favorite Way to Crack New Markets," *Wall Street Journal*, March 26, 1990, A1, A4.
6. Geert Hofstede, *Culture's Consequences: International Differences in Work-Related Values* (Beverly Hills, CA: Sage Publications, 1980): 25.
7. E. T. Hall, *The Silent Language* (Greenwich, CT: Fawcett, 1959).
8. For a more detailed definition, see A. L. Kroeber and C. Kluckholhn, "A Critical Review of Concepts and Definitions," in *Peabody Museum Papers* 47, no. 1 (Cambridge, MA: Harvard University Press, 1952): 181.
9. David Dressler and Donald Carns, *Sociology, The Study of Human Interaction* (New York: Knopf, 1969): 56–57.
10. K. David, "Organizational Processes for Intercultural Management" (Paper presented at the Strategic Management Association, San Francisco, CA, 1989).
11. www.McDonalds.com, February 20, 2001; and *Wall Street Journal*, February 2, 1990, A15.
12. Lane Kelley, Arthur Whatley, and Reginald Worthley, "Assessing the Effects of Culture on Managerial Attitudes: A Three-Culture Test," *Journal of International Business Studies* (Summer 1987): 17–31.
13. J. D. Child, "Culture, Contingency and Capitalism in the Cross-National Study of Organizations," in *Research in Organizational Behavior*, ed. L. L. Cummings and B. M. Shaw (Greenwich, CT: JAI Publishers, 1981): 303–356.
14. Jangho Lee, T. W. Roehl, Soonkyoo Choe, "What Makes Management Style Similar and Distinct Across Borders? Growth Experience and Culture in Korean and Japanese Firms," *Journal of International Business Studies* 31, no. 4 (4th Quarter, 2000): 631–652.
15. James A. Lee, "Cultural Analysis in Overseas Operations," *Harvard Business Review* (March–April, 1966).
16. E. T. Hall, "The Silent Language in Overseas Business," *Harvard Business Review* (May–June 1960).
17. "American Culture is Often a Puzzle for Foreign Managers in the U.S.,"*Wall Street Journal*, February 12, 1986, 34.
18. "One Big Market," *Wall Street Journal*, February 6, 1989, 16.
19. D. A. Ralston, Yu Kai-Ceng, Xun Wang, R. H. Terpstra, and He Wel, "An Analysis of Managerial Work Values Across the Six Regions of China" (Paper presented at the *Academy of International Business*, Boston, November 1994).
20. Philip R. Harris and Robert T. Moran, *Managing Cultural Differences* (Houston, TX: Gulf Publishing, 1987).
21. K. David, "Field Research," in *The Cultural Environment of International Business*, 3d ed., ed. V. Terpstra and K. David (Cincinnati, OH: South-Western, 1991): 176.
22. "Sharia Loosens Its Grip," *Euromoney*, May 1987, 137–138.
23. "Korea's Digital Quest," www.Businessweek.com, September 25, 2000.
24. Geert Hofstede, "National Cultures in Four Dimensions," *International Studies of Management and Organization* (Spring–Summer 1983).
25. Elizabeth Weldon and Elisa L. Mustari, "Felt Dispensability in Groups of Coactors: The Effects of Shared Responsibility on Cognitive Effort" (Unpublished manuscript, Kellogg Graduate School of Management, Northwestern University) February 2000.
26. P. Christopher Earley, "Social Loafing and Collectivism: A Comparison of the United States

and the People's Republic of China," *Administrative Science Quarterly* 34 (1989): 565–581.

27. H. K. Steensma, L. Marino, K. M. Weaver, "Attitudes towards Cooperative Strategies: A Cross-Cultural Analysis of Entrepreneurs," *Journal of International Business Studies*, 31, no. 4 (4th Quarter, 2000), 591–609.

28. Simcha Ronen and Oded Shenkar, "Clustering Countries on Attitudinal Dimensions: A Review and Synthesis," *Academy of Management Review* 10, no. 3 (1985): 435–454.

29. F. Trompenaars, *Riding the Waves of Culture* (Nicholas Brealey, London, 1993).

30. L. Hoeklin, *Managing Cultural Differences: Strategies for Competitive Advantage* (The Economist Intelligence Unit/Addison-Wesley, 1995).

31. Ross A. Webber, *Culture and Management, Text and Reading in Comparative Management* (Homewood, IL: Irwin, 1969): 186.

32. Arvind V. Phatak, *International Dimensions of Management*, 2d ed. (Boston: PWS-Kent, 1989).

33. D. Darlin and J. B. White, "GM Venture in Korea Nears End, Betraying Firm's Fond Hopes," *Wall Street Journal*, January 16, 1992, 1.

34. Geert Hofstede, *Culture's Consequences: International Differences in Work-related Values* (Beverly Hills, CA: Sage Publications, 1980).

35. George W. England, "Managers and Their Value Systems: A Five-Country Comparative Study," *Columbia Journal of World Business* (Summer 1978): 35–44.

36. Lennie Copeland and Lewis Griggs, *Going International* (New York: Random House, 1985); Boye De Mente, *Japanese Etiquette and Ethics in Business* (Lincolnwood, IL: NTC Business Books, 1989); Boye De Mente, *Korean Etiquette and Ethics in Business* (Lincolnwood, IL: NTC Business Books, 1989); George W. England and R. Lee, "Organizational Goals and Expected Behavior Among American, Japanese, and Korean Managers: A Comparative Study," *Academy of Management Journal* 14, no. 4 (1971): 425–438; R. L. Tung, *Business Negotiations with the Japanese* (Lexington, MA: Lexington Books, 1984); W. G. Ouchi and A. M. Jaeger, "Theory Z Organization: Stability in the Midst of Mobility," *Academy of Management Review* 3, no. 2 (1978): 305–314; T. Seth, "Management and Its Environment in India," in *Management in an International Context*, ed. Joseph L. Massie and J. Luytjes (New York: Harper and Row, 1972): 201–225;

Nam-Won Suh, "Management and Its Environment in Korea," in *Management in an International Context*, eds. Joseph L. Massie and Jan Luytjes (New York: Harper and Row, 1972): 226–244; Philip R. Harris and Robert T. Moran, *Managing Cultural Differences* (Houston, TX: Gulf Publishing, 1991); Fernando Quezada and James E. Boyce, "Latin America," in *Comparative Management*, ed. Raghu Nath (Cambridge, MA: Ballinger Publishing, 1988): 245–270; Simcha Ronen, *Comparative and Multinational Management* (New York: John Wiley and Sons, 1986); and V. Terpstra and K. David, *The Cultural Environment of International Business*, 3d ed. (Cincinnati, OH: South-Western, 1991).

37. R. G. Linowes, "The Japanese Manager's Traumatic Entry in the United States: Understanding the American-Japanese Cultural Divide," *Academy of Management Review*, 1993, 21–38.

38. Ibid.

39. Yumiko Ono and Wm. Spindle, "Japan's Long Decline Makes One Thing Rise —Individualism," *Wall Street Journal, December 29, 2000.*

40. Ibid.

41. E. T. Hall and M. R. Hall, *Understanding Cultural Differences*, (Yarmouth, ME: Intercultural Press, 1990): 4.

42. P. R. Harris and R. T. Moran, *Managing Cultural Differences*, 4th ed (Houston, TX: Gulf Publishing Co., 1996).

43. Robert Moore, "Saudi Arabia," Chapter 11, in Harris and Moran.

44. John A. Pearce II, Richard B. Robinson, Jr., "Cultivating Guanxi as a Foreign Investor Strategy," *Business Horizons*, January 2000, v. 43, i1, p.31.

45. M. Chen, *Asian Management Systems: Chinese, Japanese and Korean Styles of Business* (New York, NY: Routledge, 1995).

46. Anne Marie Francesco and Barry Allen Gold, *International Organizational Behavior* (Upper Saddle River, NJ: Prentice Hall, 1997).

47. J. Lee, "Culture and Management—A study of Small Chinese Family Business in Singapore," *Journal of Small Business Management*, July, 1996.

48. R. Sheng, "Outsiders' Perception of the Chinese," *Columbia Journal of World Business* 14 (2), Summer (1996): 16–22.

49. Lee.

50. Ralston.

1. E. T. Hall and M. R. Hall, *Understanding Cultural Differences* (Yarmouth, ME: Intercultural Press, 1990): 4.

2. E. Wilmott, "New Media Vision," *New Media Age*, September 9, 1999, p. 8.

3. Hall and Hall; K. Wolfson and W. B. Pearce, "A Cross-Cultural Comparison of the Implications of Self-discovery on Conversation Logics," *Communication Quarterly* 31 (1983): 249–256.

4. H. Mintzberg, *The Nature of Managerial Work* (New York: Harper and Row, 1973).

5. L. A. Samovar, R. E. Porter, and N. C. Jain, *Understanding Intercultural Communication* (Belmont, CA: Wadsworth Publishing Company, 1981).

6. P. R. Harris and R. T. Moran, *Managing Cultural Differences*, 3d ed. (Houston, TX: Gulf Publishing, 1991).

7. Samovar, Porter, and Jain.

8. Hall and Hall, 15.

9. L. A. Samovar and R. E. Porter, *International Communication: A Reader* (Belmont, CA: Wadsworth, 1988).

10. Harris and Moran.

11. Simcha Ronen, *Comparative and Multinational Management* (New York: John Wiley and Sons, 1986).

12. M. L. Hecht, P. A. Andersen, and S. A. Ribeau, "The Cultural Dimensions of Nonverbal Communication," in *Handbook of International and Intercultural Communication*, ed. M. K. Asante and W. B. Gudykunst (Newbury Park, CA: Sage Publications, 1989), 163–185.

13. H. C. Triandis, *Interpersonal Behavior* (Monterey, CA: Brooks/Cole, 1977).

14. Harris and Moran.

15. Adapted from N. Adler, *International Dimensions of Organizational Behavior*, 2d ed. (Boston: PWS-Kent, 1991); and based on M. Martin, *Adaptation to a Foreign Environment* (Ottawa: Canadian International Development Agency, to be published).

16. L. A. Samovar, Porter, and Jain.

17. D. A. Ricks, *Big Business Blunders: Mistakes in Multinational Marketing* (Homewood, IL: Dow Jones-Irwin, 1983).

18. Vern Terpstra and K. David, *The Cultural Environment of International Business*, 3d ed. (Cincinnati, OH: South-Western, 1991).

19. L. Copeland and L. Griggs, *Going International* (New York: Random House, 1985).

20. J. R. Schermerhorn, "Language Effects in Cross-Cultural Management Research: An Empirical Study and a Word of Caution," *National Academy of Management Proceedings* (1987): 103.

21. Jiatao Li, Katherine R. Xin, Anne Tsui, Donald C. Hambrick, "Building Effective International Joint Venture Leadership Teams in China," *Journal of World Business*, 34, no. 1 (1999): 52–68.

22. R. L. Daft, *Organizational Theory and Design*, 3d ed. (St. Paul, MN: West Publishing, 1989).

23. Li et al., 1999.

24. O. Klineberg, "Emotional Expression in Chinese Literature," *Journal of Abnormal and Social Psychology* 33 (1983): 517–530.

25. P. Ekman and W. V. Friesen, "Constants Across Cultures in the Face and Emotion," *Journal of Personality and Social Psychology* 17 (1971): 124–129.

26. P. Ekman and W. V. Friesen, "A New Pancultural Expression of Emotion," *Motivation and Emotion* 10 (1986): 159–168.

27. J. Pfeiffer, "How Not to Lose the Trade Wars by Cultural Gaffes," *Smithsonian* 18, no. 10, January 1988.

28. E. T. Hall, *The Silent Language* (New York: Doubleday, 1959).

29. Hall and Hall.

30. Ibid.

31. N. M. Sussman and H. M. Rosenfeld, "Influence of Culture, Language, and Sex on Conversational Distance," *Journal of Personality and Social Psychology* 42 (1982): 66–74.

32. Copeland and Griggs.

33. Hecht, Andersen, and Ribeau.

34. Li et al., 1999.

35. Pfeiffer.

36. Hall and Hall.

37. Ibid.

38. Hecht, Andersen, and Ribeau.

39. P. A. Andersen, "Explaining Differences in Nonverbal Communication," in *Intercultural Communication: A Reader*, ed. L. A. Samovar and R. E. Porter (Belmont, CA: Wadsworth, 1988); S. Scott Elliot, A. D. Jensen, and M. McDonough, "Perceptions of Reticence: A Cross-Cultural Investigation," in *Communication Yearbook* 5, ed. M. Burgoon (New Brunswick, NJ: Transaction, 1982).

40. Hall and Hall.

41. R. Axtell, ed., *Dos and Taboos Around the World*, 2d ed. (New York: John Wiley and Sons, 1985).

42. Copeland and Griggs.

43. M. K. Nydell, *Understanding Arabs* (Yarmouth, ME: Intercultural Press, 1987).

44. Harris and Moran.

45. E. T. Hall, *The Hidden Dimension* (New York: Doubleday, 1966): 15.

46. A. Almaney and A. Alwan, *Communicating with the Arabs* (Prospect Heights, IL: Waveland, 1982).

47. E. T. Hall, "The Silent Language in Overseas Business," *Harvard Business Review* (May–June 1960).

48. Ibid.

49. Based largely on the work of Nydell; and R. T. Moran and P. R. Harris, *Managing Cultural Synergy* (Houston, TX: Gulf Publishing, 1982): 81–82.

50. Ibid.

51. Copeland and Griggs.

52. Hall and Hall.

53. D. C. Barnlund, "Public and Private Self in Communicating with Japan," *Business Horizons* (March–April 1989): 32–40.

54. Hall and Hall.

55. A. Goldman, "The Centrality of "Ningensei" to Japanese Negotiating and Interpersonal Relationships: Implications for U.S.–Japanese Communication," *International Journal of Intercultural Relations* 18, no. 1 (Winter 1994).

56. Jean-Louis Barsoux and Peter Lawrence, "The Making of a French Manager," *Harvard Business Review* (July–August 1991): 58–67.

57. D. Shand, "All Information Is Local; IT Systems Can Connect Every Corner of the Globe, But IT Managers Are Learning They Have to Pay Attention to Regional Differences," *Computerworld*, April 10, 2000, 88 (1).

58. T. Wilson, "B2B Links, European Style—Integrator Helps Apps Cross Language, Currency and Cultural Barriers," *Internet Week*, October 9, 2000, 27.

59. Shand, 2000.

60. Wilmott, 1999.

61. *Business Week*, February, 1998, 14–15.

62. Wilson, 2000.

63. www.Manheimauctions.com, April, 2001.

64. Shand, 2000.

65. Ibid.

66. D. Ricks, *Big Business Blunders* (Homewood, IL: Dow Jones-Irwin, 1983).

67. Adler.

68. P. G. W. Keen, "Sorry, Wrong Number," *Business Month*, January 1990, 62–67.

69. R. B. Ruben, "Human Communication and Cross-Cultural Effectiveness," in *Intercultural Communication: A Reader*, ed. L. Samovar and R. Porter (Belmont, CA: Wadsworth, 1985): 339.

70. D. Ruben and B. D. Ruben, "Cross-Cultural Personnel Selection Criteria, Issues and Methods," in *Handbook of Intercultural Training: vol. 1, Issues in Theory and Design*, ed. D. Landis and R. W. Brislin (New York: Pergamon, 1983): 155–175.

71. Young Yun Kim, *Communication and Cross-Cultural Adaptation: An Integrative Theory* (Clevedon, England: Multilingual Matters, 1988).

72. Ibid.

73. R. W. Brislin, *Cross-Cultural Encounters: Face-to-Face Interaction* (New York: Pergamon, 1981).

CHAPTER 5: CROSS-CULTURAL NEGOTIATION AND DECISION MAKING

1. John Pfeiffer, "How Not to Lose the Trade Wars by Cultural Gaffes," *Smithsonian* 18, no. 10 (January 1988): 145–156.

2. Nancy J. Adler, *International Dimensions of Organizational Behavior*, 2d ed. (Boston: PWS-Kent).

3. Philip R. Harris and Robert T. Moran, *Managing Cultural Differences*, 2d ed. (Houston, TX: Gulf Publishing).

4. John L. Graham, and Roy A. Herberger, Jr., "Negotiators Abroad—Don't Shoot from the Hip," *Harvard Business Review* (July–August 1983): 160–168.

5. Adler.

6. John L. Graham, "A Hidden Cause of America's Trade Deficit with Japan," *Columbia Journal of World Business* (Fall 1981): 5–15.

7. Phillip D. Grub, "Cultural Keys to Successful Negotiating," in *Global Business Management in the 1990s*, ed. F. Ghader et al. (Washington, D.C.: Beacham, 1990): 24–32.

8. R. Fisher and W. Ury, *Getting to Yes* (Boston: Houghton Mifflin, 1981).

9. "Soviet Breakup Stymies Foreign Firms," *Wall Street Journal*, January 23, 1992.

10. S. Weiss, "Negotiating with 'Romans,'" *Sloan Management Review* (Winter 1994): 51–61.

11. John A. Reeder, "When West Meets East: Cultural Aspects of Doing Business in Asia," *Business Horizons* (January–February 1987): 72.

12. Adler, 197.

13. Fisher and Ury.

14. Lennie Copeland and Lewis Griggs, *Going International* (New York: Random House, 1985): 85.

15. Ibid.

16. Adler, 197–198.

17. Fisher and Ury.

18. R. L. Tung, *U.S.–China Trade Negotiations* (NY: Pergamon Press, 1982).

19. John L. Graham, "The Influence of Culture on Business Negotiations," *Journal of International Business Studies* 16, no. 1 (Spring 1985): 81–96.

20. G. Fisher, *International Negotiation: A Cross-Cultural Perspective* (Chicago: Intercultural Press, 1980).

21. Pfeiffer.

22. *Wall Street Journal*, February 2, 1994.

23. John L. Graham, "Brazilian, Japanese, and American Business Negotiations," *Journal of International Business Studies* (Spring–Summer 1983): 47–61.

24. T. Flannigan, "Successful Negotiating with the Japanese," *Small Business Reports* 15, no. 6 (June 1990): 47–52.

25. Graham, 1983.

26. Boye De Mente, *Japanese Etiquette and Ethics in Business* (Lincolnwood, IL: NTC Business Books, 1989).

27. Robert H. Doktor, "Asian and American CEOs: A Comparative Study," *Organizational Dynamics* (Winter 1990): 49.

28. Harris and Moran, 461.

29. Adler, 181.

30. These profiles are adapted from Pierre Casse, *Managing Intercultural Negotiations: Guidelines for Trainers and Negotiators* (Washington, D.C.: Society for Intercultural Education, Training, and Research, 1985).

31. D. K. Tse, J. Francis, and J. Walls, "Cultural Differences in Conducting Intra- and Inter-Cultural Negotiations: A Sino-Canadian Comparison," *Journal of International Business Studies* (3rd Quarter 1994): 537–555.

32. B. W. Husted, "Bargaining with the Gringos: An Exploratory Study of Negotiations between Mexican and U.S. Firms," *International Executive* 36, no. 5 (September–October 1994): 625–644.

33. Pierre Casse, *Training for the Cross-Cultural Mind*, 2d ed. (Washington, D.C.: Society for Intercultural Education, Training, and Research, 1981).

34. Nigel Campbell, John L. Graham, Alain Jolibert, and Hans Meissner, "Marketing Negotiations in France, Germany, the United Kingdom, and the United States," *Journal of Marketing* 52 (April 1988): 49–63.

35. Neil Rackham, "The Behavior of Successful Negotiators" (Reston, VA: Huthwaite Research Group, 1976, 1982).

36. J. Teich, H. Wallenius, J. Wallenius, "World-Wide-Web Technology in Support of Negotiation and Commmunication," *International Journal of Technology Management*, 17, nos. 1–2 (1999): 223–239.

37. Ibid.

38. Ibid.

39. Quoted in J. A. Pearce, II, R. B. Robinson, Jr., "Cultivating Guanxi as a Foreign Investor Strategy, *Business Horizons* 43, no. i1 (January 2000): 31.

40. Ibid.

41. R. L. Tung, *U.S.–China Trade Negotiations* (New York: Pergamon Press, 1982).

42. Joan H. Coll, "Sino-American Cultural Differences: The Key to Closing a Business Venture with the Chinese," *Mid-Atlantic Journal of Business* 25, nos. 2, 3 (December 1988–January 1989): 15–19.

43. M. Loeb, "China: A Time for Caution," *Fortune*, February 20, 1995, 129–130.

44. O. Shenkar and S. Ronen, "The Cultural Context of Negotiations: The Implications of Chinese Interpersonal Norms," *Journal of Applied Behavioral Science* 23, no. 2 (1987): 263–275.

45. Tse et al.

46. J. Brunner, teaching notes, The University of Toledo.

47. Ibid.

48. Joanna M. Banthin and Leigh Stelzer, "Ethical Dilemmas in Negotiating Across Cultures: Problems in Commercial Negotiations between American Businessmen and the PRC" (paper presented at 1st International Conference on East-West Joint Ventures, October 19–20, 1989,

State University of New York–Plattsburgh); and J. M. Banthin and L. Stelzer, "'Opening' China: Negotiation Strategies when East Meets West," *The Mid-Atlantic Journal of Business* 25, nos. 2, 3 (December 1988–January 1989).

49. Brunner.

50. Pearce and Robinson.

51. Ibid.

52. Ibid.

53. C. Blackman, "An Inside Guide to Negotiating," *China Busines Review*, 27, no. 3 (May 2000) 44–45.

54. Brunner.

55. Boye De Mente, *Chinese Etiquette and Ethics in Business* (Lincolnwood, IL: NTC Business Books, 1989): 115–123.

56. S. Stewart and C. F. Keown, "Talking with the Dragon: Negotiating in the People's Republic of China," *Columbia Journal of World Business* 24, no. 3 (Fall 1989): 68–72.

57. Banthin and Stelzer, "'Opening' China."

58. Blackman.

59. Ibid.

60. Lucian Pye, *Chinese Commercial Negotiating Style* (Cambridge, MA: Oelgeschlager, Gunn and Hain, 1982).

61. W. B. Gudykunst and Ting Tomey, S., *Culture and Interpersonal Communication* (Newbury Park, CA: Sage Publications, 1988).

62. L. Copeland and L. Griggs, *Going International* (New York: Random House, 1985): 80.

63. M. A. Hitt, B. B. Tyler, and Daewoo Park, "A Cross-Cultural Examination of Strategic Decision Models: Comparison of Korean and U.S. Executives," in *Best Papers Proceedings of the 50th Annual Meeting of the Academy of Management* (San Francisco, CA, August 12–15, 1990): 111–115; G. Fisher, *International Negotiation: A Cross-Cultural Perspective* (Chicago: Intercultural Press, 1980); G. W. England, "Managers and Their Value Systems: A Five-Country Comparative Study," *Columbia Journal of World Business* 13, no. 2 (Summer 1978); W. Whitely and G. W. England, "Variability in Common Dimensions of Managerial Values Due to Value Orientation and Country Differences," *Personnel Psychology* 33 (1980): 77–89.

64. Hitt, Tyler, and Park, 114.

65. B. M. Bass and P. C. Burger, *Assessment of Managers: An International Comparison* (New York: Free Press, 1979): 91.

66. D. K. Tse, R. W. Belk, and Nan Zhan, "Learning to Consume: A Longitudinal and Cross-Cultural Content Analysis of Print Advertisements from Hong Kong, People's Republic of China and Taiwan," *Journal of Consumer Research* (forthcoming).

67. Copeland and Griggs; M. K. Badawy, "Styles of Mideastern Managers," *California Management Review* 22 (1980): 51–58.

68. N. Namiki and S. P. Sethi, "Japan," in *Comparative Management—A Regional View*, ed. R. Nath (Cambridge, MA: Ballinger Publishing, 1988): 74–76.

69. De Mente, *Japanese Etiquette*, 80.

70. S. Naoto, *Management and Industrial Structure in Japan* (New York: Pergamon Press, 1981).

71. Namiki Sethi.

72. Harris and Moran, 397.

73. S. P. Sethi and N. Namiki, "Japanese-Style Consensus Decision-Making in Matrix Management: Problems and Prospects of Adaptation," in *Matrix Management Systems Handbook*, ed. D. I. Cleland (New York: Van Nostrand, 1984): 431–456.

CHAPTER 6: FORMULATING STRATEGY

1. "FedEx Forms Joint Venture in China," www.Fedex.com, November 11, 1999.

2. Ibid.

3. D. Blackmon and D. Brady, "Orient Express: Just How Should A U.S. Company Woo A Big Foreign Market?" *Wall Street Journal*, April 6, 1998.

4. A. Hill, "International Economy: UPS Granted Application to Fly Direct to China," *Financial Times*, November 27, 2000.

5. Bernard Wysocki, Jr., "U.S. Firms Increase Overseas Investments," *Wall Street Journal*, April 9, 1990.

6. Herbert Henzler and Wilhelm Rall, "Facing Up to the Globalization Challenge," *McKinsey Quarterly* (Winter 1986): 52–68.

7. "The Stateless Corporation," *Business Week*, May 14, 1990, 100–101.

8. A. E. Serwer, "McDonald's Conquers the World," *Fortune*, October 17, 1994.

9. "The Avon Lady of the Amazon," *Business Week*, October 24, 1994.

10. Ibid.

11. A. K. Gupta and V. Govindarajan, "Managing Global Expansion: A Conceptual Framework," *Business Horizons*, March/April, 2000.

12. G. Melloan, "Global Manufacturing Is an Intricate Game," *Wall Street Journal*, November 29, 1988.

13. "The Avon Lady of the Amazon," *Business Week*, October 24, 1994.

14. "The Stateless Corporation."

15. "Trinidad and Tobago," *Wall Street Journal*, May 23, 1990, special advertising section.

16. Robert Weigand, "International Investments: Weighing the Incentives," *Harvard Business Review* (July–August 1983): C1.

17. M. McCarthy, M. Pointer, D. Ricks, and R. Rolfe, "Managers' Views on Potential Investment Opportunities," *Business Horizons* (July–August 1993): 54–58.

18. Anant R. Negandhi, *International Management* (Boston: Allyn and Bacon, 1987): 230.

19. Henry Mintzberg, "Strategy Making in Three Modes," *California Management Review* (Winter 1973): 44–53.

20. Arvind V. Phatak, *International Dimensions of Management*, 2d ed. (Boston: PWS-Kent, 1989).

21. Joseph V. Micallef, "Political Risk Assessment," *Columbia Journal of World Business* 16 (Summer 1981): 47–52.

22. Mark Fitzpatrick, "The Definition and Assessment of Political Risk in International Business: A Review of the Literature," *Academy of Management Review* 8 (1983): 249.

23. M. Porter, *Competitive Strategy* (New York: Free Press, 1980).

24. D. J. Garsombke, "International Competitor Analysis," *Planning Review* 17, no. 3 (May–June 1989): 42–47.

25. A. Swasy, "Procter & Gamble Fixes Aim on Tough Market: The Latin Americans," *Wall Street Journal*, June 15, 1990.

26. W. H. Davidson, "The Role of Global Scanning in Business Planning," *Organizational Dynamics* 19 (Winter 1991).

27. Garsombke.

28. Joann S. Lublin, "Japanese Auto Makers Speed into Europe," *Wall Street Journal*, June 6, 1990.

29. K. R. Andrews, *The Concept of Corporate Strategy* (Homewood, IL: Dow-Jones-Irwin, 1979): 601.

30. A. Shama, "After the Meltdown: A Survey of International Firms in Russia," *Business Horizons* 43, no. i4 (July, 2000): 73.

31. C. K. Prahalad and Gary Hamel, "The Core Competence of the Corporation," *Harvard Business Review* (May–June 1990): 79–91.

32. Ibid.

33. M. E. Porter, "Changing Patterns of International Competition," in *The Competitive Challenge*, ed. D. J. Teece (Boston: Ballinger, 1987): 29–30.

34. P. W. Beamish et al., *International Management* (Homewood, IL: Irwin, 1991).

35. A. Palazzo, "B2B Markets–Industry Basics," www.Ft.com, Jan. 28, 2001.

36. N. S. Levinson and M. Asahi, "Cross-National Alliances and Interorganizational Learning," *Organizational Dynamics* (Autumn 1995): 50–62.

37. A. J. Morrison, D. A. Ricks, and K. Roth, "Globalization Versus Regionalization: Which Way for the Multinational?" *Organizational Dynamics* 19 (Winter 1991).

38. Ibid.

39. G. M. Taoka and D. R. Beeman, *International Business* (New York: HarperCollins, 1991).

40. Beamish et al.

41. B. Schlender, "Matsushita Shows How to Go Global, " *Fortune*, July 11, 1996.

42. Yoram Wind and Susan Douglas, "International Portfolio Analysis and Strategy: The Challenge of the 1980s," *Journal of International Business Studies* (Fall 1991): 69–82.

43. R. Gross and D. Kujawa, *International Business* (Homewood, IL: Irwin, 1989): 372.

44. P. Greenberg, "It's Not a Small eCommerce World, After All," www.ecommercetimes.com, February 23, 2001.

45. Ibid.

46. M. Porter, *The Competitive Advantage of Nations* (New York: The Free Press, 1990).

47. S. Butler, "Survivor: B2B Style," www.emarketer.com/analysis/ecommerce, April 13, 2001.

48. "eBusiness Trends," www.idc.com/ebusinesstrends, April 12, 2001.

49. "Fuji-Xerox Teams Up for New E-Marketplace." www.fujixerox.com, April 14, 2001.

50. "Online Auctions Free Procurement Savings," BHP Corporate Services, www.bhp.com, April 20, 2001.

51. "Small Business Take Part in Export Boom," *Investor's Daily*, July 10, 1991.

52. John Garland, Richard N. Farmer, and Marilyn Taylor, *International Dimensions of Business Policy and Strategy*, 2d ed. (Boston: PWS-Kent, 1990): 106.

53. Phatak, 58.

54. R. J. Radway, "International Franchising, " in *Global Business Management in the 1990s*, ed. R. T. Moran (Washington, D. C.: Beacham, 1990): 137.

55. Franklin R. Root, *Entry Strategies for International Markets* (Lexington, MA: Lexington Books, 1987).

56. Ibid.

57. S. Zahra and G. Elhagrasey, "Strategic Management of IJVs," *European Management Journal* 12, no. 1 (1994): 83–93.

58. Yigang Pan and Xiaolia Li, "Joint Venture formation of very Large Multinational Firms," *Journal of International Business Studies*, 31, no. 1 (1st Quarter, 2000), 179–181.

59. Dorothy B. Christelow, "International Joint Ventures: How Important Are They?" *Columbia Journal of World Business* (Summer 1987): 7–13.

60. Kenichi Ohmae, "The Global Logic of Strategic Alliances," *Harvard Business Review* (March–April 1989): 143–154.

61. Zahra and Elhagrasey.

62. "The Partners," *Business Week*, February 10, 1992.

63. John Templeman and Richard A. Melcher, "Supermarket Darwinism: The Survival of the Fattest," *Business Week*, July 9, 1990.

64. Many of the facts and opinions in this section are from the following sources: R. Hudson, "Investing in Euroland," *Wall Street Journal, World Business*, September 28, 1998, R. 25; Dana Milbank, "Can Europe Deliver?" *Wall Street Journal*, September 30, 1994; Tamar Almor and Seer Hirsch, "Outsider's Response to Europe 1992: Theoretical Considerations and Empirical Evidence," *Journal of International Business Studies* 26, no. 2 (2nd Quarter 1995): 223–237; S. Tully, "Europe 1992—More Unity Than You Think," *Fortune*, August 17, 1992; S. Lee, "An Impossible Dream?" *Forbes*, July 25, 1988; R. E. Gut, "The Impact of the European Community's 1992 Project," *Vital Speeches of the*

Day 65, no. 2, November 1, 1988; D. Oliver, "Antitrust as a 1992 Fortress," *Wall Street Journal*, April 24, 1989; C. W. Verity, "U.S. Business Needs to Prepare Now for Europe's Single Internal Market," *Business America*, August 1, 1988; L. H. Clark, Jr., "Europe '92? It's Mostly a Break for the Americans," *Wall Street Journal*, May 21, 1990; and Barbara Toman, "Now Comes the Hard Part: Marketing," in "World Business Special Report," *Wall Street Journal*, September 22, 1989.

65. N. G. Carr, "Managing in the Euro Zone," *Harvard Business Review*, January–February 1999: 47–57.

66. Ibid.

67. Ibid.

68. Milbank.

69. A. Cowell, "Zeneca Buying Astra as Europe Consolidates," *New York Times*, December 10, 1998.

70. L. E. Brouthers, S. Werner, and E. Matulich, "The Influence of Triad Nations' Environments on Price-Quality Product Strategies and MNC Performance," *Journal of International Business Studies* 31, no. 1 (1st Quarter, 2000): 39–62.

71. Ibid.

72. Yigang Pan and David K. Tse, "The hierarchical Model of Market Entry Modes,"*Journal of International Business Studies* 31, no. 4 (4th Quarter 2000): 535–554.

73. Gupta and Govindarajan.

74. Ibid.

75. A. E. Serwer, "McDonald's Conquers the World," *Fortune*, October 17, 1994.

76. Ibid.

77. K. R. Harrigan, "Joint Ventures and Global Strategies," *Columbia Journal of World Business* 19, no. 2 (Summer 1984): 7–13.

78. G. Hofstede, *Cultures and Organizations: Software of the Mind* (London: McGraw-Hill, 1991).

79. Pan and Tse.

80. Hofstede, 1994.

81. Pan and Tse.

82. Hofstede, 1994.

83. Pan and Tse.

CHAPTER 7: GLOBAL ALLIANCES AND STRATEGY IMPLEMENTATION

1. B. R. Schlender, "How Toshiba Makes Alliances Work," *Fortune*, October 4, 1993, 116–120.

2. D. Lei and J. W. Slocum, Jr., "Global Strategic Alliances: Payoffs and Pitfalls," *Organizational Dynamics* (Winter 1991).

3. M. A. Hitt, R. D. Ireland, and R. E. Hoskisson, *Strategic Management* (Cincinatti, OH: Southwestern, 1999).

4. Arvind Parkhe, "Global Business Alliances," *Business Horizons* 43, no. i15 (September 2000): 2.

5. www.e4engineering.com, January 4, 2001; www.Covisint.com, September 28, 2001.

6. www.businessweek.com, October 14, 2000.

7. J. E. Hilsenrath, "Tiger Trouble," *Wall Street Journal*, September 28, 1998, R.17.

8. D. Lei, "Offensive and Defensive Uses of Alliances," in *Strategic Management in a Global Economy*, 3rd ed., Heidi Vernon-Wortzel and L. H. Wortzel eds. (NY: John Wiley & Sons, 1997).

9. J. Main, "Making Global Alliances Work," *Fortune*, December 17, 1990.

10. R. N. Osborn and C. C. Baughn, "Forms of Interorganizational Governance for Multinational Alliances," *Academy of Management Journal* 33, no. 3. (1990): 503–519.

11. Lei, 1997

12. Lei, 1997

13. T. L. Wheelen and J. D. Hunger, *Strategic Management and Business*, 6th ed. (Reading, MA: Addison-Wesley, 1998).

14. Lei, 1997.

15. T. L. Wheelen and J. D. Hunger

16. Vladimir Kvint, consultant at Arthur Anderson & Co., New York, originally from Siberia.

17. A. Jack, "Russians Wake Up to Consumer Capitalism," www.FT.com January 30, 2001.

18. A. Shama, "After the Meltdown: A Survey of International Firms in Russia," *Business Horizons*, 43, no. i4 (July 2000): 73.

19. Ibid.

20. Ibid.

21. Jack.

22. Shama.

23. S. B. Novikov, "Soviet-American Joint Ventures: The problems of establishment and activities." (Paper presented to the 1st International Conference on East-West Joint Ventures, State University of New York, Plattsburgh, October 19–20, 1989).

24. K. R. Harrigan, "Joint Ventures and Global Strategies," *Columbia Journal of World Business* 19, no. 2. (Summer, 1984): 7–13.

25. M. Brzezinski, "Foreigners Learn to Play by Russia's Rules," *Wall Street Journal*, May 14, 1998.

26. M. Brzezinski and Vladimir Kvint, "Don't Give Up on Russia," *Harvard Business Review* (March–April 1994): 62–73; "The Russian Investment Dilemma," Perspectives, *Harvard Business Review* (May–June 1994): 35–44; Robert Starr, "Structuring Investments in the CIS," *Columbia Journal of World Business* (Fall 1993): 12–19; Paul Lawrence and Charalambos Vlachoutsicos, "Joint Ventures in Russia: Put the Locals in Charge," Harvard Business Review (January–February 1993): 44–54. "Investments in the CIS," *Columbia Journal of World Business* (Fall 1993): 12–19; Paul Lawrence and Charalambos Vlachoutsicos, "Joint Ventures in Russia: Put the Locals in Charge," *Harvard Business Review* (January–February 1993): 44–54.

27. A. E. Serwer, "McDonald's Conquers the World," *Fortune*, October 17, 1994.

28. Theodore Herbert and Helen Deresky, "Should General Managers Match Their Strategies?" *Organizational Dynamics* 15, no. 3 (Winter, 1987): 12. R. H. Mason and R. S. Spich, *Management—An International Perspective* (Homewood, IL: Irwin, 1987): 177.

29. E. Anderson and H. Gatignon, "Modes of Foreign Entry: A Transaction Cost Analysis and Propositions," *Journal of International Business Studies* (Fall 1986): 1–26.

30. J. L. Schaan, "Parent Control and Joint Venture Success: The Case of Mexico" (doctoral dissertation, University of Western Ontario, 1983).

31. H. W. Lane and P. W. Beamish, "Cross-Cultural Cooperative Behavior in Joint Ventures in Less Developed Countries," *Management International Review* 30 (Special Issue 1990): 87–102.

32. J. M. Geringer, "Strategic Determinants of Partner Selection Criteria in International Joint Ventures," *Journal of International Business Studies* (First Quarter 1991): 41–62.

33. J. M. Geringer and L. Hebert, "Control and Performance of International Joint Ventures," *Journal of International Business Studies* 20, no. 2 (Summer 1989).

34. Geringer.

35. P. W. Beamish, et al., *International Management* (Homewood, IL: Irwin, 1991).

36. J. P. Killing, *Strategies for Joint Venture Success* (New York: Praeger, 1983).

37. J. L. Schaan and P. W. Beamish, "Joint Venture General Managers in Less Developed Countries," in *Cooperative Strategies in International*

Business, ed. F. Contractor and P. Lorange (Toronto: Lexington Books, 1988): 279–299.

38. Oded Shenkar and Yoram Zeira, "International Joint Ventures: A Tough Test for HR," *Personnel* (January 1990): 26–31.

39. Ibid.

40. J. M. Geringer and L. Hebert, "Control and Performance of International Joint Ventures," *Journal of International Business Studies* 20, no. 2 (Summer 1989): 235–254.

41. M. Geringer, "Criteria for Selecting Partners for Joint Ventures in Industrialized Market Economies" (doctoral dissertation, University of Washington, Seattle, 1986).

42. J. L. Schaan and P. W. Beamish, 1988, op. cit.

43. R. Mead, *International Management* (Cambridge, MA: Blackwell Publishers, 1994).

44. Lisa Shuchman, "Reality Check," *Wall Street Journal,* April 30, 1998.

45. C. S. Smith, "GM Bets Billions on Shaky Car Market in China," *Wall Street Journal,* May 10, 1998.

46. Ibid.

47. Pura, "Backlash Builds Against Suharto-Lined Firms," *Wall Street Journal,* May 27, 1998.

48. P. Rosenzweig, "Why Is Managing in the United States So Difficult for European Firms?" *European Management Journal,* 12, no. 1. (1994): 31–38.

49. "In Alabama, the Soul of a New Mercedes?" *Business Week,* March 31, 1997.

50. Ibid.

51. J. Friedland and L. Lee, "The Wal-Mart Way Sometimes Gets Lost in Translation Overseas," *Wall Street Journal,* October 8, 1997

52. Ibid.

53. J. A. Pearce, II, R. B. Robinson, Jr., "Cultivating Guanxi as a Foreign Investor Strategy," *Business Horizons* 43, no. Il: (January 2000): 31.

54. Ibid.

CHAPTER 8: ORGANIZING STRUCTURE, CONTROL SYSTEMS, AND LABOR RELATIONS

1. A. D. Chandler, *Strategy and Structure: Chapters in the History of the American Industrial Enterprise* (Cambridge, MA: MIT Press, 1962); R. E. Miles et al., "Organizational Strategy, Structure, and Process," *Academy of Management Review* 3, no. 3 (July 1978): 546–562; and J. Woodward, *Industrial Organization: Theory and Practice* (Oxford Univeristy Press, 1965).

2. C. A. Bartlett and S. Ghoshal, *Managing Across Borders* (Boston: Harvard Business School Press, 1989).

2a. John M. Stopford and Louis T. Wells, Jr., *Managing the Multinational Enterprise* (New York: Basic Books, 1972).

3. D. Milbank, "Alcoa Chairman Plans to Begin Reorganization," *Wall Street Journal,* August 9, 1991.

4. P. Asheghian and B. Ebrahimi, *International Business* (New York: Harper and Row, 1990).

5. Asheghian and Ebrahimi.

6. R. H. Mason and R. S. Spich, *Management—An International Perspective* (Homewood, IL: Irwin, 1987).

7. "Heinz's Johnson to Divest Operations, Scrap Management of Firm by Regions," *Wall Street Journal,* December 8, 1997, B22.

8. A. Taylor III, "Ford's really Big Leap at the Future," *Fortune,* September 18, 1995; 134–144.

9. L. Greenhalgh, "Ford Motor Company's CFO Jac Nasser on Transformational Change, E-Business, and environmental responsibility (Interview)" *Academy of Management Executive* 14, no. i13. (August 2000): 46.

10. "Borderless Management," *Business Week,* May 23, 1994.

11. Ibid.; "Power at Multinationals Shifts to Home Office," *The Wall Street Journal,* September 9, 1994; "Big Blue Wants the World to Know Who's Boss," *Business Week,* September 26, 1994.

12. H. Henzler and W. Rall, "Facing up to the Globalization Challenge," *McKinsey Quarterly* (Fall 1986): 52–68.

13. T. Levitt, "The Globalization of Markets," *Harvard Business Review* (May–June 1983): 92–102; and S. P. Douglas and Yoram Wind, "The Myth of Globalization," *Columbia Journal of World Business* (Winter 1987): 19–29.

14. L. Kraar, "The Overseas Chinese," *Fortune,* October 31, 1994.

15. J. Kao, "The Worldwide Web of Chinese Business," *Harvard Business Review* (March–April 1993): 24–35.

16. "Asia's Wealth," *Business Week,* November 29, 1993.

17. Kao.

18. "The New Power in Asia," *Fortune*, October 31, 1994.

19. M. Weidenbaum, "The Rise of Great China: A New Economic Superpower," in *Annual Editions*, 1995–96, (Guilford, CT: The Dushkin Publishing Group): 180–185.

20. Weidenbaum.

21. Ibid.

22. Kraar.

23. Kao.

24. Weidenbaum.

25. Kraar.

26. P. M. Rosenzweig, "Colgate-Palmolive: Managing International Careers," Case Study in C. A. Bartlett and S. Ghoshal, *Transnational Management*, 2nd ed. (Boston: Irwin Publishing Co., 1995).

27. "For Levi's, A Flattering Fit Overseas," *Business Week*, November 5, 1990, 76–77.

28. Ibid.

29. B. R. Schlender, "How Fujitsu Will Tackle the Giants," *Fortune*, July 1, 1991.

30. S. Ghoshal and C. A. Bartlett, "The Multinational Corporation as an Interorganizational Network," *Academy of Management Review* 15, no. 4. (1990): 603–625.

31. R. E. White and T. A. Poynter, "Organizing for Worldwide Advantage," *Business Quarterly* 54 (Summer 1989): 84–89.

32. B. Hagerty, "Philips to Eliminate 35,000 to 45,000 Jobs by End of 1991," *Wall Street Journal*, October 26, 1990, A12.

33. C. A. Bartlett and S. Ghoshal, "Organizing for Worldwide Effectiveness: The Transnational Solution," *California Management Review* (Fall 1988): 54–74.

34. Ibid., 66.

35. R. H. Kilmann, "A Networked Company That Embraces the World," *Information Strategy* 6 (Spring 1990): 23–26.

36. R. B. Reich, "Who Is Them?" *Harvard Business Review* (March–April 1991): 77–88.

37. Ibid.

38. A. V. Phatak, *International Dimensions of Management*, 2d ed. (Boston: PWS-Kent, 1989).

39. G. Rohrmann, CEO, AEI Corp., press release, www.aeilogistics.com August, 1997.

40. Phatak.

41. W. G. Egelhoff, "Patterns of Control in U.S., U.K., and European Multinational Corporations," *Journal of International Business Studies* (Fall 1984): 73–83.

42. Ibid.

43. Ibid.

44. S. Ueno and U. Sekaran, "The Influence of Culture on Budget Control Practices in the U.S.A. and Japan: An Empirical Study," *Journal of International Business Studies* 23 (Winter 1992): 659–674.

45. Phatak.

46. P. J. Dowling, R. S. Schuler, and D. E. Welch, *International Dimensions of Human Resource Management*, 2nd ed. (Belmont, CA: Wadsworth, 1994).

47. "Taking the Pledge," *The Economist*, November 23, 1996, S15(2).

48. R. M. Hodgetts and F. Luthans, *International Management*, 2nd ed. (NY: McGraw-Hill, 1994).

49. M. R. Czinkota, I. A. Ronkainen, and M. H. Moffett, *International Business*, 3rd ed. (NY: Dryden Press, 1994).

50. C. K. Prahalad and Y. L. Doz, *The Multinational Mission: Balancing Local Demands and Global Vision* (NY: The Free Press, 1987).

51. R. Taylor, "Challenge Facing Endangered Species," *Financial Times*, August 14, 1995, 10.

52. R. J. Adams, *Industrial Relations under Liberal Democracy*, (University of South Carolina Press, 1995).

53. Dowling, Schuler, and Welch.

54. J. S. Daniels and L. H. Radebaugh, *International Business*, 6th ed. (Reading, MA: Addison-Wesley, 1992).

55. M. Poole, *Industrial Relations: Origins and Patterns of National Diversity* (London: Routledge, 1986).

56. Dowling, Schuler, and Welch.

57. Adams

58. Ibid.

59. "Unions Feel the Beat," *U.S. News and World Report*, January 24, 1994.

60. Ibid.

61. "World Wire: China to Unionize Foreign Firms," *Wall Street Journal*, May 1, 1994.

62. Ibid.

63. J. T. Barrett, "Trade Unions in South Africa: dramatic change after Apartheid ends," *Monthly Labor Review*, 119, no. 5 (May 1996): 37.

64. M. M. Lucio and S. Weston, "New Management Practices in a Multinational Corporation: The Restructuring of Worker Representation and Rights." *Industrial Relations Journal* (1999): 25, no. 2, 110–121.

65. Ibid.

66. D. B. Cornfield, "Labor Transnationalism?" *Work and Occupations* 24 no. 3 (August 1997): 278(10).

67. R. Martin, A. Vidinova, S. Hill, "Industrial Relations in Transition Economies: Emergent Industrial Relations Institutions in Bulgaria," *British Journal of Industrial Relations* 34, no. 1 (March 1996): 3.

68. "Labour Relations: Themes for the 21st Century," *British Journal of Industrial Relations* 33, no. 4 (December, 1995): 515.

69. Daniels and Radebaugh.

70. J. T. Barrett.

71. "Culture clash: South Korea," *Economist*, January 11, 1997, 35.

72. A. M. Rugman and R. M. Hodgetts, *International Business*, (New York: McGraw-Hill, 1995.)

73. This section drawn from a term project by Joy Kennley and Tim Lemos, students at the State University of New York, Plattsburgh, Spring 1995; and articles by Tim Shorrock, such as "GE, Honeywell are Focus of NAFTA Labor Complaints," *Journal of Commerce and Commercial* 399, No. 2814, February 15, 1994.

74. Daniels and Radebaugh.

75. R. Calori and B. Dufour, "Management European Style," *Academy Management Executive* 9, no. 3 (August 1995).

76. J. Hoerr, "What Should Unions Do?" *Harvard Business Review* (May–June 1991): 30–45.

77. Hodgetts and Luthans.

78. Hoerr.

79. H. C. Katz, "The Decentralization of Collective Bargaining: A Literature Review and Comparative Analysis," *Industrial and Labor Relations Review* 47, no. 1 (October 1993).

80. Adams.

81. "The Perils of Cosy Corporatism," *Economist*, May 21, 1994.

82. Wofgang Streeck, "More Uncertainties: German Unions Facing 1992," *Industrial Relations* (Fall 1991): 30–33.

83. "Germany's Economic Future Is on the Bargaining Table," *Business Week*, March 30, 1992.

CHAPTER 9: DEVELOPING A GLOBAL MANAGEMENT CADRE

1. J. L. Laabs, "HR Pioneers Explore the Road Less Traveled," *Personnel Journal*, February 1996, 70–72, 74, 77–78.

2. Ibid.

3. J. Stewart Black and Hal B. Gregersen, "The Right Way to Manage Expats," *Harvard Business Review*, March–April 1999, 52–62.

4. C. Joinson, "Why HR Managers Need to Think Globally," *HR Magazine*, April 1998, 2–7.

5. C. A. Bartlett and S. Ghoshal, "Matrix Management: Not a Structure, a Frame of Mind," *Harvard Business Review*, July–August 1990.

6. J. S. Lublin, "Foreign Accents Proliferate in Top Ranks as U.S. Companies Find Talent Abroad," *Wall Street Journal*, May 21, 1992.

7. S. J. Kobrin, "Is There a Relationship Between a Geocentric Mind-Set and Multinational Strategy?" *Journal of International Business Studies* (3rd Quarter 1994); N. J. Adler and S. Bartholomew, "Managing Globally Competent People," *Academy of Management Executive*, August 6, 1992, 52–65; P. Dowling and R. S. Schuler, *International Dimensions of Human Resource Management* (Boston: PWS-Kent, 1990).

8. G. Hedlund, "Who Manages the Global Corporation" (Unpublished working paper, Stockholm School of Economics, 1990).

9. D. Welch, "HRM Implications of Globalization," *Journal of General Management* 19, no. 4 (Summer 1994): 52–69.

10. T. T. Herbert and H. Deresky, "Should General Managers Match Their Business Strategies?" *Organizational Dynamics* 15, no. 3 (Winter 1987); and "Senior Management Implications of Strategic Human Resource Management Programs," *Proceedings of the Association of Human Resource Management and Organizational Behavior Conference* (New Orleans, November 1986).

11. D. A. Heenan and H. V. Perlmutter, Multinational Organization Development (Reading, MA: Addison-Wesley, 1979): 18–19.

12. S. B. Prasad and Y. K. Krishna Shetty, *An Introduction to Multinational Management* (Englewood Cliffs, NJ: Prentice-Hall, 1979).

13. Rochelle Kopp, "International Human Resource Policies and Practices in Japanese, European, and United States Multinationals," *Human Resource Management* 33, no. 4. (Winter 1994): 581–599.

14. Herbert and Deresky.

15. M. Mendenhall and G. Oddou, "The Dimensions of Expatriate Acculturation: A Review," *Academy of Management Review* 10, no. 1 (1985): 39–47.

16. R. L. Tung, "Selection and Training of Personnel for Overseas Assignments," *Columbia Journal of World Business* (Spring 1981): 68–78.

17. Ibid.

18. P. J. Dowling and R. S. Schuler, *International Dimensions of Human Resource Management* (Boston: PWS-Kent, 1990).

19. S. J. Kobrin, "Expatriate Reduction and Strategic Control in American Multinational Corporations," *Human Resource Management* 27, no. 1 (1988): 63–75.

20. P. J. Dowling, "Hot Issues Overseas," *Personnel Administrator* 34, no. 1 (1989): 66–72.

21. Hem C. Jain, "Human Resource Management in Selected Japanese Firms, the Foreign Subsidiaries and Locally Owned Counterparts," *International Labour Review* 129, no. 1 (1990): 73–84.

22. Bartlett and Ghoshal.

23. R. L. Tung, "Selection and Training Procedures of U.S., European, and Japanese Multinationals,"*California Management Review,* 25 (1981): 57–71.

24. R. D. Hays, "Expatriate Selection: Insuring Success and Avoiding Failure," *Journal of International Business Studies* 5, no. 1 (1974): 25–37.

25. R. L. Tung.

26. J. S. Black, "Work Role Transitions: A Study of American Expatriate Managers in Japan," *Journal of International Business Studies* 19 (1988): 277–294.

27. "They're Sending You Where?" www.businessweek.com , June 5, 1999.

28. M. Harvey, "Dual-Career Expatriates: Expectations, Adjustment and Satisfaction with International Relocation," *Journal of International Business Studies* 28, no. 3 (1997).

29. Tung, "U.S., European, and Japanese Multinationals."

30. Ibid.

31. B. Wysocki, Jr., "Prior Adjustment: Japanese Executives Going Overseas Take Anti-Shock Courses," *Wall Street Journal*, December 4, 1987.

32. Mendenhall and Oddou.

33. J. S. Black and M. Mendenhall, "Cross-Cultural Training Effectiveness: A Review and a Theoretical Framework for Future Research," *Academy of Management Review* 15, no. 1 (1990): 113–136.

34. K. Oberg, "Culture Shock: Adjustments to New Cultural Environments," *Practical Anthropology* (July–August 1960): 177–182.

35. Ibid.

36. Ibid.

37. Tung, "Overseas Assignments."

38. P. C. Earley, "Intercultural Training for Managers: A Comparison of Documentary and Interpersonal Methods," *Academy of Management Journal* 30, no. 4 (December 1987): 685–698.

39. S. Ronen, *Comparative and Multinational Management* (NY: John Wiley and Sons, 1986): 108.

40. P. R. Harris and R. T. Moran, *Managing Cultural Differences*, 4 ed. (Houston, TX: Gulf Publishing, 1996), p. 139.

41. Harris and Moran, 1996.

42. J. S. Lublin, "Younger Managers Learn Global Skills," *Wall Street Journal*, March 31, 1992.

43. "Seoul Is Supporting a Sizzling Tech Boom," www.businessweek.com, September 25, 2000.

44. Herbert and Deresky. Senior Management Implications

45. T. F. O'Boyle, "Little Benefit to Careers Seen in Foreign Stints," *Wall Street Journal*, December 11, 1989.

46. B. W. Teague, *Compensating Key Personnel Overseas* (New York: Conference Board, 1972).

47. D. Kiriazov, S. E. Sullivan and H. S. Tu, "Business Success in Eastern Europe: Understanding and Customizing HRM," *Business Horizons*, January–February, 2000, 39–43.

48. Ibid.

49. Y. Ono and W. Spindle, "Japan's Long Decline Makes One Thing Rise: Individualism," *Wall Street Journal*, Jan. 3, 2001.

50. Ingmar Bjorkman and Yuan Lu, "The Management of Human Resources in Chinese-Western Joint Ventures," *Journal of World Business* 34, no. i3 (Fall 1999): 306.

51. Ibid.

52. Charlene M. Solomon, "One Assignment, Two Lives," *Personnel Journal*, May 1996, 36–47.

53. N. J. Adler, *International Dimensions of Organizational Behavior*, 2 ed. (Boston: PWS-Kent, 1991); M. Mendenhall, E. Dunbar, and G. Oddou, "Expatriate Selection, Training, and Career-Pathing: A Review and Critique," *Human Resource Management* 26 (1987): 331–345.

54. M. G. Harvey, "Repatriation of Corporate Executives: An Empirical Study," *Journal of International Business Studies* 20 (Spring 1989): 131–144.

55. Tung, "Career Issues in International Assignments," *Academy of Management Executive* 2, no. 3 (1988): 241–244.

56. M. Harvey, "Dual-Career Expatriates: Expectations, Adjustments and Satisfaction with International Relocation," *Journal of International Business Studies* 28, no. 3 (1997): 627.

57. Tung, 1988.

58. Solomon, 1996.

59. R. Pascoe, *Surviving Overseas: The Wife's Guide to Successful Living Abroad* (Singapore: Times Publishing, 1992); and R. Pascoe, "Employers Ignore Expatriate Wives at Their Own Peril," *Wall Street Journal*, March 29, 1992.

60. J. S. Black and H. B. Gregersen, "The Other Half of the Picture: Antecedents of Spouse Cross-Cultural Adjustment," *Journal of International Business Studies* (Third Quarter 1992): 461–477.

61. J. S. Black, H. B. Gregersen, M. E. Mendenhall, L. K. Stroh, *Globalizing People Through International Assignments* (Reading, MA: Addison-Wesley, 1999).

62. www.GE.com, March 21, 2001.

63. J. Hamill, "Expatriate Policies in British Multinationals," *Journal of General Management* 14, no. 4 (Summer 1989): 18–33.

64. Based on W. Dyer, *Team Building* (Reading, MA: Addison-Wesley, 1987).

65. R. B. Reich, "Who is Them?" *Harvard Business Review* (March–April 1991): 77–88.

66. T. Gross, E. Turner, and L. Cederholm, "Building teams for Global Operations," *Management Review* (June 1987): 32–36.

67. Based largely on N. J. Adler, *International Dimensions of Organizational Behavior* (Boston: PWS-Kent, 1991).

68. C. Solomon, "Building Teams Across Borders," *Global Workforce*, November 1998, 12–17.

69. Ibid.

70. T. Brown, "Building a Transnational Team," *Industry Week*, May 16, 1988, 13.

71. Ibid.

72. R. T. Moran, "Cross-Cultural Contact: A Formula for Success in Multicultural Organizations," *International Management*, December, 1988, 74.

73. Ibid.

74. I. Ratiu, "International Consulting News," in *Managing Cultural Differences*, 3 ed., P. R. Harris and R. T. Moran eds. (Houston, TX: Gulf Publishing, 1991).

75. *Wall Street Journal*, July 26, 1995.

76. M. Kaminski and J. Paiz, "Japanese Women in Management: Where Are They?" *Human Resource Management* 23, no. 2 (Fall 1984): 277–292.

77. P. Lansing and K. Ready, "Hiring Women Managers in Japan: An Alternative for Foreign Employers," *California Management Review* 26, no. 4 (1988): 112–127.

78. "Japan's Working Mothers," *Japan Report* 37, no. 5 (August 1991).

79. "Women in Business: A Global Report Card," *Wall Street Journal*, July 26, 1995.

80. N. J. Adler and D. N. Izraeli, *Women in Management Worldwide* (Armonk, NY: M. E. Sharpe, 1988), 245.

81. Ibid.

82. M. Jelinek and N. J. Adler, "Women: World Class Managers for Global Competition," *Academy of Management Executive*, 11, no. 1 (February 1988): 11–19.

CHAPTER 10: MOTIVATING AND LEADING

1. F. Rieger and D. Wong-Rieger, "A Configuration Model of National Influence Applied to Southeast Asian Organizations," *Proceedings of the Research Conference on Business in Southeast Asia*, May 12–13, 1990, University of Michigan.

2. M. J. Gannon & Associates, *Understanding Global Cultures: Metaphorical Journeys Through 17 Countries* (Beverly Hills, CA: Sage Publications, 1994).

3. R. M. Steers, *Made in Korea: Chung Ju Yung and the Rise of Hyundai* (New York: Routledge), 1999.

4. Meaning of Work International Research Team, *The Meaning of Working: An International Perspective* (New York: Academic Press, 1985).

5. D. Siddiqui and A. Alkhafaji, *The Gulf War: Implications for Global Businesses and Media* (Apollo, PA: Closson Press, 1992): 133–135.

6. Ibid.

7. A. Ali, "The Islamic Work Ethic in Arabia," *Journal of Psychology*, 126 (1992): 507–519.

8. Yasamusa Kuroda and Tatsuzo Suzuki, "A Comparative Analysis of the Arab Culture: Arabic,

English and Japanese Language and Values" (Paper presented at the 5th Congress of the International Association of Middle Eastern Studies, Tunis, September 20–24, 1991, quoted in Siddiqui).

9. J. R. Hinrichs, "Cross-National Analysis of Work Attitudes" (Paper presented at the American Psychological Association Meeting, Chicago, 1975).

10. A. Furnham, B. D. Kirkcaldy, and R. Lynn, "National Attitudes to Competitiveness, Money, and Work Among Young People: First, Second, and Third World Differences," *Human Relations* 47, no. 1 (1994): 119–132.

11. M. Haire, E. E. Ghiselli, and L. W. Porter, "Cultural Patterns in the Role of the Manager," *Industrial Relations* 12, no. 2 (February 1963): 95–117.

12. S. Ronen, *Comparative and Multinational Management* (New York: John Wiley and Sons, 1986).

13. D. S. Elenkov, "Can American Management Concepts Work in Russia? A Cross-Cultural Comparative Study," *California Management Review* 40, no. 4 (1998): 133–157.

14. E. C. Nevis, "Cultural Assumptions and Productivity: The United States and China," *Sloan Management Review* 24, no. 3 (Spring 1983): 17–29.

15. R. L. Tung, "Patterns of Motivation in Chinese Industrial Enterprises," *Academy of Management Review* 6, no. 3 (1981): 481–489.

16. Swee Hoon Ang, "The Power of Money: A Cross-Cultural Analysis of Business-Related Beliefs," *Journal of World Business* 35, no. i1 (2000): 43.

17. *World Competitiveness Yearbook* (Lausanne, Switzerland: Institute for Management Development, 1998).

18. D. D. White and J. Leon, "The Two-Factor Theory: New Questions, New Answers," *National Academy of Management Proceedings* (1976): 358.

19. D. Macarov, "Work Patterns and Satisfactions in an Israeli Kibbutz: A Test of the Herzberg Hypothesis," *Personnel Psychology* (Autumn 1973): 483–493.

20. P. D. Machungwa and N. Schmitt, "Work Motivation in a Developing Country," *Journal of Applied Psychology* (February 1983): 31–42.

21. G. E. Popp, H. J. Davis, and T. T. Herbert, "An International Study of Intrinsic Motivation Composition," *Management International Review* 26, no. 3 (1986): 28–35.

22. R. N. Kanungo and R. W. Wright, "A Cross-Cultural Study of Managerial Job Attitudes," *Journal of International Business Studies* (Fall 1983): 115–129.

23. Ibid., 127–128

24. J. R. Lincoln, "Employee Work Attitudes and Management Practice in the U.S. and Japan: Evidence from a Large Comparative Survey," *California Management Review* 32, no. 1 (Fall 1989): 89–106.

25. J. R. Lincoln and K. McBride, "Japanese Industrial Organization in Comparative Perspective," *Annual Review of Sociology* 13 (1987): 289–312.

26. Lincoln.

27. "Detroit South," *Business Week*, March 16, 1992.

28. Hofstede.

29. M. B. Teagarden, M. C. Butler, and M. Von Glinow, "Mexico's Maquiladora Industry: Where Strategic Human Resource Management Makes a Difference," *Organizational Dynamics* (Winter 1992): 34–47.

30. T. T. Herbert, H. Deresky, and G. E. Popp, "On the Potential for Assimilation and Integration of Sub-Culture Members into the U.S. Business System: The Micro-Cultural Effects of the Mexican-American National Origin, Culture, and Personality," *Proceedings of the International Business Association Conference* (London, November 1986).

31. John Condon, *Good Neighbors: Communication with the Mexicans* (Yarmouth, ME: Intercultural Press, 1985).

32. G. K. Stephens and C. R. Greer, "Doing Business in Mexico: Understanding Cultural Differences," *Organizational Dynamics* (Summer 1995): 39–55.

33. Teagarden, Butler, and Von Glinow.

34. Stephens and Greer.

35. Ibid.

36. C. E. Nicholls, H. W. Lane, M. B. Brechu, "Taking Self-Managed Teams to Mexico," *Academy of Management Executive* 13, no. 3 (1999): 15–25.

37. Ibid.

38. Ibid.

39. Mariah E. de Forest, "Thinking of a Plant in Mexico?" *Academy of Management Executive* 8, no. 1 (1994): 33–40.

40. Ibid.

41. Ibid.

42. Teagarden, Butler, and Von Glinow.

43. Herbert, Deresky, and Popp; R. S. Bhagat and S. J. McQuaid, "Role of Subjective Culture in Organizations: A Review and Direction for Future Research," *Journal of Applied Psychology Monograph* 67, no. 5 (1982): 669.

44. Malgorzata Tarczynska, "Eastern Europe: How Valid Is Western Reward/Performance Management?" *Benefits and Compensation International* 29, no. 8 (April 2000): 9–16.

45. M. A. Von Glinow and M. B. Teagarden, "The Transfer of Human Resource Management Technology in Sino-U.S. Cooperative Ventures: Problems and Solutions," *Human Resource Management* 27, no. 2 (1988): 201–229.

46. M. A. Von Glinow and Byung Jae Chung, "Comparative HRM Practices in the U.S., Japan, Korea and the PRC," in *Research in Personnel and HRM, A Research Annual: International HRM,* ed. A. Nedd, G. R. Ferris, and K. M. Rowland (London: JAI Press, 1989).

47. A. Ignatius, "Now If Ms. Wong Insults a Customer, She Gets an Award," *Wall Street Journal,* January 24, 1989, 1, 15.

48. T. Saywell, "Motive Power: China's State Firms Bank on Incentives to Keep Bosses Operating at Their Peak," *Far Eastern Economic Review,* July 8, 2000: 67–68.

49. Steers, 1999.

50. A. Morrison, H. Gregersen, S. Black, "What Makes Savvy Global Leaders?" *Ivey Business Journal* 1999, 64, no. 2. 44–51; and *Monash Mt. Eliza Business Review,* 1, no. 2. (1998).

51. Ibid.

52. Ibid.

53. Morrison, et al. 1999; J. W. Gardner, *John W. Gardner on Leadership* (New York: Free Press, 1989); W. Bennis and B. Nanus, *Leaders* (New York: Harper and Row, 1985).

54. R. D. Robinson, *Internationalization of Business* (Hinsdale, IL: Drysden Press, 1984): 117.

55. R. H. Mason and R. S. Spich, *Management—An International Perspective* (Homewood: IL: Irwin, 1987).

56. Ibid., 184.

57. B. M. Bass, *Bass & Stogdill's Handbook of Leadership* (New York: Free Press, 1990).

58. See, for example, M. Mead, *Sex and Temperament in Three Primitive Societies* (New York: Morrow, 1935); and M. Mead et al., *Cooperation and Competition Among Primitive Peoples* (New York: McGraw-Hill, 1937).

59. L. Copeland and L. Griggs, *Going International* (NY: Random House, 1985), 131.

60. D. McGregor, *The Human Side of Enterprise* (New York: McGraw-Hill, 1960).

61. See, for example, R. M. Stogdill, *Manual for the Leader Behavior Description Questionnaire—Form XII* (Columbus: Ohio State University, Bureau of Business Research, 1963).

62. R. R. Blake and J. S. Mouton, *The New Managerial Grid* (Houston, TX: Gulf Publishing, 1978).

63. F. E. Fiedler, "Engineering the Job to Fit the Manager," *Harvard Business Review* 43, no. 5 (1965): 115–122.

64. Geert Hofstede, "Motivation, Leadership and Organization: Do American Theories Apply Abroad?" *Organizational Dynamics* (Summer 1980): 42–63.

65. Ibid.

66. Geert Hofstede, "Value Systems in Forty Countries," *Proceedings of the 4th International Congress of the International Association for Cross-Cultural Psychology* (1978).

67. Andre Laurent, "The Cultural Diversity of Western Conceptions of Management," *International Studies of Management and Organization* 13, no. 1–2 (Spring–Summer 1983): 75–96.

68. C. Hampden-Turner and A. Trompenaars, *The Seven Cultures of Capitalism* (New York: Doubleday, 1993).

69. M. Haire, E. E. Ghiselli, and L. W. Porter, *Managerial Thinking: An International Study* (New York: John Wiley and Sons, 1966).

70. S. G. Redding and T. W. Case, "Managerial Beliefs Among Asian Managers," *Proceedings of the Academy of Management,* 1975.

71. I. Kenis, "A Cross-Cultural Study of Personality and Leadership," *Group and Organization Studies* 2 (1977): 49–60.

72. F. C. Deyo, "The Cultural Patterning of Organizational Development: A Comparative Case Study of Thailand and Chinese Industrial Enterprises," *Human Organization* 37 (1978): 68–72.

73. M. K. Badawy, "Styles of Mid-Eastern Managers," *California Management Review* (Spring 1980): 57.

74. Various Newscasts, 2001.

75. A. A. Algattan, *Test of the Path-Goal Theory of Leadership in the Multinational Domain* (Paper

presented at the Academy of Management Conference, 1985, San Diego, CA).

76. J. P. Howell and P. W. Dorfman, *A Comparative Study of Leadership and Its Substitutes in a Mixed Cultural Work Setting* (Unpublished manuscript, 1988).

77. D. H. Welsh, F. Luthans, and S. M. Sommer, "Managing Russian Factory Workers: The impact of U.S.–based behavioral and participative Techniques," *Academy of Management Journal* 36 (1993): 58–79.

78. Jai B. P. Sinha and D. Sinha, "Role of Social Values in Indian Organizations," *International Journal of Psychology* 25 (1990): 705–715.

79. Hofstede, "Motivation, Leadership and Organization."

80. Jai B. P. Sinha, "A Model of Effective Leadership Styles in India," *International Studies of Management and Organization* (Summer–Fall 1984): 86–98.

81. Ibid.

82. B. M. Bass and P. C. Burger, *Assessment of Managers: An International Comparison* (New York: Free Press, 1979).

83. R. C. Tripathi, "Interplay of Values in the Functioning of Indian Organizations," *International Journal of Psychology* 25 (1990): 715–734.

84. Sinha.

85. Sinha and Sinha.

86. A. Spaeth, "India Beckons—and Frustrates: The Country Needs Foreign Investment, but Investors May Find That Hard to Believe," *Wall Street Journal*, September 22, 1989, R23–R25.

87. Ibid.

88. "Enron Switches Signals in India," *Business Week*, January 8, 2001.

89. "Enron Calls on Guarantees by India to Collect Debts," *The Wall Street Journal*, February 9, 2001.

90. S. S. Rao, "Yankee, Be Good," *Financial World*, November 7, 1995, 54–68.

91. J. J. Curran, "Why Japan Will Emerge Stronger," *Fortune*, May 18, 1992.

92. Yumiko Ono and Wm. Spindle, "Japan's Long Decline Makes One Thing Rise —Individualism," *Wall Street Journal*, December 29, 2000.

93. Kuniyasu Sakai, "The Feudal World of Japanese Manufacturing," *Harvard Business Review* (November–December 1990): 38–47.

INDEX

X

Xerox Corporation, 163, 178, 259
Xin, Katherine R., 106*n*, 108*n*
Xun Wang, 70*n*

Y

Yahoo!, 173
Yamamoto, Takuma, 230

Yatski, P., 8*n*
Young Yun Kim, 124*n*
Yu Kai-Ceng, 70*n*

Z

Zachary, G. P., 40*n*
Zahra, S., 181*n*, 182*n*
Zeira, Yoram, 209*n*

Zemin, Jiang, 8
Zeneca Group P.L.C., 185
Zenith Electronics, 199
Zetsche, Dieter, 194
Zhan, Nan, 153*n*
Zhou, Sunny, 147
Zhurakovskij, Vladimir, 218
Zimmerman, Hans Dieter, 26*n*
Zubiran, Roland, 62